Power and the
Sacred in
Revolutionary
Russia

Glennys Young

POWER AND THE SACRED IN REVOLUTIONARY RUSSIA

Religious Activists in the Village

The Pennsylvania State University Press
University Park, Pennsylvania

This book has been published with the aid of a grant from the Graduate School of the University of Washington.

Library of Congress Cataloging-in-Publication Data

Young, Glennys.
    Power and the sacred in revolutionary Russia: religious activists in the village / Glennys Young.
        p.   cm.
    Includes bibliographical references (p.   ) and index.
    ISBN 978-0-271-02837-8
    1. Russkaia pravoslavnaia tserkov'—Russia (Federation)—History—20th century. 2. Persecution—Russia (Federation)—History—20th century. 3. Communism and Christianity—Russia (Federation)—History—20th century. 4. Church and state—Russia (Federation)—History—20th century. 5. Russia (Federation)—Rural conditions. 6. Russia (Federation)—Church history—20th century.
    I. Title.
BX492.Y68   1997
281.9'47'09042—dc21   96-52408
                                                                                                                               CIP

Copyright © 1997 The Pennsylvania State University
All rights reserved
Printed in the United States of America
Published by The Pennsylvania State University Press,
University Park, PA 16802-1003

It is the policy of The Pennsylvania State University Press to use acid-free paper for the first printing of all clothbound books. Publications on uncoated stock satisfy the minimum requirements of American National Standard for Information Sciences—Permanence of Paper for Printed Library Materials, ANSI Z39.48-1992.

To the memory of my father,
a *bezbozhnik* born in the village of Edelmans, Pennsylvania

and to my mother,
a religious activist born in the town of Nazareth, Pennsylvania

Contents

List of Illustrations	viii
Glossary	ix
Acknowledgments	xi
Abbreviations	xv
Introduction	1
1 Ironic Beginnings	11
2 Perplexing Paradoxes	49
3 Burnt by the Heavens	79
4 Circling the Heavens	111
5 Unexpected Resilience	147
6 Parish Democracy	193
7 Keeping the Parish Alive	211
8 Icons of Power	233
9 Fashioning the Enemy	253
Conclusion	273
Select Bibliography	281
Index	299

Illustrations

1. Map of the Soviet Union, with details of Leningrad, Saratov, and Smolensk regions, 1924.
2. Poster: "Religion Is the Narcotic of the People."
3. Poster: "The Defiance of Youth."
4. Poster: "Fulfill Lenin's Precepts."
5. Wall newspaper (*stengazeta*) of *Bezbozhnik* (The Godless).
6. Poster: "The Clergy's Folk Dance."
7. Poster: "The Spider and the Flies."
8. Poster: "Enough Deception."
9. Poster: "Religion and the Woman."
10. Poster: "The Working Woman: Into the Battle for Socialism. Into the Battle Against Religion."
11. Poster: "The *Bezbozhnik* Is a (Scientific) Experimenter."
12. Poster: "We Will Unmask the Anti-Soviet Plans of Capitalists and *Tserkovniki*. Long Live the World Proletarian Revolution!"
13. Poster: "The Battle Against Religion Is the Battle for Socialism."
14. Poster: "Religion and the *Popovshchina* Are the Counterrevolutionary Weapons of the Bourgeoisie."
15. Cover of magazine *Bezbozhnik u stanka* (The Godless at the workbench).

Glossary

batrak. Rural laborer, hired by another peasant.
bedniak. Poor peasant.
Cheka. Extraordinary Commission for the Struggle with Counterrevolution and Sabotage; from 1917 to 1922, the national security police.
desiatina (abbr. des.). Unit of land area equivalent to 1.09 hectares (2.7 acres).
guberniia. Province. Basic administrative unit inherited from the tsarist period. Divided into *uezdy* and *volosti*.
kolkhoz. "*Kol*lektivnoe *kho*ziaistvo." Collective farm.
kombed or komitet bednoty. Committee of the Village Poor.
Komsomol. *Kom*munisticheskii *soiuz mol*odezhi; Communist Youth League.
komsomolets (pl. komsomoltsy). Member of the Komsomol.
kopeck (abbr. kop.) 1/100 of a ruble.
kulak. "Fist"; wealthy peasant.
lishenets (pl. lishentsy). An individual legally deprived of the right to vote.
mir. Peasant commune.
mirskoi skhod. A meeting of the male heads of household of a *mir*. A prerevolutionary term.
NEP. New Economic Policy. 1921–1928. Deferring ideological goals for economic productivity and political stability, the regime made concessions to the peasantry and the market. Forced requisition of grain was replaced with a tax in kind (later money); free trade in agriculture and certain forms of retail trade were permitted. The state retained control over heavy industry and credit.
NKVD. *Narodnyi komissariat vnutrennikh del.* People's Commissariat of Internal Affairs.
oblast'. Large administrative unit created at the end of the 1920s with the administrative reorganization of the USSR.
obshchii skhod. A general meeting of all enfranchised members of a peasant commune.

okrug. Administrative unit within the *oblast'*. Abolished in 1930.
pood. Unit of weight equivalent to 16.38 kg or 36 lbs.
raion. An administrative district within an *oblast'*.
RSFSR. Rossiiskaia Sovetskaia Federativnaia Sotsialisticheskaia Respublika. Russian Soviet Federated Socialist Republic.
samosud. Peasant self-adjudication, or mob law.
sel'khoziaistvennoe tovarishchestvo or TOZ (tovarishchestvo po obshchestvennoi obrabotki zemli). An association for the communal cultivation of land. Only land and some essential agricultural tools were held in common.
sel'sovet. Village or rural soviet.
seredniak. Peasant of average means.
skhod. Village assembly.
uezd (pl. uezdy). Administrative unit (subdivision of *guberniia*).
verst. Unit of linear measure equivalent to 3500 feet.
VIK. *Volostnoi ispolnitel'nyi komitet soveta (volispolkom)*; executive committee of the *volost'* soviet.
volost' (pl. volosti). Administrative unit (subdivision of *uezd*)
VTsIK. Vserossiiskii tsentral'nyi ispolnitel'nyi komitet; All-Russian Central Soviet Executive Committee of Soviets.

Acknowledgments

I am very grateful to the institutions and organizations whose financial support made this book possible. While a doctoral student at the University of California at Berkeley, I received support from the Graduate Division, the International Research and Exchanges Board (with funds provided by the Andrew W. Mellon Foundation, the National Endowment for the Humanities, and the U.S. Department of State), the Fulbright-Hays Doctoral Dissertation Research Abroad Program, and the Charlotte Newcombe Doctoral Dissertation program of the Woodrow Wilson National Fellowship Foundation. As I revised the dissertation for publication, I was lucky to receive crucial financial support from the Hoover Institution on War, Revolution, and Peace (with funds provided by the Title VIII Soviet Eastern-European Research and Training Act), the Kennan Institute, and above all, from the Henry M. Jackson Foundation. For funds to support the production and publication of the book, I thank the Dean's Mentorship Program and the Graduate School of the University of Washington.

I thank the librarians at the following institutions: the University of California, the Slavonic Library of the University of Helsinki, the Hoover Institution (especially Molly Molloy), the University of Illinois Slavic Reference Service, Keston College, the Lenin Library, the Library of the Academy of Sciences, the Library of Congress, St. Vladmir's Orthodox Theological Seminary, and the Saltykov-Shchedrin Public Library. Special thanks to Edward Kasinec, who along with his staff, always made me feel at home at the Slavic reading room of the New York Public Library and took a sincere interest in my work, alerting me to some important sources. In addition, I thank the staffs of the Central State Archive of the October Revolution (now GARF), the Central State Archive of the October Revolution in Leningrad, the Russian State Historical Archive (RGIA), the Bakhmeteff Archive at Columbia University, and the Hoover Institution Archive (especially Olga Dunlop and Carol Ledenham). Closer to home, thanks are due to the University of Washington's Slavic librarian, Michael Biggins, and it's Interlibrary Borrowing Service.

Many generous scholars read my work at various points along the way and offered invaluable suggestions for improving the manuscript. At

Berkeley, I had the very good fortune to be trained by Nicholas Riasanovsky and Reggie Zelnik, whom I thank for their support and expert intellectual guidance over many years. To Reggie, who directed the dissertation, I am particularly grateful for his faith in my capacity to defect from German to Russian history. Victoria Bonnell, who was also a member of the dissertation committee, offered incisive comments. The late Kendall Bailes was originally a member of the committee as well. He helped me tremendously in the initial stages of the project, and I have missed his broad knowledge of Soviet history and his generous spirit. Martin Malia kindled my interest in the Soviet period. I. N. Olegina, who was my Soviet adviser at what was then Leningrad State University, extended me many kindnesses. I thank the members of a Berkeley dissertation group, in particular Nancy Bristow, Anne Hyde, and Lucy Salyer, who read my earliest efforts. Daniel Peris graciously made available to me the manuscript of his forthcoming book, *Storming the Heavens: The Soviet League of the Militant Godless*. For insights, criticisms, and suggestions, I thank Helmut Altrichter, Steven Batalden, Chris Chulos, Gayla Diment, Elisabeth Domansky, Catherine Evtuhov, Anne Gorsuch, Kent Guy, David Hoffmann, William Husband, Hubertus Jahn, Cathy Kudlick, Roman Laba, Joel Migdal, Susan Morrissey, Lou Roberts, Bernice Rosenthal, Edward Roslof, Karen Sawislak, Ted Taranovski, Daniel Waugh, and James West. I am especially grateful to Joan Ullman, who took time away from her work on Spanish anticlericalism to read a chapter on short notice. Like all scholars of rural Russia in the early Soviet period, I am indebted to the work of Moshe Lewin, who was generous with his time and advice during a consultation in Philadelphia. I am also profoundly indebted to the work of Gregory Freeze, who deserves special thanks for carefully reading an earlier version of the entire manuscript and for offering invaluable criticism and suggestions. S. A. Smith, Mark von Hagen, and one still anonymous reader gave the book an extremely careful review, and it is a pleasure to be able to thank them publicly. I am very fortunate to have Penn State Press as my publisher. I am grateful to its director, Sanford Thatcher, who showed an interest in my work when he first learned of the project, and to my editor, Peter Potter, whose sharp eye improved the book and whose belief in the project sustained me. Also deserving of my gratitude is Andrew Lewis, who was an exemplary copy editor, and Cherene Holland, who as managing editor, expertly shepherded the book through the production process. It was a pleasure to work with David Barnes, who drew the maps. Cynthia Bertelsen prepared the index. None of these individuals is responsible for any errors and shortcomings that may remain.

Portions of Chapters 1 and 5 have appeared, in somewhat different form, in *Canadian-American Slavic Studies* and *Russian History / Histoire Russe*, whose editors and publishers I thank.

Much of the book was written after I joined the History Department and Henry M. Jackson School of International Studies at the University of Washington. I thank Richard Johnson, chair of the department, and Jere Bacharach and Nicholas Lardy, directors of the School, for their support of the project. I was extremely fortunate to have three excellent research assistants: Dean Bennett, Peter Frykholm, and Benjamin Hanson. Thanks to Martha Walsh, who patiently answered my proofreading queries. For advice and support, I am grateful to Marie Anchordoguy, Herbert Ellison, Susan Hanley, Steve Hanson, Ray Jonas, Richard Kirkendall, Jason Mayerfeld, Uta Poiger, Clark Sorensen, Susan Whiting, and Kozo Yamamura.

As I looked over the educational path that led me to write *Power and the Sacred in Revolutionary Russia*, I realized how much I owe to some of my high school and college teachers. At Nazareth Area Senior High School, I received an excellent education from many dedicated and talented teachers. I would particularly like to thank John Cokefair, who taught me something important about reading texts. At Lafayette College, William Dobriner helped me immensely. At the University of Pennsylvania, I was fortunate to be a student of Laurence Dickey. Without his encouragement and model of intellectual commitment, I would not have studied history or gone to graduate school.

I am very grateful to the generous individuals who offered me the personal support that I very much needed to complete the book. In St. Petersburg, the late Semën Semënovich Landa and Iuna Ianovna Zek shared their home and knowledge of Russian history with me. I would especially like to thank Karen Eikenberry, Helen Ettlinger, the late Abigail Ghumph, Boris and Baschathia Ghumph, Robert Gurval, Kathy Hendley, Paul Harvey, Deborah Meyer, Tip Ragan, Anita Tien, and Pam Weeks.

It is not easy to find the words to thank Meri Gilman, who more than anyone else, helped me finish *Power and the Sacred*. She supported me on a daily basis with her inimitable generosity and enthusiasm. I am especially grateful to her for helping me to remember, and to honor, why I was writing.

A few words on relevant aspects of my own background are, I believe, in order. I am neither Orthodox nor a practicing member of any other faith. Nevertheless, religion has been an important part of my life. I was raised in Nazareth, Pennsylvania, which was founded in 1740 by the Moravians, a German Protestant sect. Launched as a religious "commune," the political and religious boundaries of the community were identical. Although Nazareth has not functioned as a religious commune for centuries, traces of its past make it a special town today, a place where the influence of religion in daily life seems more visible than elsewhere in the United States. As I grew up, I was conscious of its unusual origins and identity, an experience that has in large part generated my interest in the relationship between religion and politics.

Finally, a word of thanks to the family in which I grew up. They, along with whoever happened to be around for lively dinner debates and pinochle games, richly shaped my views of the world and have sustained my scholarly endeavors. My sister came through for me many a time in the early stages of the project. My brother wrote me a letter that helped give me courage and inspiration. Had my father been living when I was trying to rework and publish the book, he would have surely asked many times when I was "going to be done with it." But had I not had the model of his tenacity, I doubt that I would have begun the project, let alone finished it. My mother has been a model of intellectual curiosity and patience throughout my life; and her support really helped me see this project to completion. It is to the memory of my father and to my mother that I dedicate this book.

Abbreviations

RGIA	Russian State Historical Archive. Formerly Tsentral'nyi Gosudarstvennyi Istoricheskii Arkhiv (Central State Historical Archive).
RTsKhIDNI	Rossiiskii Tsentr Khraneniia i Izucheniia Dokumentov Noveishei Istorii (Center for the Preservation and Study of Documents [Records] of Modern History). Formerly Tsentral'nyi Partiinyi Arkhiv (Central Party Archive).
TsGAOR	Tsentral'nyi Gosudarstvennyi Arkhiv Oktiabr'skoi Revoliutsii SSSR (Central State Archive of the October Revolution of the USSR). Renamed Gosudarstvennyi Arkhiv Rossiiskoi Federatsii (State Archive of the Russian Federation).
TsGAOR Leningrada	Tsentral'nyi Gosudarstvennyi Arkhiv Oktiabr'skoi Revoliutsii i Sotsialisticheskogo Stroitel'stva Leningrada (Central State Archive of the October Revolution and the Building of Socialism, Leningrad).
Smolensk WKP	Smolensk Party Archive
IVO	A general reference to the Reports of the Chief Procurator of the Holy Synod; from 1866 to 1884, *Izvlecheniia iz vsepoddaneishego otcheta ober-prokurora sviateishego sinoda po vedomstvu pravoslavnogo ispovedaniia*; from 1886 to 1915, *Vsepoddaneishii otchet ober-prokurora sviateishego sinoda po vedomstvu pravoslavnogo ispovedaniia*. Cited as *IVO* by year (e.g. *IVO za 1901 g.*).
f.	*fond* (collection)
op.	*opis'* (inventory)
d.	*delo* (file)
ed. khr.	*edinitsa khraneniia* (individual file)
l., ll.	*list, listy* (folio, folios)
ob.	*oborot* (verso)

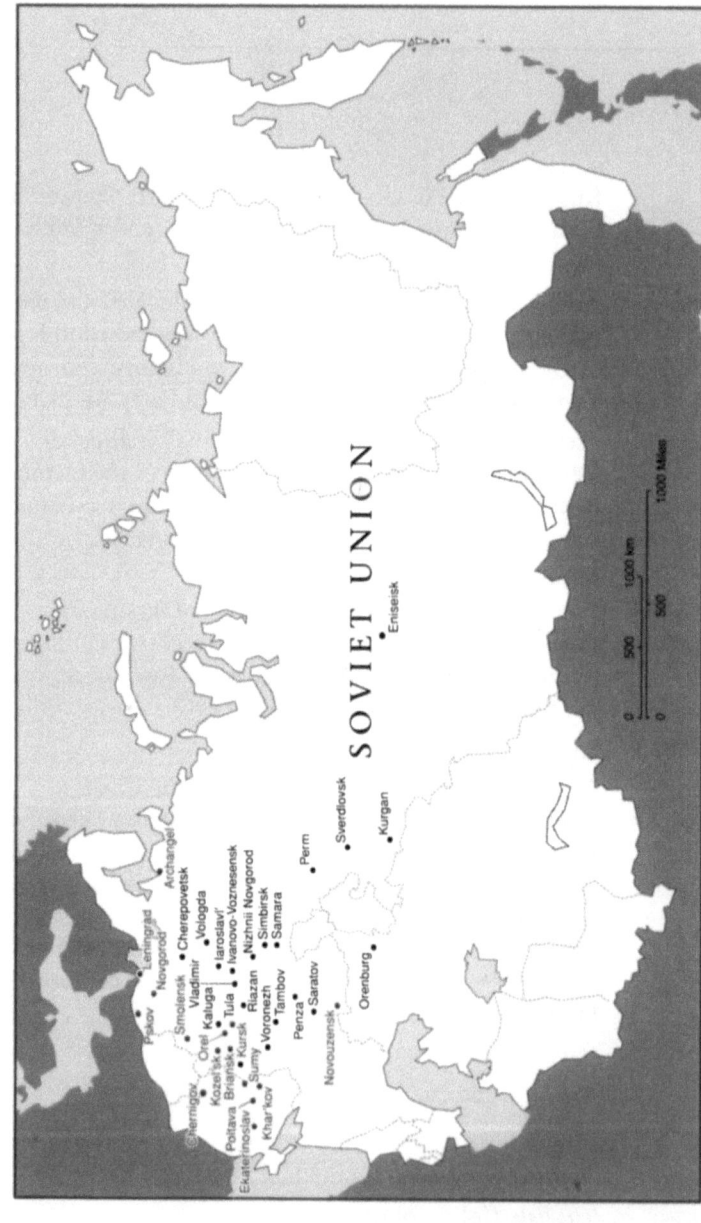

Fig. 1. Map of the Soviet Union, with details of Leningrad, Saratov, and Smolensk Regions, 1924

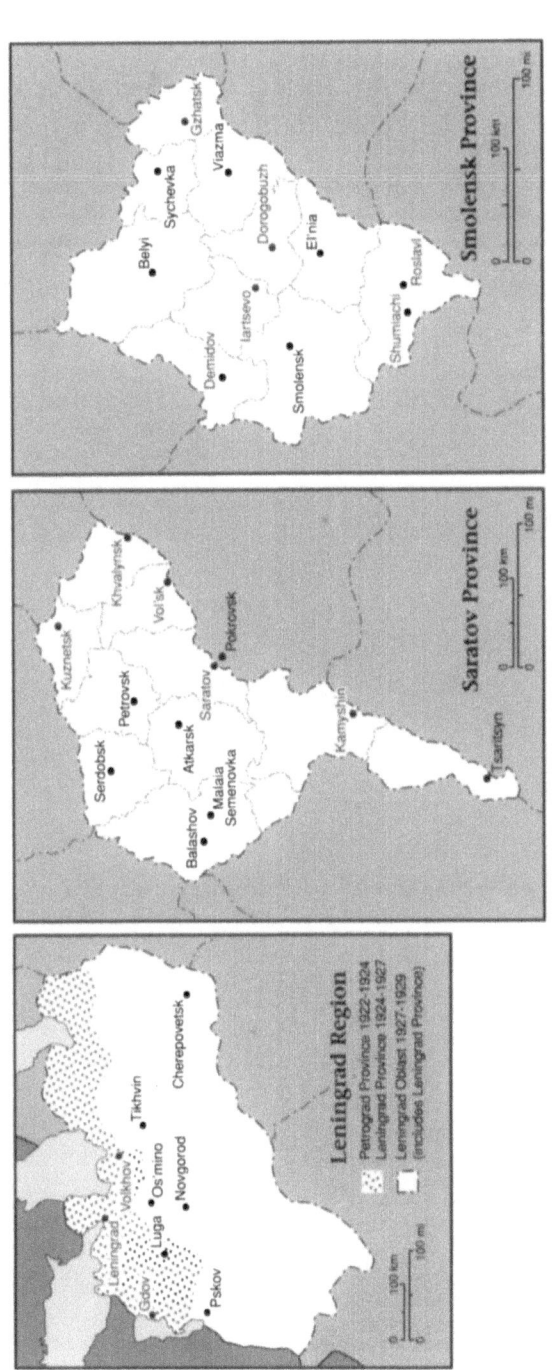

Introduction

> The separation of church and state in the conditions of Russian reality—this is absurd, not justified on any grounds. The Orthodox Church has acted as too strong a social organization within the Russian state, [and] their historical bond [of the Church and the state] is too deep, ... for this connection to be severed immediately. It seems to us that a reasonable government would not decide on this.
> —Anonymous priest in Tambov province, 1917

> The full separation of church and state—this is the demand that the socialist proletariat presents to the contemporary state and to the contemporary church.
> —V. I. Lenin

In this book I examine the relationship among Orthodox clergy, laity, and Communist Party cadres during the establishment of Soviet power in the Russian countryside in the period of New Economic Policy, 1921–28.[1] When the Bolsheviks seized power in 1917, the world turned upside down for rural Orthodox clergy and laity. Since the reforms of Peter the Great, the Orthodox Church had enjoyed complete state support at the cost of much of its independence.[2] Now the Orthodox community found itself liberated from its former captivity but forced to exist in the midst of a Party-state ideologically obsessed with the eradication of religion. The Bolsheviks' ideological

---

1. I have also occasionally included examples of sectarian villagers. Although the number of sectarians grew in the period 1917–28, some groups, such as the Dukhobors, Molokans, Subbotniki, and Khristoverie, actually lost members during this time. See A. I. Klibanov, *Religioznoe sektantstvo v proshlom i nastoiashchem* (Moscow, 1973), p. 249. In 1915, for example, there were around 2000 Baptists and Evangelical Christians in Voronezh province; by 1926–27, there were more than 5100 sectarians of the same denominations in basically the same territory. See Klibanov, *Religioznoe sektantstvo i sovremennost'* (Moscow, 1969), p. 71.

2. For challenges to the traditional assumption that the Russian state held the Orthodox Church in a position of institutional and ideological captivity, see Gregory L. Freeze, "Handmaiden of the State? The Church in Imperial Russia Reconsidered," *Journal of Ecclesiastical History* 36 (January 1985): 82–102, and "The Orthodox Church and Serfdom in Prereform Russia," *Slavic Review* 3 (Fall 1989): 361–87.

commitment spawned a massive assault on religious activity. While the Communist Party never wavered from the long-term goal of eliminating religious consciousness and practice, it shifted its short-term strategies depending on available resources and the perceived success of particular tactics.[3]

The antireligious "campaign," as friends of the regime called it, involved *de jure* legal constraint and deprivation, severe albeit haphazard physical persecution and torture, and the creation of organizations to expose villagers to antireligious propaganda.[4] The 1918 Constitution of the Russian Republic (RSFSR) guaranteed the right of religious and antireligious propaganda. However, as the new regime began to consolidate power after victory in the Civil War, it turned its attention to the "cultural front," especially to antireligious activities. State-sponsored antireligious activism was one element in the regime's project of cultural transformation.[5] The Tenth Party Congress (March 1921) called for intensified antireligious agitation and propaganda. An April 1923 Party directive called for intensive antireligious activism that would cause workers and peasants to discard religion and embrace a scientific view of the world. The leaders of two organizations, the Society of the Friends of the Newspaper *Bezbozhnik* (ODGB) (1924–25) and the League of the Godless (1925–41), under the leadership of Emel'ian Iaroslavskii, held the institutional reins of the antireligious campaign. Antireligious activists (*bezbozhniki*) included not only members of the rural cells of the ODGB and

---

3. See Dmitry Pospielovsky, *A History of Marxist-Leninist Atheism and Soviet Anti-Religious Policies* (New York, 1987), 1:8, 36.

4. For a discussion of the role of religious feeling in shaping the political activity of student radicals of the 1870s, particularly their contacts with workers, see Reginald E. Zelnik, "'To the Unaccustomed Eye': Religion and Irreligion in the Experience of St. Petersburg Workers in the 1870s," *Russian History* 16:2–4 (1989): esp. 303, 313–18.

5. This study assumes Clifford Geertz's definition of culture as "best seen not as complexes of concrete behavior patterns—customs, usages, traditions, habit clusters . . . , but as a set of control mechanisms—plans, recipes, rules, instructions . . . for the governing of behavior." To be sure, I often focus on these cultural *forms*—these "customs, usages, traditions, habit clusters"—just as the regime's leaders and cadres did. As we shall see, some antireligious leaders (e.g., Iaroslavskii) did regard cultural transformation as a project requiring the reshaping of consciousness. See Geertz's "Impact of the Concept of Culture on the Concept of Man," in *The Interpretation of Cultures* (New York, 1973), p. 44. Religion, because it offers a view of reality and the transcendental, acts as such a "control mechanism." By "religious villager" or "religious activist," I mean those villagers whose cultural commitments, in the form of religious values, plans, and recipes, motivated their everyday social, political, and even economic choices. Since the rural population did not consist exclusively of peasants, the more inclusive term "villager" also embraces former soldiers, general laborers, members of the rural "intelligentsia," craftsmen, and traders. On the expansion of rural industries during the Civil War, see Orlando Figes, *Peasant Russia, Civil War: The Volga Countryside in Revolution (1917–1921)* (New York, 1989), pp. 131, 286–89, 355. For a discussion of the literature on defining a peasant, see Joel S. Migdal, *Peasants, Politics, and Revolution: Pressures toward Political and Social Change in the Third World* (Princeton, N.J., 1974), pp. 23–25.

the League but also members of the Communist Party and Komsomol, demobilized Red Army veterans, and teachers.

Rural *bezbozhniki* carried on many different types of activity. They distributed antireligious literature such as the newspaper *Bezbozhnik* (The Godless, 1922–34), staged "secular" celebrations at Christmas and Easter, held antireligious debates and lectures, led campaigns to close village churches, and demonstrated modern agricultural techniques. They even engaged in what some leaders of the antireligious campaign called "rough methods," such as the destruction of church property and the physical and verbal harassment of clergy and laity. When *bezbozhniki* created an active antireligious cell in a particular village, they challenged the foundation of rural religious life.

Many studies, to be sure, have explored the relationship between religion and politics in the early Soviet period. Some have unearthed the tragic story of the regime's persecution of Orthodox church leaders, bishops, and parish clergy.[6] Some have examined what can be called the regime's "church politics," that is, its creation of strategies and institutions designed to cripple and eventually destroy the Orthodox Church.[7] Some have focused on the regime's efforts in antireligious propaganda and other kinds of antireligious activism, such as the League of the Godless.[8] We can learn much from these studies about how the Soviet regime mobilized against religion. But almost invariably these studies treat religion as an *object* of Soviet political mobilization. Consequently, it is easy to overemphasize the active role played by the state in a process that was necessarily two-sided. On the one hand, it is

---

6. Some important accounts are Lev Regel'son, *Tragediia russkoi tserkvi, 1917–1945* (Paris, 1977), and Anatolii Levitin and Vadim Shavrov, *Ocherki po istorii russkoi tserkovnoi smuty*, 3 vols. (Zürich, 1978).

7. Some examples include Paul Anderson, *People, Church, and State in Modern Russia* (New York, 1944); Michael Bourdeaux, *Opium of the People: The Christian Religion in the USSR* (London, 1965); John S. Curtiss, *The Russian Church and the Soviet State, 1917–1950* (Boston, 1953); William C. Fletcher, *A Study in Survival: The Church in Russia, 1927–42* (New York, 1965); Dmitry Pospielovsky, *The Russian Church Under the Soviet Regime, 1917–1982*, vol. 1 (Crestwood, N.Y., 1984); V. A. Alekseev, *Illiuzii i dogmy* (Moscow, 1991); Arto Luukkanen, *The Party of Unbelief: The Religious Policy of the Bolshevik Party, 1917–1929* (Helsinki, 1994); and Edward Roslof, "The Renovationist Movement in the Russian Orthodox Church, 1922–1946" (Ph.D. diss., University of North Carolina at Chapel Hill, 1994).

8. See, for example, Curtiss, *Russian Church*; G. V. Vorontsov, *Leninskaia programma ateisticheskogo vospitaniia v deistvii (1917–1937 gg.)* (Leningrad, 1973); Richard Stites, *Revolutionary Dreams: Utopian Vision and Experimental Life in the Russian Revolution* (New York, 1989); Stefan Plaggenborg, "Volksreligiösität und antireligiöse Propaganda in der frühen Sowjetunion," *Arkhiv für Sozialgeschichte* 26 (1992): 95–130; V. A. Alekseev, *Shturm nebes otmeniaetsia?* (Moscow, 1992); and Daniel Peris, "Storming the Heavens: The Soviet League of the Militant Godless and Bolshevik Political Culture in the 1920s and 1930s" (Ph.D diss., University of Illinois at Urbana–Champaign, 1994).

important to understand how the Soviet state went about attacking religious beliefs and institutions. On the other hand, one must recognize that Russian villagers were not simply passive recipients of state actions. This study is unique, therefore, in that it examines in detail the other side of the process. It shows how religious belief and practice of Russian villagers actually shaped both rural and national politics during the period of New Economic Policy. Thus, religious belief and practice served as an active agent of political mobilization and transformation.[9] This is not an examination of popular religiosity *per se*, though it is hoped that this study will act as an impetus for investigation along these lines.[10]

By taking this approach, I test some important assumptions about the New Economic Policy, a period whose meaning in Soviet history has been a matter of considerable debate. For instance, it is a commonplace that the Bolsheviks were preoccupied with military concerns and the creation of a centralized, bureaucratic state; and their state-building efforts extinguished the vibrant rural political life that had developed between the Revolutions of 1917 and the outbreak of civil conflict.[11] Furthermore, it is commonly argued that a vital "political society" in the countryside did not exist during NEP.[12] While granting the existence of civil society in this period, Western

---

9. Studies that offer insightful glimpses into this dynamic include Helmut Altrichter, *Die Bauern von Tver: Vom Leben auf dem russischen Dorfe zwischen Revolution und Kollektivierung* (Munich, 1984), and Moshe Lewin, *The Making of the Soviet System: Essays in the Social History of Interwar Russia* (New York, 1985). On the political strategies of clergy and lay activists during collectivization, see Lynne Viola, *Peasant Rebels Under Stalin: Collectivization and the Culture of Peasant Resistance* (New York, 1996); on their activism after collectivization, see Sheila Fitzpatrick, *Stalin's Peasants: Resistance and Survival in the Russian Village After Collectivization* (New York, 1994). Outside the Russian field, important examples of this approach include Jean Meyer, *The Cristero Rebellion: The Mexican People Between Church and State, 1926–1929* (New York, 1976); Prasenjit Duara, *Culture, Power, and the State: Rural North China, 1900–1942* (Stanford, Calif., 1988), and Suzanne Desan, *Reclaiming the Sacred: Lay Religion and Popular Politics in Revolutionary France* (Ithaca, N.Y., 1990).

10. Recent scholars and contemporaries alike have tried to subsume the rich and elusive experience of rural religiosity into a series of mutually exclusive antipodes, such as "pagan" vs. "Christian," "pious" vs. "superstitious," "backward" vs. "advanced," "*izba*" vs. "Church," "miracle" vs. "magic," and "Orthodox" vs. "Christian anti-Orthodox." Sergei Kravchinsky, *The Russian Peasantry* (1888; reprint, Westport, Conn., 1977), argues that the religion of the Russian peasantry was fundamentally pagan, rather than Orthodox, or in some cases, a dual faith (*dvoeverie*) based on a combination thereof. Pierre Pascal has claimed that peasant religiosity exemplified Christianity more than the official Orthodox creed. See his *Religion of the Russian People*, trans. Rowan Williams (Crestwood, N.Y., 1976). For a useful summary of these views, see Lewin, "Popular Religion in Twentieth-Century Russia," in *Making of the Soviet System*, pp. 59–71.

11. Figes, *Peasant Russia, Civil War*, pp. 354–55.

12. I am referring to Alexis de Tocqueville's distinction between political and civil society, as elaborated in *Democracy in America* (New York, 1966).

historians have assumed that "politics" could have occurred only in the cities, and that rural political development, if it existed at all, followed the same pattern of truncation that occurred within the urban-based Communist Party itself.[13] Historians of the Soviet countryside during the NEP period have also implicitly perpetuated this assumption of the apolitical villager, even as they have discussed villagers' involvement in the village assemblies and rural soviets, respectively the traditional and revolutionary organs of rural government. Both Western and Soviet historians have described the village assembly's *administrative* preeminence over the soviet during the NEP period.[14] They have portrayed its members' behavior as the routine and impartial execution of fixed duties, rather than as having the essential qualities of political action: to "fight," to "be passionate," and to exhibit a "feeling of responsibility" and a "sense of proportion."[15] These same historians have likewise argued that politics did not take place in the village soviet, which they have cast as ineffectual, "weak" institutions divorced from the fabric of rural life.[16] This study, however, tests whether the involvement of religious villagers in the village assemblies and rural soviets remained confined to administration or whether it contributed to the development of a vital "political society" in the countryside.[17]

This study is part of the ongoing discussion about the relationship between "state" and "society" during NEP.[18] It is about the degree of state hegemony on the one hand, and the autonomy of social groups and cultural life on the

13. Lewin recently wrote that, at NEP's demise, "there was no Bolshevik party any more, and one could even say, *no political party at all*." See his "Russia/USSR in Historical Motion: An Essay in Interpretation," *Russian Review* 50 (July 1991): 250.

14. See, for example, Dorothy Atkinson, *The End of the Russian Land Commune, 1905–1930* (Stanford, Calif., 1983), esp. p. 231; Lewin, *Making of the Soviet System*, esp. p. 86, and Yuzuru Taniuchi, *The Village Gathering in Russia in the Mid-1920s* (Birmingham, England: 1968), pp. 3–25. Both Lewin and Taniuchi tellingly describe the assembly as "managing" the affairs of the village, thereby lending it an administrative rather than political identity.

15. On the distinction between administration and politics, see Max Weber, "Politics as a Vocation," in *From Max Weber: Essays in Sociology*, ed. and trans. H. H. Gerth and C. W. Mills (NewYork, 1958), esp. pp. 95, 115.

16. See especially Lewin, *Making of the Soviet System* and *Russian Peasants and Soviet Power: A Study of Collectivization* (New York, 1968), and Taniuchi, *Village Gathering*.

17. Some attention is also given to the relationship of religious activists to the *volost'* soviets and *volost'* executive committees (VIKs). In other words, I have chosen to focus on the political institutions that villagers regarded as "theirs," that is, subject to their influence. See Mikhail I. Fenomenov, *Sovremennaia derevnia: Opyt kraevedcheskogo obsledovaniia odnoi derevni (Derevnia Gadyshi, Valdaiskogo uezda, Novgorodskoi gubernii)* (Leningrad, 1925), 2:95. See also the discussion of this issue in Chapter 4.

18. For an extremely valuable synthesis of much of the literature that examines state-society relations, see Lewis Siegelbaum, *Soviet State and Society Between Revolutions, 1918–1929* (New York, 1992).

other. That debate has usually been cast as one between adherents of two mutually exclusive positions, which can be loosely described as "creeping totalitarianism" versus "pluralism." Adherents of the creeping-totalitarian paradigm maintain that the Communist state apparatus not only sought but attained steadily increasing "control" (a term rarely defined) over Russian society prior to the abandonment of NEP and the "great break" of 1928–29.[19] "Pluralists," however, assume a relative constancy in the state's intent to achieve hegemony over Russian society during the period in question, a level considerably lower than during either the Civil War or the "great break" that followed NEP. As a consequence, they emphasize the existence and even the vitality of independent social groups and cultural life.[20] These are the paradigms of the debate that began roughly in the mid-1980s, when Stephen Cohen published his manifesto of pluralist revisionism, *Rethinking the Soviet Experience*, where he characterized NEP as an alternative prototype of Soviet socialism. How should religious activists' involvement in rural politics be synthesized with other scholarship on state-society relations during NEP? Would such a synthesis support either of the two paradigms discussed above; or should we adopt a third, alternative approach in light of the research amassed to date?

To answer these questions, we must begin our story in the years immediately following the emancipation of the serfs from the legal ownership of the nobility in 1861. Seeking to modernize the economy and society while retaining the autocratic political structure, the tsarist government enacted the "Great Reforms." It created the first independent judiciary in Russian history, set up institutions of local self-government or *zemstva*, altered the basis of military service, created new institutions of municipal self-government, and sought to transform the clerical estate (*soslovie*) into a modern, professional pastorate.[21] The emancipation, the other Great Reforms, and Russia's industrial "takeoff" in the 1890s combined to produce extremely fluid political and social relationships in the countryside. As peasants streamed into the cities to work in new and gigantic factories, the boundaries between the

---

19. Merle Fainsod, *Smolensk Under Soviet Rule* (Cambridge, Mass., 1958); Leonard Schapiro, *The Communist Party of the Soviet Union* (New York, 1960); Adam Ulam, *The Bolsheviks: The Intellectual and Political History of the Triumph of Communism in Russia* (New York: Macmillan, 1965); Martin Malia, *The Soviet Tragedy: A History of Socialism in Russia, 1917–1991* (New York, 1994), esp. p. 171.

20. Some influential revisionist accounts are Stephen F. Cohen, *Bukharin and the Bolshevik Revolution: A Political Biography, 1888–1938* (New York, 1973), esp. pp. 270–76; Cohen, *Rethinking the Soviet Experience: Politics and History Since 1917* (New York, 1985), and Moshe Lewin, *Lenin's Last Struggle*, trans. A. M. Sheridan Smith (New York, 1968).

21. The literature on the Great Reforms is voluminous. A recent and notable contribution is *Russia's Great Reforms, 1855–1881*, ed. J. Bushnell, B. Eklof, and L. Zakharova (Bloomington, Ind., 1994).

city and the countryside became more porous than ever before.

To what extent, and in what ways, were Orthodox clergy and laity drawn into the political (and administrative) arena during this period of social and political turbulence? This investigation sets up the subsequent examination of the politics of religious activism during NEP in two ways. It helps us evaluate the degree to which the political identities and experience of clergy and lay activists in the very late tsarist period shaped their perception of the political opportunities of the very early Soviet period.[22] Second, it enables us to place the politics of religious activists during NEP in comparative perspective, to highlight what was specific to the 1920s.

For too long students of early Soviet history have ignored the meaning that Soviet cadres attached to rural religious activity. If we want to understand the development of Soviet political culture and especially the background to Stalin's forced collectivization, we must explore the *image* of the rural religious as seen through the eyes of members of the Central Committee, the leadership of the League of the Godless, or rural *bezbozhniki*, and other officials.[23] The compulsion to equate the religious villager and especially the priest with the well-off peasant or "kulak," for example, prevented agents of the state from seeing the rural religious for who they "really were," from admitting and recording their actual socioeconomic identity; yet such an image acted, for the *bezbozhnik*, as his or her *reality* of the social identity of the religious villager.

Language or discourse, as reference to the highly charged category of the "kulak" suggests, both reflected and constructed this changing image of political society.[24] For this reason, my study pays particular attention to the vocabulary used in the Soviet periodical press to describe religious activity, especially the involvement of religious villagers in ostensibly "Soviet" institutions such as the rural soviets and the cooperatives.[25] I am interested in the

---

22. On the need to examine how the culture and social structure of tsarist Russia shaped Soviet society, see Lewin, *Making of the Soviet System*.

23. Along these lines, Leopold Haimson discusses the *image* of civil society that existed by the end of the 1870s, and focuses on what he calls the changing "representations" of the body politic that particular political parties, such as the Bolsheviks, held of various social groups. See his "Civil War and the Problem of Social Identities in Early Twentieth-Century Russia," in D. Koenker, W. G. Rosenberg, and R. G. Suny, eds., *Party, State, and Society in the Russian Civil War* (Bloomington, Ind., 1989), pp. 24–25, 32.

24. For an analysis of this dual significance of language during the French Revolution, see Lynn Hunt, "The Rhetoric of Revolution," in *Politics, Culture, and Class in the French Revolution* (Berkeley, Calif., 1984), pp. 19–51. Like Hunt, I am assuming that "revolutionary language ... was itself transformed into an instrument of political and social change." More specifically, as Hunt maintains, "The language itself helped shape the perception of interests and the development of ideologies." See Hunt, p. 24.

25. The distinction between perceptions (or representations) and "reality" tended to be used first by historians of the late tsarist period and of the Revolutions of 1917, such as Engelstein,

substance of the categories that the *bezbozhniki*, members of the rural apparat, antireligious correspondents, and village correspondents (*sel'kory*) used to talk about religious villagers.²⁶ The sources used in this study—provincial newspapers, newspapers and other publications of the League of the Godless, Party records, reports of ethnographic expeditions, and archival records of various cultural enlightenment organizations (such as the Union of Cultural Enlightenment Workers for the Leningrad Region or the Society to Liquidate Illiteracy) or the local *apparat*—offer excellent evidence for mapping out cadres' changing perceptions of religious activity, as reflected in the shifting discourse of the antireligious campaign.

A related but distinct issue is the *image* that rural religious activists formed of both the agents of the state mentioned above and various would-be institutions of "Soviet power," if indeed the two can be separated in practice. Like those in the state apparatus, religious villagers carried their own baggage —usually more historical than ideological, to be sure—that shaped their "representation" of bureaucratic and political officials, as well as institutions such as the village soviet. This is a study in the history of perceptions, in perceptions of how certain contemporaries construed the meaning of factional political activity in Soviet Russia of the 1920s.

The regional foci of this study are Leningrad, Saratov, and Smolensk provinces. Despite its concentration in three provinces, however, this book is not a systematic comparison of regional development. I draw together

---

Galili, Haimson, Koenker, and Rosenberg. Historians of the Soviet period have begun to follow their lead in applying such an approach, although very little of this work has been published. See Haimson's warning against "reifying," or reducing to a set of "objective" characteristics, particular social identities in his "Civil War and the Problem of Social Identities," in *Party, State, and Society*, esp. pp. 27, 32. He analyzes the labels applied by the "plebs" of urban Russia to those they voted against in elections to the Constituent Assembly. See also Ziva Galili, "Commercial-Industrial Circles in Revolution: The Failure of 'Industrial Progressivism,'" in Edith Frankel, Jonathan Frankel, and Baruch Knei-Paz, eds., *Revolution in Russia: Reassessments of 1917* (New York, 1992), pp. 188–216; idem, *The Menshevik Leaders in the Russian Revolution* (Princeton, N.J., 1989), and Laura Engelstein, *The Keys to Happiness: Sex and the Search for Modernity in Fin-de-Siècle Russia* (Ithaca, N.Y., 1992). Moshe Lewin, in "Society, State, and Ideology During the First Five-Year Plan," also hints at the important distinction between the "objective reality" and perception of the state: "For the peasant, what was 'state' [*kazennyi*] came to be seen as the product of a foreign, soulless, and oppressive force." See *Making of the Soviet System*, p. 215. He does not, however, apply this distinction consistently.

26. The same instructions and training that stressed the political mission of the *sel'kor* enjoined budding correspondents to be a "mirror" of rural life, a charge that to some extent exemplified Marxism-Leninism's apotheosis of scientific objectivity and rationality. Emel'ian Iaroslavskii, for example, called on village correspondents to reflect "how the country's heart beats." *Pravda*, May 23, 1923. Iaroslavskii became the leader of the League of the Godless in 1925. Thus the ideological "socialization" and concrete instructions that village correspondents received rendered them unlikely candidates for writing stories full of bald lies.

material from the three provinces as a common pool of information rather than as a basis for rigorous comparison. I also refer to other parts of the RSFSR and to Ukraine, when I think it is illuminating to do so.

In Chapters 1 and 2 I examine religious belief and practice as an agent of political mobilization during the period between the emancipation of the serfs in 1861 and the inauguration of New Economic Policy in 1921. Chapter 1 investigates the political consequences of religious belief from 1861 to the February Revolution in 1917. In what ways did religious commitments shape village politics—as well as attitudes toward and resistance to the state—during this period? Chapter 2 treats the politics of religious belief and practice during the social revolution of 1917–18 and the Russian Civil War. In particular, how did religious activists respond to the regime's Decree on the Separation of Church and State (January 1918)?

In Chapters 3, 4, 5, and 6 I examine how rural religious activists confronted the cultural and political conflict generated by issues of religious belief and practice during NEP. Chapters 3 and 4 explore how cultural conflict produced by the antireligious campaign divided the Russian village during NEP. To what extent did the cultural transformation sought by antireligious activists create cultural conflict, and how did it do so? Chapter 5 examines how the new political, social, and economic "conjuncture" of NEP affected the rural clergy's relationship to the parish and to the village at large. How did rural clergy respond to their changed status? Chapter 6 examines the role of Orthodox laity in sustaining parish life during NEP and in the larger cultural and political conflict surrounding religious belief and practice. If the laity played a greater role in parish affairs, what means did they use to do so? What was the influence of the new political context on the everyday religious life of rural clergy and laity? To what extent did villagers sustain religious life during the antireligious campaign, and how did they do so?

Chapters 7, 8, and 9 examine the relationship between religious activists and both traditional and Soviet political institutions. Chapters 7 and 8 examine how the various interests of religious activists shaped and transformed the content of rural politics during NEP. How effectively did clergy and lay activists use the village assembly, the cooperative, and the village soviet to garner financial and material resources for the parish? What were the political consequences of Orthodox villagers' attachment to religious ritual? Chapter 9 analyzes antireligious rhetoric in order to assess perceptions of rural religious activity, especially in the political sphere. How and why did these representations change over the course of NEP?

My intent throughout is to show why and how Russian villagers revived political life in the countryside and demonstrate that by doing so, they shaped the development of the Soviet state itself.

1

Ironic Beginnings

The "Great Reforms" struck a blow at the basic structures of power in the Russian countryside, including the Russian Orthodox Church. When the Emancipation Proclamation of 1861 demolished the old principles for constituting rural social relations, new principles had to be created.[1] Who was to wield power? What was the nature of that power to be? What symbols were to legitimate it? An air of uncertainty surrounded these questions. It was unclear who was to perform the functions previously carried out by the nobles, as well as new ones generated by the Emancipation itself.[2] In this context, the parish clergy, long the objects of the cameralist manipulations

---

1. Or at least dressed up in new garb, as the regime's increasing emphasis on *soslovie* during the "counterreforms" would illustrate. Gregory Freeze, "The *Soslovie* (Estate) Paradigm and Russian Social History," *American Historical Review* 91 (February 1986): 11–25.

2. By losing the legal right to hold other human beings in bondage, the gentry also lost other rights that accompanied that privilege: for example, the right to subject other human beings to manorial justice. For more details, see Geroid Tanquary Robinson, *Rural Russia Under the Old Regime: A History of the Landlord-Peasant Revolution of 1917* (Berkeley, Calif., 1932), pp. 42–45. To be sure, well after the Emancipation, the nobility doggedly continued to exercise considerable power on the local level, as the 1889 creation of the land captain (*zemskii nachal'nik*), who were in practice mostly drawn from the noble *soslovie*, exemplified. On Robinson's account of the nobility's tenacious clinging to local positions of political power despite their economic

of the tsarist state, were attractive candidates for assuming some of the reins of power wielded by the nobility prior to the Emancipation.³ In these shifting sands, even rural parishioners were obliged to define, on an ongoing basis, their place in the new sociopolitical order, as well as the sociopolitical significance they ascribed to both Orthodox and "pagan" beliefs and practices. In what ways were Orthodox clergy and laity drawn into the rural political (and administrative) arena during this period of turbulent political, social, and cultural change? What political identities and experience did clergy and lay activists bring to their evaluation of the political opportunities of the very early Soviet period? These are the main questions to be examined here.

The Politics of Rural Parish Life during the "Great Reforms"

On the eve of the Emancipation, parish clergy led a very difficult day-to-day existence. Obliged to spend much of their time working the land in order to survive, they to some extent shared peasants' "common existential dilemma."⁴ Like peasants, they lacked basic necessities and worried about how they would feed themselves. Yet they were also the employees of their peasant parishioners, paid in money or kind for services rendered (the per-

---

decline in the post-Emancipation period, see pp. 131–32. See also Roberta Thompson Manning, *The Crisis of the Old Order in Russia: Gentry and Government* (Princeton, N.J., 1982), pp. 38–39.

3. The "white" or nonmonastic clergy was divided into ordained and nonordained ranks. Ordained clergy had taken their holy orders through the sacrament of ordination. Their ranks included the archpriest (*protoierei*), an honorific title held by a very small number of priests in the average diocese of around several thousand clergy; Freeze estimates that no more than about a dozen priests (*sviashchennosluzhiteli*) as a rule had this title. The chief representative of the ordained clergy in most parishes was thus the priest (*ierei; sviashchennik*), who "bore primary responsibility in the parish for administering sacraments, performing private prayer services, overseeing subordinate clergy, and filing varied documents with their superiors in the Church." Deacons, beloved by parishioners for their contribution to the aesthetics of church services, existed in about half of all parishes. The nonordained clergy was comprised of the *diachok* (reader or chanter), the *ponomar* (reader or chanter), and *psalomshchik* (reader or chanter). Because they were not ordained, they could not administer sacraments; they assisted the priest by singing parts of the services, making sure parishioners behaved themselves, ringing the church bells, and performing various custodial functions. On this and the clerical estate more generally, see Gregory Freeze, *The Parish Clergy in Nineteenth-Century Russia: Crisis, Reform, Counter-Reform* (Princeton, N.J., 1983), p. 53.

4. James Scott, *The Moral Economy of the Peasant: Subsistence and Rebellion in Southeast Asia* (New Haven, Conn., 1976), p. 25.

formance of sacraments, other rites, and prayer services) and implicitly if not directly rewarded for their help in preserving their parishioners' cherished "local religion" (their attachments to particular religious places, shrines, and icons) against the encroachment of bishops and state officials.[5] Resenting this dependence, some parishioners developed strong anticlerical sentiments. As Vissarion Belinsky put it, parishioners had a long-standing tendency to view the priest as "a symbol of gluttony, avarice, sycophancy[, and] bawdiness."[6] When clergy failed to meet their needs, parishioners withheld emoluments, exercised *de facto* control over clerical appointments and tenure, and even endangered clergy's physical security. (Much of the parishioners' religious life, especially its "local" element, did *not* depend on the services or even the presence of clergy.) At the hire of their parishioners, clergy had other masters, too. Church hierarchs and state officials sought to create pastorally oriented priests and other clergy who would not only be loyal to the autocracy but mold their parishioners, who would thereby, because they were fully integrated into the national framework of the Orthodox Church, become good citizens.

By the late 1850s, church hierarchs and state officials could claim some progress in this regard. Future priests had been receiving more training in composing "short, artless talks suitable for understanding by the common people," rather than in "the composition of sermons in accordance with the rules of rhetorical art."[7] There was indeed some indication that these curricular reforms had enhanced the desired pastoral capacities; some priests displayed an increased capacity for informal communication with their parishioners, preferring informal talks (*besedy*) to prepared, highly structured sermons.[8] Nevertheless, the parish clergy remained, to Nicholas I's deep chagrin, much more defined by its liturgical than by its pastoral functions; and for this reason they also suffered the disdain of bishops, gentry, and state officials. They were in effect the "scapegoat" estate. Thus it is not surprising that in the twilight years of serfdom, one parish priest described the

---

5. I draw here on William Christian's concept of "local" religion, that is, the attachment of villagers in a very circumscribed geographical area to particular religious places (e.g., road shrines), to religious ceremonies and festivals unique to a particular village, and the like. See his *Local Religion in Sixteenth-Century Spain* (Princeton, N.J., 1981). Moshe Lewin has used "rural Christianity" to capture elements of this "amalgam of Christian symbolism welded onto a bedrock of an old agricultural civilization." See his "Popular Religion in Twentieth-Century Russia," in *Making of the Soviet System*, p. 70. On the unsuccessful efforts to create state salaries for clergy during the Nikolaevan period, see Freeze, *Parish Clergy*, pp. 65–75, 82–86, 89.

6. Vissarion Belinskii, "Letter to N. V. Gogol," in Marc Raeff, ed., *Russian Intellectual History: An Anthology* (New York, 1986), p. 256.

7. F. I. Titov, *Makarii Bulgakov, mitropolit moskovskii i komenskii* (Kiev, 1895–1903), 1:240, quoted in Freeze, *Parish Clergy*, p. 130.

8. Freeze, *Parish Clergy*, p. 130.

Russian parish clergy as a "shadow, an apparition," a sad evocation of the degree to which members of the priestly caste believed that their sense of themselves and their calling had been fashioned in reaction to the wishes of others.⁹ Whether the clergy would, in the words of that same parish priest, regain "consciousness of their own significance," appeared highly doubtful on the eve of the Great Reforms.¹⁰

Yet even before the Emancipation Proclamation the tsarist government had begun to think about ways to use clergy in the new political order. It was not only that parish priests (as opposed to *prichetniki*, or the nonordained clergy) were to read the Manifesto in church, thereby symbolically giving it religious sanction and preventing anticipated peasant unrest.¹¹ Parish priests were to have especially broad duties in relation to both nonordained clergy and former serfs. They were to counteract any erroneous popular understandings that the *prichetniki* circulated with a very literal explanation of the Manifesto.¹² Treating members of their own estate (*soslovie*) as objects of political surveillance, the clergy were obliged to inform their superintendents of any subversive behavior on the part of the nonordained clergy.¹³ Officials such as the Minister of Justice V. N. Panin, as well as diocesan archbishops, believed that the most important political task of parish clergy, however, was to remind peasants to "'zealously and continuously' fulfill their duties to the state."¹⁴ Parish priests were exhorted to fulfill this task in conversations with parishioners in church and at home.¹⁵ At least one archbishop reminded the clergy that it was incumbent upon them, as members of a "great estate of the Russian state," to fulfill these duties.¹⁶ In this the clergy were seen as a political extension of the autocracy.

Even though a "small proportion" of the parish clergy did play a significant if ambiguous role in stimulating peasant unrest, they did not, as a rule, view the state as an adversary in the early 1860s.¹⁷ Responding to the

---

9. I. S. Belliustin, *Description of the Clergy in Rural Russia: The Memoir of a Nineteenth-Century Parish Priest*, ed. and trans. G. L. Freeze (Ithaca, N.Y., 1985), p. 34.

10. Ibid.

11. On this see Aleksandr Rozanov, *Zapiski sel'skogo sviashchennika. Byt i nuzhdy pravoslavnogo dukhovenstva* (St. Petersburg, 1882), pp. 22–23.

12. "Otnoshenie ministra iustitsii gr. V. N. Panina ober-prokurora sinoda A. P. Tolstomu ot 24 noiabria 1860 g.," in I. Gurskaia, "Tserkov' i reforma 1861 g.," *Krasnyi arkhiv* 52 (1935): 183.

13. Ibid.

14. See, for example, "Otnoshenie ministra iustitsii," p. 183, and "Vozzvanie arkhiepiskopa polotskogo i vitebskogo Vasiliia k dukhovenstvu Polotskoi eparkhii," in Gurskaia, "Tserkov' i reforma 1861 g.," pp. 186–88.

15. "Vozzvanie," in Gurskaia, "Tserkov' i reforma 1861 g.," p. 187.

16. Ibid.

17. On the role of clergy in inciting peasant unrest in response to the Emancipation statute, see Freeze, *Parish Clergy*, p. 237.

questionnaire drafted by the Special Commission on Church Reforms, the clergy voiced—just as the parish priest I. S. Belliustin had a few years earlier—their aspirations to be state civil servants who enjoyed a steady and adequate salary, not to mention other benefits.[18] It may be an exaggeration to say that most parish clergy viewed the state as a beneficent Hegelian "universal bureaucracy." But clergy did believe the state could *potentially* shield them from material want and peasant animosity. Many wanted, therefore, to be subsumed to a greater degree within the state, rather than to estrange themselves from it.

The clergy had their hopes of becoming comfortable state servants raised—and dashed—by the church reforms of the 1860s. As Minister of Interior Valuev and others crafted the bureaucratic mechanisms for church reform and sought to involve Russian society in the reform process, they in general had three interrelated goals: to improve the material condition of the clergy, to liberate the clergy from the shackles of the *soslovie* straitjacket, and to fashion a clergy more effective in fulfilling a broadened pastoral role.[19] Enjoying greater support—financial and otherwise—from parishioners, the clergy was to become more "modern" and "professional." These reforms, while making some headway, largely failed to meet their stated goals.[20]

These same reforms had, nevertheless, significant yet unanticipated consequences for parish life. The service reform of 1868–69 is one case in point.[21] To ease the financial burdens on the church hierarchy and on parishioners themselves, parishes were to be merged and consolidated into, in theory, one "main church" (*glavnaia tserkov'*) and one "attached church" (*pripisnaia tserkov'*).[22] The statute thus—in theory—subordinated the parish, the needs of parishioners, and even religious practice itself to the political designs and agendas of the state;[23] but in practice, the parish reform of 1869

---

18. The Special Commission sent out its request for parish clergy's "opinions" in March 1863; by April–May, most had complied. On this see ibid., pp. 260–61ff. On clergy's desire to be state servants, see ibid., p. 272. On Belliustin's "étatisme," see ibid., p. 210, and Belliustin, *Description*.

19. By the beginning of the 1870s, several major reforms had been implemented: the 1867 decree that ended "hereditary family claims" to clerical positions; the 1869 decree that made some provisions for children of clergy to leave the clerical estate; the 1869 decree that reorganized the parish and clerical service; and the decrees of 1867 and 1869 that restructured the Church's seminaries and academies. See Freeze, *Parish Clergy*, p. 345. On May 26, 1869, Alexander II signed the aforementioned law that sought to allow children of clergy to leave the clerical estate by granting them the rank of "personal nobility." See Freeze's discussion on pp. 311–12.

20. See ibid., esp. pp. 248–347.

21. For the details of this reform, see ibid., pp. 315–19.

22. For details on the reform, see ibid., pp. 317–18. The statute made allowances for local conditions to determine whether these two churches were served by one or two priests. For details, see ibid., p. 316.

23. While apparently striking a major blow at the autonomy of clergy, laity, and the parish,

elicited clerical and especially lay initiative in defending parish needs.[24]

What parishioners cared most about defending and preserving were not the material interests of clergy threatened by the potential elimination of their positions but the church buildings themselves. Parishioners realized that the state was trying to use the parish for its own purposes. In at least one case, they reportedly exclaimed, "What right does the Tsar have to take away our church?"[25] It was not just that rural parishioners found the thought of traveling to more distant churches onerous, or viewed their churches as proverbial "old shoes" that they had grown used to attending, repairing, and renovating. All that was true. But parishioners were angry and sad about the impending loss of their churches because they practiced a highly "local" religion: "Moreover, our prayers in an alien church will be cold, for we will not see the remains of our close kin there."[26]

For these reasons parishioners expended great energy in resisting the implementation of the parish reform. They refused to attend church in the new parishes. They flooded diocesan officials with petitions to save their churches. They stepped up expressions of anticlericalism: for example, they even kicked the priest out of the parish, a decision apparently made at the village assembly. In some cases, parishioners were acting so autonomously that they reasserted the right of choosing their own priests at their village assemblies (*vybornoe nachalo*).[27] This is not surprising, given that as the commune's political and administrative organ, the village assembly remained the "center of formal political authority in the village" after the Emancipation of 1861; moreover, well before the Revolutions of 1917, the village assembly had allotted financial expenditures for religious needs.[28] Its fiscal functions not limited by the Emancipation legislation to turning over taxes to the tsarist government, the commune could also engage in building and granting financial support to churches and schools and in allotting resources to

---

the statute made the diocese—or its provincial commission—responsible for drawing up the "new registries of the parishes" (*novye rospisaniia prikhodov*). It thereby gave greater scope to local initiative in deciding how parishes were to be reorganized. For details, see ibid., p. 316.

24. Ibid., p. 365.

25. Quoted in ibid., p. 366. For relevant details, see p. 367.

26. This quotation, taken from Freeze's *Parish Clergy*, is from a statement of protest made by parishioners in Vladimir province to the diocesan committee responsible for compiling the draft *shtaty* (register of clerical positions). See Freeze, pp. 370–71. As in the eighteenth century, parishioners' attachments to local elements of their religiosity motivated them to resist the claims of the state. See Gregory Freeze, *The Russian Levites: Parish Clergy in the Eighteenth Century* (Cambridge, Mass., 1977), pp. 178–79.

27. See Freeze, *Parish Clergy*, p. 376.

28. This is Theda Skocpol's assessment as offered in *States and Social Revolutions: A Comparative Analysis of France, Russia, and China* (New York, 1979), p. 132.

other community needs.²⁹ After 1861, the peasants' "rural society" (*sel'skoe obshchestvo*) chose individuals to collect voluntary contributions for the construction and improvement of churches.³⁰

Parish clergy, too, had reason to see themselves and their calling in new ways in the aftermath of the Emancipation and other reforms. In the 1870s and 1880s the new tasks and sociopolitical roles that clergy assumed in the wake of the Emancipation and other "Great Reforms" began to crystallize. Their new and enhanced duties came from two sources.

The first taskmaster was the Russian state. Its officials tried once again to make the clergy effective shepherds of their flocks' moral and political behavior.³¹ Invoked rhetorically in official synodal publications of the 1870s and 1880s (and beyond), the ambiguous term "religious-moral situation" meant, on the one hand, clerical vigilance in shielding parishioners from competitive threats to Orthodox belief and practice, such as pagan traditions, the doctrines of the Old Belief, and sectarian movements.³² On the other hand, it meant clerical vigilance in monitoring parishioners' social comportment. In the yearly reports of the Holy Synod from the 1870s and 1880s, excessive alcohol consumption was portrayed as a prime example of the "overt unscrupulousness and disorderliness" that clergy had to be vigilant about. Aleksandr Rozanov, a parish priest in Saratov province, stated emphatically in his autobiography: "The entire life of a village priest—all of his activity, all of his thoughts, his entire soul—should be dedicated to the religious-moral condition [*religiozno-nravstvennoe sostoianie*] of his parishioners."³³

Parish clergy of Rozanov's generation employed a number of tools to fulfill this mandate. They relied in particular on religious instruction offered in formats (*besedy, chteniia, vnebogosluzhebnye sobesedovaniia*) distinct from liturgy and religious services themselves.³⁴ Discussions were held in locations

29. Atkinson, *Russian Land Commune*, p. 25. According to law, however, taxes levied for such concerns had to be approved by the peasant *volost'*. See also Donald Male, *Russian Peasant Organisation Before Collectivisation* (New York, 1971), pp. 56–57. Of course the primary (and historically the earliest) function of the commune was the redistribution of land and the regulation of crop rotation.

30. See, for example, *IVO za 1901 g.* (St. Petersburg, 1905), p. 21. A decree of the Holy Synod in 1881 stated that collectors of such voluntary contributions should be chosen with the consent of the lower clergy and approved by the local police chief. See ibid. On the *sel'skoe obshchestvo*, see Atkinson, *Russian Land Commune*, pp. 23–26, 57, 235.

31. While the application of the parish counterreform took some pressure off parishioners and clergy alike, other counterreforms enhanced the claims of the state on all members of the parish. For details, see Freeze, *Parish Clergy*, pp. 413, 414–17, 429–30, 433–40.

32. See, for example, *IVO za 1887 g.*, p. 129. More details can be found in my "'Into Church Matters': Lay Identity, Rural Parish Life, and Popular Politics in Late Imperial and Early Soviet Russia, 1864–1928," *Russian History / Histoire Russe* 23:1–4 (1996).

33. Both of these quotations are from Rozanov, *Zapiski*, p. 26.

34. Popular subjects of an explicitly religious nature included explanatory remarks on the

other than the church building itself—in church lodges and courtyards, schools, and even outdoors during the summer months.[35] Parishioners frequently punctuated clergy's remarks with questions on a variety of matters, sometimes related and sometimes not to the topic at hand.[36] While extraliturgical instruction had taken place since the beginnings of Christianity in Russia, parish clergy began to increase their efforts along these lines in the post-Emancipation period.[37] Even before an 1890 decree of the Holy Synod made conducting extraliturgical instruction a formal clerical obligation, parish clergy had demonstrated considerable initiative in doing so.[38] To be sure, even official publications (such as diocesan serials and episcopal reports), interested in portraying the achievements of the clergy and the piety of their parishioners in the best possible light, admitted that attendance at the extraliturgical discussions rarely exceeded 10 percent of all parishioners.[39] Nevertheless, parish clergy played, over the course of the last three decades of the nineteenth century, a considerable role in making extraliturgical instruction a routine part of rural parish life.[40]

---

symbols of belief, biblical mysteries, the sacraments, the Ten Commandments, and Orthodox liturgy and prayers. *IVO za 1903–4 gg.* (St. Petersburg, 1909), p. 118; A. A. Papkov, *Tserkovnye bratstva. Kratkii statisticheskii ocherk o polozhenii tserkovnykh bratstv k nachalu 1893 godu* (St. Petersburg, 1893), p. 74. Clergy were especially eager to hold discussions that explained the Old Testament, because more and more "half-literate" peasants were able to acquire copies. Papkov, p. 74. As parish clergy tried to fulfill their new pastoral roles, they were obliged to take into account new historical trends such as the spread of literacy and the development of a reading culture, even among the peasantry. On these developments, see especially Jeffrey Brooks, *When Russia Learned to Read: Literacy and Popular Literature, 1861–1917* (Princeton, N.J., 1985). These forms of religious instruction are also discussed in Chris J. Chulos, "Peasant Religion in Post-Emancipation Russia: Voronezh Province, 1880–1917," 2 vols. (Ph.D. diss., University of Chicago, 1994).

35. To be sure, some were held in parishioners' homes. See Papkov, *Tserkovnye bratstva*, p. 72.

36. On the form of extraliturgical discussions, see ibid., pp. 77–78. For examples of questions asked by peasants at the discussions, see ibid., p. 78. When discussions were held in locations other than the church building itself, parishioners were more willing to ask questions and, tellingly, to engage in "religious debates." The implication in the text is that the broad and ambiguous term "religious debates" included those on the existence of God, and so on. If so, they adumbrated and possibly served as a model for the antireligious disputes of the 1920s, which are discussed at length in Chapter 3.

37. Chulos, "Peasant Religion," p. 109. In Voronezh diocese, clergy began in the 1870s to offer extraliturgical instruction, sometimes petitioning their consistory in order to do so. See ibid., esp. pp. 115–16.

38. On the Decree, see also ibid., pp. 116–17.

39. Ibid., pp. 117–18. The extent of extraliturgical instruction and clerical involvement therein no doubt varied from diocese to diocese, if not on an even more microscopic level, depending on factors such as the existence and wealth of the church brotherhoods. See ibid.

40. Only two years after the decree had been issued, parish priests, with considerable assistance of the church brotherhood (*bratstvo*) of Saints Mitrofan and Tikhon, conducted extraliturgical instruction in about half of all churches in Voronezh diocese. *IVO za 1892–93 gg.*

Frequently offering readings and discussions on topics not of an explicit theological or dogmatic nature, clergy showed that parish life was enmeshed in broader sociohistorical developments. Obvious cases in point included extraliturgical discussions on aspects of Russian history and on "prominent contemporary events in aspects of social life that affected the church."[41] Other popular topics illustrated the impact of the dynamic social change of the post-Emancipation era on village social relations, as well as on the contours of popular piety. Clergy, for example, chose topics for extraliturgical instruction that revealed a deep concern about the increased tensions plaguing peasant families as well as about what they perceived to be pathological behavior exhibited by village youth (such as vagrancy) and the dangers of alcohol.[42] The content of these discussions betrayed clergy's doubtless correct perception that some parishioners—and especially younger ones—were being lured away from "traditional" public displays of religiosity by the very types of public sociability that often evoked priestly ire: evening merrymaking, frequenting taverns, and the like. Extraliturgical instruction was, therefore, not just a barometer of such cultural conflict but an integral part of it.

Extraliturgical instruction was also woven into the fabric of village politics. Some parish priests offered extraliturgical instruction at the village assembly. In Smolensk province, for example, a priest conducted a "discussion" (*beseda*) with its members. Warning them of the dangers of drunkenness, he went on to describe the proper way for Orthodox Christians to celebrate their holidays.[43] Parish priests thus regarded the village assembly as a legitimate forum for fulfilling their pastoral role, a practice that they would repeat in this organ, albeit in quite different circumstances, in the 1920s.

What did clergy gain from the varied efforts they expended in giving extraliturgical instruction? In some ways, their gains appeared meager: the percentage of parishioners attending the discussions and readings was low;

(St. Petersburg, 1895), p. 164. By 1903–5, claimed the official report of the Holy Synod, extraliturgical instruction was being conducted "in many parishes and in almost all dioceses." *IVO za 1903–4 gg.* (St. Petersburg, 1909), p. 118.

41. *IVO za 1903–4 gg.* (St. Petersburg, 1909), p. 118; Papkov, *Tserkovnye bratstva*, p. 74.

42. Papkov, *Tserkovnye bratstva*, p. 75. As they offered extraliturgical instruction, clergy also exhorted parishioners not to engage in slander, display envy, or treat animals in a "coarse or brutal" way. They also "gave [villagers] advice on using fires" and provided information on the basic elements of nature. See ibid., pp. 74–75. On forms of sociability among village youth during this period, see Stephen Frank, "Simple Folk, Savage Customs: Youth Sociability and the Dynamics of Culture in Rural Russia, 1856–1914," *Journal of Social History* 25 (Summer 1992): 711–36. On developments within the rural family, see Barbara Engel, *Between the Fields and the City: Women, Work, and Family in Russia, 1861–1914* (New York, 1994), and Christine Worobec, *Peasant Russia: Family and Community in the Post-Emancipation Period* (DeKalb, Ill., 1995).

43. Papkov, *Tserkovye bratstva*, p. 72. The incident took place in Sychevsk *uezd*; Papkov did not specify the year.

the "religious-moral condition" of the parish was not "healed";[44] some parishioners nevertheless continued to shift elements of religious practice to the private sphere;[45] rural "social pathologies" such as hooliganism continued unabated and even worsened.[46] In fact, there is good reason to believe that extraliturgical instruction at times backfired in that it gave "dissenting" villagers a public forum in which to challenge religious practice and clerical authority. But clergy did, for their part, get something from the deal. They learned how to interact with parishioners in new ways, and in new places; and this was a skill that would, as we shall see, serve them well down the line.

Needy parishioners were the second source of the increased demands faced by overwhelmed clergy in the counterreform years. In his autobiography Rozanov described what he perceived as the considerable additional demands placed on clergy in the wake of the Great Reforms. When peasants distrustful of "local authorities" received an "overbearing order," they often went to their parish priest for advice on whether or not to obey it.[47] Somewhat analogously, rural parish clergy provided nobles with counsel on a variety of secular matters:

> One parish priest went to see an old noble, and flattered him as much as possible. . . . The priest became his lecturer and adviser in all of his affairs: if the miller needed to lease some land from him, [the noble] would first ask the priest about it; if he wanted to buy some forest land, he would first try to see the priest; if a peasant committed an offense—he would go for protection to the clergy; if he wanted to get his son exempted from military service—he would go to the priest for a petition.[48]

Serving as a *de facto* surrogate local administrator and legal counsel for their parishioners, rural clergy also had new official administrative obligations outside their parishes, such as serving on statistical commissions of the *zemstva*.[49] If the priest had become a "leader in social affairs," if he was to

---

44. On the persistence of peasant superstitions, see Lewin, "Popular Religion in Twentieth-Century Russia," in *Making of the Soviet System*, and Chulos, "Peasant Religion," esp. vol. 2.

45. Chulos, "Peasant Religion," chap. 5.

46. See Joan Neuberger, *Hooliganism: Crime, Culture, and Power in St. Petersburg, 1900–1914* (Berkeley, Calif., 1993).

47. Rozanov, *Zapiski*, p. 15.

48. Ibid., p. 99.

49. Ibid., p. 8. Father Georgii Gapon's father, Apollon Fedorovich, was a village sexton who repeatedly won election to the post of village elder and also served as a *volost'* clerk for close to thirty-five years. See Walter L. Sablinsky, *The Road to Bloody Sunday: Father Gapon and the St. Petersburg Massacre of 1905* (Princeton, N.J., 1976), p. 35.

fulfill tasks set by the state such as teaching the *Zakon Bozhii* in secular schools, if his "mission" consisted of "unifying the heterogenous parts of society into one whole," then why, Rozanov asked, could the priest not be a paid civil servant?[50] Clergy based their ever louder demands for a state salary on their enhanced sociopolitical roles in the post-Emancipation village. It did no good.

The clergy were handicapped by more than just the lack of a state salary as they tried to meet the demands placed on them by the state and by their parishioners. By the 1870s and 1880s they were also experiencing a variety of new and long-standing pressures on the parish level. These included difficult material and living conditions. Rozanov, for example, sought to draw attention to the fact that parish clergy found it difficult to police the behavior of peasants, let alone nobles and others of a higher social standing, because they were very dependent on their flock for emoluments and other basic needs: censuring a parishioner for a drunken binge could result in the loss of much-needed income. They were dependent on their parishioners' goodwill for other material needs as well: seeking an apartment from the village commune, Rozanov had to appear before the village assembly and make his request to each member "almost one by one."[51] Parish clergy had, in other words, to endure the humiliation of begging for basic living necessities from a political body in which they had no formal legal right to participate.[52] Moreover, parishioners, angry at their clergy for their relentless financial demands, were reluctant to accord the degree of respect and authority this policing presupposed.[53] Peasants also did not accord clergy respect and authority because they often dressed like peasants.[54]

Overwhelming demands and maddening constraints: it might seem as though parish clergy had nothing to show for their efforts. This was not the case. We have already seen that clergy acquired new skills as they fulfilled their pastoral duties under these difficult conditions. But what distinguished the parish clergy of the Rozanov generation from their fathers and grandfathers was not simply the honing of skills. For the rural parish clergy had begun to construct and elaborate a new sociopolitical identity. Not without significance, for example, is the fact that members of the clergy actually

---

50. For his claim that clergy had become leaders in rural society, see Rozanov, *Zapiski*, p. 15. On the clergy's mission, see ibid., p. 7. For his desire to be a paid civil servant, see ibid., pp. 136, 171, 173–75.

51. Ibid., p. 33. In the end the assembly did vote to grant him the apartment.

52. For a bishop's complaint about the fact that clergy did not have the right to participate in the village assembly, see Arkhimandrit Evdokim, "Na zare novoi tserkovnoi zhizni! (Dum'e i chuvstva)," *Bogoslovskii vestnik*, May 1905, p. 164.

53. Rozanov, *Zapiski*, p. 26ff.

54. Ibid., p. 242.

petitioned the diocesan authorities for permission to conduct extraliturgical instruction, a telling sign of the seriousness with which they viewed the responsibility of insuring the religious-moral "health" of their parishioners. The clergy did not invest so much effort in extraliturgical instruction just because the Decree of 1890 called on them to do so. Rozanov, for example, related his difficulties in fulfilling what he considered to be the chief duty of the priest—to care for the religious-moral situation of his parishioners—in a tone of thinly veiled anger and sadness.[55] He took his children out of the seminary not only to protect them from future poverty but also to spare them from the psychological pain of being unable to fulfill these pastoral duties.[56] Assuming we can take Rozanov's account at face value and regard it as representative of his generation of parish clergy, then we should interpret this frustration, sadness, and grief as evidence of the degree to which at least some of his counterparts had come to view themselves as "pastors," as opposed to "priests." As Rozanov put it: "My view of society is entirely different than the one that my grandfather and father had; the way that society itself looks at the clergy has changed, perhaps even more. Now it is a different education, situation, requirements—[really] a different life, than my parents had."[57]

Indeed, because clergy could not fulfill this new pastoral role and became increasingly frustrated as they tried to do so, they stopped identifying with the state and believing it would provide for them.[58] Trying to fulfill their pastoral roles, they had to become cultural entrepreneurs, luring parishioners away from competing models of religious piety, forms of sociability, and even belief systems. Ironically, clergy and especially parishioners demonstrated increasing autonomy not despite but *because* political elites treated them as extensions of the state.

Lay Activism and Parish Politics During the Counterreform Era

In the 1880s and especially in the 1890s, the new skills and emerging identities of rural clergy and lay activists were put to the test. During the dark years of state oppression that followed Alexander II's assassination in 1881,

55. Ibid., p. 26.
56. Ibid., p. 132.
57. Ibid., p. 118.
58. Freeze, *Parish Clergy*, p. 468.

the autocracy recaptured its intrusive hold on the countryside. Villagers felt the constraining grip of such measures as the institution of the Land Captain in 1889, the *zemstvo* counterreform in 1890, and a number of new counterreforms in the Church.[59] Moreover, as peasants flocked to urban factories during Russia's great industrial takeoff, the boundaries between the village and the world beyond became more porous than ever before. One thinks here of Semën Kanatchikov, the young peasant lad accompanied by his father to a Moscow factory in the spring of 1895.[60] When they intermittently returned to their villages, these "yesterday's peasants," like other peasants who engaged in other types of seasonal labor outside the village ("outmigrants" or *otkhodniki*), brought with them the culture and habits of the city; and like other *otkhodniki*, they rejected religion and other ways of the village. In this new context, what forms did lay activism take? What meanings did it come to have? And how did parish clergy respond to the concurrent challenges of increased lay autonomy and rejection of religion by villagers who had ventured into the world beyond? What did it mean for these villagers to challenge clerical authority and religious belief?

Lay activists became involved in church councils (*popechitel'stva*) in ways that revealed how differently they saw their place in the parish. Intended largely to provide financial and material support for the impoverished parish clergy, legislation calling for the creation of parish councils was signed by Alexander II on August 2, 1864.[61] The legislation (*Polozhenie o prikhodskikh popechitel'stvakh* or Regulation on Parish Councils) delineated clear legal boundaries for the activities of the councils and their members.[62] Clergy, church, and *volost'* elders were automatically permanent members. The chair, elected by a lay assembly, could be the priest. Directly (in theory) under the supervision of the diocesan administration, the council was housed in the parish but did not belong to it; it could not dispose of parish funds, although it had its own treasury. Councils had the following tasks: caring for church buildings; providing for the material needs of the priest, including housing; founding church schools and other charity activities, such as homes for the

---

59. On the high politics of the parish counterreform, see ibid., pp. 417–33.

60. Reginald Zelnik, trans. and ed., *A Radical Worker in Tsarist Russia: The Autobiography of Semën Ivanovich Kanatchikov* (Stanford, Calif., 1986), p. 6.

61. For details of the legislative process, see Freeze, *Parish Clergy*, pp. 248–60. The *tserkovno-prikhodskie sovety*, descendants of the *popechitel'stva*, were created by the Holy Synod in November 1905 (Old Style). On this see John Shelton Curtiss, *Church and State in Russia: The Last Years of the Empire, 1900–1917* (New York, 1965), p. 220, and Igor Smolitsch, *Geschichte der russischen Kirche, 1700–1917* (Berlin, 1990), 2:102–3. The *bratstva* differed from both institutions in that their activities were not confined to the boundaries of the parish. On the distinction between *popechitel'stva* and *bratstva*, see Papkov, *Tserkovnye bratstva*, p. 10.

62. The provisions can be found in Smolitsch, *Geschichte*, p. 99.

elderly; supervising parish cemeteries and the burial of the poor; and performing charity work in general. Parishioners made donations for specific goals, which could not be changed by the councils. Parish councils were to report yearly to the diocesan authorities on their activities and had to have the approval of the diocesan administration to engage in activities beyond those listed above. The number of councils in the empire climbed from 7,596 in 1871 to 20,059 at the beginning of 1910.[63] It was during the period between 1890 and 1909 that the number of *popechitel'stva* rose dramatically, from 13,924 to 20,059.[64]

Did parish clergy, who in theory stood to benefit from the establishment of new councils, take the lead in creating, maintaining, and reopening them? Even when diocesan officials or clergy took the lead in suggesting that a council be launched, it was villagers who actually brought them to life at the "assembly of laity" (*obshchestvo grazhdan*) and also at the village assembly.[65] Given the key role that peasant parishioners often played in creating the councils, it is not surprising that they often comprised a significant percentage of their "permanent" membership.[66] Church councils often included a mix of representatives of all four estates.[67]

Why, then, did parishioners—and peasants in particular—invest so much energy in creating and maintaining parish councils, especially during the repressive years of counterreform? The answer to this question may lie in how they used these councils. From the 1870s until the last years of the tsarist period, the yearly reports of the Holy Synod praised the involvement of church councils in charity activities.[68] Not only did villagers specifically mention charity goals in their resolutions to create councils, but donations for charity and parish schools increased seven-fold from 1869 to 1913.[69] The principal activity of the church councils during this period, however, was

63. *IVO za 1871 g.*; *IVO za 1908–1910 g.*, p. 352. Moreover, interest in creating new councils varied significantly within this period. By 1868, only four years after Alexander II's legislation, more than 5,000 councils existed. After this promising start, however, interest in the *popechitel'stva* fell. Between 1871 and 1881, only 2,970 new parish councils appeared. See *Pravoslavnogo obozreniia. Zametki*, February 1865, pp. 101–3.

64. *Pravoslavnogo obozreniia. Zametki*, February 1865, pp. 101–3. By comparison, the number of parish churches (including *edinoverie*) in 1898 was 37,502. See *IVO za 1899 g.*, p. 121. In 1898, there were 48,002 churches of all kinds in the Empire.

65. See *Pravoslavnoe obozrenie. Zametki*, May 1865, pp. 2–5.

66. Ibid., pp. 2–14. More details can be found in my "Into Church Matters."

67. *Pravoslavnoe obozrenie. Zametki*, May 1865, pp. 2–14. See also Smolitsch, *Geschichte*, p. 99.

68. On church councils' support of parish schools, see *IVO za 1871 g.*, p. 90, and *IVO za 1886 g.*, p. 229. For references to their charity activities, see *IVO za 1871 g.*, p. 90; *Pribavleniia* no. 35 (August 27, 1905), p. 1488; and *IVO za 1911–12 g.*, p. 216.

69. See *Pravoslavnoe obozrenie. Zametki*, May 1865, p. 3.

contributing to the upkeep of churches. Donations "for the maintenance and decoration of churches" far exceeded those "for the [material] support of clergy."⁷⁰ Donations for the upkeep of churches ranged narrowly from 74 percent to 75.5 percent of total contributions. Funds targeted for supporting clergy totaled 4 percent in 1869 and never exceeded 7.8 percent for the period through 1912.⁷¹ To be sure, parish councils in Samara diocese did provide sizable donations for the material support of clergy.⁷² That diocese, however, was exceptional. Throughout the tsarist period the councils failed to attain the main goal of the 1864 legislation: to provide the parish clergy with a more stable source of income.⁷³

In other ways, too, parishioners used the church councils for their own purposes rather than those of either the clergy or the state. Overstepping the statutory boundaries of their authority, members of church councils actually joined clergy in mounting efforts to improve the "religious-moral condition [*sostoianie*]" of the parish, such as the attempt to eliminate pagan practices. Church councils also attempted to improve the level of "morality" in the parish by trying to decrease parishioners' consumption of alcohol.⁷⁴ Members of church councils also relied on a third strategy in their efforts to curb the consumption of alcohol: anti-alcohol "propaganda" in the form of books, brochures of a "religious-moral content," readings, and

---

70. While total donations increased more than five-fold between 1869 and 1912, percentage breakdowns in the respective subcategories (e.g., upkeep of churches, support for clergy) varied inconsequentially. On this see, for example, *IVO za 1903-4 gg.*, p. 86. For further statistics on donations to *popechitel'stva* by category, see my "Into Church Matters."

71. Most of these resources went to providing apartments for clergy or to making repairs on their lodgings. On this see, for example, *IVO za 1903-4 gg.*, p. 86. For a firsthand report from Saratov diocese, see Rozanov, *Zapiski*, p. 62.

72. In 1879, for example, parish councils in Samara bishopric collected 96,435 rubles for the material support of clergy and 290,691 rubles for the maintenance of churches. See *IVO za 1879 g.*, p. 133; for similar evidence, see *IVO za 1877 g.*, p. 164. In other words, the ratio of donations for the upkeep of churches to those for the material support of clergy was approximately 3:1. Other dioceses that proved exceptions to the general pattern included Viatka, Vologda, and Podol'sk. On this see *IVO za 1899-1900 gg.*, p. 54. The diocese of Samara also stood out in terms of the high amount of parishioners' contributions, which rose from 399,437 to 504,891 r. in 1899–1900 alone. For other dioceses that demonstrated a significant increase during the same year, see *IVO za 1899-1900 gg.*

73. See, for example, *IVO za 1871 g.*, p. 90; *IVO za 1873 g.*, p. 90; *IVO za 1875 g.*, p. 148; *IVO za 1877 g.*, p. 163; *IVO za 1879 g.*, p. 132; and *IVO za 1911-12 gg.*, p. 216. In some cases, parishioners made their donations "in kind" in the form of bread, potatoes, meat, wood, bricks, and the like. See *IVO za 1900 g.*, p. 50.

74. For other examples, see *IVO za 1871 g.*, p. 91, and *IVO za 1887 g.*, pp. 129–30. On church councils' battles against pagan practices, see *IVO za 1887 g.* On drinking in rural Russia, see Patricia Herlihy, "'Joy of the Rus': Rites and Rituals of Russian Drinking," *Russian Review* 50 (April 1991): 131–47.

discussions (*sobesedovaniia*).⁷⁵ Some councils, as funds allowed, opened reading rooms in the libraries of parish church schools.⁷⁶

Beginning in the 1880s, in fact, the yearly reports of the Holy Synod complained of the hostility demonstrated by members of the councils to the clergy and church elders. Accused of "wrangling" with the clergy and the church elders, church councils "got into church matters, demanded an accounting from clergy and the elders in the parish and in the spending of church sums."⁷⁷ The Holy Synod's yearly report for 1887 complained that the majority of church councils "consider themselves complete managers of everything that has to do with the church, imperious masters over the clergy and uncontrollable administrators of church funds; consequently many parish councils have developed a hostile relationship to the clergy, if the latter doesn't consider it better to be quiet and [just] let them do what they want."⁷⁸ The same report expressed alarm that some parish councils were "censuring the actions of church elders and priests."⁷⁹ Hoping that such lay insubordination had resulted simply from not knowing the provisions of the 1864 Regulation, diocesan officials in Poltava ordered that two copies be sent to each church.⁸⁰ Even if parishioners had known the details of the legislation, it is unlikely that they would have followed these rules; they "overstepped their bounds" not in ignorance but in defiance of (perceived) clerical privilege and power.⁸¹

But what was the nature of their resistance? If we want to understand its meaning, we must examine not just the dynamics of parish life (e.g., anticlericalism) but also the broader sociohistorical context. In the post-Emancipation era in general, and especially in the decades immediately preceding the Revolution of 1905–7, the church council was by no means the only arena in which rural parishioners voiced a demand for more power in parish affairs. During the years of counterreform in Russian society and in church affairs in particular, lay initiative in parish affairs continued to increase. Demonstrating that the reach of their memories of parish affairs extended far into the past, parishioners began to demand that the practice of lay election of clergy (*vybornoe nachalo*) be restored.⁸² In some cases, as

75. *IVO za 1890–91 gg.*, p. 93.
76. Ibid.
77. *IVO za 1886 g.*, pp. 228, 230.
78. *IVO za 1887 g.*, p. 126.
79. Ibid., p. 127.
80. *IVO za 1886 g.*, p. 229.
81. Had parishioners known that the legislation limited their scope of action so narrowly, they very well may have been even *more* inclined to use the councils to take over clerical functions and express hostility toward their priests.
82. Freeze, *Parish Clergy*, pp. 376, 468; Rozanov, *Zapiski*, pp. 180ff.

Rozanov recalled them, parishioners even went a step further: demanding that the state abolish the clerical *soslovie* and all ecclesiastical institutions, they sought to make the village assembly responsible for training suitable clerical candidates, from which that body would make the final selection![83] It is indubitable that parishioners had begun to demand such powers in order to avoid the kinds of financial claims that state-appointed clergy were making on them. Writing in 1888, the populist Sergei Kravchinsky maintained that the fact that churches were perceived "not [as] houses of prayer, but houses of plunder" had caused a deep estrangement between the clergy and laity.[84] He claimed that parishioners viewed their clergy "as a class of tradesmen, who have wholesale and retail dealings in sacraments, not as guides or advisers."[85] Certainly rural parishioners were reacting to this image of clergy in voicing their demands for the restoration of *vybornoe nachalo* and in seeking more autonomy in other parish affairs. But when parishioners used the church councils to counter clerical power in parish affairs, were they only trying to resist clergy's financial demands?

These rural parishioners probably did view their priests as "a symbol of gluttony, avarice, sycophancy [and] bawdiness," but it is too limiting to call their actions "anticlerical" and leave it at that.[86] When members of church councils became unruly, and when the village assemblies presumed to take responsibility for training and electing clergy, they were going beyond the comparatively passive resentment of clergy described by Belinskii and others. For these parishioners had transformed their resentment of clerical power and privilege—their "anticlericalism"—into a positive vision of a more equitable relationship between clergy and parishioners. When, as in the case of the church councils or village assemblies, parishioners put this vision into practice, they were, in objective terms, not only contesting the claims of a particular priest or other members of the clergy. They were also resisting the state power that clergy sometimes brought to the village. It is more difficult to tease out the subjective meaning with which parishioners infused such actions. Given the parish clergy's close if not invariable association with the tsarist state in the minds of parishioners, it is logical that parishioners experienced, on at least an unconscious or latently conscious level, such active assertions of autonomy and clerical power as having a political meaning, as being thinly veiled acts of political resistance. The case of the church councils

---

83. Rozanov, *Zapiski*, p. 180.
84. Kravchinsky, *Russian Peasantry*, p. 375.
85. Ibid., p. 373. See also Maureen Perrie, "Folklore as Evidence of Peasant Mentalité," *Russian Review* 48 (1987): esp. 124–27. On analogous anticlericalism during the French Revolution, see Michelle Vovelle, *Les métamorphoses de la fête en Provence de 1750 à 1820* (Paris, 1976), p. 113.
86. Belinskii, "Letter to N. V. Gogol," in Raeff, *Russian Intellectual History*, p. 256.

thus exemplifies a general dynamic in Church-state relations in late imperial Russia: as Gregory Freeze has put it, "elite attempts to refurbish the religious bond unwittingly proved counterproductive, tending to dissolve rather than bolster the spiritual legitimacy of the regime."[87]

If, in the dark counterreform years, parishioners were making a political statement when they asserted their autonomy in parish affairs, how then should we "read" the actions of those villagers who sought to challenge in even more radical ways the traditional religious life of the village? This is an important question to ask about the apparently evaporating religiosity of the aforementioned increasing number of *otkhodniki*, or villagers who engaged in seasonal industrial work outside the village, shuttling back and forth between what became to them benighted rural backwaters (*glush'*) and alluring urban centers, such as Moscow and St. Petersburg.[88] At the end of the nineteenth century, bishops frequently asserted that villagers employed as seasonal industrial workers often became irreligious. A bishop's report from Orel diocese, for example, reads as follows: "A part of the population leaves its birthplace to work in far-away regions, especially in southern provinces. Peasant youth, having spent time in those places, return having not only been changed externally but having a different internal life, which expresses itself in the nonobservance of fasts and every kind of free thought."[89] Although this bishop faulted the out-migrants for engaging in "free thought," these wayward souls did not, in fact, formulate clearly articulated rejections of Orthodoxy. Rather, they refused to take part in Orthodox sacraments, rituals, and holiday celebrations and stopped attending church.[90] In sum, those (usually) younger villagers with industrial work experience

---

87. Gregory Freeze, "Subversive Piety: Religion and the Political Crisis in Late Imperial Russia," *Journal of Modern History* 68 (1996): 312. For a powerful challenge to the assumption that the Orthodox Church and its parish clergy invariably acted as an extension of the tsarist state, see Freeze, "Orthodox Church and Serfdom." Karl Marx in fact interpreted peasant anticlericalism (i.e., "becoming irreligious") in nineteenth-century France as an expression of resistance against state power: "The priest then appears as only the anointed bloodhound of the earthly police—another '*idée napolienne.*'" See his *Eighteenth Brumaire of Louis Bonaparte* (New York, 1981), pp. 129–30. My reference to "resistance" is based on the definition offered by James C. Scott in his *Weapons of the Weak: Everyday Forms of Peasant Resistance* (New Haven, Conn., 1985), p. 290. See also his *Domination and the Arts of Resistance: Hidden Transcripts* (New Haven, Conn., 1990), p. xii.

88. On *otkhodnichestvo*, see, for example, Robert E. Johnson, *Peasant and Proletarian: The Working Class of Moscow in the Late Nineteenth Century* (New Brunswick, N.J., 1979).

89. RGIA, f. 796, op. 440, d. 1206, l. 11, as quoted in the tendentious though informative discussion of the impact of *otkhod* on village religiosity in L. I. Emeliakh, *Istoricheskie predposylki preodoleniia religii v sovetskoi derevne (Sekuliarizatsiia derevni nakanune Velikogo Oktiabria)* (Leningrad, 1975), esp. pp. 19–21.

90. Ibid., pp. 20–21.

outside the village generally wanted to reduce, if not extinguish, the presence of Orthodox (and pagan) ritual in everyday village life.

As the out-migrants tried to implement this agenda, they came into conflict with other villagers in a variety of arenas.[91] Affording us a glimpse of the kind of conflict about religious practice that often occurred in families in which a member had engaged in seasonal out-migration, the bishop of Smolensk diocese wrote in 1902: "Seasonal out-migration spoils the morality of young people, . . . and there are cases when, upon returning home, they bring to their families new views on belief and the decisions of the Church."[92]

While the domestic sphere was a well-trod field of conflict, villagers also contested religion's presence in public arenas and spaces. Casting aside traditional expressions of religiosity, younger *otkhodniki* instead opted for fairs, bazaars, and especially fairground shows (*balagany*), some of which were held at the same time as church services.[93] As village priests and church officials saw it, villagers who opted for these new types of entertainment liked not only their secular form but also their content, which "never approved of nor sanctified the Holy church."[94] Alarmed by the threat of such new forms of popular entertainment to traditional village religiosity, an increasingly pastoral clergy took a variety of measures to lure wayward parishioners away from these new cultural forms—if not back to the Church itself. The widow of a certain N. F. Bunakov, who had been instrumental in arranging theatrical performances in the 1880s and 1890s in the village Petino, described such clerical techniques:

> As the theater more and more attracted peasants, both as actors and spectators, priests and psalmists came out fervently and openly as opponents [*protivniki*] of the theater. During both rehearsals and performances, the priest, taking advantage of the fact that his home was located across from the theater, sat on the bench at his hut or stood on the path and excommunicated all of the actors and spectators; he threatened them with all of the tortures of hell, [and] . . . [told them] that he would not give communion or burial rites to them or their parents. In church the priest gave sermons in which he cursed the actors and spectators; he threatened that the building that housed

---

91. I draw here on the useful notion of a "field of conflict" elaborated in James Davison Hunter, *Culture Wars: The Struggle to Define America* (New York: Basic Books, 1991).

92. RGIA, f. 796, op. 440, no. 1205, l. 24, as quoted in Emeliakh, *Istoricheskie predposylki*, p. 21.

93. Ibid., esp. pp. 22–23. See also A. Shevelev, *Tserkov' i zrelishcha* (Moscow, 1892); Arkhimandrit Nikodim, *O teatral'nykh predstavleniiakh s tserkovnoi tochki zreniia* (Kazan, 1899); and *O zrelishchakh i razlichnykh teatral'nykh predstavleniiakh* (Perm, 1906).

94. Emeliakh, *Istoricheskie predposylki*, p. 24.

the theater would fall down; he called the theater sinful, the devil's amusement.[95]

Rural clergy also played a significant role in making the muddy streets of the village the site of cultural conflict about the role of traditional forms of religiosity in village life. As this quotation demonstrates, one of the main tools of their trade was a discourse of damnation and apocalypse, which drew on the very cultural forms that wayward parishioners were in the process of contesting: younger villagers (often *otkhodniki*) and clergy were, in such cases, "talking past each other."[96] Each "side" was indirectly expressing its position through the use of competing cultural forms, through language that did not invite reciprocal dialogue.

To return to our original question, How are we then to "read" this cultural conflict ostensibly generated by differing visions of religion's role in village life? Should we take it at face value? More to the point, why were so many younger villagers, often out-migrants, bent on reducing if not extinguishing the "space" in village life occupied by traditional religious practice? Damning religion as "old-fashioned," were they simply attracted to modern pleasures?

When younger villagers rejected religious belief and practice, they were expressing the generational conflict especially acute in regions of widespread out-migration. Beginning in the last decades of the nineteenth century, returning out-migrants challenged not only the traditional religious practices of their fathers—one thinks here of Semën and Ivan Kanatchikov—but also openly contested their fathers' authority in marital and financial matters.[97] For out-migrants, independent experience outside the village and the rejection of the patriarchal authority of their elders went hand in hand, a dynamic visible in other industrializing societies as well.[98] Why, in the Russian case, did returning out-migrants judge the rejection of religious practice to be so crucial to their challenge to the patriarchal order and to the bid to define their lives?

These questions were never directly posed to nor answered by out-migrants themselves, but they are issues refracted indirectly in one especially revealing worker autobiography, that of Semën Ivanovich Kanatchikov. That

---

95. The actors' parents said their children would have to be baptized again because they had been "defiled." Ibid., p. 23.

96. Karl Mannheim, *Ideology and Utopia: An Introduction to the Sociology of Knowledge* (New York, 1936).

97. A point made by David Hoffmann in *Peasant Metropolis: Social Identities in Moscow, 1929–1941* (Ithaca, N.Y., 1994), p. 22.

98. Frances Rothstein, "The New Proletarians: Third World Realities and First World Categories," *Comparative Studies in Society and History* 2 (1986): 218–24.

autobiography can be read, on one level, as an expression of Kanatchikov's recollection of his experience of the "bad" patriarchal village father, a father "bad" because his frequent drinking binges, among other things, render him emotionally unavailable to his son.[99] Ivan Kanatchikov was not an uninvolved, silent father, however, but a tyrannical, abusive one. Early in the autobiography, for example, the young Kanatchikov states: "My father was strict in disposition and despotic in character. He kept the entire family in mortal fright. We all feared him and did everything we could to please him."[100] Here Semën leads us to believe that he lived in perpetual fear of his father. When we read the autobiography more closely, however, we find that Semën's fears abated when his father was drunk. They returned when his father sobered up. "Gloomy and morose," his father would beat his mother. When Semën tried to protect his mother, he became the object of his father's blows.[101]

Kanatchikov perceives this emotional unavailability—probably typical of village fathers of Ivan's generation—as being legitimized by the patriarchal village elders (*bol'shaki*) as well as by his father's cherished religious beliefs and practices.[102] To be sure, there were, as the young Kanatchikov was proud to report, some limits to his father's religiosity: "He was a religious believer, but he wasn't superstitious. He did not believe in demons, household spirits, or magic spells, he made fun of village wise women and healers, and he didn't like priests."[103] Kanatchikov's father nevertheless drew on religious belief and practice to underwrite his own power within the family, as well as power in Russian society more generally. On the momentous day that the young Kanatchikov departed for Moscow, his father gathered the entire family and "lit icon lamps in front of the images of the saints. When the prayer was over, Father addressed me with his parting words, once more reminding me not to forget God, to honor my superiors, to serve my employer honestly, and, above all else, to be mindful of our home."[104]

As this quotation suggests, Kanatchikov is repeatedly contemptuous of how his father used religion to keep him from creating an independent self, and to bind him to the village more generally.[105] Once Semën had moved to

---

99. In the following discussion of the "good" and the "bad" father, I draw on Lynn Hunt's *Family Romance of the French Revolution* (Berkeley, Calif., 1992). On Kanatchikov's troubled relationship with his father, see Zelnik, *Radical Worker*, esp. pp. 4–6; Zelnik, "Introduction: Kanatchikov's *Story of My Life* as Document and Literature," in *Radical Worker*; and his "Russian Bebels: An Introduction to the Memoirs of Semën Kanatchikov and Matvei Fisher," *Russian Review* 35 (July 1976) and (October 1976).
100. Zelnik, *Radical Worker*, pp. 4–5.
101. Ibid., p. 5.
102. Ibid., p. 6.
103. Ibid., p. 5.
104. Ibid., p. 6.
105. See Zelnik, "Introduction," p. xxiv, and *Radical Worker*, p. 94.

St. Petersburg, for example, his father nevertheless tried to maintain his hold through letters: "I received two more letters—mailed from the village—from my father; both were full of anxiety. Apparently someone had told him all kinds of fables and horror stories about me. In the first letter he called on me to attend church, to pray to God, to serve my employer, and so on . . ."[106] Religious practice, as he saw it, provided the symbolic and ideological legitimacy for the limits placed on human autonomy in the patriarchal family, in village government, in the factory, and in the autocracy.[107] In other words, it was the source of these "bad fathers."

While Kanatchikov's autobiography is thus a narrative about various kinds of bad fathers, it is also a narrative in which the "good father" occupies a rather large "absent presence." Not unlike French authors of the eighteenth century, Kanatchikov seems increasingly aware that the "good father" is out there, only to be found, if not constructed. Of course, if religious practice both accounted for and legitimized the bad father, then the good father would, for Kanatchikov, be distinguished by his *lack* of formal religiosity. Kanatchikov's own father remains both unavailable and religious to the day he dies.

Nevertheless, Kanatchikov's narrative recounts a process of separating from his internalized father, a process coterminous with his formal rejection of religion. The young Kanatchikov broke with formal religion, achieved emotional independence from his father, and adopted the identity of a "conscious" worker all at the same time.[108] Having taken the first step in rejecting the hold of the "bad father" (by not fulfilling his father's wish that he marry), Kanatchikov is then able to break more rules and become a "conscious" (that is, politically radical) worker. Indeed, the adoption of the latter identity was Kanatchikov's way of creating the "good father." As he did so, he in effect reparented himself by offering himself a new model of power and authority that, as he saw it, allowed the flourishing of human autonomy. The disappearance of religion was both a precondition and result of the autonomy he was seeking.

106. Zelnik, *Radical Worker*, p. 94.
107. This is the essence of the point Kanatchikov makes during the debate with his family on God's justice, a debate that occurred after his father died. See Zelnik, *Radical Worker*, p. 147. See, for example, the poem, which Kanatchikov "liked very much" and cites from memory on ibid., p. 99. Kanatchikov came by this perception honestly; as Christine Worobec has put it: "The patriarchal Russian family was but a microcosm of a hierarchical social order that extended from God to his representative on earth, the *batiushka* (little father) tsar to all other fathers." See her *Peasant Russia*, p. 175.
108. It was after reading Plekhanov's *Russian Worker in the Revolutionary Movement*, for example, that Kanatchikov "stopped going to the priest for 'confession,' no longer attended church, and began to eat 'forbidden' food during Lenten fast days." He nevertheless continued to cross himself "for a long time to come." See Zelnik, *Radical Worker*, p. 34.

Since most out-migrants and village youth did not become Bolsheviks, how can Kanatchikov's narrative shed light on their motivations for rejecting religious practice? Though Kanatchikov arrived at a different destination than many village youth of his generation, he started at much the same place. For the out-migrant's experience of an emotionally unavailable, quasi-alcoholic, and formally religious father, who wielded considerable power in the family and the village, was, as noted above, unfortunately quite prevalent, if not universal.[109] The patriarchal family was not, to be sure, the only reason younger villagers rejected religious practice. To that list we must add mere exposure to secular environments and secular literature, as well as antireligious propaganda offered workers by Populists and Bolsheviks.[110] While these experiences may account for an individual's disinterest in engaging in religious practice, they cannot really explain the *particular* agenda of out-migrants, which, after all, was to reduce and extinguish the place of religious practice in the *public* life of the village, to remove it from the public world of the village elders.[111] To do this, younger villagers had to transform the cultural life of the village. If, for example, public religious practices such as processions of the cross no longer took place, there would be no display of the power of the village elders (*bol'shaki*), who typically occupied a prominent place in such processions, along with the clergy, who were perceived as local "handmaidens of the state."[112] Kanatchikov's description of the "theological arguments" he picked with his father when he visited his village on holidays in fact adumbrated the antireligious disputes and debates of the 1920s.[113] Village youth of Kanatchikov's day sang a song that asked rhetorically:

> What thief or demon came from hell,
> What dark magician cast a spell,
> Squeezed the worker, sucked him dry,
> Takes my money, lets me die?
> Why, that's no thief or being from hell,
> Or sorcerer who casts a spell,

---

109. On the patriarch's power within the rural family, see Worobec, *Peasant Russia*, pp. 44–46, 175ff. For literary evidence, see, for example, Anton Chekhov, "Peasants," in *Selected Stories* (New York, 1982), pp. 242–74. On the role of drinking in village culture and in the construction of masculinity, see Olga Semyonova Tian-shanskaia, *Village Life in Late Tsarist Russia*, ed. David L. Ransel (Bloomington, Ind., 1993), pp. 109–14. See also Herlihy, "Joy of the Rus."

110. See, for example, Zelnik, "To the Unaccustomed Eye."

111. See, for example, Kanatchikov's description in Zelnik, *Radical Worker*, pp. 171–72, of the celebration of Nicholas Day (December 6, Old Style), during which village elites—"local tradesmen and kulaks . . . all the clergymen of the local church, the village police inspector, and the steward from the nearby estate"—gathered together.

112. See Fenomenov, *Sovremennaia derevnia*.

113. For more details, see Zelnik, *Radical Worker*, p. 35.

> That takes my money every day
> And sucks the worker's blood away.
> It's just the merchant and the priest,
> It's just the tsar—our father pure.[114]

Returning villagers and village youth of Kanatchikov's generation believed that the extinction of public religious practice and the making of new forms of authority—new icons of power—had to go hand in hand.

In sum, the hostility of out-migrants toward religious practice in village life should not be taken "at face value." This is not to suggest that returning villagers were feigning a hostility to public and even private religious practice. What is being claimed here is that their hostility to private and especially public religious practice had political origins, significance, and potential (though not necessarily actual) instrumental value.

Thus, during the counterreform years, villagers reinterpreted the meanings of religious belief, practice, and parish social relations. To be sure, religious belief and practice had long had political significance in the local political culture of the village, as the role of local religion as a political tool in eighteenth-century peasant rebellions (for example, the Pugachev rebellion) demonstrates.[115] To be sure, peasants continued to express deference to the tsarist state through collective displays of public religiosity; when villagers built and rebuilt churches—one of (if not *the*) most important ways of demonstrating popular piety—they often named them in honor of a tsar. But one searches in vain to find prior examples of villagers seeking to extinguish public religious practice in order to "win" generational and political struggles, or of using religious ritual to express—even if in latent form—a *generalized* resistance to tsarist political authority.[116] It was thus in the counterreform years that villagers drew on religious belief and practice to refract the increasingly deep political and cultural cleavages *within* a "rural nexus" that was feeling the shock waves of life beyond the village to an unprecedented degree.[117]

---

114. See ibid., p. 49.

115. During peasant disturbances of the late eighteenth century, parishioners sanctified their exhortations of political resistance in the presence of icons. For examples, see Freeze, *Russian Levites*, pp. 181–82.

116. See, for example, Chekhov's depiction of a peasant religious procession in "Peasants," analyzed in depth in the beginning of Chapter 8.

117. On the "rural nexus," see Lewin, *Making of the Soviet System*.

The Politics of the Parish and the Revolution of 1905–1907

Through the lens of these often new and increasingly conflicting political meanings of religious belief, ritual, and parish organization, clergy and parishioners evaluated the political challenges and opportunities of 1905–7. The year 1905 brought a *political* crisis in which strikes, peasant rebellions, a professional "liberation" movement, assassinations, executions, and right-wing counterrevolutionary violence not only imperiled the existence of the Russian autocracy but posed the even more fundamental questions of who would have political power in Russia and why. Because religion and politics were intertwined institutionally, ideologically, and symbolically from the local to the national level, Russians necessarily wrestled, during this political crisis, with an almost endless series of questions about the relationship of religious organization, belief, and practice to political power. The rural parish was a case in point.

It was uncertain, for example, what political stance the village clergy would take toward the autocracy. Reflecting an anachronistic attachment to cameralist principles, the embattled autocracy sought to use rural parish clergy to reestablish state power and stem the revolutionary tide. Given this goal, it might appear incongruous that Imperial Decrees exhorted clergy to stay out of politics, and that the Holy Synod at first forbade priests to join any political parties (in the Duma).[118] Yet this injunction was consistent with the autocracy's general aversion to "modern" party politics and with its general championing of the notion that it was the job of the state to define the political (or rather, administrative) duties of members of a given *soslovie*.[119] Exemplifying this latter principle, the Synod called on the clergy at particularly turbulent moments in the revolutionary drama (such as following Bloody Sunday, and during the momentous month of December 1905) to make speeches and offer prayers designed to reestablish parishioners' loyalty to the autocratic regime.[120] Quoting from the Bible (1 Tim. 4:2), the Synod called on "Pastors of the Holy Orthodox Church!" to "preach the word, be instant in season, reprove, rebuke, exhort with all long suffering and doctrine."[121] It also tried to encourage the clergy to use *besedy* (and extraliturgical instruction more generally), to increase the political loyalty

---

118. See Curtiss, *Church and State in Russia*, p. 241; see also Abraham Ascher, *The Revolution of 1905: Authority Restored* (Stanford, Calif., 1992), 2:329.

119. See Freeze, "*Soslovie* (Estate) Paradigm."

120. Curtiss, *Church and State in Russia*, esp. pp. 237, 240; Ascher, *Authority Restored*, 2:329.

121. *Tserkovnye vedomosti*, January 15, 1905, quoted in Curtiss, *Church and State in Russia*, p. 237.

of parishioners.[122] By recognizing those parish clergy who actually did perform valuable political services for the regime, the Synod was no doubt hoping to set up such reliable priests as a corrective model for those priests who had succumbed to the temptations of liberalism.[123] Through these various efforts, the Synod enhanced the political significance of those aspects of religious life it deemed politically useful, such as sermons, prayers, and *besedy*.

To what extent did rural clergy act as the regime (and especially the Holy Synod) sought? Besides offering *besedy*, prayers, and sermons designed to ensure political loyalty, the clergy distributed antisocialist and/or pro-regime propaganda, thereby implicitly enhancing the political significance of literacy itself.[124] There were village priests who attempted, sometimes successfully, to quiet agrarian disturbances and to stop the mutiny of soldiers returning from the Manchurian front.[125] They sometimes actively defended nobles' land from peasant attack.[126] In these various efforts, rural clergy drew also on religious symbols, such as icons and crucifixes, as tools in the reestablishment of civil order.[127] To be sure, clergy did not necessarily act in these ways out of true political loyalty to the regime.[128] Nevertheless, such actions solidified parishioners' already close identification of parish clergy—as well as Orthodox doctrine, symbolism, and ritual—with the autocracy.

Thus, clerical actions gave parishioners cause to make them targets of political resistance. To be sure, it would be too simplistic to say that when the clergy lent their support to the autocracy, they automatically made themselves the target of peasant resistance.[129] Sometimes clergy actually *succeeded*, their often limited influence in the village notwithstanding, in convincing villagers to stop their resistance and/or rebellion.[130] There were, moreover, cases in which priests played a neutral role during the revolutionary process itself and peasants still rebelled. Thus it would be fair to say that in some cases, clerical action was indeed the proximate cause of peasant political resistance targeted against clergy during these revolutionary years.

In some cases, villagers made the clergy the targets of political resistance simply because they wanted their land. Villagers tried to obtain what has been estimated as the 337,206 *desiatin*s of clerical land through a variety of

122. Ibid., p. 238.
123. On clerical liberalism, see Curtiss, *Church and State in Russia*, esp. p. 242, and Freeze, *Parish Clergy*, pp. 42, 50, 389–96, 465, 467–68.
124. Curtiss, *Church and State in Russia*, pp. 252–53.
125. Ibid., pp. 247–49.
126. Emeliakh, *Istoricheskie predposylki*, p. 45.
127. For examples, see Curtiss, *Church and State in Russia*, pp. 248–49.
128. See ibid., p. 249.
129. To be sure, some peasants expressed exactly this perception. For a vivid example, see ibid., p. 281.
130. See ibid., esp. pp. 276–77.

arenas and means, including violence.[131] Even religious gatherings were not out of the question in this regard: when clergy tried to conduct *besedy*, villagers started talking about the land question.[132] By far the most frequent and most effective arena parishioners used to assuage their land hunger at the expense of clergy was the village assembly. In 1905–7, village assemblies frequently passed resolutions calling for the seizure of church and monastery lands, as well as land in the personal possession of clergy.[133] As demonstrated by these resolutions as well as others canceling priestly salaries, it was during the Revolution of 1905–7 that some villagers invested the village assembly with a new function in religious affairs: it was now to be used to limit as well as support (through allocations for church building and repair) the religious life of the parish. At the same time, villagers (and perhaps even those who passed such "anticlerical resolutions") continued to use the village assembly to carry out its long-standing functions in parish affairs, a telling index of the new ambiguity inherent in the relationship between parish life and village political institutions.[134]

The issue of the village assembly's role in parish affairs was, in fact, part of a broader debate on what villagers and national contemporaries called the "parish question" (*prikhodskii vopros*). Discussed in national journals—and in cities and villages throughout Russia—the "parish question" really embraced two sets of questions concerning the relationship of the parish to the political process. The first fundamental question was the following: who would control various aspects of parish affairs? Setting up the conciliar principle in opposition to the control exercised by diocesan authorities (namely, bishops and the consistories) over the parish, parish priests, laity, and even in rare cases bishops, sounded the call for "parish democracy," or what

---

131. In 1905, the Russian Orthodox Church possessed 1,871,858 *des*. of land; the clergy had an additional 337,206 *des*. "*v lichnoi sobstvennosti*." Monasteries had 739,779. Even Emeliakh, however, admits that these statistics were not based on "complete information." See his *Istoricheskie predposylki*, p. 44. From February to May 1906 alone, villagers are alleged to have killed thirty-one priests and burned twelve churches and two monasteries to the ground. See ibid., p. 45.

132. For an example from Kiev diocese, see Emeliakh, *Istoricheskie predposylki*, p. 57.

133. Presenting statistics that may have been inflated for ideological purposes, the Soviet historian Emeliakh claims that village assemblies passed 350 such resolutions. Diocesan reports, even those offered retrospectively, commented on the actions of village assemblies in this regard. See ibid., esp. pp. 44, 98, as well as Curtiss, *Church and State in Russia*, pp. 280–81, and Robinson, *Rural Russia*. These resolutions were thus congruent with those of the First Peasant Congress, held in Moscow in July of 1905.

134. For examples of parishioners donating money for church repair and for decorating icons on the eve of the Revolution of 1905, see *Iaroslavskie eparkhial'nye vedomosti*, January 23, 1905, p. 53. For a vivid description of a village assembly's debate on allocating funds for building a new church, see "Iz zhizni odnogo sviashchennika," part 1, "Ostraia Luka," p. 73. Hereafter cited as "Keston ms."

contemporaries liked to call parish "revival" (*ozhivlenie*).¹³⁵ Parish priests and laity were generally united in sounding the call for the elimination of diocesan control over such parish matters as finances and the appointment of priests.¹³⁶ They parted company, however, on who, in the absence of the diocese, was to control such matters. On the matter of priestly appointments, for example, laity generally favored the restoration of *vybornoe nachalo*, a demand that was part of a broader cry to grant the village assembly greater control over parish affairs. Priests, however, often thought otherwise.¹³⁷

These debates on parish reform generated their own political momentum. The Synod's decree of October 18, 1905, which established parish councils (*prikhodskie sovety*), is a case in point. This decree was, in effect, a concession to the broadly articulated demand for parishioners to have an elected body that would have at least some control over the parish's property and other financial resources. (Prior to the decree, it was the priest and the church elder [*tserkovnyi starosta*] who controlled these matters.)¹³⁸ Partially addressing this demand for greater control over parish financial matters, the Synod permitted the convocation of parish meetings, where councils of twelve *men* could be elected. The Synod's decree expressed a reluctance, lamented by contemporaries, to give parishioners a clearly articulated legal basis for control of parish finances: "The members of the vestry may be asked by the clergy and the parish elder to participate in the handling of church finances."¹³⁹ Moreover, the limits and vagueness of the decree only contributed to further debate and politicization of the parish question. A case in point was Perm diocese, where, in June 1906, parishioners petitioned for women to be included in the councils and to have the same rights as men therein.¹⁴⁰ The Perm petitioners were in fact successful in their bid to eliminate gender as an exclusionary category in parish affairs, thus illustrating a

---

135. For an example of the call for parish revival, see, for example, Sviashchennik Dmitrii Silin, "K voprosu ob ozhivlenii tserkovno-obshchestvennoi deiatel'nosti," *Bogoslovskii vestnik* (September 1905), and "Okonchanie," ibid. 3 (October 1905): 324–47, and "Bishop of Saratov," in Gregory L. Freeze, ed., *From Supplication to Revolution* (New York, 1988), p. 233.

136. On the details see Curtiss, *Church and State in Russia*, pp. 218–20.

137. Ibid., pp. 219–20.

138. Although parishioners elected the elder for a three-year term, they could neither impeach him nor censure his actions for the duration of the term. See ibid., p. 220.

139. Quoted in ibid. As Curtiss notes, "The powers of these vestries and of parish meetings were not defined, and their decisions were to be subject to the approval of the diocesan authorities, who were to have the power to decide all cases in which misunderstandings arose" (p. 220). For an example of contemporary criticisms of the Synod's decree, see V. N. Myshchena, "Iz periodicheskoi pechati," *Bogoslovskii vestnik* (December 1905), esp. p. 830. While lamenting these and other limitations of the Decree, Myshchena deemed the councils a "a first desired step in creating the foundation of *sobornost'*."

140. For details, see *Pribavleniia k tserkovnym vedomostiam*, December 16, 1906, p. 3131.

dynamic that played itself out in other revolutionary contexts: once human rights are articulated to any degree, limitations upon them become, in Lynn Hunt's words, "harder and harder to justify."[141]

The second component of the "parish question" was the political role of the parish itself. For it was not just that the parish was transformed politically by the revolutionary process of 1905–7. As participants in the debate on parish reform confronted these issues, they sometimes considered how the parish could be an agent of political transformation. Some champions of "parish democracy," of the diffusion of power over parish affairs, we can infer, saw parish reform as contributing to a more democratic village and a more democratic Russia. "Conservatives" (defined loosely as opponents of revolutionary agitation of any sort), however, invested parish reform and the parish itself with a very different kind of political agency. They made a connection between the absence of parish autonomy, the withering of parish religiosity, and the eruption of political turmoil (such as the Revolution of 1905–7). Along these lines, the conservative commentator Arkhimandrit Evdokim called for the resurrection of the control of parish life that the village commune had had prior to Peter the Great's church reforms. Why, he implicitly asked, should the commune regain its status as a "lively and self-sufficient unit"? Why should the commune (and its village assembly) be restored to its pre-Petrine apogee, when it "built its own church, chose its priest, and . . . judged its own members and had the right to interfere in family life"?[142] Why should the parish receive the rights of a corporation (*iuridicheskoe litso*)?[143] As Arkhimandrit Evdokim saw it, only the restoration of parish autonomy—the restoration of the parish's identity as the "first cell of the free, conciliar, and apostolic Church"—could stop the revolutionary "sedition" imperiling Russia.[144] Thus, as this brief survey suggests, contemporaries invested parish reform and even parish democracy with varied and contradictory political meanings.

In this ambiguous context, the clergy seized the opportunity to articulate claims about their own political role vis-à-vis the state. Even as early as 1904,

---

141. A point made by Lynn Hunt in "The Revolutionary Origin of Human Rights," Stice Lecture, University of Washington, May 1995. In choosing not to justify excluding women from enjoying such rights, the local *preosviashchennyi* noted that women possessed the necessary qualifications for election to the councils: "piety and devoted belief." (In other words, religious criteria were being viewed as the basis for legal rights!)

142. Episkop Evdokim, "Na zare novoi tserkovnoi zhizni," *Bogoslovskii vestnik*, June 1905, p. 209.

143. Evdokim, "Na zare," *Bogoslovskii vestnik*, June 1905, p. 226. At stake in the demand for *iuridicheskoe litso* was the parish's right to buy and sell property. The government, however, refused to grant it this power. See Curtiss, *Church and State in Russia*, p. 220.

144. Evdokim, "Na zare," July–August 1905, p. 419.

Metropolitan Antonii of St. Petersburg, a rare example of liberalism among what one historian has described as "an exceedingly conservative upper clergy," called for the clergy to have a greater role in state political institutions.[145] It was not, however, only clerical liberals who voiced demands for the clergy to have a greater political role. Arkhimandrit Evdokim was an important example of a conservative who also spoke out loudly in favor of clerical political autonomy and power. Making a rather blatantly self-interested case for a greater political role for bishops, Evdokim based his argument on historical precedent, the routinely important political contributions they made in the pre-Petrine period.[146] Yet Evdokim also extended this claim to the parish clergy, one member of which implicitly articulated his desire for true *political* agency (as opposed to administrative service) as follows: "For a long time the clergy has been deprived of initiative, and only carries out orders, decrees, and judgments of the higher authorities.... The clergy has been turned into a modest bureaucracy, dutifully carrying out the will of the authorities."[147] In other words, both Evdokim and the priest were rejecting the cameralist identity foisted on them by the state. To be sure, it is impossible to determine how widespread and how consciously articulated such a desire for independent political agency actually was. There is no denying, however, that it was common for rural parish clergy to experience the underlying dynamic generating the desire for true political agency. On the one hand, they played an increasingly important "social role" in the village. Yet on the other hand, they had very little legally encoded political power: they even lacked, as Evdokim reminded the readers of *Bogoslovskii vestnik*, the right to participate in the village assembly.[148] This belief in the "right" to political agency was the common denominator that underlay—and was strengthened by—the especially varied political roles that rural clergy played in the revolutionary process, whether that of bulwark of the autocratic regime, agitator of peasant insurrection, advocate of clerical liberalism, or supporter of the Black Hundreds.[149]

---

145. He made this plea at a specific conference of Russian state ministers. See Curtiss, *Church and State in Russia*, pp. 210, 212.
146. Evdokim, "Na zare," May 1905, esp. p. 161.
147. Evdokim, "Na zare," July–August 1905, p. 412.
148. Evdokim, "Na zare," *Bogoslovskii vestnik*, May 1905, p. 164.
149. As Freeze notes, clerical political behavior was "less predictable" outside the major urban centers. See *Parish Clergy*, p. 470. There is no definitive assessment of the relative strengths of these political loyalties among parish priests, let alone among the rural parish clergy. Rejecting Freeze's (and also Curtiss's) emphasis on the unpredictability of clerical political loyalties and identities on the parish level, Ascher has asserted that "among the parish clergy, sympathy for the Union of Russian People was certainly stronger than support for liberal movements, as is suggested by the numerous press reports on the involvement of priests in the URP and other right-wing movements and even in pogroms" (*Authority Restored*, 2:336). I am

Deepening Conflict, 1907–1914

By 1907 the revolutionary turmoil was over, but the clergy, other villagers, and political elites had by no means forgotten it. In the new political landscape, whose reactionary cast Prime Minister Pëtr Stolypin personified for many, tsarist officials once again tried to use the parish clergy to shore up rural parishioners' political loyalty to the autocracy. As in 1861 and 1905–7, the Holy Synod instructed parish clergy to preach loyalty to the tsar and the autocracy in sermons and extraliturgical instruction.[150] While responding in the often tried (but not necessarily true) way, the Synod also emphasized other aspects of the rural parish clergy's pastoral role, aspects tailored to the particular social, cultural, and political challenges faced by the Orthodox Church in the rural parish. Its religious monopoly now officially dissolved by both the October Manifesto and the Edict of Toleration (April 17, 1905, Old Style), rural Orthodoxy was also threatened by an increasingly visible secular village intelligentsia and growing ranks of seasonal out-migrants. Even the Stolypin reforms themselves created new challenges for the rural parish. Those peasants who separated from the commune and lived on enclosed farms (*khutory*) now found themselves located a greater, and a seemingly insurmountable distance, from the parish church. What were the politics of the rural parish in this new sociopolitical context?

Some rural clergy continued to do their part in the autocracy's latest "wager on the pious."[151] After 1907, bishops emphasized the clergy's pastoral role in those rural areas in which anticlerical, antireligious, and revolutionary activity had been especially great; the Synod even instructed the clergy to study socialist and atheist ideas in order to be able to convince parishioners to reject them![152] Diocesan authorities issued parish clergy explicit instructions to remind those parishioners who had engaged in agrarian disturbances that unlawfully seizing another's property went against church teachings.[153] To be sure, bishops were wont to characterize the results of such efforts in an overdramatic, exaggerated way, claiming, for example,

---

skeptical of this conclusion because it is an argument "from silence," and it is not based on a careful scrutiny of the content and discourse of those reports.

150. Curtiss, *Church and State in Russia*, p. 319.

151. I am here adapting Stolypin's phrase "wager on the strong and sober," applied to the agrarian reforms of 1907–11 that sought to create an independent landholding peasantry that would be politically conservative.

152. For an example from the diocese of Ekaterinburg and Irbitsk, see Bishop Mitrofan's diocesan report of 1912, as quoted in Emeliakh, *Istoricheskie predposylki*, p. 48. The full text can be found in RGIA, f. 796, op. 442., no. 2516, l. 14.

153. See Emeliakh, *Istoricheskie predposylki*, p. 49, for an example from a 1909 diocesan report from Penza, which can be found in RGIA, f. 796, op. 442, no. 2346, l. 27 ob.

that they had put "a rebellious peasantry [back] on the path of reverence for God and tsar."[154] But there is no doubt that some clergy followed diocesan instructions of this sort, even if those efforts ultimately backfired as they increased peasant anticlericalism and political resistance.

Moreover, the Synod's efforts to get clergy to engage in other types of pastoral activity also bore some fruit. As early as 1906, in response to agrarian unrest and competition from *zemstvo* specialists, diocesan authorities emphasized that the clergy had to play a much more active role in encouraging new forms of peasant economic activity.[155] This emphasis outlived the Revolution; throughout the postrevolutionary period, diocesan journals (*eparkhial'nye vedomosti*) routinely lauded the efforts of clergy who offered peasants agronomic assistance.[156] Diocesan authorities in particular sang the praises of those clergy who assumed leadership roles and otherwise participated in cooperative credit societies (*kreditnye tovarishchestva*), agricultural councils (*sel'sko-khoziaistvennye sovety*), and consumers' societies (*potrebitel'nye obshchestva*).[157] A significant number of parish clergy likewise heeded the Synod's 1909 injunction to combat alcoholism by forming temperance societies and church brotherhoods (*bratstva*), and by giving appropriate sermons.[158] In these and other efforts, such as the missionary work that now assumed increasing urgency, the clergy were to save parishioners from threats to their "religious-moral condition."[159]

Yet the rural clergy increasingly recognized that their job was not just to protect and reform but to entice. A rural parish priest in Samara diocese, for example, spent a good deal of time trying to convince male villagers to attend church on holidays.[160] In offering parishioners the religious discussions (*besedy*) that proved so popular in the years between the 1905 Revolution and World War I, rural parish priests, drawing on skills developed during the counterreform years, tried to compete with popular theater, cinema, and even secular literature.[161]

---

154. See the 1908 report from Kherson diocese in Emeliakh, *Istoricheskie predposylki*, p. 49.

155. For a discussion of the efforts of Archbishop Anastasii of Voronezh diocese, see Chulos, "Peasant Religion," pp. 369–71.

156. For examples from Voronezh, see ibid., p. 370.

157. Curtiss, *Church and State in Russia*, p. 363; for examples from Voronezh diocese, see Chulos, "Peasant Religion," pp. 121, 370–71.

158. Curtiss, *Church and State in Russia*, pp. 362–63; Chulos, "Peasant Religion," pp. 361–63.

159. On rural clergy's missionary work, see, for example, Curtiss, *Church and State in Russia*, pp. 319–28.

160. Keston ms., p. 78.

161. On the popularity of *besedy*, see Keston ms., p. 39, and the cautious interpretation offered by Chulos, "Peasant Religion," p. 117. On the popularity of religious-moral readings (*chteniia*) in the village, see *IVO* (St. Petersburg, 1911), p. 278. On the competition between

Although clergy tried to protect, entice, retain, and convert, village youth and/or out-migrants continued to prove resistant to clerical entreaties. During the years of 1907–14, bishops commonly singled out youth, out-migrants, former soldiers, the village intelligentsia (teachers, *zemstvo* workers), and to some extent older male villagers for their rejection of icons and Orthodox ritual, for their "evasion of communion and confession."[162] Some villagers, such as those whom a bishop in 1911 described as being "indifferent to the church," now preferred working in the fields to attending church on Sundays and holidays.[163] Noting that some villagers openly proclaimed their rejection of the sacraments, worried bishops characterized such behavior as evidence of the growth of atheism, which they in turn attributed to the influence of revolutionary exiles, village intelligentsia, as well as the socialist and antireligious propaganda they distributed.[164]

Had these villagers really stopped believing in God? Although there is no way to know for sure, there is reason to be skeptical that they had. It is always dangerous to deduce beliefs from behavior; there is much evidence that declining church attendance and atheism do not necessarily go hand in hand. If declining belief did not generate the behavior described above, what did?

Younger villagers and seasonal factory workers who appeared to be "antireligious" were not as good at disguising their underlying motivations as we might think. Even brief excerpts from bishops' yearly diocesan reports render these villagers more transparent—at least to the historian—than they probably wanted to be. We get a useful clue, for example, from a 1911 report from Chernigov diocese. Lamenting that youth "attended church . . . in order to leave," the bishop also noted that they "left for effect when the preacher appeared at the altar."[165] The youth wanted to stage an open challenge to

---

balagany and church services, see Emeliakh, *Istoricheskie predposylki*, p. 90; on the popularity of cinema in Voronezh diocese, see Chulos, "Peasant Religion," pp. 365–66. On the spread of literacy and secular literature in the countryside, see Brooks, *When Russia Learned to Read*. On the increasing availability of irreligious literature, see Emeliakh, pp. 83–84.

162. For examples from a variety of dioceses, see Emeliakh, *Istoricheskie predposylki*, esp. pp. 60, 76, 78, 86–87, 90–91, and passim. In the discussion that follows, I have regrettably had to conflate the irreligious behavior of these different social groups, since the bishops' reports themselves often do not make such distinctions.

163. The phrase was used in the 1911 report from Kiev and Chernigov dioceses (RGIA, f. 796, op. 422, no. 2497, l. 50). See Emeliakh, *Istoricheskie predposylki*, p. 87.

164. Soviet historians, for obviously different reasons, became uncritical proponents of this interpretation. For an example, see Emeliakh, *Istoricheskie predposylki*, as well as Emeliakh, *Antiklerikal'noe dvizhenie krest'ian v period pervoi russkoi revoliutsii* (Moscow, 1965) and *Krest'iane i tserkov' nakanune Oktiabria* (Leningrad, 1976).

165. RGIA, f. 796, op. 442, no. 2497, ll. 52 ob.– 53, as quoted in Emeliakh, *Istoricheskie predposylki*, p. 76.

clerical authority, a stance that did not necessarily reflect antireligiosity. What these youth in Chernigov diocese communicated by the timing of their action, their counterparts in Tambov diocese chose to express through cultural forms tailored specially for the purpose at hand. As described in a 1908 diocesan report, Tambov village youth composed "street songs" in which they made fun of clerical "clothing, hair, gait, and voice intonation."[166] To be sure, these challenges to clerical authority had much in common with other ways in which villagers expressed their hostility to parish clergy (such as refusing to receive them on holidays, reducing or completely eliminating their payments of *ruga*, attempting to seize clerical land, withholding financial support for parish schools).[167] Yet they differed from these other cases as well. For what underlay them was the villagers' desire to devise their own cultural forms to express their hostility to clergy (and possibly to ritual) in as publicly visible and provocative a way as possible. During the reactionary years following the Revolution of 1905–7, village youth (and probably other villagers) created, or at least maintained, a public culture of disrespect for and abuse of clerical authority, appropriating for their purposes a variety of public village spaces, even the village church.[168] Moreover, unlike the second group of anticlerical actions, those of the Tambov and Chernigov youth were not attempts to resist a particular claim that clergy were trying to exact from them (such as *ruga* and emoluments); rather, they were expressions of complete rejection of clerical authority, with all the implicit political meanings elaborated previously. This suggests the possibility that the other cases of "antireligious" behavior we have seen should also be interpreted as attempts to challenge clerical authority and the institutional prestige of the parish church, rather than necessarily as expressions of pure atheism.

Whatever their meaning, these different types of anticlerical behavior had a significant impact on daily life in the village. To be sure, in most villages only a relatively small minority of villagers engaged in such anticlerical acts, and there is now compelling evidence that at least in Voronezh diocese "Orthodox peasants remained nearly as observant of annual sacramental obligations in 1914 as they had in 1860."[169] The impact of the anticlerical "faction," however, was far greater than its relatively small size

166. RGIA, f. 796, op. 442, no. 2303, ll. 43, 54, as quoted in Emeliakh, *Istoricheskie predposylki*, p. 95. An analysis of the content of such songs and peasant verse (*chastushki*), though I have not attempted it here, would no doubt reveal a great deal about the motivations of these youth and other ostensibly antireligious villagers.

167. Emeliakh, *Istoricheskie predposylki*, passim.

168. For another example, see ibid., p. 69.

169. Chulos, "Peasant Religion," p. 399. As he points out, the statistics from Voronezh on the fulfillment of communal and confession obligations do not allow us to conclude that church attendance remained constant as well. See his discussion in ibid., pp. 397–403.

might suggest. As in 1905–7, its impact continued to be felt in the village assembly, where anticlerical villagers, whom one bishop referred to as the "younger generation," sometimes used their influence to refuse traditional communal expenditures such as *ruga*, church upkeep, and support for church schools.[170] It would seem unlikely that these were village "youth," since only male heads of households were voting members of the village assembly at this point. They were probably younger heads of households who now had enough political clout to derail the agenda of their seniors, possibly evoking heated debate and even violence. As suggested above, there is good reason to believe that younger heads of households, many of whom had worked as seasonal laborers outside the village, were in fact taking such stands against the clergy and the institutional life of the parish *in order* to challenge the power their elders wielded in village affairs. In other words, during the years following the revolutionary upheaval of 1905–7, certain villagers not only continued to define the power structure of the village by contesting the legitimacy of its symbols. They expanded the cultural forms (e.g., songs) and arenas (e.g., the church) in which they did so.[171]

This challenge did not, of course, go uncontested. To be sure, as exemplified by some clergy's new aversion to even making traditional requests before hostile village assemblies, the "anticlerical faction" was able to win some skirmishes in the battle to define the cultural bases of power.[172] Clergy and other villagers faced limits in the direct defense they could mount at a given moment of cultural confrontation, let alone in a particular institutional setting such as the village assembly. Yet they had at their disposal an array of institutions and networks that they could use to work behind the scenes. While the *tserkovnye sovety* born in 1905 languished in the years before 1917, parishioners continued to use the *popechitel'stva* to build and maintain churches.[173] Although they may have been preaching to the converted,

170. For a discussion of the influence of anticlerical villagers in the village assemblies of Ekaterinoslav and Mariupol'sk dioceses, see the 1912 report of Bishop Agapit, partially reprinted in Emeliakh, *Istoricheskie predposylki*, p. 69. On the tendency of *otkhodniki* to reject patriarchal authority and village customs (such as marriage and sexual norms), see Barbara Alpern Engel, "Peasant Morality and Pre-Marital Relations in Late Nineteenth-Century Russia," *Journal of Social History* 4 (1990): 695, and Hoffmann, *Peasant Metropolis*, p. 7.

171. Here I am adapting Duara's useful concept of the "cultural nexus of power." See *Culture, Power, and the State*, esp. p. 15.

172. On the clergy's newly displayed aversion to making requests to unresponsive and even hostile village assemblies, see Emeliakh, *Istoricheskie predposylki*, p. 69 (Bishop Agapit, Ekaterinburg and Mariupol'skii, RGIA f. 796, op. 442, no. 2517, ll. 9–11).

173. On the "weakness" of the church councils created in 1905, see Curtiss, *Church and State in Russia*, pp. 301–2. Maintaining that "the parish councils never proved to be strong," he then goes on to give examples of elite perceptions of clerical disinterest in forming them. Clergy were disinterested in part because parishioners wanted to "capture" them, like the *popechitel'stva*, for their own purposes.

clergy could use *besedy* to mobilize support against those villagers who contested clerical authority and the institutional strength of the parish church.[174] Drawing on the authority they still commanded among some villagers, clergy actively enlisted key segments of the village population—even youth—in their missionary work. Of course, this required some ingenious planning and enticement. To give but one example, a rural parish priest in the Lower Volga followed rehearsals for his youth choir with discussions about religious matters, gradually succeeding in getting youth to do missionary work among Old Believers and sectarians. "It's always easier to attack than defend," stressed the priest as he urged the young peasants, whom he called his "helpers," to take the lead during such conversations.[175] It is quite possible that parish priests also recruited willing youth to exert a positive influence on their anticlerical, often "hooligan" counterparts.[176] If so, it was not just that the battle to control the cultural underpinnings of power pitted one generation against another; rather, that conflict fell along intragenerational lines as well.

The Politics of Parish Religiosity During World War I

When Russia entered World War I in August 1914, it seemed to contemporaries that villagers were less interested in challenging clerical authority and the institutional prestige of the parish church. Bishops and parish priests alike noted what they described as a rise in "religiosity."[177] To be sure, it is always dangerous to accept contemporaries' perceptions, especially when expressed in such global terms, at face value. In this case, however, there are reasons to take such claims seriously, if not literally. For the combined processes of military mobilization and seasonal labor diminished the ranks of the anticlerical, anti-church faction.[178] Ignoring or dismissing the impact of these demographic processes on parish life, bishops of course attributed this perceived religious revival to the heroic efforts of parish clergy, once again instructed by the Holy Synod to mobilize parishioners through nationalistic sermons. Synthesizing these two types of explanations for a

---

174. In fact, it may have been that rural parish clergy engaged in pastoral work in these arenas not because of the directives they received from the Holy Synod but because of the anticlerical challenges they experienced on an everyday basis.

175. Keston ms., pp. 19–21. To prepare them, the priest instructed them in the history of Old Belief as well as the "basic attitudes and retorts of Old Believers at *besedy*."

176. See Keston ms.

177. Ibid., p. 161; Emeliakh, *Istoricheskie predposylki*, pp. 124–27.

178. Emeliakh, *Istoricheskie predposylki*, pp. 124–27.

resurgence in rural parish life, it may be that because those villagers who were not mobilized—women and older men—were most likely to be receptive to such "propaganda," there really was a connection between clergy's pastoral efforts and religious revival. In any case, rural parish clergy did enthusiastically contribute to the war effort, leading parishioners in providing financial, medical, and religious support.[179] Although some parishioners continued to engage in anticlerical actions, such as refusing to pay *ruga*, on the whole rural clergy found that the hostility of the prewar years had abated somewhat.

They soon found that their brief reprieve had come to an end. By 1916, bishops' reports' routinely lamented a resurgence of what they deemed the pathologies of rural parish life. They bemoaned the growing numbers of villagers disinclined to fulfill their obligations to take communion and confession, to attend church on Sundays and holidays, and to provide financial support for their clergy.[180] Rejecting in apparently increasing numbers the liturgical aspects of parish Orthodoxy, villagers (especially the younger ones) instead, if bishops' reports are to be trusted, preferred theater productions, bazaars, and films to Sunday services and holiday celebrations.[181] As we might expect, those same reports noted that villagers intensified their contestation of clerical authority and the institutional basis of parish life. Village assemblies, for example, passed resolutions that placed a tax on clerical financial demands, while hostile (and sometimes physically violent) altercations between clergy and parishioners over *ruga* and emoluments ostensibly increased.[182]

Why did the attack on the clergy and, more generally, the cultural underpinnings of village power, reach if not exceed its prewar dimensions? This happened in part because as the war went on, the demographic processes that had been kind to clergy and to parish life reversed themselves. Seasonal laborers returned to their villages as the war brought economic deterioration, shutting down some factories.[183] They were joined in their attack on clergy and on the Church by another very important social group: deserting

---

179. For details, see Curtiss, *Church and State in Russia*, pp. 377–79.

180. For examples, see Emeliakh, *Istoricheskie predposylki*, especially pp. 117–22, and Keston ms., p. 163.

181. Emeliakh, *Istoricheskie predposylki*, pp. 121–22; *Saratovskie eparkhial'nye vedomosti*, January 21, 1917, p. 106.

182. See the 1915 report on the condition of Tambov diocese (RGIA, f. 796, op. 442, no. 2734, ll. 66–67ob), quoted in Emeliakh, *Istoricheskie predposylki*, p. 130; *Saratovskie eparkhial'nye vedomosti*, January 11, 1917, p. 57. To be sure, they had also passed such resolutions before the outbreak of the war.

183. On the connection between military mobilization and increased seasonal labor (and surging numbers of newly minted *otkhodniki*), see Emeliakh, *Istoricheskie predposylki*, pp. 124–27.

and demobilized soldiers, many of whom had been exposed to antireligious propaganda while at the front.[184] These demographic processes, though highly important, cannot alone explain what contemporaries (bishops and parish priests) described as a profound deterioration in clerical-lay relations by 1916. By 1916, bishops were reporting that even "old men of sixty to seventy years of age were not going to confession or taking communion."[185] Such deterioration was, ironically, brought on in part by clergy themselves. Through their extensive contributions to the war, they hinged their own prestige and authority to the fate of the conflict. Exemplifying the degree to which parishioners identified clergy with the devastating conflict, villagers in the Lower Volga region claimed that "clergy had started the war."[186]

The daughter of a parish priest in the Lower Volga gave a retrospective account of the difficulties her father experienced as the war went on. She lamented that "it was more and more the case that when either Sergei or my mother left the house, hostile barbs were aimed at him. A hostile mood had even emerged among members of the parish council."[187] This rather poignant description captures one of the key processes we have traced in this chapter: the increasing degree to which villagers were at odds with each other over the role of religious practice in village life. It was probably only in his peasant hut, if anywhere, that Father Sergei and his family could avoid anticlerical insults and the underlying cultural and political conflict that they reflected and deepened. Well before the Bolsheviks inaugurated yet another round of subordinating rural Orthodoxy to political ends, Russian villagers were contesting religion's role in providing the cultural underpinnings of village power and, implicitly, the national political order it supported and shaped.

---

184. Ibid., pp. 138–40. Some former soldiers became sectarians. A missionary conference held in 1916 in Novgorod diocese devoted attention to the problem of soldiers who had become vehemently anticlerical and ostensibly irreligious during the wartime stints. See ibid., p. 140.

185. In fact, one parish priest maintained that it was only during the war that a crisis in clerical-lay relations occurred. See Keston ms., p. 163.

186. Ibid. On the extensive wartime charity efforts of the clergy in Saratov diocese, see *Saratovskie eparkhial'nye vedomosti*, January 1, 1917, p. 27.

187. Keston ms., p. 163.

2

Perplexing Paradoxes

Russian peasants had launched a social revolution even before the Bolsheviks came to power in October 1917.[1] They had shattered the autocratic order in the countryside, seizing the land and otherwise destroying the property of the gentry, creating their own political institutions and laws in the process. Although the Bolsheviks were able to gain the passive support of the peasants—in part because they tolerated this blossoming of rural political activity—they were well aware that this support had shallow roots. In part because Lenin had denounced all peasants as capitalists who threatened to block the building of socialism, the Bolsheviks believed they had to penetrate the village and transform it economically, culturally, and politically.[2] That agenda became especially urgent once the Civil War began in the early summer of 1918. The Bolsheviks sought to establish "soviet power" in the village through legislation (e.g., on the place of the Orthodox Church under the new regime), through new village institutions (e.g., rural Party cells, soviets, and the committees of the village poor or *komitety bednoty*), agitation

---

1. Skocpol, *States and Social Revolutions*.
2. To be sure, Lenin did believe in the possibility of an alliance between the poor peasantry and the proletariat. On Lenin's views of the peasant, see Esther Kingston-Mann, *Lenin and the Problem of Marxist Peasant Revolution* (New York, 1985).

and propaganda (versus the Church), and terror. As they knew only too well, their success in these arenas depended on having enough qualified cadres to do the work.

It was not only the Bolsheviks (from 1918 the Communist Party), however, who sought to control the village. Even before the Revolutions of 1917, some villagers—especially seasonal labors and demobilized veterans—had begun to challenge the authority of the parish clergy, and of rural Orthodoxy more generally, for their own political purposes. Representatives of these social groups streamed back into the villages in increasing numbers during the Revolution and Civil War. But did they, whether or not they became Party members, continue to challenge the traditional political structures of the village and the role that village Orthodoxy played in legitimizing them? How, and with what success, did they do so?

This chapter examines the dimensions and impact of these various attempts to establish the relationship of the rural parish to the village political structure. What were the social identities—as well as goals, strategies, and tools—of the respective "factions" that emerged in this ongoing process of negotiation? With what political meanings did villagers invest religious symbols, belief, practice, and parish organization? This chapter investigates how the religious identities (or lack thereof) of clergy and other villagers shaped rural politics in revolution and Civil War, that is, during three distinct periods: from March to October 1917, or what Orlando Figes has aptly called the "emergence of rural political autonomy"; from October 1917 to early summer of 1918, the "six months of peasant rule"; and from May 1918 to early 1921, the span of Russia's Civil War.[3]

Social Revolution, Peasant Political Autonomy, and Parish Life, March–October 1917

As Russian villagers began to shatter the old order during the spring and summer of 1917, they necessarily created new social and political relations (including those that involved the clergy and the rural parish). When the Provisional Government refused to satisfy the peasants' now ravenous "land hunger," the peasants seized a good deal of the land and other property of the gentry and the Orthodox Church. Although to gentry and urban observers this may have seemed like a spontaneous, elemental process, nothing could have been further from the truth. For even as the peasants

---

3. This is the chronological breakdown adopted by Figes in his magisterial *Peasant Russia*; I have quoted the titles of chapters 2 and 3.

destroyed the rural state apparatus of the tsarist autocracy (e.g., the *zemstva*, the land captains, the rural police, the *volost'* administration, provincial governors), they realized that they needed to devise new institutions that could carry out the agrarian revolution and at the same time form the basis of the newly emerging rural political order.[4] To that end, peasants created "ad hoc peasants committees (and later soviets), elected by the communal or village assemblies," through which, as Figes has skillfully shown, they passed their own laws, some of which "authorized" them to seize and distribute land formerly held by the Church and the gentry.[5]

Seeking to exercise their political autonomy, the peasants held village assemblies to discuss local, national, and international issues generated by the revolutions in Petrograd and in the countryside. These assemblies differed from prerevolutionary village assemblies in two important ways. First, at these assemblies, villagers discussed "a much wider range of issues than the village assemblies before 1914," including "the position of the church."[6] Second, these new village assemblies (tellingly called *obshchie skhody* rather than *mirskie skhody*) were comprised of not just the heads of peasant households but *all* the residents of a given village.[7] The male peasant elders had to negotiate power with "junior members of the peasant households (including the female members), landless labourers and craftsmen, village *intelligenty* (e.g., scribes, teachers, vets, doctors), soldiers on leave, and other 'respected citizens' (e.g., the clergy and well-loved gentry squires)," who had heretofore not been able to participate in the village assembly.[8] Clergy (as well as religious activists such as members of church councils) thus had to operate in a new political world. It was a world in which they now had a direct voice. But it was also a world in which an increasing number of villagers, not to mention new types of villagers, had the potential to decide matters affecting rural parish life.

The village population, and consequentially the social basis of village politics, was in a state of flux during the months between the February and October Revolutions. Especially from May onward, the number of refugees—a group that included such diverse elements as unemployed factory workers, political refugees, and prisoners of war—increased significantly.[9] As was the case during the last decades of the tsarist regime, these in-migrants (and especially the former factory workers) tended to be hostile

---

4. Ibid., p. 40.
5. On this see ibid., p. 31.
6. Ibid., p. 32.
7. Orlando Figes, "The Russian Peasant Community in the Agrarian Revolution, 1917–18," in Roger Bartlett, ed., *Land Commune and Peasant Community in Russia: Communal Forms in Imperial and Early Soviet Society* (New York, 1990), p. 238.
8. This list is taken from Figes, *Peasant Russia*, p. 33.
9. On deurbanization, see Diane Koenker, "Urbanization and Deurbanization in the Russian

to the clergy and to organized religion more generally, in part because they had a higher level of literacy. Although they had the desire and the skills necessary to challenge the position of the parish church, at least in the period under consideration they lacked the necessary clout. In fact, most refugees found themselves on the fringes of village society; many villages refused to house them or give them land and probably disregarded anything they said at the general village assemblies.[10] If the villages shunned the in-migrants, they accorded returning peasant soldiers, whom the villages also began to reabsorb in the summer of 1917, a great deal of respect. This is because they were native sons who had made good in the world beyond the village, generally acquiring high levels of literacy, leadership skills developed in a large organization, and familiarity with new political ideologies (e.g., Bolshevism). In fact, on returning to their native villages, those peasant soldiers who had been exposed to Bolshevik propaganda generally proclaimed themselves atheists or at least voiced considerable hostility to clergy and Orthodox parish life.[11] Although these returning native sons did not yet have a voice at the *mirskie skhody*, which were still dominated by peasant smallholders, their views no doubt commanded great prestige at the more inclusive *obshchie skhody* and *obshchie sobraniia*.[12]

How did the clergy and the rural parish church fare in this new political world? As noted above, even before the Bolsheviks' Decree on Land of October 1917, peasants passed resolutions that empowered the commune to confiscate the property of the rural parish and of the clergy.[13] Were such resolutions anticlerical, and did they, furthermore, reflect a deep hostility to parish Orthodoxy? To be sure, as we have seen, anticlericalism had a long lineage in the Russian village; in 1917, with the return of former soldiers to

---

Revolution and Civil War," in Diane P. Koenker, William G. Rosenberg, and Ronald Grigor Suny, eds., *Party, State and Society in the Russian Civil War* (Bloomington, Ind., 1989), esp. pp. 90–91. For statistics on the number of refugees in Saratov province, see Orlando Figes, "Peasant Farmers and the Minority Groups of Rural Society: Peasant Egalitarianism and Village Social Relations During the Russian Revolution (1917–1921)," in E. Kingston-Mann and T. Mixter, eds., *Peasant Economy, Culture, and Politics of European Russia, 1800–1921* (Princeton, N.J., 1991), pp. 391–92.

10. For details, see Figes, "Peasant Farmers," pp. 392–93.

11. See Allan K. Wildman, *The End of the Russian Imperial Army*, 2 vols. (Princeton, N.J., 1980, 1988). On the impact of Bolshevik propaganda on the religiosity of soldiers, see A. Okninsky, *Dva goda sredi krest'ian: vidennoe, slyshannoe, perezhitoe v Tambovskoi gubernii s noiabria 1918 goda do noiabria 1920 goda* (Newtonville, Mass., 1986), p. 231. Once a tsarist official, Okninsky occupied a post in the Podgornoe VIK (Tambov province). For more on him, see Figes, *Peasant Russia*, p. 83.

12. On the political dominance of the heads of the small-scale family farms, see Figes, "Peasant Farmers," pp. 378–79.

13. For an example from Voronezh diocese, see Chulos, "Peasant Religion," pp. 413–14. See also Figes, *Peasant Russia*, pp. 40–41.

their native villages, its social base increased. While anticlericalism no doubt played a significant role, especially in those villages in which the priest was perceived to have played a particularly "extortionist" role, other motivations often operated as well. For one, those resolutions reflected the reassertion of the communal landholding principle that no one was to be exempt from the authority of the repartitional commune.[14] Thus in 1917–18, the commune typically granted rural parish clergy an allotment of land, as well as voting rights at the more circumscribed *mirskoi skhod*; unlike the marginal elements of rural society such as urban refugees, the clergy were regarded as part of the village.[15] The seizure and repartition of church property reflected the increasingly prominent role that village assemblies, in the "inter-revolutionary months," played in deciding nearly all important aspects of parish life.[16] In addition to confiscating and redistributing land and other church property, often village assemblies in essence reinstituted the pre-Petrine practice of *vybornoe nachalo*, a desire that parishioners had voiced during the last decades of the tsarist regime: they kicked out particularly loathsome parish priests (and sometimes parish elders) and usually replaced them with more promising candidates.[17] Adumbrating the even greater democratization of parish life that would emerge in the 1920s, they sometimes made do without a replacement and performed the liturgy themselves.[18] Although not necessarily hostile in a categorical way to the clergy or to village Orthodoxy more generally, village assemblies sought to establish their control over parish affairs.

Some villagers, however, *were* openly hostile to the clergy and sometimes to parish Orthodoxy as well. Violence against the clergy, as well as against parish property, was apparently quite common in 1917–18.[19] Yet there was no one meaning that can be ascribed to these various types of violence. Sometimes villagers committed violence against the clergy—even going so far as murdering them—because they resented the wealth they perceived them to have.[20] When the clergy were harassed and physically attacked in public places, it was often at the hands of hooligans who may have been expressing a general rejection of authority.[21] Was this also the case when villagers (of unspecified social backgrounds) destroyed cemeteries and desecrated other parish places and spaces? The answer is unclear, but it may very

14. Figes, *Peasant Russia*, pp. 56–61.
15. Figes, "Peasant Farmers," p. 395.
16. Chulos, "Peasant Religion," p. 423.
17. Ibid., pp. 418–20.
18. For an example, see ibid., p. 420. Actually, this example was reported in a diocesan publication of January 21, 1918 (Old Style), so it may have occurred after the October Revolution.
19. For cases from Voronezh, see ibid., pp. 413–17.
20. For a case from Voronezh, see ibid., p. 414.
21. See Neuberger, *Hooliganism*.

well be that such acts were committed by marginalized in-migrants, who for all intents and purposes did not have a voice in village politics.[22]

Peasants not only publicly mourned but actively protested and resisted particular cases of violence against clergy and church property. In Voronezh diocese, peasants apprehended the hooligans who had attacked their priest as he was heading home after church and beat one of them to death.[23] Lay organizations, such as the circles of Orthodox zealots (*kruzhki revnitelei pravoslaviia*), were formed during this period, quite possibly in direct response to the violence against clergy and church property.[24] As had been the case in the final decades of the tsarist autocracy, villagers were at odds with each other over the role of the clergy and of parish Orthodoxy.

In sum, villagers began, during the months between the February and October Revolutions, to create a fundamentally new relationship between the rural parish and the brave new world of rural politics. What motivated villagers as they discussed church issues and passed relevant measures was the application of what Figes has called the "democratic driving force" of the social revolution under way in the village, a force from which no institution—not even the Church—was exempt.[25] Propelled by this leveling principle, villagers sought to place parish affairs squarely and completely under the jurisdiction of the commune; in this, they satisfied a desire that long predated the Revolutions of 1917. And as had also been the case during the last decades of the tsarist autocracy, it was those not fully integrated into the economic and political structures of the villages—in-migrants and youth (not necessarily mutually exclusive categories)—who were most likely to express, often through violent means, their rejection of clerical authority and parish life. As had been the case during the last decades of tsarist rule, villagers played out this conflict in the cultural arena: when young "hooligans" desecrated a cemetery, they were trying to subvert the cultural underpinnings of village life. As exemplified by the degree to which parishioners mobilized in retaliation, and by the reports of the vitality of public religious life (e.g., the frequent *krestnye khody*), rural parish life emerged intact—if changed—from this first phase of the social revolution in the village.[26]

22. If so, they may have selected religious places and objects as the targets—which they may have associated with the smallholder peasants who essentially ran village affairs—in order to express their anger about not being integrated into the village. There is some evidence to suggest that peasants continued to perceive the church building as the prime physical symbol of the commune and, in turn, the village: when communes seized gentry estates in 1917, it was routine for peasants to assemble in front of the parish church before heading off to the manor. This "ritual" is described in Figes, *Peasant Russia*, p. 52.

23. Chulos, "Peasant Religion," pp. 416–17.

24. Ibid., p. 416.

25. Figes, *Peasant Russia*.

26. Evidence of the solid place of the church in village life can be drawn from villagers' treat-

The October Revolution and Parish Politics, October 1917–May 1918

Following the Bolsheviks' seizure of power, villagers continued and completed the social revolution that had begun to reconfigure the relationship between parish life and the rural political structure. In the absence of a fully formed centralized state apparatus whose reach extended into the countryside, the *volost'* soviets, which villagers established in the winter of 1917–18, the village assemblies, and the village soviets, which villagers created during the first months following the October Revolution, handled the economic, political, social, and cultural issues facing rural society. Despite the increasing number of in-migrants and peasant-soldiers who continued to stream into the countryside, it was the smallholding peasantry that wielded power in the newly emerging political structure, deciding the principles that would guide the allotment and repartition of land, the distribution of food, and so forth.[27] One of the key issues raised in this new political context was what social and political terms the politically and economically dominant smallholding peasantry would accord the increasing numbers of those who did not belong to the land commune. This group comprised former gentry landowners, landless laborers, in-migrants and refugees, peasant-soldiers, "craftsmen, traders, occasional laborers, [and] members of the rural intelligentsia," such as teachers and clergy.[28] Prior to the outbreak of the Civil War in the early summer of 1918, the smallholding peasantry created a social and political system that amounted to "neither a peasant dictatorship, nor a village democracy." The patriarchs remained dominant, but they shared power with an increasing number of social groups in the village, in part because they needed the skills they offered.[29]

For the time being, the Bolsheviks had to accept the village social and political structure created by a smallholding peasantry at long last politically autonomous. They did so in order to keep the passive support (or at least to preserve the guarded neutrality) of the peasantry. But even as they did so, they began to create the legal infrastructure they deemed necessary to penetrate the village; and they took what could only be halting steps to put it into practice.

---

ment of "separators," those who possessed private farms (*khutora*) and enclosed holdings (*otruba*). The commune barred them from using the church, as well as roads, wells, and other key public spaces of the village, a telling index of both the importance of the church building and religious experience in villagers' lives. See ibid., p. 57.

27. Ibid., p. 131.
28. For a detailed discussion of how each of these groups fared, see ibid., pp. 131–53.
29. Ibid., p. 152.

The legislation that the Bolsheviks enacted to establish the relationship between religion and the Soviet state was an important case in point. To be sure, not every piece of that legislation was radical: the Decree on Land (October 26, 1917), which nationalized all land belonging to the churches and monasteries, merely gave national legal form and validity to the land seizures that peasants had already carried out. But three other significant pieces of legislation concerning the relationship between religious activity and the Soviet state—the Decree on the Separation of Church and State (February 1918) and the Soviet Constitution (July 1918), as well as an addendum to the Decree known as the "Instruction" (August 1918)—were, unlike the Decree on Land, far-reaching attempts to use law to transform society and align it with a "socialist" ideal. What, if any, was the impact of the Decree in the context of the village sociopolitical structure that emerged during the "six months of peasant rule," a structure neither dictatorial nor democratic? Did clergy, lay activists, and other peasants resist the new claims that the legislation, as well as Bolshevik attacks on clergy, churches, and monasteries, sought to make upon them? If so, how?

Before the implementation of the Decree became an issue in village life, the politically dominant smallholding peasants had decided on the main principles guiding the place of the clergy (and the church) in the village social structure. The smallholders' treatment of the clergy and the church was a particular application of the general "moral standards and conceptions of social justice" that guided their relations with other social groups in rural society.[30] The smallholders distinguished between those social groups whose skills and qualities they prized, and those whom they deemed to be a drain on village resources or otherwise unwelcome. This crucial distinction determined the economic and political "rights" each social group received.

Economically, the parish clergy fared relatively well during the commune's application of land reform during the social revolution of 1917–18. Clergy always received an allotment of land, land that was "sometimes ... of particularly good quality, since it served in part payment for the priest's religious services."[31] Moreover, it was "not unusual for the commune to organize a collective labour team to work the priest's allotment, in the nineteenth-century tradition of *pomoch'*."[32] As for political "rights," the clergy, unlike peasant women and the "free riders" (e.g. vagabonds, "idlers," in-migrants), were no longer politically disenfranchised as they had been prior to 1917 but allowed to have a voice in village politics (e.g., in the *obshchii skhod*).[33] While the commune as a rule valued the skills and social contributions of clergy (e.g., literacy,

30. Ibid.
31. Ibid., p. 147.
32. Ibid., p. 148.
33. Ibid., p. 152.

religious services, charity), those clergy whom parishioners perceived as having treated them well and as having played a particularly strong role in village life prior to 1917 no doubt fared particularly well. (The converse is no doubt also true.)[34] Or to put it a bit differently, those parish clergy who had played a visible social role in the post-emancipation village fared well during the village social revolution of 1917–18. Some exceptions notwithstanding, the parish clergy, unlike former tsarist officials and many in-migrants, were integrated into the village social and political structure—even if the Revolution left many questions about their social role in the village unanswered.

Thus rural parish clergy and the parish church had a recognized, if somewhat precarious place, in the village when the Bolsheviks promulgated the February 1918 Decree on the Separation of Church and State.[35] It was not until 1929 that the Decree, which sought to redefine the relationship between religious activity and sociopolitical life, was substantially modified.[36] The Decree deprived the Church of its lands, capital, and numerous trade enterprises and stripped religious bodies of their legal and juridical status; moreover, it authorized the Soviet state to confiscate the Church's investments and cash reserves, an act that damaged the church hierarchy and bishops much more than the parish clergy.[37] It ordered the cessation of religious teaching (the *Zakon Bozhii*) in the schools. It made religion a "private affair" and ritual optional.[38] Another law granted exclusive recognition to civil marriage and divorce and ordered that parish record books (*metricheskie knigi*) be turned over to governmental bureaus.[39] Religious organizations were forbidden from engaging in educational activities.[40] Articles 10 and 13 of the Decree prohibited the Church from possessing property not specially intended for worship (e.g., houses, candle factories, inns) and declared all property of church and religious societies part of the public domain.[41] The

34. See Okninsky, *Dva goda*, p. 231.
35. By the "Decree," I mean not only the initial legislation of February 1918 but a subsequent directive for its implementation, the Instruction (*Instruktsiia*), "O poriadke provedeniia v zhizn' Dekreta 'Ob otdelenii tserkvi ot gosudarstva i shkoly ot tserkvi,'" which was promulgated on August 24, 1918. See also Pospielovsky, *Russian Church*, 1:31–32. Joan Delaney claims that a "special commission" attached to the Central Committee was responsible for the "execution" as opposed to "actual implementation" of the decree. See her "Origins of Soviet Antireligious Organizations," in R. H. Marshall, Jr., ed., *Aspects of Religion in the Soviet Union, 1917–1967* (Chicago, 1971), p. 105.
36. A point made in M. N. Persits, *Otdelenie tserkvi ot gosudarstva i skholy ot tserkvi v SSSR* (Moscow, 1958), p. 125.
37. Curtiss, *Russian Church*, p. 46.
38. *Sobranie uzakonenii i rasporiazhenii rabochego i krest'ianskogo pravitel'stva*, 1918, no. 18, art. 272–73. (Hereafter cited as *SU*.)
39. Curtiss, *Russian Church*, p. 46.
40. See *SU*, 1917, no. 9, art. 126.
41. See I. A. Trifonov, *Likvidatsiia ekspluatatorskikh klassov v SSSR* (Moscow, 1975), p. 69.

People's Commissariat of Justice ordered local soviets to confiscate all church property not used for worship services. The Decree revoked state subsidies and juridical status from religious societies and prohibited the Church and its representatives from demanding payment for religious services.[42] It forbade the execution of religious rituals that "damaged the social order" or "encroached upon the rights of Soviet citizens" (Article 5). It also banned religious rituals and objects from state and public buildings and removed "religious societies" from public life in the sphere of education, ritual, and finance.

But the Decree also obliged religious activists to have contact with the state and its administrative organs. It stipulated that representatives of the Church had to prepare three copies of an inventory of church property for the local soviet, which would then allow the religious organizations free use of the buildings or objects. To this end, at least twenty members of the congregation had to conclude an agreement (*dogovor*) with the local soviet. By signing the contract, clergy and laity undertook to fulfill a series of obligations concerning the property in their use, such as upkeep and repair. They were legally obliged to allow Soviet officials to inspect the property periodically. Upon any infringements of the agreement, the contracting agents had to relinquish the property to the state. For the rural religious, the operation of a church required, at least *de jure*, the fulfillment of a series of strict administrative procedures.

The Instruction further delineated and clarified the legal infrastructure in which the rural (and urban) parishes were to operate. To form a religious society (*religioznoe obshchestvo*), at least twenty members of a congregation had to conclude an agreement with the local soviet.[43] The rural religious community also found itself saddled with new limitations for maintaining church buildings and property. A subsequent Instruction for implementing the Decree on the Separation of Church and State (August 24, 1918) ordered parishes to relinquish the property used in religious ceremonies to their local soviets. These bodies, after receiving an inventory from the parishes, could return the property to religious representatives, provided that twenty clergy or laity assumed responsibility for its use and upkeep. This legislation also allowed the construction of new churches, which would become the property of the state. The Instruction required villagers to make repairs for insurance purposes. According to the Instruction

---

42. For a discussion of the consequences of these financial restrictions, see Figes, *Peasant Russia*, p. 147.

43. See point 8 of the Instruction, "O poriadke provedenniia v zhizn' Dekreta 'Ob otdelenii tserkvi ot gosudarstva i shkolu ot tserkvi'" (August 24, 1918); for a sample of the standard from the contract, see "Dogovor" ("Prilozhenie 1-e k st. 685") of the Instruction, which appeared in *SU*, 1918, no. 62, art. 757–65.

of August 1918, the agreement on the use of religious buildings and objects obliged contracting clergy and laity to "undertake repair of the designated property and expenditures connected with the use of property, such as those for heating, insurance, upkeep, the payment of taxes and of local levies, and similar items."[44] The renewal of the church's lease depended on making the necessary repairs. The initial legislation empowered either the district or provincial executive committee to make the final decision to close a church.[45] Thus the Instruction offered rural clergy and laity a legal way to ensure the continued physical existence of their church but established obligations (e.g., repairs) that could entail financial burdens that would render that task difficult, if not impossible.[46]

Priests, although affected by these legal constraints, themselves received almost no attention in early Soviet legislation on the relationship between Church and state.[47] Neither the initial Decree nor the Instruction employed any of the Russian terms for "priest" or "clergy." Instead, these documents used phrases such as "representatives of the former [church] administration or individuals of the corresponding creed," "members of religious societies," or the "group of individuals who had concluded an agreement [to use religious buildings and/or objects]" to refer to all committed members of religious denominations. Placing clergy and laity on the same footing, neither piece of legislation subjected priests themselves to direct legal discrimination. This is not to say that the legislation did not have great potential to affect the financial position of the clergy. For by revoking the clergy's right to charge for religious services (the elimination of *treby* and *ruga*), the legislation, at least in theory, increased the clergy's dependence on their own agricultural labor.[48]

In sum, these three major pieces of early Soviet legislation laid out the means for transforming the relationship of religious practice to every aspect of Soviet life. They staked out arenas of cultural conflict in law, administration, electoral politics, family, education, and semiotics.[49] They gave legal form to the disparate efforts of some villagers—usually those on the fringes of village society and politics—to sever the connections between Orthodoxy

44. *SU*, 1918, no. 62, art. 758.
45. An "Instruction of the NKIu and NKVD" of July 19, 1923, stated the following: "On the basis of a decision of the VTsIK of April 19, 1923, matters concerning the breach of contracts with groups of believers on the use of church buildings and matters concerning the closing of temporary or permanent temples and prayer houses of all cults are resolved by decisions of the presidiums of provincial executive committees without distinction." See F. Oleshchuk, *Kto stroit tserkvi v SSSR* (Moscow-Leningrad, 1929).
46. Curtiss, *Russian Church*, p. 46.
47. On this see also Pospielovsky, *Russian Church*, 1:32.
48. On this see Figes, *Peasant Russia*, p. 147.
49. These categories or their equivalents are used by Hunter in *Culture Wars*.

and the rest of village life. They tied the successful resolution of this cultural conflict to particular institutions; in the case of the rural parish, the Decree and the subsequent Instruction, for example, placed considerable responsibility on the village soviets and the *volost'* executive committees (VIKs).

The role of the village soviets was particularly important. Assuming that as laid out by the Constitution, clergy would neither hold office in them nor significantly influence their work from behind the scenes, the legislation empowered the rural soviets to confiscate church property and to conclude the agreement with the religious society of twenty lay members concerning the use of this property, among other rights discussed above. As an ostensibly socialist institution, the village soviet was to transform village social and political relations so that a socialist consciousness could begin to emerge among the peasants (who would then cease to be peasants after joining cooperatives, collective farms, and other socialist agricultural institutions). How successful were the clergy and lay activists in stopping the soviets—and the VIKs—from implementing measures aligned with the letter and spirit of the Decree, as well as in applying pressure once such measures had been passed?

The Constitution of July 1918 defined the form of the rural state apparatus for the entire RSFSR.[50] According to VTsIK instructions adopted in 1918, rural settlements with at least one hundred "adult" residents could elect a soviet. All male and female village residents over the age of eighteen, with the exception of disenfranchised groups such as clergy, could vote. The VTsIK's instructions stipulated that there was to be one member of the soviet for each hundred voting inhabitants of the rural settlement.[51] The size of the soviets, as mandated by Article 57 of the 1918 Constitution, was to range between three and fifty members.[52] The rural soviet was also to serve as the building block of the basic units of state organization on the county or *volost'* level: one of every ten members of the soviet was to attend the *volost'* assembly. According to Article 57 of the Constitution, the assembly, which was to meet at least once a month, was the "highest authority within the *volost'*."[53] It was to be the members of the *volost'* assembly who elected an executive committee (*volispolkom* or *VIK*) which exercised authority between convocations of the assembly.[54]

50. Figes, *Peasant Russia*, p. 71.
51. Ibid., pp. 199–200.
52. In practice, at least prior to the introduction of NEP, villagers ignored the size of the rural settlement in determining how many members could be legally elected. See ibid., pp. 75–76.
53. Ibid., p. 72.
54. "The VIK was answerable to the *volost'* soviet assembly, but it was expected to carry out the orders of the higher soviet and military authorities, particularly the district (*uezd*) soviet, which was attended by rural soviet delegates (one for every 1,000 inhabitants) and representa-

The Constitution also delineated the relationship of clergy and parishioners to this new state structure. In fact, it was the Constitution of July 1918 (the "fundamental law" or *osnovnoi zakon*) that inflicted the most severe legal blow on the clergy. Article 65 deprived the clergy of legal rights, a discriminatory stance that the Mexican Constitution of 1917 also inflicted on clergy during the Mexican Revolution. As *lishentsy*, they were subject to limits on rations and housing and had to pay higher taxes.[55] This meant, for example, that they did not have the right to obtain bread from the state bakery, a severe material disadvantage, since private bakeries did not exist at the time.[56] Like other *lishentsy*, they could not serve in the regular army (i.e., bear arms), yet were obliged to serve in a nonmilitary capacity.[57] They could not vote or be elected to public office, whether those of the VIKs, the rural soviets, rural cooperatives, or *kombedy*.[58] The 1918 Constitution's prohibition of electing clergy to Soviet institutions obliged believers, in theory if not in practice, to promote the election of lay leaders. On a general level, the Constitution granted voting rights to "workers" and denied them to "exploiters." It subdivided the category of "worker" into three groups: productive and socially useful laborers, soldiers and sailors, and those no longer able to work.[59] Those deprived of voting rights comprised seven major groups: members of the tsarist police (including Okhrana agents), employers

---

tives of the factories and towns (usually one for every 200 electors). This dual obligation of the VIKs was to play a crucial role in the social and political history of the early Soviet period." Ibid., p. 72.

55. See Curtiss, *Russian Church*, p. 61. For a description of taxes paid by village clergy over the course of the 1920s, see *Vestnik russkogo khrist'ianskogo dvizheniia*, no. 150, 2d ser. (1987): 229–30.(Hereafter cited as *VRKhD*. The original title of this journal was *Vestnik russkogo studentcheskogo khrist'ianskogo dvizheniia*, which is hereafter cited as *VRSKhD*.) On the Mexican case, see Meyer, *Cristero Rebellion*, pp. 13–14.

56. Father Trophimus, "Russian Religion on the Defensive," *Slavonic and East European Review* 12 (July 1933): 82.

57. Although sons of clergy could not bear arms, they still had to serve in a nonmilitary capacity. They could not bear arms. See Elise Kimerling, "Civil Rights and Social Policy in Soviet Russia, 1918–1936," *Russian Review* 41 (January 1982): 35.

58. Clergy could not be elected to the *volost'* soviet assembly, which was in turn to elect the VIK. They could not be elected to the executive committees (*ispolkomy*) of the village soviets, which, according to the Constitution, were to be comprised of a maximum of five members in villages with a population over 1,000. (The executive committees included chairs and secretaries of the soviets, discussed below.) Nor could they be elected as general members of the soviets. On this see Figes, *Peasant Russia*, pp. 76–78, 214–18. Clergy could not serve on the board (*pravlenie*), council (*sovet*), or inspection commission (*revizionnaia komissiia*) of a cooperative. On the creation of the *kombedy*, see V. N. Aver'ev, ed., *Komitety bednoty: Sbornik materialov* (Moscow-Leningrad, 1933), 1:52–54, and Figes, "Russian Peasant Community," pp. 249–50.

59. Article 64 of the Constitution.

of hired labor, those living on unearned income, private merchants and commercial brokers, the insane and those under guardianship, convicts, and "monks and spiritual servitors of all Churches and religious cults." Social and political criteria shaped the construction of civil rights, creating significant ambiguities that would arise in conjunction with determining the voting rights of clergy and laity.[60]

The Party set standard procedures for all elections, including those for the village soviets. Preelection preparations and the voting process itself took place from December to January. In other words, they coincided roughly with the New Year's and Christmas holidays, traditionally occasions for major celebrations in rural (as well as urban) Russian society. The elections themselves, in which oral voting obtained, were to be held on a nonworking day. Preparatory activities included "meetings of account before voters" (the *otchetnoe sobranie*), at which members of the village soviets provided voters with a summary of their work for the preceding year. In some provinces, officials gave their reports at the village assembly.[61]

The village electoral commission (*izbirkom*) was to oversee the implementation of these procedures. Some of the designated functions of the commission, such as providing the ballots and writing materials and posting electoral lists, were mechanical in nature, or at least so it would seem. But the voting commissions also had key political functions, such as arresting anti-Soviet agitators and chairing electoral meetings at which the candidates were voted on.[62] Given the political importance of this work, it was hardly surprising that three or four citizens, distinguished by "clearly [showing] themselves, through their public activity, to be steadfast defenders of the interests of the working masses," were to make up the commission.[63] Each commission was also to include "at least one member who had been nominated by the electoral commission at the higher level."[64] For this reason higher Soviet officials, Party "instructors," and Red Army personnel often staffed the commission.[65]

The rural parish stood to benefit from the fact that neither the form nor the social composition of the village soviets, *volost'* assemblies, or even the

---

60. On this see Kimerling, "Civil Rights," p. 30. The Soviet Constitution thus represented a transposition into a Marxist idiom of the conditional granting of social and economic "rights" by peasant smallholders to other social groups in the village: both the smallholders and the drafters of the Constitution made "productive and socially useful labor" the basis for granting civil and economic rights.
61. See, for example, TsGAOR Leningrada, f. 748, op. 1, d. 3, l. 2.
62. See Figes, *Peasant Russia*, p. 201.
63. Quoted in ibid.
64. Ibid.
65. Ibid.

VIKs met the rigid script set forth in the Constitution. In many villages, soviets were not elected until the autumn of 1918, and sometimes not even for the duration of the Civil War.[66] Those village soviets that did exist were often far larger than the size legally stipulated by the Constitution; and the actual size of the VIKs often exceeded the five-member maximum set forth in an NKVD circular of April 1918.[67] Although the meetings of the soviet were usually smaller than those of the *skhod*, they were generally held in the same place, attended and dominated by the same villagers, and devoted to a similar range of issues.[68] It was, thus, the farming members of the village who dominated the village soviets. Landless peasants, such as in-migrants who were more likely to be hostile to the clergy and to the parish church more generally, "occupied only a secondary role in the village soviets."[69] Thus social groups friendly to the clergy and the Church wielded power in the village soviets, one of the key institutions designated by the Decree to impose new constraints on religious activity.

In fact, from the earliest days of the Soviet state, members of the clergy held positions in the rural soviets.[70] Like the village soviets, the *volost'* assemblies and even the VIKs, as Figes has shown, "remained essentially 'peasant' in their composition."[71] But the qualifier "essentially" is an important one. This is because the soviets and especially the VIKs very much needed the administrative experience and literacy that "members of the former propertied classes"—including the clergy—had to offer.[72] While villagers valued the contributions of the clergy to the village and *volost'* soviets, the clergy, for

---

66. Ibid., p. 73. Those villages that did not form soviets did elect a "commissar, a chairman, or a *starosta* who, together with a scribe, served as the executive of the communal or village assembly," which acted as the *de facto* village soviets. Ibid.

67. On the reasons for this, see ibid., pp. 75–76. The *volost'* assemblies, like the village soviets, bore certain similarities to the meetings of the village assemblies: like the latter, they were usually held on a Sunday afternoon, and in an open field. It was also rare for the VIKs to be elected by the *volost'* assembly, as legally stipulated in the Constitution. See ibid., p. 76.

68. See ibid., pp. 73–74.

69. Ibid., p. 83.

70. According to an intelligence report submitted by nineteen-year-old Pavel Rybakov, a Communist political worker (*agitator-organizator*), as of 1919 the secretary of the soviet in Novo-Ivanovko (Aleksandrovsk *uezd*, Ekaterinoslav province) was a deacon. Hoover Institution Archives, Wrangel Collection, "Shtab Glavnokomanduiushchego razred. otdel." Peasant Revolts, Intelligence Reports, 1919. Biulleten' no. 18, "K kharakteristike 'makhnovshchiny.'" For examples of priests who served as members and chairs of district executive committees in Kursk province, see PAKO (Partarkhiv Kurskoi oblasti), f. 5. op. 1, d. 1, l. 20; *Kurskii krai*, April 5, 1917; *Izvestiia Kurskogo gubernskogo obshchestva kraevedeniia* 5 (1927): 37; and GATO, f. 1058, op. 1, d. 21, l. 82, as cited in V. N. Dunaev, "Sotsial'no-politicheskaia orientatsiia" (candidate diss., Voronezh University, 1972), p. 50.

71. Figes, *Peasant Russia*, p. 83.

72. Ibid., p. 82.

their part, were only too happy to oblige, for doing so gave them a chance to champion their interests—and those of the Church. Along these lines, the Tambov bishopric explicitly urged its clergy to enter the VIKs "in order to defend the interests of its estate."[73]

Given the degree to which the village soviets and the VIKs thus diverged from the structure laid out for them in the Constitution, how effective were they in performing the crucial functions charged to them by the Decree? By the spring of 1918, only one *volost'* soviet in Penza province had set up a department to handle the registration of births, deaths, and marriages; we can thus infer that the *metricheskie knigi* remained under the control of the other parishes in the province.[74] The soviets, for their part, lacked not only the means but the will: in the first few months after the Decree had been issued, some did "take measures to keep the profits of the clergy to a minimum," but a good many "allowed the priests to charge what were considered [by the Soviet press] to be extortionate prices."[75] Some village soviets even passed resolutions to allot funds for maintaining the church, in direct violation of the Decree.[76]

Perhaps hoping that members of the VIKs and the soviets were failing to implement the Decree's provisions out of ignorance, Party members made occasional visits to villages to "explain" the Decree's provisions and convince villagers that it was in their interests to implement it.[77] These efforts were necessarily sporadic, however, because Party members were overburdened with a variety of tasks, and the structure of the rural (and even urban) Party apparatus was still extremely fragile.[78] Party members lacked not only time and energy to enforce the Decree but—in many cases—a clear understanding themselves of its provisions.[79]

These various constraints handicapped Party members in their "implementation" of the Decree, if indeed it can be called that. On the one hand, perhaps owing to their own religious attachments, some Party members proved surprisingly permissive of (and even themselves encouraged) clear infringements of the Decree, a pattern that continued during the Civil War

---

73. See *Tambovskie eparkhial'nye vedomosti* 17 (1917): 397, as cited in Dunaev, "Sotsial'no-politicheskaia orientatsiia," p. 50.

74. Figes, *Peasant Russia*, pp. 77, 148.

75. Ibid., p. 148.

76. Ibid., p. 74.

77. Persits, *Otdelenie*, p. 114. For an account of villagers' reaction to Party members' reading of a lecture on the Decree, see *Perepiska sekretariata TsK RKP(b) s mestnymi partiinymi organizatsiiami* (Moscow, 1957–72), 6:395.

78. Daniel Thorniley, *The Rise and Fall of the Soviet Rural Communist Party, 1927–1939* (New York, 1988).

79. V. A. Kozlov, *Kul'turnaia revoliutsiia i krest'ianstvo, 1921–27 (po materialiam Evropeiskoi chasti RSFSR)* (Moscow, 1983), p. 22.

and beyond.⁸⁰ Party officials on the district level could demonstrate a surprising degree of complacency toward rural clergy. At an unspecified point during the Civil War, a priest from the village Sablino (Shatsk *uezd*, Tambov province) was not punished for spreading anti-Soviet propaganda. The district branch of the Cheka explained its leniency as follows: "[We have decided] to drop the matter because the agitation did not provoke a counterrevolutionary demonstration." On the other hand, whether because they simply misunderstood the Decree or impatiently ignored its clearly delineated administrative procedures for "separating" Church and state, other Party members far exceeded its provisions in their conduct toward the rural parish and religious life. Some Party members harassed, persecuted, tortured, and even murdered members of the clergy—especially bishops.⁸¹ Party members also ignored the law in their treatment of other aspects of rural parish life. While it is difficult to isolate general patterns within the broad category of such extremist acts, Party members often exceeded the legal provisions of the Decree in their treatment of religious property. This was the case, for example, when in April 1918 the Bolshevik Party cell in a village in Saratov province removed icons from the parish church.⁸² At the May 1918 diocesan congress in Tambov, an unidentified speaker decried five cases of "force" against representatives of the Orthodox Church, among them the "local Soviet deputy's" accusation that the reception of Vyshenskii's miracle-working icon of Our Lady Mary could be used to launch a counterrevolutionary uprising.⁸³ In other words, overzealous Party members often focused their extralegal efforts on the very elements of religious life—its external trappings—that had so captured the anger, disdain, and disrespect of some *otkhodniki* and other villagers prior to 1917. This is hardly surprising since some of these Party members had indeed been *otkhodniki* prior to 1917.

In resisting such threats to religious life, rural parishioners both drew on and broadened the "parochialization of power" in parish life that had begun to develop prior to 1917. Church councils played a more significant role in parish affairs than ever.⁸⁴

It was by no means only members of church councils who mounted significant resistance to Party members' abuses of the legal provisions of the

---

80. As cited in Dunaev, "Sotsial'no-politicheskaia orientatsiia." On the continuing religious attachments of Party members in rural areas, see Chapter 3.

81. See the discussion at the beginning of Chapter 5.

82. See Figes, *Peasant Russia*, p. 150, esp. n. 288.

83. *Protokoly eparkhial'nogo sobraniia dukhovenstva i mirian Tambovskoi eparkhii maiskoi sessii 1918 g.* (Tambov, 1918), p. 10.

84. On the aggressive role of parish councils in 1917 and early 1918—and beyond—see Gregory L. Freeze, "Counter-reformation in Russian Orthodoxy: Popular Response to Religious Innovation, 1922–1925," *Slavic Review* 54 (Summer 1995): 329–33.

Decree. When the Bolsheviks confiscated church property, they often catalyzed peasant uprisings on a significant scale.[85] A case in point is the considerable resistance that villagers staged in April 1918 in response to the Bolshevik party cell's seizure of icons from a village church in Saratov province, an episode already mentioned briefly. A crowd of at least five hundred peasants, "most of them women," carried out a *samosud* (self-adjudication) against both the "Bolshevik leaders" and a detachment of mounted police who later appeared in order to quell the uprising.[86] But *samosud* was by no means the crowd's only weapon of resistance: the villagers, who were willing to use violence against the armed Bolsheviks ("scuffles broke out"), eventually drove the intruders from their village.

An analysis of the *form* that the resistance took can explain why villagers defended religious property so powerfully and effectively. Why, for example, did the villagers subject the Bolsheviks and the police to a *samosud*? It was not just that the attempted seizures were undesirable; to the villagers, they were fundamentally unjust.[87] Peasants throughout the world have formulated their own conceptions of justice; moreover, the practice of *samosud* was hardly new to the Russian village. But it was particularly ironic that Russian villagers were applying a *samosud* to Bolsheviks, whose actions were prompted by another set of legal principles, those embodied in the Decree on Church and State. In fact, in staging the *samosud*, the villagers were not just resisting the seizures but engaging in a fascinating inversion, trying to exact claims on the Bolsheviks by applying their own unwritten decree, as it were. (This suggests that the villagers knew that the intruders' actions had been occasioned by the Decree.) This raises the important question of exactly what conception of peasant justice—what peasant "decree" (or "Bill of Rights" if you will)—the intruders had violated. Was it the right of villagers to engage in religious practice, to possess property they had acquired through their own labor, or simply to manage their affairs as they wished? The answer is unclear, but it would be a mistake to dismiss motivations other than the defense of religious property *per se*. Put another way, there is good reason to believe that these villagers regarded the icons as precious symbols of *both* their religious identity and their political autonomy.

The depth and power of such resistance notwithstanding, the typical village did not, as a rule, stand as one against Bolshevik abuses of the Decree. Given their hostility toward religious practice, those villagers whom Figes has called free riders ("e.g., [landless laborers] vagabonds, 'idlers',

---

85. Figes, *Peasant Russia*, p. 150.

86. Given the Bolsheviks' tendency to view (and, more consequentially, to *want* to view) religious experience as the women's domain, we should not take at face value the claim that "most" of the rebels were women.

87. On peasants' conceptions of justice, see Scott, *Moral Economy*.

in-migrants") did not participate in such resistance. Excluded from the structures of village power, they would not have been consulted in decisions about whether—and how—to mount such resistance. There is every reason to believe that this exclusion only fueled their animosity to religious practice and parish life, with which they ever more closely associated the patriarchs of the village, as well as its power structures more generally. (These uprisings, even if carried out in large part by women, most likely only cemented such an association.) Although prior to the outbreak of the Civil War the "free riders" continued to dissent from the village powerholding elite on a variety of matters, including the place of religious life in the village, they as yet had no institutional base from which to act on their dissent. In short, the fact that the village "was neither a peasant dictatorship nor a village democracy" sustained and probably increased intra-village conflict on the role of religious practice in village life.[88] By late summer, when the Civil War broke out, these tensions were percolating within the Russian village, indeed begging for resolution.

Counterrevolution and Civil War: May 1918–Early 1921

When the Civil War began in May 1918, most Russian peasants wanted as little as possible to do with it.[89] This is not to say that they categorically refused to take up arms. To be sure, they needed no prompting to fight former landlords, form peasant brigades, or even, under certain circumstances, join the Red Army.[90] But they were only willing to join and fight to defend the social revolution in the village. They were highly indifferent to the national causes (e.g., in the case of the SRs, of national democracy) championed by the parties in the conflict. Indeed, they sought to insulate the rural political autonomy they had won over the previous six months from the corrosive influences of a Civil War fought for national causes that interested them little. As they exercised rural political autonomy, they integrated, albeit in a precarious way, the priest and parish life more generally into the newly transformed sociopolitical order in the village.

Despite their persistent efforts, the smallholder peasants who dominated the commune and even the village soviets could not control the impact of the Civil War on village social and political relations. Unwanted urban

88. Quoted in Figes, *Peasant Russia*, p. 152.
89. See the assessment to this effect of a recruitment officer of the People's Army in Simbirsk province, as reprinted in ibid., p. 175.
90. These causes are discussed in ibid.

refugees streamed into their villages, resulting in an 8 percent increase in the rural population during the Civil War. (The northern and Lower Volga regions were especially popular destinations of these urban out-migrants.)[91] Moreover, the smallholders had to face the fact that the Bolsheviks had, in the previous six months, tolerated rural political autonomy not out of principle but of necessity. Now, however, it was the exigencies of war—and especially the need for food to feed the Red Army and the urban population —that guided the Bolsheviks, whose organization in the countryside remained extremely weak.[92] The exigencies of war made it even more urgent for the Bolsheviks to gain political, economic, and cultural control of the countryside, and one step in implementing that agenda was enforcement of the Decree on the Separation of Church and State.

To this end, throughout the Civil War, the Bolsheviks (from March 1918, the Communists) invested considerable efforts in "state-building" in the Russian countryside. Even though the village soviets remained "essentially 'peasant' organs of power," the number of Bolshevik Party members in the village soviets—and especially in the village soviet executive committees—increased beginning with the 1919 elections.[93] Especially dramatic was the Bolsheviks' transformation of the VIKs into "bureaucratized state organs, run by three to five executive members, most of them in the Bolshevik party, and a team of salaried officials."[94] Thus the Bolsheviks achieved a greater presence in precisely those rural institutions (the village soviets and the VIKs) legally designated to play a chief role in implementing the Decree.

This political transformation was by no means the only ominous challenge facing rural clergy and parishioners during the Civil War. For the Bolsheviks, cultural transformation and political transformation went hand in hand. Thus *Glavpolitprosvet* (Political Education Department, Commissariat of Enlightenment) had, prior to the end of the Civil War, established schools, courses, rural reading rooms, and workers' universities in which antireligious propaganda was conducted, thereby contributing to the

91. Koenker, "Urbanization and Deurbanization," p. 91.
92. For statistics on the Bolshevik Party organization in the Volga Region (1918–19), see Figes, *Peasant Russia*, p. 226.
93. This is Figes's characterization, as offered on ibid., p. 211. Demands for new elections to the village soviets during the anti-Soviet rebellions of 1919–21 cast doubts on his contention that "stable peasant farmers, who dominated the communes, sought to isolate themselves from the outside world by turning their backs on the soviets, which were increasingly seen as organs of government taxation and Communist rule," a claim Figes makes on p. 355. On the presence of clergy and other (lay) religious activists in the executive committees of the village soviets, see Chapters 5 and 6.
94. Ibid., p. 220. For details, see ibid., pp. 220–22. In 1920, in fact, the number of VIK members who were also registered members of the Bolshevik Party was higher than during the mid-1920s. See ibid., pp. 223–24.

training of antireligious cadres, all of which, to be sure, had a limited and haphazard impact on the village.[95]

How did clergy and parishioners respond to the threat that this political and cultural transformation, however incomplete, posed to parish life? It is important to keep in mind that parish life itself was undergoing significant structural changes. According to one relatively unbiased observer, rural church attendance was weak in 1918 and the first half of 1919; moreover, anticlericalism "flourished" during the Revolutions of 1917 and the Civil War, albeit in "sporadic" fashion. In fact, there is compelling evidence to suggest that church attendance began to increase significantly from the "second half" of 1919 onward.[96] During the Civil War, parishioners' control over parish affairs continued to increase significantly and consistently. At times they used their growing power to limit that of the clergy, demanding, for example, the expulsion of parish priests; at others, they used it to generate revenue desperately needed by a financially emasculated church (diocesan and central) bureaucracy, and by the rural parish clergy itself.[97] The center of power in these and other parish matters was now in the parish council, whose membership was known sometimes to overlap that of the village soviet.[98] The parish council was an institutional resource that parishioners (and even clergy) could draw on as they responded to the attempted implementation of the Decree and to other antireligious measures in the new political context.

One of the basic claims of the Decree was the secularization of land allotted to churches and to monasteries. To be sure, during the Civil War, the Soviet authorities made considerable progress in implementing this provision of the Decree. By the end of 1920, 673 monasteries, which held 828,000

---

95. Narkompros had been involved in antireligious affairs prior to the creation of *Glavpolitprosvet* in November 1920. On this see Delaney, "Origins," pp. 106–7.

96. On anticlericalism, see Richard Stites, *Revolutionary Dreams: Utopian Vision and Experimental Life in the Russian Revolution* (New York, 1989), p. 105, and Okninsky, *Dva goda*, pp. 231ff.

97. See Freeze, "Counter-reformation," pp. 330–31, for these and other examples. These aggressive measures against clergy notwithstanding, parishioners still valued the latter's services. In approximately 1919, several villagers from Chernoiaro (Shatsk *uezd*, Tambov province) wrote their archbishop that "our church is without a priest. Especially in the present dark and troubled times [*smutnoe vremia*] it is imperative that we have defenders of the church in the person of a priest, [who can] support the fallen souls of us, the laity." GATO, f. 181, op. 145, d. 4., l. 4., as quoted in Dunaev, "Sotsial'no-politicheskaia orientatsiia." See also GATO, f. 181, op. 145, d. 62, l. 11.

98. See, for example, *Derevenskaia kommuna*, May 3, 1919. When the Commissariat of Justice learned in 1919 that all the members of the Gorlovo village soviet (Riazan province) entered the parish council, it ruled that members of soviets could only join parish organizations (i.e., parish councils and "groups of believers") as "private individuals." See Persits, *Otdelenie*, pp. 165–66.

des. of land, had been "liquidated"; organs of Soviet power had confiscated over 7 million rubles of property and other church valuables.[99] But in so doing, they faced considerable resistance from the church administration, as well as from rural clergy and parishioners. The 1917–18 All-Russian Council (*Sobor*) of the Russian Orthodox Church, for example, condemned the Decree as "open persecution of the Orthodox Church, as well as of all religious societies, whether Christian or not."[100] Sometimes specifically expressing their formal approval of the Sobor's resolution on the Decree, diocesan congresses (*s"ezdy*) also issued their own protests against its claims, and in particular its provisions on the seizure of church land and other property. Held in June 1918, the diocesan congress in Nizhni-Novgorod, for example, decided to place in its journal a call to "rise up against the seizure [*otobranie*] of church land and other property."[101] District meetings of clergy and parishioners (*sobraniia dukhovenstva i mirian*) and parish organizations echoed such sentiments.[102] Parish meetings of laity adopted resolutions protesting the nationalization of the property held by monasteries.[103] Parish clergy, for their part, sometimes tried, during church services themselves, to mobilize parishioners not to recognize the Decree and, in particular, its claim to secularize church lands and property.[104] In general, however, these strategies had little impact on most villagers, who often seized church lands themselves instead of local soviets.[105] More successful in the short run in resisting the Decree were those monks who, for a time, reorganized their monasteries as agricultural communes or *artel*s in an attempt to hold onto their land and other property.[106]

Whereas villagers saw the secularization of church lands as an application of the "democratic driving force" of the social revolution in the village, they perceived the state's claim to control church property (e.g., the church building) and religious objects as a threat to parish life as they knew it. Revealing the depth of their fears, they spread rumors about the consequences of signing the contract (*dogovor*) for the use of church property, one

99. Trifonov, *Likvidatsiia*, p. 89.
100. Quoted in Persits, *Otdelenie*, p. 140.
101. TsGAOR, f. 353, op. 2., d. 696, l. 111 ob., quoted in Persits, *Otdelenie*, p. 144.
102. For excerpts of the protocols of a meeting of clergy and parishioners in Kashinsk *uezd*, Tula province (held on July 20, 1918), see Persits, *Otdelenie*, p. 145.
103. Ibid., pp. 146–67. On the formation of "unions for the defense of Orthodox churches and cloisters," as well as *bratstva* to defend monasteries and their property, see ibid., p. 144 n. 15.
104. See ibid., pp. 176–77.
105. For examples, see ibid., pp. 160–61.
106. For specific cases and their investigation by the Eighth Section of the Commissariat of Justice, see ibid., pp. 162–63. Some sectarian communes reorganized themselves as "false communes," orphanages, and almshouses. See ibid., p. 162.

such rumor being that believers would be subject to "excessive taxes."[107] Like those constructed during collectivization, these rumors had two interrelated functions: to represent the state's demands as fundamentally unjust, and to convince other villagers to resist.[108] Although it is very difficult to gauge the overall effectiveness of such rumors, we do know that in some cases they did stop believers from signing the requisite contract.[109] By far the most effective resistance in this regard, however, was mounted by the village soviets, which often failed to play the role in the administrative disposition of church property the Decree had laid out for them.[110] Contemporaries and Soviet historians attributed the typically errant record of the village soviets to a shortage of Communist cadres. In doing so, they refused to admit the deeper cause—the continuing political dominance of the peasant smallholders, whose religious attachments remained "traditional" and strong.

With the creation of the *kombedy* in May/June of 1918, however, the irreligious on the margins of village life now had something of an institutional base. Their chief purpose was to obtain grain and other foodstuffs allegedly hoarded by "kulaks." But the *kombedy* were given rather "sweeping political powers" so that they could successfully challenge the authority of the village soviets.[111] Able and even encouraged to pursue social and political agendas that went far beyond class struggle on the "agricultural front," many *kombedy* attempted to seize the property of parish churches.[112] In sum, one of the key agendas pursued by the *kombedy* was to subvert the place of parish life in the village.

Clergy and parishioners alike resisted this agenda in a variety of ways. Village soviets commonly ignored directives of the *kombedy*.[113] Thus the

---

107. See ibid., p. 174.

108. See Lynne Viola, "The Peasant Nightmare: Visions of Apocalypse in the Soviet Countryside," *Journal of Modern History* 62 (December 1990): 747–70.

109. A case in point occurred in the village Sergacha, Riazan province. See Persits, *Otdelenie*, p. 174.

110. Ibid.; Figes, *Peasant Russia*, p. 149. In several areas, as a result of the precarious conditions of the Civil War and the "licentiousness" (*razgul*) of "banditism," the inventories of church property and the contracts concerning the transfer of worship buildings and objects to religious societies were lost. It was necessary to renew them in 1922, when the famine in the Lower Volga region impelled the confiscation of church valuables. See Dunaev, "Sotsial'no-politicheskaia orientatsiia."

111. For this characterization, and a detailed description of the activities of the *kombedy*, see Figes, *Peasant Russia*, pp. 196–97.

112. There is good reason to believe that *kombedy* also, against the wishes of villagers, tried to close churches. One indirect piece of evidence in favor of this point is that 1918 and 1919 circulars required the closing of churches to reflect the "demand of the working masses." Proper observance of this legislation required proof of such popular consent, testimony often sought (or imposed) at the village assembly (*skhod*).

113. In Alekseev *volost'*, for example, officials of the soviets shrugged their shoulders at

opposing agendas of the soviets and *kombedy* on the religious question only heightened conflict between the two institutions. Although no doubt grateful for the efforts of village soviets, in some instances the clergy tried to take control of the *kombedy* by either organizing such institutions themselves or otherwise becoming involved in them.[114] To be sure, clergy comprised a very small percentage of *kombedy* members. But the point that still needs to be underscored is that they attempted to harness these rural political institutions for their own purposes, as opposed to those of the regime.

Villagers were just as determined to resist the financial claims of the Decree as they were to resist its administrative procedures for the use of church property. In theory, as we saw above, the village soviet was to prevent the parish priest from obtaining his traditional sources of revenue. Here again it was the *kombedy* that often took the lead in trying to hinder if not prevent the clergy from receiving emoluments.[115] Even though the number of Bolsheviks elected to the executive committees (*ispolkomy*) of the soviets increased in 1919 and 1920, these institutions typically continued to allow parish priests to collect revenue in ways prohibited by the Decree.[116] Even those soviets which did try to reduce clerical revenues still levied "a tax on the population to pay for the upkeep of the church, its property, and its personnel"; they simply made the payment of emoluments voluntary.[117]

A case in Shenkursk *uezd* (Arkhangel province) nicely illustrates the symbiotic relationship that developed between parish priests and village soviets during the Civil War. In 1919, an impoverished parish priest appeared at a

---

evils targeted by the VIKs, such as food-hoarding. See Figes, *Peasant Russia*, p. 240.

114. For a case of a parish priest and deacon managing the affairs of a "false" *kombed*, see *Derevenskaia kommuna*, October 20, 1918. For statistics on clerical involvement in the *volost'* and village-level *kombedy* of Tambov province, see Aver'ev, *Komitety bednoty*, 1:176–79. Clergy comprised 1.2 percent of all *kombedy* members prior to the outbreak of the Civil War in Tambov province, and 1.2 percent thereafter. The only two districts in which clergy became members of the *kombedy* were Usmansk and Morshansk, where clergy comprised 2.3 percent and 0.7 percent of all *volost' kombedy* members during the Civil War. (It is not clear why they were so exceptional in this regard.) Clergy also served as chairs and secretaries of the *volost' kombedy*. Unfortunately, I have not been able to obtain statistics on the percentage of *clergy* who became *kombed* members or otherwise served in these institutions.

115. Seeking to break the church's "hold over the village poor," they also tried to outlaw the "charity schemes of the churches." On this see Figes, *Peasant Russia*, p. 197. On the (apparently successful) efforts of Samara *kombedy* in reducing clerical emoluments, see *Derevenskaia kommuna*, October 24, 1918.

116. For statistics on Bolshevik party members elected to the executive committees of the village soviets, see Figes, *Peasant Russia*, pp. 216–17. For examples of village soviets in the Volga Region allowing priests to collect revenue, see ibid., p. 148. See also *Derevenskaia kommuna*, May 3, 1919.

117. Village soviets in the Tatar and Bashkir regions were especially resistant to imposing the Decree. See Figes, *Peasant Russia*, p. 148.

meeting called by the chair of the village executive committee (*ispolkom*). Complaining that he could not buy potatoes anywhere, the priest asked the soviet to provide him with as many "potatoes and other foodstuffs" as possible. All those present at the meeting agreed to do so, and presumably a levy was taken up.[118] There are several striking aspects to this interaction. Just as priests routinely made requests for personal needs to the village assembly, now they made similar requests to the village soviets. In fact, given the considerable overlap in personnel between the village soviets and village assemblies (even during the Civil War), there is every reason to believe that the priest perceived the village soviet as more or less a village assembly.[119] For those attending the meeting, the priest's request most likely elicited memories of similar interactions in the village assemblies of tsarist times. Given the way in which the priest and the other villagers connected the present to the past, it makes sense that the village soviet rescued the priest from his desperate material situation, in complete violation of the Decree.

If the Decree's claims on church resources met with significant resistance, what of those legal claims of the state to take over functions previously performed by the church and the clergy (such as marriage and the registration of births and deaths)? In executing the Decree, members of the rural *apparat* were especially willing to tolerate infringement of the *akty grazhdanskogo sostoianiia* (the legal obligation for civil as opposed to church registration of births and deaths). The parish record books (*metricheskie knigi*), for example, continued to be kept in the church until 1919 in the Zadonsk and Bobrov districts of, respectively, Voronezh and Kursk provinces.[120] Still more surprising, in 1919 the *volost'* soviet in Morshansk district (Tambov province) filed a request with the Eighth Department of the Commissariat of Justice to "make the [lower] clergy [*pricht*] of local churches responsible" for keeping track of the *akty grazhdanskogo sostoianiia*.[121] With this gesture, in complete violation of the decree, local Party officials invited rural priests to help them carry out the bureaucratic procedures of a secular Soviet state. This decision makes some sense, however, if we recall that prior to their "bureaucratization" in 1919–20, very few VIKs had been able to set up the necessary department to register births, deaths, and marriages.[122] Thus even during the Civil War, as counterrevolutionary forces threatened the very existence of the Soviet state, local authorities sometimes tolerated the

118. See *Derevenskaia kommuna*, December 4, 1919, p. 4.
119. For an example of a priest making a similar request before a village assembly in the late tsarist period, see Chapter 1.
120. See Dunaev, "Sotsial'no-politicheskaia orientatsiia."
121. Ibid. See Figes, *Peasant Russia*, p. 148.
122. Figes, *Peasant Russia*, p. 148. There is good reason to believe that VIKs implemented the *akty grazhdanskogo sostoianiia* once they had become "bureaucratized."

customary practices of rural Orthodoxy; they cooperated with rural priests on matters that spanned religious and political categories, a practice to continue, in various forms, throughout the NEP years and beyond.

There was also a wide gap between the Decree's provision on civil marriage and rural realities. Although statistics compiled by the Eighth Department of the Commissariat of Justice showed a significant rise in civil marriages in cities and in factories, Lenin himself admitted in November 1918 that "in the countryside . . . church marriage prevails."[123] In 1918, for example, there were twenty-five civil marriages in Mikhailovskoe *volost'* of Tula province, as compared (supposedly) to thirty-five church marriages.[124]

Evidence indicates that those inclined toward civil marriages were younger villagers and often Communists.[125] Thus the very state-building efforts that brought Communists (often former Red Army soldiers) and young urban workers into the countryside also increased the numbers of those social groups inclined toward civil marriage. In March 1919, for example, *Bednota* reported the case of a chair of the "local executive committee [VIK]," a Communist and former soldier who fell in love with a girl from what was described as a "kulak" family in Kursk province. To the great consternation of the woman's parents and siblings, the couple decided on a civil marriage.

Following the civil ceremony that took place in the soviet, the angry father set out to his son-in-law's home, demanding the return of his daughter. Aping the practice of villagers who in tsarist times subjected female adulteresses and thieves to *charivaris*, he forcibly removed the infractor's clothing (including her boots!), commenting that "if you want to live with a Communist, go naked to him."[126] By beginning the "ritual" typically reserved for those subjected to *charivaris*, the father implicitly accused his daughter of having violated the established norms of the community as seriously as any adulteress or thief.[127] He stripped his daughter to shame her into leaving a man he most surely did not regard as her legitimate husband and to impress on her that she deserved to be temporarily expelled from the community, like all those subjected to *charivaris*.[128] The daughter and her husband could hardly have failed to understand what the father was trying to get across. Yet instead of acceding to the norms of the community invoked by elements of the ritual

123. Lenin, *Polnoe sobranie sochinenii*, 28:160–61, quoted in Persits, *Otdelenie*, p. 171.
124. Persits, *Otdelenie*, p. 172.
125. See ibid.
126. For examples of villagers stripping off the clothing of women subjected to *charivaris*, see Stephen P. Frank, "Popular Justice, Community, and Culture: 1870–1900," in B. Eklof and S. P. Frank, eds., *The World of the Russian Peasant: Post-Emancipation Culture and Society* (London, 1991), esp. pp. 137, 139.
127. Ibid., p. 140.
128. On the functions of *charivaris*, see ibid., pp. 140–41.

of *charivari*, the young bride defied her father, ran to the neighboring peasant homestead (*dvor*), dressed, and rejoined her husband. The young Communist, for his part, not only joined the daughter in defying the norms of the community (that only church marriages are legitimate) but implicitly sought to establish new ones by inviting guests to celebrate his marriage (to have a collective event that sanctioned the civil marriage).

The father, daughter, and husband no doubt walked away from the confrontation more certain than ever that the political, social, and cultural differences between them were irreconcilable.[129] It is hard to imagine the father and his new son-in-law tolerating each other's presence, let alone cooperating in working out issues facing the village. If this example is taken as representative, the relatively anomalous occurrences of civil marriage heightened the unresolved social and political tensions between those who had defined the structure of the village social and political order that emerged during the rural social revolution of 1917–18 and those who sought to undermine it.[130] Their occurrences both reflected and generated deep cultural and generational conflict, the shock waves of which continued to reverberate long after the civil ceremonies.

Rural cadres likewise faced the acute challenge of dissolving well-established traditions as they implemented the Decree's claim to usurp the Church's long-standing role in village education. At the time of the October Revolution, the Church operated most of Russia's village schools.[131] Another obstacle facing those who would implement the Decree was the continuity in the rural teaching staff on both sides of the 1917 divide.[132] The third and probably the greatest obstacle was the invariable dependence of impoverished village schoolteachers on the financial support of the village communes. What this last factor meant in practice was that teachers inclined to eliminate religious influences from the classroom faced the financial punishment of their "employers," who often wanted to maintain religious aspects of education such as the teaching of the *Zakon Bozhii*. As of the summer of 1919, some teachers were leaving icons in the schools to cater to the cultural sympathies of the local populace.[133]

---

129. I have transposed the title of Helmut Altrichter, "Insoluble Conflicts: Village Life Between Revolution and Collectivization," in S. Fitzpatrick, A. Rabinowitch, and R. Stites, eds., *Russia in the Era of NEP: Explorations in Soviet Society and Culture* (Bloomington, Ind., 1991), pp. 192–209.

130. This assertion also obviously assumes the father was a smallholder peasant.

131. Figes, *Peasant Russia*; on parish schools, see also Ben Eklof, *Russian Peasant Schools: Officialdom, Village Culture, and Popular Pedagogy, 1861–1914* (Berkeley, Calif., 1986).

132. On the reasons for this, see Figes, *Peasant Russia*, p. 151.

133. See Larry E. Holmes, *The Kremlin and the Schoolhouse: Reforming Education in Soviet Russia, 1917–1931* (Bloomington, Ind., 1991), p. 15.

Thus villagers began to mobilize in response to the *threat* of a secular education alone. One example can suffice to illustrate this point. On September 27, 1918, a joint meeting of the *kombedy* and *volost'* soviet in Babavesk *volost'* of Tambov province was to address the matters of public education and the supply of foodstuffs (*prodovol'stvie*). Members (presumably) of the *kombedy* read the section of the Decree prohibiting the *Zakon Bozhii* in the schools. Villagers (presumably members of the soviet) responded defiantly: "How can this be, that our children have forgotten God? We won't allow [this], let them teach [our children], just as we were taught."[134] To defend the traditional religious elements of village education—and to resist the *kombedy* in their attempt to implement the Decree—villagers elected three "fervent advocates" of teaching the *Zakon Bozhii* to the *volost'* soviet's department of public education. Hardly content to allow villagers opposed to secular education to acquire an institutional base from which to pursue their interests, their opponents somehow arranged for a "reelection" of the department's membership. Villagers (again, presumably members of the *kombedy*) who supported the Decree, and especially secular education, were elected. In other cases, however, opponents of the Decree—and, in fact, clergy themselves—succeeded in their bid to "capture" the *volost'* departments of public education.[135] How clergy (and, presumably, lay activists) used this power is unclear, although there is some indication that such departments engaged in strategic "foot-dragging": when villagers spread rumors that children would be "branded" (*kleimit' detei*) in secular schools, a *volost'* department of education that was headed by a psalmist of course failed to dispel such catastrophic predictions.[136]

Rural clergy and lay activists faced an especially acute threat when rural cadres abused the Decree. Some interpreted the Decree as a kind of *carte blanche* sanctioning any kind of antireligious measures whatsoever. Moreover, as had been the case prior to the outbreak of the conflict, rural Party members still did not always understand the Decree.

Throughout the Civil War, rural cadres' abuses of the Decree were frequent and varied. The torture, murder, and illegitimate arrest of clergy are well-known and tragic examples of such abuses.[137] But cadres and even non-Party villagers abused the Decree in other important ways. Overstepping the legal parameters of the Decree, in 1919, for example, Party members in

---

134. Details of this meeting can be found in Persits, *Otdelenie*, pp. 177–78 (quoting *Bednota*, November 21, 1918).

135. For the case of a psalmist chairing a *volost'* department of public education in Pskov province, see *Derevenskaia kommuna*, December 2, 1919, p. 4.

136. Ibid. It is unclear whether or not the schools in question had been secularized.

137. See the discussion at the beginning of Chapter 5.

Sychevka district of Smolensk province prohibited villagers in two counties from carrying out any religious rituals at burials, an error that was said to engender an "anti-Soviet mood" among the peasants.[138] Another pervasive type of abuse was the illegal confiscation and thievery—by local cadres often said to be in a drunken state—of religious property and other items.[139] Any conclusions concerning a "typology" of such abuses must remain very tentative. But there is no doubt that cadres (and non-Party villagers) targeted public and collective expressions of religiosity (or symbols thereof, such as religious property). Perpetrating such extralegal abuses, they acted much like the apparently irreligious *otkhodniki* and hooligans of the very late tsarist period.

A close and careful examination of one such case can shed light on the motivations of abusive cadres. When President M. I. Kalinin conducted "explanatory work" on the Decree with peasants in Samara province, he faulted those "young Communists, who, with caps on their heads enter a church."[140] They of course knew very well that they were not to cover their heads inside an Orthodox church; such cases were hardly acts of ignorance. Rather, the act of wearing a cap was a statement of identity, of not being bound by Orthodox ritual, and, in fact, of not being part of the peasant community itself. The cap was the badge of the outsider. By wearing it, these young Communists were defying the notion that there are certain behaviors that are inappropriate in holy places. In fact—and this takes us to the second fundamental purpose of the provocation—the young Communists were, as outsiders, asserting the authority to *define* the purpose of the space, and the code of behavior that applied therein. Seeking a kind of instantaneous secularization, they were asserting that the church was in fact not a church at all, but a secular space. The young Communists sought to invert one of the basic truths of Russian peasant life: that only those who are *part* of the community have a right to define its norms and its structures of power. The young Communists expressed, in symbolic form, the desire for village power asserted by (usually irreligious) outsiders since the counterreform decades.

Party leaders offered implicit testimony of widespread resistance to such provocative abuses. The Eighth Party Congress, held in March 1919, called for "thoughtfully avoiding any kind of abuse of believers' feelings, which only lead to the strengthening of religious fanaticism."[141] Two months later,

---

138. *Perepiska sekretariata TsK RKP(b)*, 7:294–98.
139. See M. I. Kalinin's admission to this effect in *Krasnyi arkhiv* 1:86 (1938): 111, as reprinted in Persits, *Otdelenie*, p. 167.
140. Ibid.
141. *KPSS v rezoliutsiiakh i resheniiakh s"ezdov, konferentsii i plenumov TsK*, pt. 1 (Moscow, 1954), pp. 420–21, as quoted in Persits, *Otdelenie*, p. 188.

during his "conversations" with peasants in Samara province, Kalinin went a step further. He stated that Communists who acted in disrespectful and abusive ways were to be held legally accountable.[142]

From the first days of the rural social revolution of 1917–18 to the last days of the Russian Civil War, no one social group, political party (or faction), or institution defined the relationship of parish life to the emerging sociopolitical order. To be sure, the peasant smallholders who made that social revolution and continued to dominate the emerging rural political order had the greatest say in deciding religious issues. Yet they found their institutional and symbolic nexus of power increasingly challenged by the Bolsheviks and by village outsiders, overlapping but not identical groups. During the Civil War, Bolshevik state-building efforts, however limited, provided some institutional toeholds for those committed in principle to the legal claims of the Decree on the Separation of Church and State, the Constitution, and the Instruction.

Yet the Decree on the Separation of Church and State played no small role in bringing on the very phenomenon it was to avert: a symbiotic relationship between clergy, lay activists, and rural political institutions. They created that symbiotic relationship with precisely those rural political institutions the Decree had designated to *enforce* its claims (and, on a broader level, engineer a social, political, and cultural transformation): the VIKs and the village soviets. Almost equally as paradoxical was the fact that the Decree, intended as a piece of social and political engineering that would insure the smooth functioning of socialist society, ultimately catalyzed a great deal of social, cultural, and political conflict in the village.

At this point in our story, it is tempting to view these paradoxes of the Bolsheviks' cultural and political transformation as unique to the period of Revolution and Civil War. For the roots of the Soviet state in the countryside were at their shortest and (presumably) the imprint of the social identities fashioned during the tsarist period the freshest. But were these paradoxes really unique to the Civil War? Would the political activism of clergy and committed parishioners continue during the "strategic retreat" of the New Economic Policy? If so, what would be the consequences for village social and political relations, and also for the national political structure and culture?

---

142. Persits, *Otdelenie*, p. 167.

3

BURNT BY THE HEAVENS

The Soviet regime's secularizing mission in the countryside was one of the most ambitious projects of cultural transformation undertaken during the NEP period. It would be hard to imagine a more daunting crusade than the project to separate Russian villagers from their Orthodox and pagan religious beliefs and practices. Their very low literacy rates and deep suspicion of outsiders rendered them a very difficult and elusive audience for the *bezbozhnik*'s antireligious propaganda and agitation. It was not just a matter of reaching and converting this audience to a new way of thinking but of doing so in the face of growing hostility, a hostility that had already erupted in the Tambov uprising of 1921.[1]

The Soviets, for their part, brought their own considerable limitations to the antireligious "front," as it was often called. The Communist Party's reach into the Russian countryside remained thin and erratic throughout NEP.[2] Seven years of war had taken their toll on Russia's industrial and agricultural production, leaving the regime with very limited resources to conduct

---

1. An influential Western account of the Tambov uprising is Oliver H. Radkey, *The Unknown Civil War in Soviet Russia: A Study of the Green Movement in the Tambov Region* (Stanford, Calif., 1976).
2. Thorniley, *Rise and Fall*.

its utopian projects of cultural transformation.³ Even if the Soviets had had all the financial and material resources they needed, they would have brought other equally consequential limitations to their antireligious efforts. Within the Bolshevik Party, for example, there were already divergent and competing understandings of religion—and of the relationship between religion and socialist transformation—prior to the October Revolution; Lenin's intolerance for "Godbuilders" such as Bogdanov is one well-known case in point.⁴ These differences were only compounded once the Bolsheviks seized power; those cadres who joined the Party during the Civil War (Sheila Fitzpatrick's "Civil War generation") lacked the theoretical erudition in Marxism-Leninism—and its stance toward religion—that "Old Bolsheviks" generally commanded, tending instead to see cultural transformation in general as a military project.⁵ There was thus a tremendous potential for conflict within the antireligious "front," especially because these different understandings of religion could find institutional toeholds during the state-building efforts that continued during NEP.⁶

The prospects for successful cultural transformation in the antireligious sphere were not, to be sure, entirely gloomy. As we have seen in the preceding chapters, some villagers had begun to contest the place of religious belief and practice in village life in the late tsarist period, a conflict that had continued to reverberate as the demographic shifts of the social revolution of 1917–18 and the Civil War made the boundaries between the village and the world beyond increasingly porous. During NEP, the potential social base of this irreligious and often anticlerical faction only widened. Hungry and unemployed, workers and other citydwellers continued to flee to the Russian countryside throughout the 1920s. Only in 1926 did the tide begin

3. On the place of antireligious activism in Russian utopianism, see Stites, *Revolutionary Dreams*, esp. chap. 5.

4. For pertinent remarks on the Godbuilding controversy, see ibid., pp. 101–3.

5. Sheila Fitzpatrick, "The Civil War as a Formative Experience," in Abbott Gleason, Peter Kenez, and Richard Stites, eds., *Bolshevik Culture: Experiment and Order in the Russian Revolution* (Bloomington, Ind., 1985).

6. Within the Party-state, there was no one institutional center in charge of antireligious efforts during NEP. In fact, those efforts were highly dispersed and only minimally coordinated. Prior to 1922, several subunits within or attached to the Central Committee were involved. Other key players were the Commissariat of Justice (whose role in antireligious activities was ended in 1924), the Central Executive Committee of the Soviets (VTsIK), and the OGPU. In 1922, the Central Committee unified some of these disparate efforts with the creation of the Anti-Religious Commission, chaired by Iaroslavskii. Eventually abolished in 1929, the Anti-Religious Commission was charged with supervising the dissemination of antireligious propaganda; as this suggests, it was to supervise the League of the Godless. Vorontsov, *Leninskaia programma*, p. 59. For more on organizational matters, see Peris, "Storming the Heavens, pp. 71–73.

to turn.⁷ At the same time, seasonal out-migration of peasants seeking work not only resumed but reached considerable proportions, climbing to several million each year.⁸ When such opportunities began to dry up in the mid-1920s in some pockets of the countryside, such as Saratov province, poorer peasants challenged the power of the *bol'shaki*.⁹ The social base of the potential antireligious faction also included Red Army veterans returning to their villages stoked with a potentially powerful combination of significant exposure to antireligious propaganda, independent experience outside the village, and a fierce determination to challenge the traditional leadership of the village patriarchs.¹⁰ Often unable to create economically viable peasant households, returning veterans and urban refugees were highly dissatisfied with village life. Viewing themselves as under a kind of forced internal exile, urban refugees, frustrated *otkhodniki*, and Red Army veterans often felt contemptuous and even ashamed of village religiosity. The way in which these former soldiers, urban residents, and *otkhodniki* spoke, dressed, and otherwise behaved set them apart from those villagers who had not spent a significant amount of time away from the village. Their "presentation of self" and religious iconoclasm no doubt won them the awe of many restless younger villagers, especially their own brothers and sisters.¹¹

The Bolsheviks knew well of these developments. Successive generations of Party members had themselves participated—e.g., as *otkhodniki*, or as members of urban delegations sent to the countryside—in negotiating this social, cultural, and political conflict. But could they harness this popular irreligiosity for their own purposes? Could they channel it into the institutional forms (e.g., the regime's premier antireligious organization, the League of the Godless) through which they sought to engineer cultural transformation? What impact would these efforts have on the religious and political life of the village?

7. See Koenker, "Urbanization and Deurbanization."
8. Lewin, "Society, State, and Ideology," in *Making of the Soviet System*, p. 215. Otkhod had declined during the Civil War itself.
9. Sheila Fitzpatrick, "The Problem of Class Identity in NEP Society," in Sheila Fitzpatrick, Alexander Rabinowitch, and Richard Stites, eds., *Russia in the Era of NEP: Explorations in Soviet Society and Culture* (Bloomington, Ind., 1991), pp. 23–24.
10. On generational conflict, see Hoffmann, *Peasant Metropolis*, pp. 21–23. On demobilized soldiers' attempts to reshape rural politics and cultural life during NEP and collectivization, see Mark von Hagen, *Soldiers in the Proletarian Dictatorship: The Red Army and the Soviet Socialist State, 1917–1930* (Ithaca, N.Y., 1990), pp. 295–325; *Krest'ianskaia pravda*, February 22, 1928; and TsGAOR Leningrada, f. 6307, op. 13, ed. khr. 9, l. 39.
11. The restless mood of village youth in the 1920s was a recurring theme in the ethnographic and Party studies produced in the 1920s; see, for example, V. A. Murin, *Byt i nravy derevenskoi molodezhi* (Moscow, 1924), and Fenomenov, *Sovremennaia derevnia*, vol. 2, passim; see also Fitzpatrick, *Stalin's Peasants*, pp. 36–37, and Hoffmann, *Peasant Metropolis*, pp. 25–31.

A Vision Launched

Several years after the end of the Civil War, rural Communists began to lead the way in the creation of the institutional building blocks of the rural antireligious network.[12] The "circle" (*kruzhok*), the organizational building block of the antireligious campaign during this period, crept slowly into the isolated crevices of the Russian countryside in 1923, that is, approximately one year after the crisis over church valuables and the regime's fomenting of a schismatic movement within Russian Orthodoxy called the Renovationist Church.[13] In 1923–24, Party organizations on the district and county levels created functioning antireligious circles, for example, in Leningrad, Saratov, and Smolensk provinces.[14]

The birth of an antireligious circle in Sychevka district of Smolensk province nicely illustrates the process of creating the most basic unit of rural antireligious activity. On January 14, 1924, a meeting of the board of the Agitprop department of the Sychevka *uezd* committee of the RKP(b) discussed organizing an antireligious circle and, not surprisingly, decided in favor. It recognized that this decision would require the training of qualified antireligious workers and the selection of material for a circle, showing that the institutional organization of the cell, which the Party imposed "from

---

12. In the years immediately following the Civil War, several antireligious groups appeared in Voronezh, Severodvinsk, and Moscow. An "Association of Active Atheists" was founded in 1921 in Moscow. Two years later, a new group, the "All-Union League of Active Atheists," appeared there, supposedly taking the "Association" as its model. The Moscow Party Committee created the Moscow Society of the Godless in 1923. For more details on these early urban groups, which with the exception of the Moscow "Society" were isolated endeavors, see V. N. Konovalov, "Soiuz voinstvuiushchikh bezbozhnikov," *Voprosy nauchnogo ateizma* 4 (1967): 67, and V. Shishakov, "Soiuz voinstvuiushchikh bezbozhnikov," in M. Enisherlov, ed., *Voinstvuiushchee bezbozhie v SSSR za 15 let* (Moscow, 1932), p. 324; Peris, "Storming the Heavens," p. 79.

13. In February of 1922, following on the heels of famine in Ukraine during the previous summer, the regime ordered that all church valuables, including sacramental vessels, be confiscated, an action that met widespread opposition from the Church. Three months later, the authorities arrested Patriarch Tikhon on the grounds that he had played a counterrevolutionary role in encouraging resistance to the decree. Archival material recently made available has confirmed Lenin's ruthless role in crushing vehement opposition to the seizures in Shuia, located to the northeast of Moscow. They show that he did in fact order clergy and laity to be arrested and shot. See Dmitrii Volkogonov, *Lenin: A New Biography* (New York, 1994), pp. 376–78. On the crisis over church valuables, see, for example, Curtiss, *Russian Church*, pp. 106–28, and Alekseev, *Illuzii i dogmy*, pp. 191–200. On the Renovationists, see Roslof, "Renovationist Movement," and Freeze, "Counter-reformation."

14. *Bezbozhnik*, July 15, 1923, and June 17, 1923; *Izvestiia Saratovskogo soveta rabochikh i krest'ianskikh deputatov*, November 14, 1923; *Serp i molot*, March 29, 1924, p. 3, and October 14, 1924, p. 2; TsGAOR Leningrada, f. 7576, op. 6, d. 5, ll. 6, 16–17; and on the district level, TsGAOR Leningrada, f. 7576, op. 6, d. 5, l. 21.

above," preceded the existence of personnel or antireligious literature. In fact, the group charged the chair of the cultural department of trade unions (*predsedatel' kul'totdela profsoiuza*) with the organization of the cell and the development of its program.[15]

The network of antireligious circles grew very slowly, however. In Leningrad province, for example, as of 1924, both Kotel'sk and Os'mino *volosti* had only one antireligious circle each. If these two counties were typical, then there were only 143 antireligious circles in Leningrad province as of 1924, and 312 religious societies. (Since the creation of an antireligious circle on the level of the county was more an exception than the rule, 143 is most likely a generous estimate.)[16] As these figures demonstrate, rural Orthodoxy appeared more powerful than the fragile and scattered network of antireligious circles.

The creation of the Society of the Friends of the Newspaper *Bezbozhnik* (ODGB) in 1924 did represent a step toward creating an effective, centralized antireligious structure, but it did not rid this ailing network of its organizational weakness. While the antireligious leader A. Lukachevskii claimed that the development of this organization, and of its successor, the League of the Godless, proceeded "spontaneously on the local level," there is abundant evidence to the contrary.[17] Indeed, as Lukachevskii and his colleagues launched the Society and subsequently struggled to build a corresponding network at the provincial and local levels, they executed what might be called an atheistic "revolution from above." The development of the ODGB thus replayed, on a much grander scale, the dynamic noted in the creation of rural antireligious circles: cells existed—or were planned—before there were enough (qualified) cadres to run them, not to mention a receptive audience.

Antireligious workers, especially representatives sent to meetings of the ODGB, directly and indirectly confessed this discrepancy between agenda and infrastructure. On May 7, 1925, the executive bureau of the ODGB, which met following a conference of that organization, tellingly emphasized

---

15. Smolensk WKP 10, Protokol no. 10—zas. kollegii Agitpropotdela Sychevskogo ukoma RKP(b) ot 14/I-24 g.

16. During the period from December 1923 to October 1924, there were thirty-nine Orthodox religious societies (*pravoslavnye religioznye obshchestva*) in Novoladozhsk district. Multiplying that figure by eight (the number of districts in the province), we obtain the figure of 312 religious societies. TsGAOR Leningrada, f. 1010, op. 1., ed. khr. 103, l. 12. There were sixty-four religious societies in the district. The actual number of churches per district may have been greater. As of September 1924, for example, there were twenty-nine religious societies but forty-two churches in Volodarsk district (*raion*). See ibid., ll. 86–87. The number of counties is based on a 1921 state publication, *Spisok gubernii i uezdov R.S.F.S.R.* (Moscow, 1921). In other provinces far removed from major metropolitan centers, there may very well have been even fewer antireligious circles.

17. *Antireligioznik* 2 (February 1926): 3; *Bezbozhnik*, November 8, 1925, p. 2.

the imperative of "the quickest [possible] realization of the resolutions of the congress," or the "expansion and deepening of the existing organization." In less euphemistic terms, participants understood this agenda as the "definitive creation" of councils of the ODGB at the level of the *oblast'*, province, and district.[18] Although an antireligious correspondent from Tver' province claimed in early 1925 that "there is not one province without at least ten cells of the ODGB,"[19] official surveys revealed the absence of *councils* (as opposed to scattered, isolated cells) of the organization in certain provinces, districts, and many counties.[20] Eleven provincial councils, six provincial organizational bureaus, and sixteen *okrug* and *uezd* councils existed as of November 1925.[21] As late as January 1925, the Agitprop section of the provincial Party organization (*gubkom*) in Orel was sending groups of antireligious workers to *uezdy* in order to organize local sections (*otdeleniia*) and cells. In fact, as the mere deployment of the aforementioned survey suggests, antireligious leaders were acutely conscious of tremendous variation in the health, not to mention the existence, of the ODGB in the RSFSR.

The often frustrated participants in these surveys, meetings, and conferences also lamented the weak connections between the various components of the antireligious network. One antireligious correspondent, writing in 1925 on the occasion of the first anniversary of the ODGB, invidiously compared the persistent activity of "hundreds of clerical and sectarian performers, who covered the entire USSR," with the inability of district and provincial antireligious workers to "find the time to link together cells that had already been spontaneously organized by [a process of] drift [*samotek*]."[22] He demanded the connection of cells in the village with the higher organizational levels of the ODGB, a cry echoed by participants in the first meeting of the ODGB executive bureau in May, as well as by local antireligious workers.[23] As of November 1925, for instance, 287 cells were without provincial- or district-level supervision. Instead they were directly connected to the Central Committee of the ODGB itself.[24] The two ODGB cells of Bronnitsy *volost'* (Novgorod *uezd* and province), which local antireligious workers kept alive in 1925 "without [direction from] provincial or

18. *Bezbozhnik*, May 17, 1925, p. 6.
19. *Bezbozhnik*, April 19, 1925, p. 2.
20. *Bezbozhnik*, July 19, 1925, p. 3.
21. *Bezbozhnik*, November 8, 1925, p. 2. In addition, the ODGB could claim three councils and three organizational bureaus on the level of the region (*oblast'*), four organizational bureaus on the level of the district (including the *okrug*), one urban organizational bureau, three councils, and two organizational bureaus on the district (*raion*) level. There were fifty-one provinces in the RSFSR in 1921.
22. *Bezbozhnik*, November 8, 1925, p. 2.
23. *Bezbozhnik*, May 17, 1925, p. 6.
24. *Bezbozhnik*, November 8, 1925, p. 2.

district councils," "represented [only] themselves," in the words of the local antireligious correspondent.[25]

Decoded, the "spontaneous" development of the ODGB thus referred to the layering of a centrally imposed antireligious organizational structure on a substratum of preexisting antireligious circles or cells, holdovers from the period before 1924. Yet since local Party members had often taken the initiative in establishing these cells or circles, these randomly located vestiges of an earlier stage of antireligious activity were not spontaneous either, if by "spontaneous" we mean "popular," unofficial, and non-Party in origin.[26] The organization of the ODGB, contrary to the assertions of its leaders, was not the culmination of "mass" desire to raze rural religion, even if villagers subsequently supported its cells to varying degrees and for varying reasons. As we will see, the antireligious "pioneers" in the provinces continued to falter in their organizational efforts in part because of a lack of qualified colleagues and literature. The provincial committee of the ODGB in Orel admitted that because of a lack of experienced propagandists antireligious work had proceeded "haphazardly" until the creation of the provincial bureau in October 1925.[27] An anonymous member of the Orel provincial ODGB inadvertently betrayed the slow penetration of the antireligious forces into the countryside when he proudly reported the existence of cells "even" in villages.[28]

Who coordinated the activities of these isolated circles and cells of the ODGB? It was overburdened Party members for the most part.[29] Statistics on the composition of the ODGB, for example, demonstrate the overlap of Party membership and commitment to antireligious work. In 1925, for example, of the 964 members of the ODGB in Smolensk province, approximately 51 percent could claim some affiliation to the Party.[30] Komsomoltsy also comprised a very significant if elastic percentage of ODGB cell membership.[31] In addition to the members of the Party and Komsomol, Red Army

25. *Bezbozhnik*, July 19, 1925.
26. For an example, see *Bezbozhnik*, March 1, 1925. Nor, Vovelle claims, was the French dechristianization campaign "spontaneous," as defined above. See *Religion et révolution: La déchristianisation de l'an II* (Paris, 1976), p. 300.
27. *Bezbozhnik*, May 17, 1925, p. 6, and July 19, 1925, p. 3.
28. *Bezbozhnik*, March 1, 1925.
29. *Serp i molot*, March 29, 1924, p. 3; for an example of Party members' leadership of antireligious cells and circles in Leningrad province, see TsGAOR Leningrada, f. 7576, op. 6, d. 5, l. 4. Henceforth I will be using "cell" and "circle" interchangeably.
30. *Serp i molot*, May 17, 1925. Of the 964 members of the ODGB at that time, 315 were members of the Party, while 173 belonged to the Komsomol.
31. The 1,266 members of the ODGB in Moscow province included, in July 1925, 525 members (417 men and 108 women) of the Komsomol. *Serp i molot*, May 17, 1925. Of the 964 members of the ODGB in Smolensk province in 1925, 173 were Komsomoltsy. Ibid. For

veterans and young villagers who did not yet have a Party affiliation typically filled out the cells.[32] It was rare for antireligious and provincial newspapers to report that adult peasants had joined an antireligious cell. As during the last decades of the tsarist period, the social revolution of 1917–18, and the Civil War, it was the younger villagers who led the way in antireligious activities. Their antireligious energies were in turn one expression of the generational conflict that was such an important dynamic in village social relations during the 1920s.[33]

This youthful energy did not, however, transform the cells into vital centers of antireligious activity. Cells on the county level often hovered around 12 to 15 members, while those on the district level were sometimes considerably larger. The antireligious circle in Kingisepp *uezd* (Leningrad province), for example, boasted a membership of 70 unidentified persons and drew 396 people to its meetings.[34] Antireligious cells on the county level in Leningrad province typically met about twice a month. Although the evidence is not conclusive, it appears that the members conducted antireligious "lessons" among themselves at such meetings.[35] There is some indication that cells on the district level, on the other hand, did indeed engage in outreach activities (i.e., antireligious lessons) among nonmembers.[36] Very little direct information is available concerning the content of these lessons, as well as the kinds of social interactions (and social conflict) that they generated. We do know that whether conducting antireligious lessons among themselves or other villagers, members of the cells had very little antireligious literature (e.g., the newspaper *Bezbozhnik*, whose first issue appeared at the end of 1922) at their disposal.[37]

In sum, the rather modest and infrequent activities of scattered antireligious cells hardly constituted a significant direct threat to parish life. Preaching their antireligious creed almost exclusively to the "converted," so

---

statistics on the county level, see Smolensk WKP 25, "Sostoianie i rabota opornoi Slishchenskoi volostnoi iacheiki VKP(b), za period s oktiabria 1925 g. po 1-e avgusta 1926 goda," pp. 7–8.

32. *Serp i molot*, March 29, 1924, p. 3; *Bezbozhnik*, July 15, 1923. Antireligious activists in the Mexican Revolution were often army officers and teachers. See Meyer, *Cristero Rebellion*, p. 26.

33. On this see Hoffmann, *Peasant Metropolis*, pp. 22–23, and Fitzpatrick, *Stalin's Peasants*, pp. 35–37.

34. TsGAOR Leningrada, f. 7576, op. 6, d. 5, l. 6; *Serp i molot*, March 29, 1924, p. 3; TsGAOR Leningrada, f. 7576, op. 6, d. 5, l. 21.

35. See, for example, TsGAOR Leningrada, f. 7576, op. 6, d. 5, ll. 6, 16–17.

36. The Kingisepp district cell, for example, conducted thirty-three lessons among villagers during January 1925. See ibid., l. 21.

37. On the very limited availability of *Bezbozhnik* and other antireligious propaganda, see *Bezbozhnik*, May 1, 1923, p. 5; June 3, 1923, p. 3; and May 1, 1925, p. 3.

to speak, the activities of cells on the county level (or even on the district level) could not have had much of an impact on the religiosity (however defined and measured) of the adult smallholding peasants. It is, of course, possible and even probable that members of both *uezd* and *volost'* cells engaged in antireligious activities apart from their attendance at meetings. To be sure, rural Party members and Komsomoltsy engaged in a wide range of antireligious activities outside the institutional jurisdiction of the cell. Rural Communists randomly distributed antireligious leaflets, organized antireligious disputes, and conducted sporadic antireligious campaigns.[38] This impressive list of contributions notwithstanding, Party members' efforts in their capacity as leaders and members of cells were quite limited.

The indirect and long-term impact of these antireligious cells, however, was no doubt greater. Attending meetings and interacting with those who shared their hostility to parish life most likely solidified the identity of the antireligious activist (*bezbozhnik*), thereby laying the basis for subsequent social, cultural, and political conflict. Although villagers had in fact experienced such conflict over the place of religion in village life for decades, never before had an organization devoted *solely* to the exacerbation of such conflict existed in the Russian village. And villagers did carry out a wide range of irreligious or at least anticlerical activities—such as burning icons and setting fire to churches. But even perceptive antireligious leaders and correspondents realized that their antireligious organizations could not always take credit for inspiring them to do it.[39]

Thus rural cadres had, relative to the Civil War, made progress in setting up an antireligious institutional network. Yet that organizational structure remained, as a rule, fragile. Why, then, were antireligious cadres unable to create a complete and vital network of antireligious cells during precisely those years when the potential social base of an antireligious faction was arguably at its apogee?

Unbroken Ties

For one reason, a significant number of Party members, Komsomoltsy, and returning Red Army veterans (not mutually exclusive categories, to be sure) themselves had close and active ties to the world of Russian Orthodoxy.

---

38. *Bezbozhnik*, February 25, May 27, August 5, and June 3, 1923.
39. Examples can be found in *Bezbozhnik*, March 18, 1923, p. 5; and May 6, 1923, p. 5.

Judging from surveys published in provincial and antireligious newspapers, as well as the records of the Communist Party in Smolensk province, a considerable number of rural Party members continued to practice Orthodox rituals, especially those of marriage and baptism.[40] To give just one of many possible examples, in 1924, in the village of Il'men' (Balashov *uezd*, Smolensk province), local Communists were accused of receiving a priest and having their children baptized.[41] Like some of their older colleagues in the Party, some Komsomoltsy retained active ties to the Orthodox faith. A report on the Komsomol cell in Matavina, for example, revealed that "one of the Komsomoltsy ... went to the priest to be married. For that he was excluded from the Komsomol."[42] A 1929 report of the Leningrad Regional Committee on Public Education claimed that "we found waverers and believers not only in non-Party ranks but even within the Komsomol."[43] Provincial newspapers and Party records from Smolensk province frequently condemned members of the Komsomol for participating in traditional religious ceremonies, especially marriage and baptism, as well as for attending church services.[44] Upon discovering such religious ties, condemned rhetorically as a violation of Communist "ethics" or "discipline," many rural Komsomol cells resolutely and promptly purged the errant member from their ranks.[45] Some district Komsomol cells may have overturned such decisions, however, because they believed that it was possible to reconcile Komsomol membership and formal expressions of religiosity.[46]

---

40. For a typical indictment of a candidate Party member who had his children baptized, see Smolensk WKP 13, "Doklad o sostoianii Zabolotskoi volpartorganizatsii i ee rabote." See also I. A.Trifonov, *Klassy i klassovaia bor'ba v SSSR v nachale NEPa, 1921–23 gg.* (Leningrad, 1964), p. 37.

41. *Sovetskaia derevnia*, March 2, 1924.

42. TsGAOR Leningrada, f. 3106, op. 1, d. 327, l. 45; Pospielovsky, *Russian Church*, 1:179; Isabel Tirado, "The Revolution, Young Peasants, and the Komsomol's Anti-Religious Campaign (1920–1928)," *Canadian-American Slavic Studies* 26:1–3 (1992): 114. On the persistence of religious sentiment and practice among youth, see Holmes, *The Kremlin and the Schoolhouse*, p. 102.

43. TsGAOR Leningrada, f. 6307, op. 12, ed. khr. 455, l. 66.

44. *Bezbozhnik*, August 9, 1925, p. 5; Smolensk WKP 25, "Akt obsledovaniia leninskoi opornoi iacheiki VKP(b) za period s I/XII-25 g. po I/VI-26 goda," and "Otchet Bel'skogo ukoma VKP(b) za period s XIX partkonferentsii po 1-e maia 1926 goda."

45. See, for example, *Sovetskaia derevnia*, April 6, 1924, p. 4. Some Komsomol cells staged public trials of colleagues married in church. See *Sovetskaia derevnia*, April 9, 1924, p. 4. In March 1921, the Central Committee called for an open discussion of the issue of Communists who practiced religious rituals and even avowed religious beliefs. Although neither the clergy nor devout believers could be Party members, the Central Committee ruled that those practicing rituals because of family pressures could remain in the Party. See Vorontsov, *Leninskaia programma*, p. 48.

46. *Krasnye rezervy*, October 15, 1922, p. 2.

Religious commitments did, in some instances, diminish a Party or Komsomol member's participation in the life of the cell, and in antireligious activities in particular. Cases of such interference were clustered around major religious holidays, such as Easter and Christmas. While his comrades attended a Komsomol meeting on Easter 1924 in a village in Saratov province, one young Communist instead headed to church and prayed.[47] Some of his peers in Smolensk province also made the same choice. A 1927 report on the Komsomol cell in Velikie Luki quoted a religiously oriented member as saying: "On April 13 I cannot come to the Komsomol evening . . . since I have to prepare for Easter." Another proudly exclaimed: "We will eat Easter eggs and go to church; it isn't such a great offense since on Easter they have an excellent service."[48] It is likely that Komsomoltsy who attended Easter services shied away from participation in Komsomol antireligious activities, especially from activities timed to coincide with traditional religious holidays, or else participated without much enthusiasm. There were certainly reports that members of rural Party cells who remained faithful to certain Orthodox rituals did not engage in any antireligious activity.[49]

To digress a bit from our main theme, why were Party and Komsomol members able to reconcile these ostensibly conflicting identities?[50] To be sure, for some committed believers, especially sectarians, the identities of Komsomol-*bezbozhnik* and believer proved psychologically incompatible. The cell in the Molokan settlement of Astrakhanka (Kashirinsk *uezd*, Orenburg province) disintegrated in part because some members could not reconcile their sectarian identities with Komsomol activism. At one point the settlement hosted a Komsomol cell of thirteen members.[51] By December of 1927, however, the membership of the cell had dwindled to three. One member from a Baptist family, who had been seen crying on several occasions, repeatedly reassured his comrades that "my stay in the Komsomol is creating hellish conditions of [everyday] life for me. But in spite of everything I remain a Komsomol member."[52] This tortured individual eventually found himself unable to maintain this delicate balance of his religious and political identities. Later, while serving in the Red Army, he left the Komsomol

---

47. *Sovetskaia derevnia*, May 24, 1924, p. 4.
48. Fainsod, *Smolensk Under Soviet Rule*, p. 413.
49. See, for example, *Sovetskaia derevnia*, March 2, 1924.
50. On this new *dvoeverie*, see also Siegelbaum, *Soviet State and Society*, p. 162. During the Party purge of May 1929 to May 1930, "defects in personal life and conduct," a category that included adherence to religious rituals, accounted for 21.9 percent of the approximately 170,000 purged. See Hiroaki Kuromiya, *Stalin's Industrial Revolution: Politics and Workers, 1928–1932* (New York, 1988), p. 38.
51. See *Bezbozhnik*, December 11, 1927.
52. Ibid. See also Tirado, "The Revolution," p. 100.

and wrote his Baptist congregation letters of repentance (*pokaiannye pis'ma*). One of his sectarian compatriots, vulnerable to the pleas of his religious parents, also resolved to favor the claims of religion over those of politics:

> My father and mother, who got down on their knees, had been [trying to] persuade me for a long time [to leave the Komsomol]. . . . I could not look indifferently at my parents, who had crawled to me on their knees and shed bitter tears. My heart could not bear [this] . . . and [so] I left. But in terms of beliefs and disposition I am still a Komsomol member now.[53]

Why were these individuals in such emotional pain? Did the psychic strain come only—or at least predominantly—from the pressure exerted by sectarian parents unable to tolerate the "dual faith" espoused by their children? Or was it the case that parental pressure only exacerbated the already considerable psychic strain produced by the attempt to reconcile Party or Komsomol identity with a more inner-directed form of Christianity? One thinks here of the Dukhobors (Spirit-Wrestlers), who believed that the spirit of human beings incorporated the Father, the Son, and the Holy Spirit; many Russian sectarian movements regarded the inner life or the "soul" of the individual as sacred.[54] By making a powerful and in fact all-encompassing claim on the individual's inner life, sectarian identity left little space for the adoption of other identities or even affiliations, let alone identification with a totalistic political ideology that nominally demanded atheism. When parents and sectarian communities applied acute pressure, they intensified the conflicting internal claims that resounded inside the Komsomol-sectarian.

Parental pressure played a different role in the case of Party and Komsomol members who practiced Orthodox rituals. To be sure, parents of Party and Komsomol members did exert considerable pressure on their children to have church marriages, baptize their own children, and engage in

---

53. Tirado, "The Revolution," p. 100.

54. The "Father" was human memory; the "Son" was human reason; the "Holy Spirit" was human will. The soul, believed the Dukhobors, progressively entered the human body during ages six through fifteen; the body itself could not be resurrected. The Dukhobors in turn gave rise to other sects whose members preserved in somewhat subdued form this radical spiritualism, including the *Molokane* (Milk Drinkers), *Subbotniki* (Saturday observers), *Voskresniki* (Sunday observers), and *Pryguny* (Jumpers). Each member of the *Khlysty* sect (from which the *Skoptsy* derived) claimed to be an incarnation of God. (*Khlyst* means "whip" or "flagellant.") *Skoptsy* engaged in various forms of self-mutilation. The *Dukhobors* first appeared in the eighteenth century, and the *Molokane* split off from them in about 1770. This information and other useful sketches of sectarian movements can be found in Donald W. Treadgold, "The Peasant and Religion," in W. S. Vucinich, ed., *The Peasant in Nineteenth-Century Russia* (Stanford, Calif., 1968), pp. 89–91.

other Orthodox practices.⁵⁵ The pressure was no doubt especially acute in the case of those Komsomoltsy who came from clerical families, such as Aleksandr Makkaveev, son of a deacon in the village of Storozha (Tula province).⁵⁶ Parents of sectarian-Komsomoltsy tried to get their children to abandon their newly chosen political identities; parents of those individuals who tried to balance Orthodoxy and Party membership, on the other hand, focused their efforts on having their children *maintain* key religious practices.⁵⁷ To be sure, this latter agenda makes sense, given the emphasis on the (proper) observance of ritual in Russian Orthodoxy.

Why, though, did parental and community pressure often work? (To be sure, rural Communists may have exaggerated those pressures in order to avoid taking responsibility for their actions.) In answering this question, it is important to understand how that pressure resonated inside the Komsomolets or Party member. While the theological beliefs held by Russian sectarians made powerful religious claims on an individual's inner life, Russian Orthodoxy's stress on ritual and form made much greater claims on behavior. Conversely, especially given the relative lack of theological sophistication of the typical Russian peasant, it made relatively fewer claims on an individual's internal life.⁵⁸ In sum, it was actually easier to compartmentalize one's attachment to Russian Orthodoxy, which ostensibly involved no more than observance of the major sacraments, crossing oneself in front of icons, and attendance at key holiday celebrations, than one's attachment to sectarian belief. Having compartmentalized one's Orthodoxy as something one *did* on specific occasions, the Party or Komsomol member was thus free to believe what he or she wanted about social and political realities. This explanation is consonant with the fact that Red Army veterans, for example, typically shed their antireligious stance a couple years after they returned to their native villages.⁵⁹

It would be a mistake, however, to assume that Party and Komsomol members made such adjustments only under the duress of community and

55. See Fainsod, *Smolensk Under Soviet Rule*, pp. 413–14, and Vorontsov, *Leninskaia programma*, pp. 46–69.

56. *Bezbozhnik*, May 24, 1925; see also ibid., November 15, 1925.

57. This is not to ignore parental disapproval of their children's political choices. Family conflict on this issue could be intense. But the chief target of parental pressure appears to have been the maintenance of religious ties, rather than the abandonment of Communist political identity. See, for example, the case of the church elder and his Komsomol son, discussed later in this chapter.

58. For revealing examples of the large gaps in peasants' theological knowledge, see Belliustin, *Description*.

59. See, for example, TsGAOR Leningrada, f. 6307, op. 13, ed. khr. 9, l. 99. For a similar assessment, see also Fitzpatrick, *Stalin's Peasants*, p. 36; Okninsky, *Dva goda*, p. 231; and von Hagen, *Soldiers in the Proletarian Dictatorship*, p. 302.

family pressure. As in the case of sectarians, such pressure no doubt landed on fertile ground. In other words, there is good reason to believe that Party and Komsomol members were intrinsically inclined to maintain their religious attachments. In the late tsarist period, religious sensibility shaped the construction of identity in "conscious" workers; workers' pursuit of religious asceticism drew them to "activism and molded their conceptions of 'consciousness' and 'revolutionary,'" even as they rejected the external trappings of Orthodox religiosity.[60] Their anticlericalism notwithstanding, did many rural (and urban) Bolsheviks of the 1920s, too, think of themselves as "saints of the Revolution," taking the model of the ascetic saint as their psychic blueprint? That Bolshevism for some was a product and even extension of their religious sensibility is not at variance with the still vehement anticlericalism of Party and Komsomol members. In fact, it in part explains such anticlericalism. For those implicitly taking the ascetic saint as their internal model would have no doubt been very disappointed in the all too imperfect conduct of drunken, greedy priests. They very well may have even viewed certain antireligious acts as a kind of purification of religiosity; indeed, speaking retrospectively, Mikhail Shakhnovich, who served as an antireligious correspondent in the 1920s, characterized the antireligious campaign as "our reformation."[61] Alternatively, religiously observant Communists may have made the strategic calculation that dutifully displaying the requisite attachment to Orthodoxy would help a Communist or Komsomolets ingratiate himself with the village patriarchs, thereby increasing his political effectiveness.[62]

Serving Without Support

Even those Party and Komsomol members who *had* shed their formal religious attachments faced other significant obstacles to carrying out antireligious activities. The Civil War, as well as the very weak penetration of the

60. Dave Pretty, "The Saints of the Revolution: Political Activists in the 1890s in Ivanovo-Voznesensk and the Path of Most Resistance," *Slavic Review* 54 (Summer 1995): 304. See Zelnik, *Radical Worker*, and the discussion of this issue in Chapter 1.
61. Interview by the author on October 2, 1987, at Leningrad State University, where Shakhnovich was a professor. He is the author of *Lenin i problemy ateizma* (Moscow-Leningrad, 1961), as well as *Zapiski bezbozhnika* (Leningrad, 1933). To be sure, there is an important distinction to be drawn between the emulation of religious models of behavior (i.e., the ascetic saint) and the kind of innate religiosity that expressed itself in the observance of ritual and other traditional religious practices. (The existence of the former can not be automatically presumed to be evidence for the latter.)
62. For examples, see Chapters 5 and 6.

Party into the countryside prior to its outbreak, left the rural Party apparatus and network of Soviet institutions fragile and incomplete. Between April 1920 and September 1921, the number of Bolshevik Party members in Saratov province fell from 20,699 to 10,383 as a result of anti-Soviet peasant uprisings, party purges, mobilization, and famine.[63] By 1924, the organizational network of the Party had still not penetrated into many areas of the Soviet countryside. As late as 1925, the Party committee in Iaroslavl' province had not even *begun* to organize county executive committees (*volkomy*).[64] And even in those areas graced by the existence of these bodies, cadres were confused about the proper relationship between the Party cell, county committee, and district committee.[65]

The Komsomol's strong presence in the countryside—usually greater than the Party's—had significant implications for antireligious activism. In 1924, the Seventh Komsomol Congress adopted a new policy, "turn to the village," which sought to increase peasant membership in the organization. Over the course of the next three years, the Komsomol succeeded in swelling the number of peasant members, although it was only at the end of NEP that the League's network extended beyond towns and large villages into smaller rural settlements.[66] By the end of the 1920s, the ratio of rural Komsomoltsy to rural Party members was between three and four to one.[67] The rapid growth of the Komsomol organization diminished the Party's capacity to provide proper direction for its younger colleagues, which in turn weakened both organizations' control over the involvement of its cadres in antireligious activity.[68] While the membership ranks of the Komsomol were swelling overall, substantial outflow, apparently unrelated to members having reached the

---

63. Figes, *Peasant Russia*, pp. 226–27.

64. Khataevich section in Ia. Iakovlev and M. Khataevich, eds., *Iacheika i sovety v derevne* (Moscow-Leningrad, 1925), p. 15. As of 1925, more than half of the 13,558 rural Party cells comprised only five to eight people. See *Bol'shevik* 3–4 [19–20] (1925): 74.

65. G. Rylkin and V. Truntaev, in Iakovlev and Khataevich, *Iacheika i sovety*, p. 9. Both appear to have traveled to the countryside and investigated the rural *apparat* sometime during early or mid-NEP.

66. By June 1925, Komsomol membership was 1,503,000. For more statistics on membership, see Ralph Talcott Fisher Jr., *Pattern for Soviet Youth: A Study of the Congresses of the Komsomol, 1918–1954* (New York, 1955), p. 409. On the penetration of the Komsomol into the countryside, see especially Tirado, "The Revolution," pp. 100, 108. She notes that peasant membership climbed from 37.6 percent in May 1924 to 53.7 percent in 1926 of the total Komsomol membership. See also Smolensk WKP 15, "Iartsevskii volostnoi komitet RKP(b)—1/II 1926 goda—Smolgukomu VKP(b)/ORGOTDEL," and TsGAOR Leningrada, f. 3106, op. 1, d. 327, l. 4.

67. Fitzpatrick, *Stalin's Peasants*, p. 34.

68. "O nekotorykh zadachakh momenta," *Bol'shevik*, June 30, 1925; *Pravda*, January 9, 1926, p. 1. See also Smolensk WKP 13, "Plan rabot Zabolotskogo volkoma na dek., ianv., fev. mesiatsy 1924 i 25-i god."

maximum age for membership, also existed.[69] In sum, neither the Party nor the Komsomol could supply the cadres or offer the institutional infrastructure needed to extend the network of antireligious cells beyond district towns and large villages.

Constrained by this weak institutional infrastructure, rural Party and Komsomol members often lacked the skills that sustained antireligious propaganda and other antireligious activities required. Although Komsomoltsy had a high level of education and literacy relative to the rest of the population, they still lacked the knowledge and the verbal skills that effective antireligious cadres needed, e.g., solid knowledge of the Bible, of the history of science, and of Soviet antireligious propaganda. As of September 1, 1922, for example, 79.2 percent (3,210) of all Saratov Komsomoltsy had received only an elementary education, while 1.4 percent (fifty-nine) were illiterate.[70] Nor were the educational and literacy levels of Party members themselves entirely adequate to the task.[71] Not surprisingly, rural Party leaders complained frequently of the political ignorance of rural Komsomoltsy, of the relatively low level of grounding in Marxist-Leninist and antireligious theory. Party leaders were very aware of and concerned about this problem and their failure to solve it.[72] For Party members themselves often lacked the requisite "political literacy"; moreover, Komsomoltsy often proved indifferent to becoming better educated in this regard.[73]

Party members, as suggested by their default role in supervising Komsomoltsy, had to juggle the creation of antireligious cells and other antireligious activities with a daunting number of other duties and responsibilities.[74] Within the cell itself, a shortage of personnel overburdened even capable and willing cadres, thereby diluting their effectiveness at any given

69. *Pravda*, January 3, 1926. Although in January and August 1926, 565,000 new members joined the organization, 110,000 left it in the same period. Of these, 75 percent left voluntarily, and 25 percent were purged. In Saratov province, the number of rural Komsomol cells "greatly decreased" during the summer and winter of 1921–22. *Krasnye rezervy*, December 17, 1922.

70. For more on the educational profile of the 4,053 members, see *Krasnye rezervy*, October 1, 1922, p. 1. On attempts to bring literacy to the countryside, see TsGAOR Leningrada, f. 6307, op. 7, d. 394, l. 8.

71. As of 1920, 82.5 percent of all district Party members in Saratov, Simbirsk, and Penza provinces had received an elementary or domestic education. See Figes, *Peasant Russia*, p. 229.

72. See the protocol of the Zabolotsy *volost'* Party committee from February 15, 1925, in Smolensk WKP 13, "Plan rabot."

73. See Smolensk WKP 13, "Protokol no. 11-zasedaniia Zabolotskogo volkoma RKP(b) ot 20/I-25 goda"; Protokol no. 4-zasedaniia Zabolotskogo volkoma ot 21 marta 1925 goda"; and "Protokol 5 Obshchego ob"edinennogo sobraniia chlenov i kandidatov RKP i RLKSM 30 aprelia 1925 g."

74. This condition was termed *peregruzka* (overload) in Party discourse. The legally delineated responsibilities of Party members were called their "party load" (*partnagruzka*).

task. One example will suffice to illustrate this general condition. A beleaguered candidate of the Party in the village of Petrovskoe (Orenburg *uezd*, Moscow province) found himself saddled with the multiple duties of director of readers at a reading hut, director of a Komsomol *propkollektiv*, village organizer of work among women, member of the presidium of the county political enlightenment committee, juror (*narodnyi zasedatel'*), and member of the village soviet.[75] Burdened with this daunting list of responsibilities, this individual had little time or energy left over for antireligious activities. Joining antireligious activities (and, eventually, the League of the Godless) in competing for the time and energy of Party members were other mass, "voluntary" organizations such as MOPR, Obshchestvo Doloi negramotnost', and Osoviakhim.[76] Given these excessive demands on a Party member's time, it is not surprising that "only a small part of the especially progressive village cells and Party committees, where there happened to be sensible and strong workers, could align its work with the spirit of the last directives of the Party" (namely, its policy vis-à-vis the countryside).[77]

Given all of these obstacles, it is easy to see why rural Party and Komsomol members could not create vital antireligious cells in significantly larger numbers. These same obstacles—especially inadequate levels of literacy and education—in fact rendered many Party and Komsomol members uninterested in the main task for which antireligious cells existed: conducting antireligious propaganda among the converted and the not-yet-converted. The very obstacles that rendered rural cadres disinclined to engage in antireligious propaganda also attracted them to other antireligious activities that did not demand so much knowledge, so much steady investment of effort over a long (and seemingly indefinite) period of time, and so much tolerance for not being able to see immediate and visible results of one's labors. Not only was it physically impossible to become anything close to a twenty-four-hour *bezbozhnik* engaging in patient dialogue about antireligious propaganda with hostile or indifferent peasants, the prospect of it was psychologically intolerable.[78]

---

75. *Pravda*, July 5, 1926. The cell consisted of sixty members and candidate members of the Party, of whom six were severely overworked. The article noted that thirty of its members carried on no Party work at all.

76. "MOPR" was the International Organization for Aid to Imprisoned Fighters for the Revolution. For details on the history of Osoaviakhim, see von Hagen, *Soldiers in the Proletarian Dictatorship*, pp. 246–47. Obshchestvo Doloi negramotnost' was the "Down with Illiteracy" Society.

77. Rylkin and Truntaev, in Iakovlev and Khataevich, *Iacheika i sovety*, p. 9.

78. This is an adaptation of Stephen Hanson's concept of the "twenty-four-hour revolutionary." See also his *Time and Revolution: Marxist Ideology and the Design of Soviet Institutions* (Chapel Hill, N.C., 1997), esp. pp. 205–8.

Rural *bezbozhniki* were, therefore, irresistibly attracted to a *style* of antireligious activism called the "campaign" or "campaignism" (*kampaneishchina*) in Party discourse. In other words, Party and Komsomol members applied intense and very concentrated efforts to one particular type of antireligious activity (usually one that was designed to attract a large group of the rural population), and then stopped—until the next and chronologically distant round. In between, rural cadres gave similarly intense and concentrated efforts to a different subsections of the general political, social, and cultural transformation sought by the regime (such as the literacy campaign).[79] The "shock brigades of rural groups of godless [*bezbozhniki*]," as one rural correspondent called them, also adumbrated the form taken by the shock work (*udarnyi trud*) of the 1930s, that is, the gang or the brigade.[80]

Particular activities exemplified this campaign style especially well. Especially important examples were Komsomol Christmas and Easter celebrations and antireligious disputes.[81] Both activities had considerable visibility in the countryside prior to the establishment of the League of the Godless in 1925; the first "secular" holiday, Komsomol Christmas, was celebrated in 1922–23, with a week-long Komsomol Easter carnival following in 1923. Antireligious disputes were typically focused on a particular theme or question (e.g., Did Christ Exist?) and featured a face-to-face confrontation between an often motley contingent of *bezbozhniki* on the one hand and clergy and lay activists on the other, with the contested support of a crowd of potential converts to atheism hanging in the balance.[82] Clergy and

79. There is compelling evidence that some perceptive rural cadres were aware of the limitations of the "campaign" style of antireligious activity, rather than resigned, as Peris claims on p. 116 of "Storming the Heavens," to "seemingly hollow organizational achievements over substantive social change." See, for example, *Bezbozhnik*, February 25, 1923, p. 2, and August 5, 1923.

80. On the origins of the term "shock work," see Lewis Siegelbaum, *Stakhanovism and the Politics of Productivity in the USSR, 1935–1941* (New York, 1988), p. 40, and idem., "Shock Workers," in *The Modern Encyclopedia of Russian and Soviet History* (Gulf Breeze, Fla., 1983), 35:23–27.

81. Another prominent example of the campaign style was the opening of reliquaries (*vyskrytie moshchei*) of Orthodox saints. According to popular belief, the bodies of Orthodox saints are imperishable. The Commissariat of Justice directed that clergy, especially bishops, were to be present when a saint's tomb was opened, unwrap the corpse, and sign an inventory list of the actual contents. Government officials and members of scientific commissions were also to be present. The openings were widely publicized and sometimes led to judicial proceedings against clergy, who were charged with resistance to taking part in the openings or having deceived the population by claiming the bodies of Orthodox saints would not decay. Although exemplary of the "campaign" style analyzed above, I have not included them here because they tended to involve church and political "elites," as opposed to parish clergy and rural officials. See F. I. Garkavenko, ed., *O religii i tserkvi: Sbornik documentov* (Moscow, 1965), pp. 105–9, and Vorontsov, *Leninskaia programma*, pp. 72–74.

82. Such was the title of an antireligious debate held in Orel in 1925. For more details, see *Bezbozhnik*, February 1, 1925, p. 7.

contemporary observers alike (e.g., Maurice Hindus) noted the tremendous popularity of antireligious disputes. City auditoriums and rural fields "teemed with talk of religion," said Hindus.[83] Indeed, antireligious disputes were in some respects ironic inversions of Orthodox missionaries' debates against Old Believers in the nineteenth and early twentieth centuries, as well as of *besedy* and extraliturgical instruction of the late tsarist period; all were efforts to reshape (or, in the case of debates, to extinguish) popular piety for political purposes.[84] Secular holiday celebrations, which featured processions replete with blasphemous acts, mockery, inversion of church ritual and liturgy, and other "rituals of a counterfaith," also had prerevolutionary precedents.[85] Both kinds of events, however, represented public and collective antireligious activity on an unprecedented scale.

It is one thing to list the kinds of activities that antireligious activists engaged in during these events and another to capture the heady excitement with which they anticipated such mini-campaigns. The Party and Komsomol members who organized and carried them out, some of whom did have special training as antireligious lecturers, realized that they were events that were guaranteed to bring into direct conflict the "plans and recipes" of Bolshevism with those of village Orthodoxy.[86] In fact, they welcomed such total cultural confrontation as part of a secular apocalypse that would ultimately produce a new society. They regarded such confrontation as the prerequisite to successfully neutralizing patriarchal opposition to their project.

Antireligious cadres structured disputes to produce the maximum bearable amount of confrontation. The format was itself ritualized: first an antireligious activist would deliver an atheistic sermon for one to two hours, then he—it was almost invariably a male—would engage in an intentionally provocative debate with the priest, and finally, he would take up the same theme with a lay member of the audience, namely, a worker or peasant.[87] Within this general format, the activist's intent was to engage the priest or

---

83. Quoted in Stites, *Revolutionary Dreams*, p. 107.

84. Disputes on religious themes were a format that appeared in Orthodox seminaries in the eighteenth century.

85. For an extremely perceptive elaboration of this concept, see Stites, *Revolutionary Dreams*, 109–14. Stites, for example, notes that "Ivan Pryzhov, a radical of the 1860s, so hated religion that he would conduct his drinking bouts in a parody of Orthodox ritual" (p. 101). The prerevolutionary "Godbuilding" movement created in large part by Anatole Lunacharsky, who was Commissar of Enlightenment, can also be considered a precedent. On Lunacharsky, see especially Sheila Fitzpatrick, *The Commissariat of Enlightenment: Soviet Organization of Education and the Arts under Lunacharsky, October 1917–1921* (New York, 1970).

86. See also Stites, *Revolutionary Dreams*, p. 108.

87. See the vivid if perhaps somewhat embellished description of the typical format of antireligious debates in Father Trophimus, "Russian Religion," pp. 84–85. Trophimus was a pseudonym. At the time of the article's publication, the author was a parish priest in the USSR.

layperson in a series of rapid-fire questions, questions usually designed to expose the empirical unsupportability of religious belief.[88] These intentionally provocative verbal exchanges, however, were only one element of the cultural confrontation that took place at disputes. For *bezbozhniki* incorporated visual demonstrations of the nonexistence of God into their performances. They also bombarded the audience and their avowed opponents with banners and flags bearing provocative slogans such as "the merciless war with God and his visible Church by means of scientific proof and the logic of common sense."[89] Antireligious disputes were to engage as many of the senses and faculties as possible.[90]

What was the impact of such spectacles on the often large and utterly engrossed audiences that had "had no food for hours, but [did] not wish to eat?"[91] To be sure, *Bezbozhnik* and various provincial newspapers frequently offered examples of how disputes drained support for the religious cause. Some peasants expressed an interest in *Bezbozhnik*.[92] Some disputes apparently swelled the membership of antireligious cells: in 1925, a correspondent for *Bezbozhnik* claimed that a dispute in the ODGB cell in Orel had increased the number of non-Party members from thirteen to thirty-six.[93] Attending disputes catalyzed epiphanies in which villagers left religious organizations (e.g., the collective of believers) and were "born again" as *bezbozhniki*.[94] Antireligious correspondents alleged that Komsomoltsy successfully confronted rural clergy during disputes. One correspondent, for example, noted that the priest in the village Soglasovka (Serdobsk *uezd*, Saratov province) was "living well" until the organization of the Komsomol began. As evidence of this institutional development on the life of the priest, he cited the staging of disputes. During the winter of 1923–24, he maintained, the priest "had to listen to many unpleasant things" at these events. In fact, this priest, aware that revenues from his parishioners had decreased and that the number of faithful was declining, fled to a neighboring village, where he received land and 1,000 poods of bread.[95] Antireligious correspondents also provided less concrete and therefore less convincing indications of the contributions of disputes to the antireligious cause. In 1923, a writer for

88. See Stites, *Revolutionary Dreams*, p. 107.
89. Father Trophimus, "Russian Religion," pp. 84–85.
90. Trotsky believed that cinema could easily satisfy workers' need for visual stimulation and entertainment, a need previously satisfied by Orthodoxy. See his "Vodka, Cinema, and the Church," in William G. Rosenberg, ed., *Bolshevik Visions: First Phase of the Cultural Revolution in Soviet Russia* (Ann Arbor, Mich., 1984), pp. 371–74.
91. Father Trophimus, "Russian Religion," pp. 84–85.
92. *Bezbozhnik*, July 29, 1923.
93. *Bezbozhnik*, February 1, 1925, p. 7.
94. *Bezbozhnik*, May 27, 1923, p. 3, and May 17, 1925, p. 6.
95. *Sovetskaia derevnia*, May 22, 1924, p. 4.

Bezbozhnik claimed that "the army of *bezbozhniki* grows after each dispute" but gave no examples to support his assertions.[96] Following an antireligious discussion on January 7, 1925, "many peasants" in the village Buchka (Chernigov province) "took to the side of the *bezbozhniki*."[97] According to another correspondent, in 1925 *bezbozhniki* "won" a well-attended dispute, "Did Christ exist?" which concluded the anti-Christmas campaign in Orel. Villagers, he claimed, "were dissatisfied" that local clergy failed to make an appearance.[98] Provincial correspondents may have reverted to such abstract claims because the *actual* effectiveness of such disputes was so much less than they hoped, some relatively small successes notwithstanding.

Antireligious disputes, as a rule, hardly proved to be the celebrations of cultural transformation that activists so hoped (and even believed) they would be. The activists who staged and "performed" at these disputes had themselves partly to blame for this disappointing record, for they often arrived unprepared—if they arrived at all.[99] Speaking in 1929 at the Second All-Union Congress of the League of the Militant Godless, its leader Emel'ian Iaroslavskii felt compelled to remind his audience that antireligious workers had to prepare for disputes.[100] Even when antireligious workers did show up and came well prepared, they often proved to be no match for the clergy and for the lay members of the community who came to their aid.[101] (Diocesan gazettes, such as *Permskie eparkhial'nye vedomosti*, instructed parish clergy to prepare for antireligious disputes by reading antireligious literature.)[102] During the rapid-fire question-and-answer exchanges, antireligious activists were often unable to give the crowd convincing answers; moreover, some of their answers and nonanswers sent the audience into hysterical, shaming fits of laughter.[103]

One very interesting strategy adopted by the clergy and laity involved attempts to synthesize religious beliefs and scientific findings. During a debate in the town of Sumoe in 1925, a member of an evangelical sect maintained that ancient Egyptian priests had discovered electricity. Making quite a

---

96. *Bezbozhnik*, May 27, 1923, p. 4.
97. *Bezbozhnik*, January 18, 1925, pp. 4–5.
98. *Bezbozhnik*, February 1, 1925, p. 7.
99. For examples of poor turn-outs of *bezbozhniki* themselves, see, for example, *Bezbozhnik*, May 10, 1925, p. 7.
100. E. Iaroslavskii, *Razvernutym frontom. O zadachakh i metodakh antireligioznoi propagandy. (Doklad na vtorom vsesoiuznom s"ezde soiuza bezbozhnikov)* (Moscow, 1929), p. 96.
101. For an example see *Bezbozhnik*, January 18, 1925, pp. 3–5. According to Pospielovsky, Renovationist priests participated in disputes more visibly and frequently than their Patriarchal counterparts. See *Russian Church*, 1:86.
102. See *VRSKhD*, October 1928, p. 16.
103. For an example of Archbishop Vvedensky's astute performance and the crowd's reaction, see Stites, *Revolutionary Dreams*, p. 107.

logical leap, he claimed that Jesus had ascended to heaven with the aid of electricity.[104] Disputes also catalyzed clergy to make syncretic pronouncements on the compatibility of religious belief and elements of Bolshevik political culture. On May 15, 1925, at a dispute on the theme "Religion—the Narcotic of Humanity," a priest asserted that Lenin admitted the existence of God.[105]

Leaders of the antireligious campaign were well aware of the various factors that handicapped *bezbozhniki* at disputes. Recounting the discussion at the 1925 conference of the ODGB, Mikhail Gorev (a member of its Central Committee) claimed that demonstrating the effectiveness of modern agricultural techniques "would attract the sympathies of peasants to us one hundred times faster than ten disputes with priests, which are still badly organized."[106] What Gorev and others were much less willing to admit openly was the *damage* that antireligious disputes did to their cause. Notwithstanding the small successes that they yielded, in the main, antireligious disputes turned out to be celebrations not of young *bezbozhniki*'s heroic overcoming of patriarchal religiosity and of the birth of a new society but painful lessons in the difficulty—and the ironies—of cultural transformation. Even when *bezbozhniki* declared themselves the victors in a particular debate, they probably still lost the war, their provocative techniques causing in many deeper alienation from the godless and their goals of cultural transformation. Disputes brought into the open the conflict over religious practice and belief, an issue brewing in the Russian village since the last decades of the tsarist period. But our limited evidence suggests that the *bezbozhniki*, by using intentionally provocative techniques, only hardened the increasingly irreconcilable stances of the opposing contingents.[107]

Practicing Pious Atheism

Secular holiday celebrations proved to be even more intense episodes of cultural confrontation than antireligious debates. During the first Komsomol Christmas, held in January 1923 in cities, towns, and even large villages

---

104. *Bezbozhnik*, January 18, 1925, p. 3.
105. *Petrovskaia kommuna*, May 21, 1924, p. 4.
106. *Bezbozhnik*, May 17, 1925. For more biographical details on Gorev, a former priest, see Daniel Peris, "Commissars in Red Cassocks: Former Priests in the League of the Militant Godless," *Slavic Review* 54 (Summer 1995), esp. 344–48.
107. For one such evaluation, which *may* have reflected the biases of the observer, see Father Trophimus, "Russian Religion," pp. 84–85.

throughout Russia, Komsomoltsy and other participants carried out activities that mocked and blasphemed both Orthodox and pagan religiosity. Festivities varied somewhat from place to place, but burning religious effigies, performing skits that ridiculed and mocked religious belief, delivering lectures on the absurdity of the biblical story of creation, and carrying out processions of atheistic "icons" (e.g., antireligious posters and caricatures of Orthodox priests) were consistently popular activities.[108] Both the Central Committee and the Komsomol leadership issued directives to subdue various elements (such as street processions) of what appeared to be harsh episodes of pure antireligiosity.[109]

Even as the secular clergy, like their French revolutionary forebears, mocked and blasphemed religion, they exhibited a fidelity to certain aspects of religious belief, feeling, and ritual. One extremely fascinating case in point was in fact the burning of religious effigies: Komsomoltsy were almost certainly invoking the popular Orthodox notion of fire as a purifying agent in order to cleanse Russian cities and villages of profane adoration of transcendent beings. Nor was this the only case of ritualistic inversion. As James von Geldern has noted, "Readings from enlightened scientists replaced the scriptures, agit-verses stood in for the old hymns, and modern medicine and technology were forwarded as a substitute for backwardness."[110] The "secular" substitution for the traditional procession of the cross and icons (*krestnyi khod*) was the procession, which featured antireligious posters and caricatures of religious figures as secular icons. Developing and executing this secular liturgy and holiday celebration, antireligious activists preserved the form and function that had existed in the original religious version. Fire still purified, antireligious posters were designed to lead the viewer instantaneously to a secular state of grace, and secular hymns and scriptures were to produce faith in the "plans and recipes" of Bolshevism.[111] In other words, the architects and executioners poured a secular content into formal structures that had their origin in Orthodox Christianity, especially village Orthodoxy. The "deep structure" of Komsomol Christmas and Easter celebrations was religious.[112]

---

108. See, for example, *Sovetskaia derevnia*, January 18, 1924. A perceptive discussion of the futurist origins and of the process of Komsomol Christmas, which informs some of my analysis, can also be found in James von Geldern, *Bolshevik Festivals, 1917–1920* (Berkeley, Calif., 1993), p. 217. See also Curtiss, *Russian Church*, p. 203. Likewise, during the French Revolution (1793–94), mockery, especially of religion, sometimes characterized revolutionary festivals in villages. See Mona Ozouf, *Festivals and the French Revolution* (Cambridge, Mass., 1988), esp. pp. 88–89, 93–94.
109. Curtiss, *Russian Church*, pp. 202–3; Alekseev, *Shturm nebes otmeniaetsia?* pp. 30–32, 40.
110. Von Geldern, *Bolshevik Festivals*, p. 217.
111. Orthodox icons were said to lead their viewers to an instantaneous state of grace.
112. This is an adaptation of Martin Malia's distinction between the "formal tenets" and

Why, then, did antireligious leaders and rural (as well as urban) religious activists grant Komsomol Christmas and Easter celebrations this quasi-religious deep structure? Were this deep structure and this ritualistic inversion merely coincidental, the product of an attempt to offer the masses carnivalistic entertainment at the holidays? Or can the festivities be read for information about the identities of their creators, as well as for information about how they perceived the task of cultural transformation that lay before them? Finally, what was the impact of Komsomol Christmas and Easter celebrations on village religiosity, and also on rural social relations?

Antireligious leaders had, to be sure, pragmatic reasons for launching Komsomol Christmas celebrations. At least to some extent the creation of the antireligious activist Ivan Skvortsov-Stepanov, the general plan for a Komsomol Christmas "carnival" was approved at a "special conference of Communist antireligious workers" held in 1922.[113] What was behind this decision? To be sure, antireligious and Komsomol leaders were well aware of the increased drinking and "hooliganism" (directed against the clergy and the church) of Komsomoltsy during the holidays. They thus faced the challenge of how to channel effectively the often overzealous energies of Komsomoltsy, some of whom had indeed served in the Red Army, into the antireligious campaign.[114]

But why channel those energies into antireligious carnivals timed to coincide with traditional Orthodox holidays? In exploring this issue, we should remember that many Komsomol and antireligious leaders had only recently broken their own formal attachments to Orthodox belief, ritual, and "feeling," if, indeed, they had indeed done so at all. A significant number of antireligious leaders and rural activists were former members of the clergy.[115] The deep structure of Komsomol Christmas and Easter celebrations thus in part reflected this lack of a complete separation from attachment to religious belief, feeling, and ritual. For some of the scriptwriters and performers, it may also have reflected their underlying conception of "secular" holiday celebrations as a *purification* of religion, which echoes Shakhnovich's description of the antireligious campaign as "our reformation."[116]

They incorporated this deep structure for practical reasons as well. Some Russian Marxists, taking their cues from Marx himself, had long conceived

---

"deep structures" of Marxism, as elaborated upon in *Soviet Tragedy*, pp. 36–38 and passim.

113. Curtiss, *Russian Church*, p. 202.

114. Demobilized Red Army soldiers who had been Komsomoltsy or Communists had an erratic commitment to Party organizations when they returned to their villages. See *Izvestiia Atkarskogo uezdnogo ispolkoma*, November 25, 1922, and *Izvestiia Saratovskogo soveta*, December 5, 1923, p. 4. For more on the demobilization of Red Army soldiers, see von Hagen, *Soldiers in the Proletarian Dictatorship*, esp. pp. 295–308.

115. Peris, "Commissars in Red Cassocks," p. 341.

116. Interview with Shakhnovich of October 2, 1987.

of religion in instrumental terms.[117] Locating the emotionally cathartic (and addictively numbing) properties of Russian Orthodoxy in its rich visual texture and pageantry and its sociability, Trotsky claimed that cinema could replace it.[118] When antireligious activists and fellow travelers imbued Komsomol Christmas and Easter with theatrical and carnivalistic elements, they were most likely drawing on this conception of religion.

Taken by itself, however, this conception of religion cannot explain the form and content of these theater-like events. It cannot explain such phenomena as the ritualistic inversions, the elaborate substitution of secular for sacred liturgy, the burning in effigy of pagan and Orthodox deities. If the purpose of Komsomol Christmas and Easter celebrations had only been to provide surrogate visual stimulation and convivial sociability, then other kinds of public entertainment—such as cinema—could have sufficed. What distinguished the kind of entertainment that Komsomol Christmas and Easter celebrations offered was the "concentration of hostile extremes" in form and content: the juxtaposition of the secularized shell of Orthodox rituals (e.g., the *krestnyi khod* with blasphemous costumes and antireligious posters, and so on.).[119] (As Figure 2 suggests, even the antireligious posters themselves inverted elements of Orthodox iconography.) Thus, Komsomol Christmas and Easter celebrations were the descendants of Russian futurists' artistic works, plays and poems that expressed the notion that revolutionary apocalypse can emerge only out of intense conflict between inherently polar opposites.[120] And only out of revolutionary apocalypse, presumed the futurists as well as the scriptwriters and performers of Komsomol Christmas and Easter celebrations, could utopia finally burst forth.[121] The secular rituals of Komsomol Christmas and Easter—e.g., the processions, the burning of religious effigies—were thus designed to mark and to create the transition to a utopian society.[122] Taken as a whole, Komsomol Christmas was a ritualistic celebration of a "secular" birth of a religious society, while Komsomol Easter signified the redemption of the new society. In theory, Komsomol Christmas and Easter were thus not only agents of social transformation but also the symbolic celebration of and legitimization of the new order.

    117. See, for example, G. V. Plekhanov, "Materialisticheskoe ponimanie istorii," "O knige L. I. Mechnikova," "Ocherki po istorii materializma," "Neskol'ko slov v zashchitu ekonomicheskogo materializma," and "Pis'ma bez adresa," in *O religii i tserkvi: izbrannye proizvedeniia* (Moscow, 1957), and Lenin, "Sotsializm i religiia," *Novaia zhizn'*, December 30, 1905. Lunacharsky's Godbuilding movement incorporated—with obviously very different results—this belief in religion's emotionally cathartic properties. See his *Religion and Socialism* (St. Petersburg, 1908–11).
    118. "Vodka . . ." in Rosenberg, *Bolshevik Visions*, pp. 371–74.
    119. Von Geldern has used this phrase to describe the content of Mayakovsky's "Mystery-Bouffe." See *Bolshevik Festivals*, p. 66.
    120. On this see ibid., pp. 64–71.
    121. On the unique "utopian strain" in Russian futurism, see ibid., p. 65.
    122. See von Geldern, *Bolshevik Festivals*, p. 142: "Rituals, like drama, mark transition: a change in season, a change in status, a key moment in history."

Fig. 2. "Religion Is the Narcotic of the People." 1920–40. Note the inversion of the icon into an antireligious poster. The page of the "Bible" reads: "The church is a kulak prop. / Endure the kulak levy." The off-center eyes are a deliberate blasphemy. Note also the contrast in shoes: the peasant is wearing peasant shoes made from bast (*lapti*); the priest is wearing shoes that easily cost one hundred times as much. (My thanks to James West for suggesting these points to me.) At the bottom, a quotation from Lenin reminds viewers that "religion teaches humility and patience to those who work their whole lives. Courtesy, Poster Collection, Hoover Institution Archive, Stanford University.

Violence and Redemption

Out in the streets and in the fields, however, some Komsomoltsy and fellow travelers took this notion of the redemptive value of intensely concentrated conflict to a tragic extreme. During secular holiday celebrations, Komsomoltsy and ostensibly non-Party peasant youth—the line was often very difficult to draw—departed from the theatrical script of the carnivalistic festivities and engaged in a variety of extremely intrusive and often violent acts against clergy, lay activists, and religious objects or buildings. (See Figure 3.) Youth of peasant origin in a village in Saratov province, for example, in 1924 staged a confrontation with believers during the celebration of Komsomol Easter. Just as bearded men were leaving the village church, a "battalion" of peasant youth emerged from the nearby people's house (*narodnyi dom*)—the secular analogue of the village church—and confronted them.[123] In other cases the "impatient militants" destroyed or confiscated religious objects ranging from graves to panes of glass in local churches.[124] Why were Party and non-Party youth so intrusive and violent? To be sure, the attacks of these "impatient militants"—to some extent the analogue of the "persecutors" in the dechristianization campaign of the French Revolution—attested to the powerful legacy of the militaristic emphasis on heroic deeds characteristic of the Civil War.[125]

This legacy, however, cannot explain the form of the confrontational and violent acts. What motivated the impatient militants, after all, was not a desire for the maximum possible obliteration of the property of the "enemy." Rather, drawing on and expanding the repertoire of the village hooligans in the very late tsarist period, Party and non-Party youth performed an array of skit-like acts, skits in which violence and confrontation had symbolic meaning. In the case described above, for example, the peasant youths' emergence from the people's house was a hostile inversion of the adult peasants' simultaneous departure from the village church. That carefully orchestrated

---

123. *Petrovskaia kommuna*, May 11, 1924, p. 3.
124. See, for example, *Bezbozhnik*, March 8, 1925, p. 7, and July 18, 1926.
125. Categorizing dechristianizers during the French Revolution, Michel Vovelle distinguished between "persecutors" and "apostles," the latter desiring to eliminate superstition through propaganda. See *Religion et révolution*, pp. 261–65. As most of these Komsomols would not necessarily have served in the Red Army, their violently confrontational stance, we can speculate, reflected their memory of the violence of the Civil War and/or displaced anger toward the power structure of their elders. On the preference of Komsomoltsy for direct and sometimes violent action, see, for example, Smolensk WKP 10, "Protokol no. 17 (zasedanii kollegii agitpropa ot 15-go maia 1924 goda) -2. (Ob uchastii partii i komsomoltsev v prop. rab. Doklad uezdnogo agronoma Timofeeva. Tezisy)."

Fig. 3. "The Defiance of Youth." 1931. A Komsomol member gestures to the heavens in a show of repressed violence. Courtesy, Poster Collection, Hoover Institution Archive, Stanford University.

moment contained the "concentration of hostile extremes."[126] Perpetuating the futurists' theatricalization of the revolution, these "impatient militants" acted out a conviction that the "concentration of hostile extremes" had to be violent. The "impatient militants" thus believed that only a "[*violent*] concentration of hostile extremes" could produce apocalyptic transformation and, later, utopia. For them, violence became a ritual that registered and effected the transition to the new society, allowing them to overcome their elders' opposition.[127]

What, prior to 1925, was the social, cultural, and political impact of Komsomol Christmas and Easter celebrations in the Russian countryside? As a rule, we cannot know directly what we most want to know: What did peasants and other villagers think and feel as they watched or heard about Komsomol Christmas and Easter celebrations? What we do have, however, is evidence about how villagers acted in response to such events. As with debates, there is little doubt that these early celebrations of Komsomol Christmas and Easter brought some small successes, the boastful exaggeration of antireligious and provincial newspapers notwithstanding. To be sure, an antireligious correspondent in Tula province was most likely exaggerating when, discussing the 1922–23 celebrations of Komsomol Easter and Christmas in Tula district, he claimed that "the broad antireligious movement" was "also attracting the adult peasantry."[128] Even if the occasional adult peasant who attended such festivities did not leave them fully "de-converted," his or her attendance was by itself a victory for the antireligious cause.[129] This was especially so because many of the activities were intentionally focused on youth (as well as soldiers and workers), rather than those who because of their strong religious commitments, real or presumed, required patience and persistence on the part of the *bezbozhnik*—e.g., women, older male peasants.[130] Antireligious activists took heart when older male peasants showed up at such events; clergy, of course, were alarmed.

These small successes paled, however, next to the overwhelmingly hostile reaction of most peasants and other villagers. It is, of course, very difficult to distinguish between the impact of the violent and intrusive confrontations

---

126. On ritualistic inversion, see Natalie Davis, *Society and Culture in Early Modern France* (Stanford, Calif., 1975).

127. On the communicative functions of violence, see Davis, "Rites of Violence," in *Society and Culture*, pp. 152–87.

128. *Bednota*, July 17, 1923; *Bezbozhnik*, July 19, 1925, p. 3. On the failure of antireligious holidays such as Komsomol Christmas and Easter to attract adult peasants, see Murin, *Byt i nravy*, pp. 42–43.

129. *Bednota*, July 17, 1923. See also *Bezbozhnik*, June 27, 1923, p. 4.

130. See, for example, *Bezbozhnik*, May 1, 1923 and *Krasnye rezervy*, January 4, 1923, p. 2.

of the "impatient militants" and the offensive form and content of the carnivalistic festivities themselves. When villagers murdered Communists during the secular holiday celebrations, their sense of justice had most likely been inflamed by a combination of such confrontational and violent activities.[131] To be sure, most reactions were not this extreme. One striking feature of Komsomol Christmas and Easter celebrations was the on-the-spot mobilization and defensive tactics of clergy. During the 1923-24 celebration of Komsomol Christmas in Novouzensk (Saratov province), unidentified *bezbozhniki* gave daily antireligious lectures on such topics as "the creation of the world in six days," "with fire and blood in the name of God," and "on the immaculate conception." While Komsomoltsy, non-Party youth, peasants, and white-collar workers (*sluzhashchie*) listened to the talks, clergy filed by "and tried to defend religion."[132] Rather than eliminating social difference and alienation, as antireligious leaders and rural activists hoped and assumed they would, Komsomol Christmas and Easter debates produced intensified social, cultural, and (eventually) political conflict.

These same leaders and rural activists became, in fact, quite worried about the celebrations' intense and sometimes tragic polarization of village life.[133] Occasionally, a provincial antireligious correspondent would cheer the violent and intrusive acts of Komsomol and non-Party youth. But most shared one correspondent's anxiety that "these incidents do not qualify as [part of] the battle against religion, but rather as its consolidation."[134] Such perceptions were echoed in the highest echelons of the Communist Party; a resolution of the Twelfth Party Congress (1923) asserted that "rough methods [and] the ridicule of objects and ceremonies . . . do not accelerate, but aggravate the liberation of the toiling masses from religious prejudice."[135] Convinced that Komsomol Christmas and Easter were not only sabotaging the antireligious campaign from within but also polarizing rural social and political relations, antireligious leaders such as Iaroslavskii chose to discontinue such activities after 1923-24.[136] Even Skvortsov-Stepanov eventually

---

131. For cases of murder in connection with Komsomol Christmas, see von Geldern, *Bolshevik Festivals*, p. 217.

132. *Sovetskaia derevnia*, January 18, 1924.

133. See, for example *Bezbozhnik*, May 10, 1925, p. 7.

134. For an example of an antireligious correspondent praising rural Komsomoltsy for destroying a chapel, see *Bezbozhnik*, March 8, 1925, p. 7. For correspondents' critiques of such tactics, see ibid., May 10, 1925. At the Second All-Union Congress of the League of the Godless in 1929, Iaroslavskii recounted the case of a Communist from Kaluga province who was expelled from the Party for playing a harmonica in the street on Easter morning. See *Stenograficheskii otchet vtorogo vsesoiuznogo s"ezda soiuza voinstvuiushchikh bezbozhnikov* (Moscow,1930), p. 50.

135. *KPSS v rezoliutsiiakh* (Moscow, 1970), 2:470.

136. *Bezbozhnik*, April 26, 1925, p. 5. On some Smolensk province Komsomol leaders' opposition to secular holiday celebrations, see Tirado, "The Revolution," p. 104.

branded Komsomol Christmas and Easter celebrations failed experiments.[137] To be sure, Komsomol activists in the provinces chose to disregard Moscow's new policy, which combined the de jure abandonment of such celebrations with emphasis on distributing antireligious literature of a "popular-scientific nature," as well as material "illustrating the history and origin of religion."[138] The central Komsomol leadership only called for the renewal of Komsomol Easter and Christmas celebrations in 1928.[139]

In sum, prior to the creation of the League of the Godless in 1925, what was the impact of antireligious activities on religious life and village sociopolitical relations? As we have seen, Party and Komsomol members, as well as members of other rural antireligious cells and circles, conducted very little day-to-day antireligious activity. Rather, most antireligious activity— whether antireligious "conversations" in the village, lectures, debates, the opening of relics, and Komsomol Christmas and Easter celebrations—followed a "campaign" model. Sporadic in its nature, such varied activity nevertheless did score some small successes, especially in larger villages and towns. There were certainly cases, although rather isolated, of professed "conversions" to atheism, though many appeared to be short-lived. There is some evidence that adult smallholder peasants were among those who began to pass through the stages of conversion to atheism: flirtation with the sporadically present subculture, doubts about religious belief and practice, rejection of elements of religious belief and practice, and—in rarer cases— participation in antireligious activities. Taken by themselves, such small successes did not pose a significant threat to the viability of the rural parish, but they caused significant anxiety in the clergy and lay activists. Yet in some cases, they even created the very results they were designed to avert: a strengthening of religious commitment. In fact, to varying degrees such activities only increased the social, cultural, and political conflict that the issue of religious belief and practice had been generating in the village since the end of the tsarist period. Komsomol Christmas and Easter celebrations, as well as the violent and intrusive skirmishes of the "impatient militants," exemplified these dynamics in a more pronounced way than other antireligious activities.

The overwhelmingly young and male antireligious activists were not, prior to 1925, the heroic creators of a utopia of the irreligious sons. No new society, distinguished by the absence of social, cultural, and political difference and alienation, formed around the antireligious activists.[140] Rather, they were

137. See I. I. Skvortsov-Stepanov, *Izbrannye ateisticheskie proizvedeniia* (Moscow, 1959), p. 489.
138. *KPSS v resoliutsiiakh* (Moscow, 1970), 2:470.
139. See Pospielovsky, *Soviet Antireligious Campaigns*, 2:42–44.
140. This analysis incorporates insights from Hunt, *The Family Romance of the French Revolution*. See especially p. 44.

left feeling the longing for social, cultural, and political transformation more deeply than at the outset of NEP. (Analogously, activists probably also felt this longing *more* acutely at the conclusion of a given type of antireligious activity or round of antireligious "campaigning.") In the process of their efforts to achieve such transformation, the opposition of the patriarchs (and the matriarchs) had become more determined and potent. Would the outcome be different after 1925, the year the League of the Godless was founded and the Party adopted its "face to the countryside" policy?

4

CIRCLING THE HEAVENS

The creation in 1924–25 of the League of the Godless, an all-Union "voluntary" organization to disseminate antireligious propaganda, was part of a fundamental shift in the Party's policy toward the peasantry. With the alliance (*smychka*) between workers and peasants jeopardized by the so-called "scissors crisis" of 1923–24, Party leaders reevaluated policy toward the peasantry and Party strategy for long-term economic growth.[1] One cornerstone of this policy shift was the "revival of the soviets," which Kalinin called "one of the enormous political campaigns." The "revival of the soviets" was part of a plan to make the village soviet the center of the "building of socialism" in the countryside. (See Figure 4.) The policy sought to empower the soviet at the expense of the village assembly, thereby eliminating "dual power" in the village. Through greater participation in the village soviets, poor and middle peasants would "acquire the skills necessary for the

---

1. During the so-called scissors crisis, as the gap between the increasingly high prices for industrial goods and the increasingly low prices for agricultural goods widened, the regime faced the danger that procurement levels of grain would fall dangerously low. The worst point of the crisis was October 1923. On what came to be called the "industrialization debates," see Moshe Lewin, *Political Undercurrents in Soviet Economic Debates: From Bukharin to Modern Reformers* (Princeton, N.J., 1974); E. H. Carr, *Socialism in One Country*, vol. 1 (London, 1958); and Siegelbaum, *Soviet State and Society*, pp. 165–80.

Fig. 4. "Fulfill Lenin's Precepts." 1929. This poster was part of the Party's campaign to make the village soviet the center of the building of socialism in the countryside. The slogan in the upper right reads: "The Village Soviet Is the Master of the Countryside." The bottom slogan reads: "Strengthen the Alliance of the City and the Countryside." Courtesy, Poster Collection, Hoover Institution Archive, Stanford University. Artist: P. Smukrovich.

business of state administration." They would in turn develop the political consciousness that was both the precondition for, and result of, their "growing into socialism."[2]

Closely related in spirit was a sloganistic policy known as "Face to the Countryside." On one level, "Face to the Countryside" consisted of a series of short-term economic concessions to the peasantry (e.g., a lower tax rate and increased provisions for hiring labor and leasing land).[3] But the economic concessions were not only to patch up the *smychka*. They qualified as part of a long-term strategy for generating the agricultural productivity needed to support industrial development. At the same time, "Face" was to provide the general political framework out of which peasants would ultimately, as Bukharin put it, "grow into socialism."

One component of that political framework was the formal renunciation of the methods of War Communism at the Fourteenth Party Congress (April

2. The first quotation is from Siegelbaum, *Soviet State and Society*, p. 141. See also *Vlast' sovetov*, January–June 1925, p. 7.
3. See Siegelbaum, *Soviet State and Society*, p. 140.

1925).⁴ Worried, as Bukharin put it, about "losing the masses," the Party instructed rural Party cadres to replace the tendency to give the population harsh orders (*prikazy*) with a policy of persuasion, proof, example, and the demonstration of its agenda for rural politics.⁵ Another important component of "face to the countryside" was the voluntary association. Bukharin, one of (if not *the*) chief architects of "face to the countryside," called for the creation and expansion of "all types of voluntary circles, societies . . . and groups for agricultural propaganda, for fighting alcoholism, against smoking, societies for rural amenities, for cooperative assistance, and so forth."⁶ Just as peasants' involvement in cooperatives would dissolve peasant economic "pettiness" and the pernicious influence of the kulak, so too would their involvement in other voluntary organizations alter the structure of their mental calculations and link them more and more to the state.⁷ Shedding the local attachments so characteristic of peasant life, they would instead think of themselves as national political actors, as members of a Soviet "civil community."⁸ The voluntary associations thus exemplified the key premise underlying "face to the countryside": the abandonment of the quest for instantaneous control of behavior (e.g., rejection of War Communist methods, rough tactics in antireligious work, restrictions on use of hired labor) in favor of peasants' (and others') involvement in formal structures (cooperatives, village soviets, voluntary societies that would gradually produce a transformation in consciousness).⁹ The creation of the League of the Godless—only one of the many voluntary associations that appeared in the mid-1920s—was thus part of what Bukharin and others thought of as a policy that would yield greater, not less, control of society.¹⁰ Was this

---

4. Although not technically correct, the policy of "revival of the soviets" was often equated rhetorically with abandoning the methods of War Communism. For examples, see *Bol'shevik*, September 15, 1926, pp. 5–6; ibid., July 30, 1925, p. 3; and B. Levin and I. Suvorov, "Sovety i stroitel'stvo sotsializma," in E. Pashukanis, ed., *15 let sovetskogo stroitel'stva* (Moscow, 1932), p. 422.

5. Bukharin, in *Bol'shevik*, 7–8 (1924): 24. Similarly, Mendel M. Khataevich, leader of the *apparat* in Ukraine and elsewhere, criticized Party cells for their lack of persistent everyday work "toward the attraction of support, toward the rallying of the best strata of the countryside around us." Khataevich, in *Bol'shevik*, 3–4 (1925): 80. He was secretary of the Party in Odessa province in 1923 and in 1925 was elected secretary of the Tatar *oblast'* Party Committee. From 1928 to 1932 he served as secretary of the Central Volga *krai* Party Committee. See also "Voprosy provedeniia," ibid., July 30, 1925, p. 3.

6. Quoted in Siegelbaum, *Soviet State and Society*, pp. 139–40.

7. The classic treatise on the unique forms of peasant economic rationality is A. V. Chaianov, *Chayanov: The Theory of Peasant Economy*, trans. and ed. D. Thorner, B. Kerblay, and R.E.F. Smith (Homewood, Ill., 1966; reprint, Madison, Wis., 1987).

8. Siegelbaum, *Soviet State and Society*, p. 139.

9. *Korenizatsiia*—"implanting" ethnic nationals on a quota basis within the Party, state apparatus, educational institutions, and judiciary in any given national territory (e.g, Soviet Armenia)—was also an example of this approach.

10. Siegelbaum, *Soviet State and Society*, p. 136. Those voluntary associations included the

expectation justified? This chapter examines the League's impact on the village from 1925 to the Party's abandonment of NEP in 1928–29.

The avowed goals of the League of the Godless reflected this Bukharinist vision of the role of the voluntary society in socialist transformation. To be sure, in the short run League members were to conduct antireligious activities—distributing the newspaper *Bezbozhnik* and other antireligious publications, holding antireligious lectures (often called "evenings"), facilitating the closing of churches, and so on—in order to combat religious behavior. But the League was to do much more than combat these external signs of religiosity. True victory, at least according to the official manifestos of the League's leadership, meant a transformation in consciousness; it meant exchanging the "plans and recipes" of rural Orthodoxy for those of "scientific materialism."[11] More was involved than just giving up religious practice and belief: the "godless agenda" also implicitly and often explicitly mandated that peasants learn to read, practice modern agricultural techniques, and acquire a new, sometimes Taylorist conception of time.[12] In other words, the leaders of the League were after a cultural transformation in the Geertzian sense of the concept of culture.[13]

The intended structure of the League in turn reflected this ambitious goal.

---

following: ODSK (Obshchestvo druzei sovetskogo kino, or Society of the Friends of Soviet Film); ODN (Obshchestvo Doloi negramotnost' or Society for the End of Illiteracy, founded in 1923); and ODVF (Obshchestvo druzei vozdushnogo flota, or Society of the Friends of the Air Force, 1923). Other voluntary associations included the ODD (Obshchestvo druzei detei, or Society of the Friends of Children); Dobrokhim (Society of the Friends of Chemistry, 1924); ODR (Obshchestvo druzei radio, or Society of the Friends of Radio); Novyi byt—New Everyday Life; ODP (Obshchestvo doloi prestupnost', or the Society to End Crime); Obshchestvo smychka goroda s derevnei, or Society for the Alliance of the City and the Countryside; and OPS (Obshchestvo pomoshchi studenchestvu, or Society to Aid Students). On Osoaviakhim, a voluntary society of 1927 that represented a merger of the ODVF and DobroKhim, see William Odom, *The Soviet Volunteers: Modernization and Bureaucracy in a Public Mass Organization* (Princeton, N.J., 1973). Some voluntary associations, such as the International Organization to Assist Fighters of Revolution (MOPR), created in 1922, had appeared significantly before the shift in Party policy of 1924–25. Even those associations having an ostensibly "apolitical" theme, such as the Society of the Friends of Children (ODD), were to contribute to political, social, and cultural transformation in the ways that Bukharin and others anticipated. Siegelbaum, by contrast, claims that some voluntary associations "were composed primarily of non-communists and were essentially apolitical" (*Soviet State and Society*, p. 136). This may have been true in practice. But in theory all voluntary associations had a clear political purpose.

11. See, for example, E. Iaroslavskii, *Religiia i R.K.P.* (Moscow, 1925), and *Protiv religii i tserkvi*, 3 vols. (Moscow, 1932–35).

12. On Lenin's interest in Taylorist notions of time, see Hanson, *Time and Revolution*, pp. 97–98, 109, 124–25.

13. Even before the League was created, there was extensive controversy over the means, goals, and institutional incarnation of antireligious activism. The major antagonists were Iaroslavskii, who believed that the dissemination of antireligious propaganda would ensure the

The League was to be a pyramid-like structure whose various organizational units—a Moscow national office, regional councils, and local cells—were to paper the entire USSR.[14] According to the organizational charter (*ustav*) of the League, cells were to be supervised by councils on the district (*uezd*) or *raion* levels, which were in turn to be directed by councils at the level of the *guberniia* (province) and *oblast'*.[15] The structure of the League thus presumed the existence of a kind of antireligious vanguard, whose already considerable scientific-materialist consciousness would prompt them to join the League voluntarily. The antireligious activities of this vanguard, composed of some Party members but mostly non-Party activists, would both purify their own scientific materialism and help others make the same journey. The implicit vision of the League's charter was that no individual—and certainly no Russian peasant—was to remain untouched by the antireligious campaign.

The Hapless Crusaders

To what extent did the actual structure of the League replicate this vision during NEP? Was it an improvement over the ODGB? At the highest level,

---

victory of a "scientific-materialist world view," and the Moscow Party activist Mariia Mikhailovna Kostelovskaia, who favored "rough methods" such as closing churches and eliminating priests—that is, actions designed to bring a quick secularization. While Iaroslavskii and his backers insisted on the need to train antireligious cadres (*bezbozhniki*) specially equipped for antireligious agitation by their knowledge of Orthodoxy, religious history, and science, Kostelovskaia countered that Party members with no special training could do the job. Kostelovskaia was the editor of the journal *Bezbozhnik* (later *Bezbozhnik u stanka*), which toed her line on religion and on the creation of the atheistic society from its appearance in January 1923. Each of the antagonists had an institutional power base; Kostelovskaia's was the Moscow Party, Iaroslavskii's, the Antireligious Commission, the ODGB, and eventually the League. See Delaney, "Origins," pp. 103–30. More details can be found in Peris, "Storming the Heavens," pp. 83–103. On the reemergence of the Iaroslavskii-Kostelovskaia antagonism at the League's second conference in 1929, see Daniel Peris, "The 1929 Congress of the Godless," *Soviet Studies* 43:4 (1991): 711–32.

14. Periodically reelected "councils" (*sovety*) were to exist on the level of the *uezd*, *raion*, and province. *Uezd* and *raion* councils were to range between five and seven individuals. Provincial councils were to be larger. The League was to be financed in good part from the collection of dues, which were set at five kopecks per month; in practice, members were very remiss in paying their dues. There were fifty or more salaried activists paid in part with funds controlled by the Central Committee of the League. Other income was to come from selling anti-religious propaganda. For these and other details, see Curtiss, *Russian Church*, esp. p. 206; *Kak stroit' soiuz bezbozhnikov* (Moscow, 1927); and Adolf Ziegler, *Die russische Gottlosenbewegung* (Munich, 1932), pp. 51–64.

15. See *Ustav soiuza bezbozhnikov SSSR* (Moscow, 1925).

this unfinished business involved the creation of bureaus of the League for the provinces. The first efforts in this regard followed the creation of the League in February–March 1925 and its first conference in April of that year.[16] During the first few months of 1925 antireligious cadres established such organizational bureaus in several provinces; the first provincial council appeared in Leningrad.[17] In February, representatives who attended a meeting of the Agitprop department of the provincial Party committee in Pskov created a provisional provincial council of the League.[18] By March, unnamed personnel were in the process of establishing an analogous organization in Kursk.[19] A provisional organizational bureau appeared in Briansk province in June.[20] Another organizational spurt followed the Central Committee's Anti-Religious Conference, held in April 1926, and lasted until the end of that summer; in fact, the ineffectiveness of the League was one of the main themes of that conference.[21] Yet the creation of provincial councils continued over the next several years. Thus a provincial council of the League did not appear in Saratov until the beginning of 1927.[22] The creation of councils on the district and *okrug* levels followed the same general rhythm but at a slower pace.[23] It was common for members of councils on the level of the district or *okrug* to feel ignored by their supervisory councils.[24]

Cadres struggling to create cells in the village were even more isolated. Red Army veterans often began to spread the godless "message" even before an antireligious cell existed; a former antireligious correspondent claimed that the creation of an antireligious network went most smoothly in those regions with a high percentage of former soldiers; it met with great resistance in Riazan province, whose villages had reabsorbed few former soldiers.[25]

16. *Antireligioznik*, May 1926, p. 18; for more details, see Peris, "Storming the Heavens," pp. 116–25.
17. *Bezbozhnik*, May 15, 1927, p. 7.
18. *Bezbozhnik*, February 21, 1926, p. 8. For more details on the development of the League's organizational structure in Pskov, see also Peris, "Storming the Heavens," pp. 118–19.
19. *Bezbozhnik*, March 7, 1926.
20. *Bezbozhnik*, November 1, 1925.
21. See A. Lukachevskii, "Antireligioznoe soveshchanie pri agitprope TsK VKP(b)," *Antireligioznik*, May 1926, p. 18. On this organizational flurry, see Peris, "Storming the Heavens," p. 116.
22. *Sovetskaia derevnia*, December 30, 1926, p. 3.
23. For example, antireligious workers in the newly formed Lower Volga region (*krai*) did not establish councils of the League on the *okrug* level until the end of 1928 and the beginning of 1929. *Povolzhskaia pravda*, March 8, 1929, p. 3. In Leningrad province, some district councils formed as early as 1925. For details, see *Bezbozhnik*, May 17, 1925. See also Peris, "Storming the Heavens," chap. 4.
24. For an example, see *Povolzhskaia pravda*, May 23, 1929, p. 3.
25. See, for example, *Krest'ianskaia pravda*, February 22, 1928; interview of October 2, 1987, with Mikhail Shakhnovich. When pressed, even Shakhnovich admitted that a large

There was no uniform way in which these veterans and other antireligious activists—mainly Party members and Komsomoltsy, but also teachers—created cells.[26] In a good many cases, Party members created cells of the League that were attached to existing Party cells and reading huts, an effort in which district and county Agitprop departments led the way.[27] Most likely prompted by Party members and Komsomoltsy, villagers sometimes decided to create cells of the League at meetings of the village assembly or general gathering.[28] Yet the impact of such cadres (often outsiders in the village) was indeed erratic, for in other cases village *bezbozhniki* suggested the formation of cells and the acceleration of antireligious work, only to find their initiatives ignored by cadres higher up in the Party.[29] Just as prior to the proclamation of "face to the countryside" and the creation of the League, Party members and Komsomoltsy continued to be constrained in creating cells (and in other antireligious efforts) by their own religious commitments, weak institutional infrastructures, chronic overwork (*peregruzka*), and low levels of political literacy and education.[30]

Given these constraints, it is hardly surprising that the creation of antireligious cells in rural areas proceeded slowly and unevenly. By January 1, 1926, there were 2,421 cells and 87,033 members. Between January 1, 1926, and January 1, 1927, the number of cells increased by 700 and the number of members by 51,369. During the next year, the number of members actually decreased from 138,402 to 123,007.[31] Although the structural development of the League varied significantly from province to province

---

supply of veterans could not assure the smooth functioning of the campaign; when asked in which areas godless work proceeded without difficulty, he replied: "It was never easy." He also commented that antireligious work met with great resistance in Tambov province, as a result of the uprisings in 1920–21.

26. See, for example, *Sovetskaia derevnia*, April 25, 1929. On surveys by Narkompros, the League of the Godless, and the Komsomol that revealed the persistence of religious consciousness and practice, see Holmes, *The Kremlin and the Schoolhouse*, p. 102. Even by the mid-1920s, 50 to 70 percent of pupils did not attend school on religious holidays.

27. For examples from Smolensk province, see Smolensk WKP 25, "Akt obsledovaniia leninskoi opornoi iacheiki VKP(b) za period s I/XII-25 g. po I/YI-26 goda," and Smolensk WKP 17, "Zasedaniia agitpropkollegii pri Dukhovshchinskoi volkome VKP(b) 18 sentiabria 1926 goda."

28. For examples, see *Bezbozhnik*, April 25, 1926, and *Izvestiia saratovskogo soveta*, April 14, 1928.

29. See, for example, *Izvestiia saratovskogo soveta*, October 8, 1927, p. 4.

30. On the religious attachments of Party members during the twilight years of NEP and even thereafter, see, for example, *Krest'ianskaia pravda*, May 28, 1929, p. 5.

31. These figures are taken from Curtiss, *Russian Church*, p. 206. In 1929, there were 8,928 cells and 465,498 members. From 1927 to 1931, the number of cells of the League rose from 266 to more than 50,000. See TsGAOR, f. 5407. op. 1, ed. khr. 72, l. 19, as cited in Vorontsov, *Leninskaia programma ateizma*, p. 129.

(or region to region), as a rule parish churches greatly outnumbered the cells.[32] Even as late as 1929, the League's 1,200 cells did not provide an equal institutional counterweight to the roughly 2,000 churches and 2,000 additional prayer houses in the Lower Volga Region.[33] In the years 1925–28, the distribution of cells varied significantly, not only from province to province, but from district to district and even county to county: "Our Prechistoe *volost'* is hardly the most backward in Smolensk province. In many *volosti* there are cells of the League of the Godless, and in some, such as, for instance, Shumiachi, with which we share a border within Roslavl *uezd*, there even are five cells. But in our *volost'*, [which has] an area of twenty versts and six huge parishes, there is not one godless cell."[34] As this candid admission suggests, by 1928, the last year of NEP, antireligious activists still had not created cells of the League in many villages.[35] Antireligious cells varied significantly not only in distribution but in size; there is evidence to suggest that cells in Leningrad province, for example, were considerably larger than those in Saratov province.[36]

In many cases cadres involved in antireligious work at the most basic level of the cell, circle, or club hungered for a closer connection to their supervisory institutions. In 1928, the director of the cultural department (*kul'totdel*)

---

32. A few examples of this disparity must suffice. In 1925, there were 742 "church and religious organizations" in Smolensk province, 648 of them Orthodox and 16 Old Believer, with the rest Protestant, Catholic, and Jewish. As of the same year, the antireligious "army" could claim 964 members. By 1926, this figure had climbed to 2,158; as of January 1, 1927, the Smolensk branch of the League proudly claimed a membership of 4,011, with 389 cells. See *Bezbozhnik*, May 17, 1925. A 1925 survey of the NKVD revealed that during the period from January 1 to November 1, 1925, the number of religious societies increased, with the number of Orthodox parishes, for example, growing by 9 percent. A. Veshchikov, "Etapy bol'shogo puti," *Nauka i religiia* 11 (November 1962). The survey was based on data from twenty-nine provinces of the RSFSR.

33. *Povolzhskaia pravda*, August 14, 1929, p. 3.

34. *Bezbozhnik*, November 15, 1925, p. 6.

35. *Izvestiia Saratovskogo soveta*, January 25, 1928, p. 4, and January 31, 1928, p. 4; *Sovetskaia derevnia*, January 22, 1928.

36. To be sure, this conclusion is only tentative because it is based on a rather small amount of data. The cell in Mikhailova (Mokshan *uezd*, Leningrad province) in 1925 boasted fifty-seven members. Such a large size was not an isolated occurrence: the Kolchanovo cell (Volkhov *uezd*), which had been established in 1925, could claim a membership of fifty-three only one year later. The cell in Petrovsk (Budogoshch' *uezd*, Leningrad region) surpassed all of these with a membership of 130 in 1929. Corresponding information for the Lower Volga region, although based on estimation rather than direct figures, shows an average size of forty-three per cell in Astrakhan *okrug*, thirty-two in Balashov *okrug*, and twenty-seven in Pugachev *okrug* during the year 1929. These statistics on the size of cells in Leningrad province (and region) are drawn from *Bezbozhnik*, May 3, 1925, p. 8, and January 31, 1926, p. 8; the calculation of the sizes of cells in Saratov province is based on figures taken from *Povolzhskaia pravda*, March 8, 1929. Of course this manner of calculation obscures the true size of individual cells.

of the club "Trud i nauka," located in the Lower Volga Region, admitted that "we don't know what to do in that area [antireligious work], we don't know how to begin. The League of the Godless doesn't give us any direction, and we ourselves don't know how to undertake this [kind] of work. We have an antireligious cell, but it still hasn't lifted a finger."[37] Lacking supervision from councils on the level of the district and province, some cells languished and died, only to be resuscitated at a later date during another flurry of organizational activity.[38]

Thus the rural antireligious network remained fragile, erratic, and incomplete right up to the eve of collectivization.[39] While most towns and many large villages had antireligious cells by the very end of NEP, the small village that had, during the first three years of the League's existence, a functioning antireligious cell was the exception, not the rule. To focus only on the limitations of the League's infrastructure in the countryside, however, is to miss the impact of the antireligious "campaign," as it continued to be called, on village life. What, then, was the social, cultural, and political impact of these antireligious cells, as well as of other antireligious activities conducted outside the cells?

Atheism and Power in the Village

The list of activities that cells carried out was, to be sure, often impressively long. Just as they had prior to the League's creation in 1925, cells conducted a variety of activities that fell under the rubric of antireligious activism. They conducted antireligious lessons and lectures, often earmarking these offerings to coincide with religious holidays.[40] Implicitly representing religion as unjust rather than merely superstitious, the Sumsk *okrug* council of the League in 1925 held "agitational trials of religion" that were said to draw

37. *Povolzhskaia pravda*, December 14, 1928, p. 5.
38. On the establishment, disappearance, and reestablishment of the League in the Krasnyi Perekop textile mill (Iaroslavl' province), see Peris, "Storming the Heavens," pp. 147–52.
39. This confirms the reigning historiographical portrait of the underinstitutionalization of the Russian countryside throughout the tsarist and early Soviet periods. On "underinstitutionalization" in the Soviet period, see, for example, Lewin, *Russian Peasants and Soviet Power* and *Making of the Soviet System*, and Taniuchi, *Village Gathering in Russia*. On the late Imperial period, see, for example, S. Frederick Starr, *Decentralization and Self-Government in Russia, 1830–70* (Princeton, N.J., 1972), and George L. Yaney, *The Urge to Mobilize* (Urbana, Ill., 1982).
40. See, for example, *Sovetskaia derevnia*, December 30, 1926, p. 3, and TsGAOR Leningrada, f. 6307, op. 13, ed. khr. 9, ll. 160–61.

Fig. 5. A 1929 wall newspaper *(stengazeta)* of *Bezbozhnik* (The Godless). A special anti-Easter issue. Courtesy, Poster Collection, Hoover Institution Archive, Stanford University.

audiences of 450 on the average.[41] Some rural cells made available copies of *Bezbozhnik*, usually by displaying them as "wall newspapers" (see Figure 5) in the reading hut.[42] On returning to his native village in Voronezh province, one Red Army veteran even took out his own subscription; and reading *Bezbozhnik* was said to have convinced him "that there is no supernatural, god, or devil, and that everything in nature has an explanation."[43]

This soldier's rather formulaic testimony raises a terribly important issue: what impact was *Bezbozhnik* designed to have on the relatively small percentage of villagers who were literate and curious enough to take a look at it?[44] Readers were exposed to a variety of regular features and themes. The newspaper chronicled clerical depravity and greed.[45] It represented religious belief and practice as the pernicious tool of the "kulak." It praised those

41. *Bezbozhnik*, August 23, 1925.
42. Smolensk WKP 13, "Doklad o sostoianii Zabolotskoi Volpartorganizatsii i ee rabote."
43. *Bezbozhnik*, May 17, 1925, p. 3.
44. On *Bezbozhnik*'s limited circulation, see Curtiss, *Russian Church*, p. 206. In 1926, it was claimed, the literacy rate of the rural population in European Russia was 38.8 percent, an increase of 9.4 percent from 1920. For these and other statistics, see Kozlov, *Kul'turnaia revoliutsiia i krest'ianstvo*. Even by 1932, almost half of the rural population as a whole was illiterate. See Hoffmann, *Peasant Metropolis*, pp. 43–44.
45. Villagers attended theatrical productions that portrayed clergy as hypocrites. For some

Fig. 6. "The Clergy's Folk Dance." 1919. This poster depicts clerical hypocrisy and corruption. Courtesy, Poster Collection, Hoover Institution Archive, Stanford University.

villagers who had already broken with religion. It illustrated the instrumental value of secular culture, especially modern agricultural techniques.⁴⁶ On one level, of course, the point of these detailed and colorful articles was to cause the reader to stop believing in God and dispense with religious practice. But *Bezbozhnik* was to convey other important messages as well. To appreciate them, we must recognize that antireligious correspondents fashioned a discourse that incorporated prevailing conceptions of peasant justice—or the correspondents' perceptions thereof.⁴⁷

Articles in *Bezbozhnik* and other newspapers thus portrayed clergy and other religious activists as having taken more from other villagers—and the resources of "the village" more generally—than they gave back in turn.⁴⁸ (See Figure 6.) Barely if at all hiding his anger, a correspondent complained that peasants in Stavropolsk *volost'* had spent 75,210 rubles on religion in the preceding year "from their economy [*khoziaistvo*] without [gaining] any use [in return]."⁴⁹ A 1925 article in *Sovetskaia derevnia* quoted a peasant who condemned the village church as a "'machine' for emptying out peasants' pockets."⁵⁰

Correspondents also portrayed this religious "front," as it was often called, as having intentionally endangered the very subsistence of other

---

glimpses into the "antireligious repertoire of village theater," see Murin, *Byt i nravy*, p. 48. See Figure 6 for an antireligious poster that portrays this theme.

46. For examples of condemnations of clerical greed, see *Bezbozhnik*, January 17, 1925, and April 19, 1927. The close identification of the kulak with religious belief and practice is discussed at length in Chapter 9. For an example of a correspondent praising converts to atheism (i.e., for having "finally understood the irrelevance of the clerical narcotic") see ibid., March 8, 1925, p. 7. An article by Oleshchuk, for example, reminded readers that one of the main goals of the League of the Godless was to demonstrate "the connection of agricultural [practices] with religious beliefs," as well as to engage in "sanitary enlightenment." See ibid., August 28, 1927, p. 7. Claims of success can be found, for example, in ibid., January 29, 1928. The Central Cooperative Council sought to enlist cooperative organizations in distributing antireligious propaganda and, by 1927, could claim some successes along these lines. See "Kooperatsiia i rabota s antireligioznoi knigoi," ibid., July 3, 1927. As discussed below, from its inception, the League was involved in policy and in practice with the attempt to get peasants to adopt more modern agricultural techniques and attain greater levels of agricultural productivity. See, for example, *Bezbozhnik* 3 (December 1925): 13. While Peris is right to stress that after 1929 the League's involvement in collectivization was a cornerstone of its identity, its "agricultural mission" had become "predominant" before that date. See "Storming the Heavens," pp. 294–95.

47. This analysis draws heavily on Scott's *Moral Economy*, esp. chap. 6.

48. Putting it in Scott's terms, the religious contingent, then, was guilty of violating other villagers' "right of reciprocity." See *Moral Economy*, esp. pp. 167–76.

49. See *Bezbozhnik*, August 23, 1925.

50. *Sovetskaia derevnia*, May 17, 1925, p. 5. See also "Velikopostnye kombinatsii," *Bezbozhnik*, April 10, 1927.

villagers.⁵¹ A few examples of this kind of indictment must suffice here. By demanding excessively high payments for various services rendered, for example, clergy were placing the poor peasant dangerously close to the subsistence line—or pushing them over that line. In 1928, a correspondent for *Bezbozhnik* pointed out that peasants had paid the priest so much that they had neglected to outfit themselves with a firefighting brigade. He ended the article by pointing out the danger in which clerical financial extractions had placed the peasants: "Well, and what if there is a fire? Then it will surely be too late [to think about this.]"⁵² By allotting village resources to church repairs, upkeep, and other parish needs, the peasant smallholders who dominated the village assembly were ignoring the fundamental economic needs of the village—to include better schools and roads and modern agricultural implements—and thus making peasants vulnerable to famine and other threats to their daily existence.⁵³ One antireligious poster likened the priest to a spider who sucked the blood of the flies ("parishioners") in his grasp (see Figure 7). Another depicted a well-fed priest roping in an emaciated parishioner (see Figure 8).

Popular verse and rhetoric also indicted clergy—and the parish more generally—for threatening villagers' subsistence. Numerous popular verses (*chastushki*) with antireligious themes existed in the 1920s. Their tone and content varied from region to region: those in agricultural provinces (e.g., Riazan province) tended to be quite caustic, a characteristic "entirely" absent from those particular to northern provinces (e.g., Cherepovets, Vologda).⁵⁴ Making essentially the same point as a *Bezbozhnik* article that shamed a priest for taking the "last kopecks" from a poor family as payment for funeral services,⁵⁵ one verse asked: "But tell us why, for example, / You need the priest so much / Without him you will have / Both your supper and your lunch."⁵⁶ Did writers for *Bezbozhnik* and other rural newspapers lift such

---

51. I am thus referring to what Scott calls the "right to subsistence," which, along with the "right of reciprocity," constitute the "active moral principle[s]" of the village. See *Moral Economy*, p. 176.

52. *Bezbozhnik*, January 29, 1928.

53. For examples from *Bezbozhnik*, see "Ne poladili" in the April 17 and October 9, 1927, issues, and "Chernigoshchiny proedaiut sotni shkol" in the January 28, 1929, issue.

54. On these regional and subregional variations, in turn reflecting differences in political attitudes as well (e.g., the "in comparison to the south, the striking restraint in expressing sociopolitical *vozzrenii*"), see Fenomenov, *Sovremennaia derevnia*, 2:96–97.

55. See *Bezbozhnik*, January 11, 1925.

56. "A skazhi, zachem, k primeru, / On tebe tak nuzhen: / Bez nego imeesh' ty / I obed i uzhin." (To keep the rhyme in the English translation, I have reversed the order of two words in the last line.) For this and twenty-three other *chastushki* on specifically antireligious themes, see Murin, *Byt i nravy*, pp. 140–41.

Fig. 7. "The Spider and the Flies." 1919. The spider is the priest who sucks the blood from his parishioner flies. Courtesy, Poster Collection, Hoover Institution Archive, Stanford University. Poem by Demian Bednyi. Artist: Viktor Deni.

Fig. 8. "Enough Deception." 1925–35. Again mimicking an icon, this poster shows a priest using the church to exploit parishioners. Courtesy, Poster Collection, Hoover Institution Archive, Stanford University. Artist: P. P. Skala.

themes and rhetoric from popular verses? Or were popular verses repeating themes that had appeared in *Bezbozhnik*? It is impossible to make a general conclusion. Because some of these *chastushki* predated *Bezbozhnik*'s debut in the countryside, we can infer that its correspondents were in fact influenced by these popular cultural forms. Along these lines, drawing on the work of the acclaimed ethnographer Vladimir Bogoraz, Sheila Fitzpatrick has rightly emphasized that "urban Komsomols and Communists . . . [took on] characteristics of the traditional [prerevolutionary] village freethinker, the 'godfighter' [*bogoborets*]."[57]

In any case, two consequences followed from *Bezbozhnik*'s indictment of the clergy and parish for their violation of the fundamental moral principles of peasant life. First, because the clergy and religious activists (e.g., the smallholders and *bol'shaki*) had violated these rights, their claims to power were illegitimate. So too were the social and political relations (e.g., the political culture of the village assembly) that such claims generated. These discursive strategies were intended to resonate with what was assumed to be villagers' latent experience of exploitation by clergy and other village elites, and with their growing perceptions of the illegitimacy of the claims in question. To further inflame this sense of exploitation, correspondents for *Bezbozhnik* (and other antireligious and provincial newspapers) adopted a variety of refrains in which they rhetorically shamed clergy and religious activists for having violated the basic principles of peasant justice. Clergy who overcharged their clients were told to be ashamed of themselves.[58] This discourse of shame was also applied to antireligious activists who, by failing to be vigilant in their antireligious work, allowed clergy and religious activists to continue their exploitative practices. A 1927 article in *Sovetskaia derevnia* shamed the secretary of a *volkom* and the chair of a VIK, who with others left a lecture on religion to attend church: "Can this behavior serve as a good example for Komsomols and non-Party [peasants]?"[59] This discourse thus sought to construct and enforce a new set of community norms—now transposed to a national scale—for the relationship of newly emerging village political elites to the other villagers they served. *Bezbozhnik* was thus to be a kind of journalistic *samosud*, a rhetorical shaming of those who had violated the rights and norms of the community.

While these themes could appeal to villagers of both genders, antireligious publications also offered messages for women only. A good example of the

---

57. See Fitzpatrick, *Stalin's Peasants*, p. 37.

58. Village theatrical productions also shamed clergy for their hypocritical behavior, as noted in Murin, *Byt i nravy*, p. 48.

59. See, for example, "Zvali k sebe, a sami ushli v tserkov'," *Sovetskaia derevnia*, May 8, 1927, p. 2.

gendered themes of antireligious propaganda is the antireligious poster "Religion and the Woman" (see Figure 9). Its images and verses portrayed peasant (and urban) women as having endured a "submissive slavery" (*pokornoe rabstvo*) to the Church, to the clergy, to their husbands, and to housework itself. Women suffered even more than men the humiliation of giving more to the powers in their lives than they received in return. For by verbally describing women as slaves, and by visually representing them as being swept along by the serpent-maelstrom of the Church, the visual images and verses of the poster denied women agency. Their lack of agency was epitomized by the scene in the upper left-hand corner, which—like Kanatchikov's autobiography—depicted domestic violence as being sanctioned by religion. In this women had to suffer a particularly humiliating threat to their very existence. (See also the depiction of domestic violence in Figure 10.) But the poster offered a way out of the earthly slavery sanctioned by the Church. Women, too, could find true justice; and the last two stanzas of its verse told them how. They had only to "go, go, to the soviets / to the factory committees, to the RIKs, to the Profsoiuz / listen to lectures, study, read newspapers." Women could regain agency—a kind of earthly redemption—by participating in such activities and throwing off their "slavish belief in priests and in God." The low literacy of the population and the very limited availability of *Bezbozhnik* and other printed material like this poster severely restricted, to be sure, the actual impact of such discursive strategies—even when transmitted in colorful and provocative images.[60]

Owing in part to these limitations of antireligious propaganda, members of cells opted for techniques with a potentially larger impact. In the village Malaia Semënovka (Balashov *uezd*, Saratov province), doctors and teachers took part in the antireligious cell's "social work," a category that included the repair of bridges.[61] By undertaking such activities, members of antireligious cells were trying to portray themselves as the new political elites of the village, discharging tasks (e.g., repair of bridges) typically assigned by the village assembly, or else performed by *zemstvo* activists of the late tsarist period.[62] Their implicit assumption seemed to be that if they performed tasks typically executed by Russian village elites, villagers would—eventually—accord them such status, as well as its corresponding loyalties and

---

60. Laments about the unavailability of *Bezbozhnik* in the countryside (and elsewhere) resounded on its pages and at antireligious conferences throughout the 1920s. See, for example, *Bezbozhnik*, June 3, 1923, p. 3; ibid., February 15, 1925, p. 5; "S"ezd bezbozhnikov," ibid., February 20, 1927, p. 7; and *Stenograficheskii otchet*, pp. 67, 103–4.

61. See *Bezbozhnik*, August 16, 1925, p. 7.

62. See Terence Emmons and Wayne Vucinich, *The Zemstvo in Russia: An Experiment in Local Self-Government* (New York, 1982).

Fig. 9. "Religion and the Woman." 1917–20. Some antireligious propaganda was directed specifically at women, telling them that they had been enslaved to the church and clergy as well as to housework and their husbands. Courtesy, Poster Collection, Hoover Institution Archive, Stanford University.

Fig. 10. "The Working Woman: Into the Battle for Socialism. Into the Battle Against Religion." 1931. This poster offers women an escape from the domestic violence supposedly sanctioned by the Church. The lower caption reads: "Religion is a tool for the enslavement of the working woman." Courtesy, Poster Collection, Hoover Institution Archive, Stanford University. Artist: B. Klinch.

obligations.⁶³ Improbable as it may seem, the repair of a bridge was thus a political act, a symbolic attempt to create political legitimacy.

Another important component of the League's "social work" was the demonstration of modern agricultural techniques and, more generally, the instrumental value of science. Challenging the commune's prerogative to make decisions about agricultural methods, members of antireligious cells staged agricultural competitions. "Godless fields" or "godless hectares" were planted with specially selected seeds and farmed using modern agricultural techniques; and they were to compete with fields farmed by believers in traditional ways and blessed by priests. (See Figure 11.) To challenge the belief that saints were responsible for the weather, antireligious activists demonstrated "godless meteorology."⁶⁴ An article in *Bezbozhnik* laid out the activities that cells were to offer for the *prazdnik urozhaia* (Harvest Day) in 1925.⁶⁵ Cells were to provide lectures and conversations on the general theme of "agriculture and religion," followed by "antireligious plays with an agricultural theme." Especially recommended was the play "Who Is Going to Help the Peasant—The Agronomist or God?"⁶⁶ The plan for Harvest Day reflected Gorev's statement, made earlier that year, that demonstrating the effectiveness of modern agricultural techniques "would attract the sympathies of peasants to us one hundred times faster than ten disputes with priests, which are still badly organized."⁶⁷ The purpose of such activities was twofold. They were obviously meant to convince peasants and other villagers of the value of scientific explanations for natural phenomena, thereby stimulating a break with religion. By rivaling the commune's traditional role in agricultural matters, antireligious activists challenged the legitimacy of the *bol'shaki* who ran it. What such activities underscored, then, was how antireligious efforts were so inextricably intertwined with the regime's attempt to reshape virtually every other aspect of rural life.

Antireligious activists had a fairly varied repertoire of antireligious activities, but they carried them out rather infrequently. Many cells sprang into action only during religious holidays—if then—only to slip into paralysis during the intervals between them.⁶⁸ The same factors that inhibited the growth of the League's rural network hindered many cells that did exist from becoming a vital presence in rural life. Overworked, lacking the necessary

---

63. On the cost to village elites of violating the "right of reciprocity," see Scott, *Moral Economy*.
64. Curtiss, *Russian Church*, p. 212.
65. Part of what Stites has called a "whole new counter-festival calendar," Harvest Day was to replace the Feast of the Intercession. See *Revolutionary Dreams*, p. 110.
66. "Iacheiki SB i den' urozhaia," *Bezbozhnik*, August 23, 1925.
67. *Bezbozhnik*, May 17, 1925.
68. For examples, see *Bezbozhnik*, May 1, 1923, and *Povolzhskaia pravda*, December 14, 1928, p. 5.

Fig. 11. "The *Bezbozhnik* Is a (Scientific) Experimenter." 1925–40. Members of antireligious cells staged agricultural competitions to show that modern agricultural techniques surpassed traditional methods sanctioned by the Church. Courtesy, Poster Collection, Hoover Institution Archive, Stanford University.

skills, and often still quite attached to religious beliefs and practices themselves, a significant number of rural Party members and Komsomoltsy remained reluctant to engage in antireligious propaganda, not to mention other kinds of antireligious activities, after the League's establishment.[69] Party members tended to take into account the personal qualities of the local members of the clergy in deciding whether or not to engage in antireligious activities. Allowing a priest to keep money that he had won in a bond in 1929, Party members in Murmansk explained: "How can [we] conduct antireligious propaganda here, he's a good priest you know, how could we really do anything against him?"[70] Not without reason, then, did a village priest in the Novgorod region, who had baptized the offspring of a candidate member of the Party in January of 1929, smugly dismiss Party members with the comment "all of them are *bezbozhniki* only on paper."[71] Because rural Party members and other villagers could not sustain their own vital antireligious cells, central antireligious or cultural enlightenment organizations were

69. For examples, see Glennys Young, "Rural Religion and Soviet Power, 1921–1932," (Ph.D. diss., University of California, Berkeley, 1989), pp. 64–66, 70–71, 155–59.
70. TsGAOR Leningrada, f. 6307, op. 13, ed. khr. 9, l. 159.
71. *Krest'ianskaia pravda*, May 28, 1929, p. 5.

obliged—when resources permitted—to import antireligious crusaders to "backward" rural areas.[72] Even as late as 1930, the Leningrad regional council of political enlightenment sent seventy antireligious workers to the countryside before the Christmas holiday, a figure even an antireligious supervisor admitted was "not enough."[73] The Party's proclamation of "face to the countryside" had failed to cure the cells of the League of "campaignism" and general weakness. Using adjectives such as "weak," "feverish," "sporadic," "bad," "unsystematic," and "neglected," antireligious activists and correspondents offered a rather honest and accurate appraisal of the League's rural cells.[74]

Flirting with the Godless

How, then, are we to gauge the impact of these often far-flung and sputtering cells on the religiosity of peasants and other villagers? One difficulty in measuring this impact is that our definitions of religiosity are woefully inadequate for the task at hand. Indexes such as attending church, participating in celebrations and festivals during religious holidays, executing religious rituals, observing the sacraments, and avowing religious belief do not do justice to the fluid and "messy" constructions of religious identity in the Russian countryside of the 1920s. To be sure, ethnographic reports stressed that throughout the 1920s, peasants continued to attend church on holidays, observe fasts (especially Lent), to invite clergy to the village to lead prayers (e.g., for rain, and upon pasturing cattle), and to celebrate holidays (especially local ones established "on precept," (*po zavetu*)—the backsliding of some youth and other, often marginalized villagers notwithstanding.[75] But as Lewis Siegelbaum has noted, there were peasants who clung to a good

---

72. Forty-five "antireligious shockworkers," for example, were sent to Atkarsk *okrug* on December 25, 1929. They stayed until January 10, 1930. See TsGAOR, f. 5462, ed. khr. 366, op. 12, l. 15.

73. TsGAOR Leningrada, f. 6307, op. 13, ed. khr. 9, ll. 160–61.

74. See, for example, *Povolzhskaia pravda*, May 23, 1929, p. 3; *Sovetskaia derevnia*, December 30, 1926, p. 3; and *Povolzhskaia pravda*, March 8, 1929, p. 3, and 13 September 1928, p. 4.

75. See, for example, Fenomenov's *Sovremennaia derevnia*, 2:79, and *Trudy obshchestva istorii arkheologii i etnografii pri Saratovskom universitete* 34:1 (1923): 13–15. Journals and other publications produced by the many remaining societies conducting "studies of local lore" (*kraevedenie*) also took this view. See *Poznai svoi krai. Izdanie Pskovskogo obshchestva kraevedeniia*, 1925, p. 89. To be sure, there were in fact ethnographers who in the 1920s came to very different conclusions, stressing the decline of traditional religious practices (e.g., ritual, prayer,

many localistic pagan beliefs—for example, that house-spirits resided in the stove—yet took down the icons of Orthodox saints that hung in those same huts, putting up icons of secular saints such as Lenin and Kalinin in their place.[76] Explaining that they were hedging their bets, even some members of antireligious cells continued to go to church.[77] As these examples indicate, it is misleading to deduce either an individual's "religiosity"—or "atheism"— from one particular indicator, such as church attendance. Peasants' "conversion" to atheism did not follow a linear progression.[78] Rather, what characterized peasants' religiosity was the delicate integration of behavior, beliefs, and institutional loyalties that we would assume to be incompatible.

The case of Malaia Semënovka, a village in Saratov province, illustrates well these interpretive quandaries. In an article published in *Bezbozhnik* in 1925, an antireligious correspondent sang the praises of the village's allegedly thriving antireligious cell.[79] Although in cells such as the one in Malaia Semënovka it was peasant youth who comprised the core membership, that particular cell integrated a seemingly ever-expanding number of villagers, including doctors and teachers, into the "social work" discussed above, such as the repair of bridges.[80] It was the vitality of the cell, claimed the correspondent, that alone accounted for the declining church attendance of villagers: only twelve to fifteen "older women" attended church on a regular basis, while "bearded peasants" converted themselves to *bezbozhniki*. The interpretive ambiguities—which pervade archival documents no less strongly—are seemingly endless. Did these same "bearded peasants" have icons in their huts? Did they believe in the spirits that animated the Russian countryside? Did they cling to localistic pagan beliefs while eschewing Orthodox beliefs? Did women continue to attend church because parish life was an arena in which they could be "actors" rather than "victims," the messages of antireligious propaganda notwithstanding?[81] When villagers were making choices about their religious identities, did they take into account the presence and activities of an antireligious cell? For example, was it the

---

church attendance). For one such view, see L. E. Karunovskaia, "Selo Novoselka-Ziuzino Roslavskogo uezda," in V. G. Tan-Bogoraz, ed., *Revoliutsiia v derevne (ocherki)*, vol. 1 (Moscow, 1924), esp. p. 71. For a convincing portrait of the continued strength of village religiosity in Tver' province, see Altrichter, "Insoluble Conflicts" and *Die Bauern von Tver*.

76. Siegelbaum, *Soviet State and Society*, p. 162.
77. Ibid.
78. For more examples and discussion of such religious "syncretism," see Stites, *Revolutionary Dreams*, pp. 100–105.
79. *Bezbozhnik*, August 16, 1925, p. 7.
80. On the predominance of peasant youth in cells of the ODGB and the League, see *Bezbozhnik*, February 15, 1925, p. 5, and November 20, 1927.
81. Christine Worobec, "Victims or Actors? Russian Peasant Women and Patriarchy," in Kingston-Mann and Mixter, *Peasant Economy, Culture, and Politics*, pp. 177–206.

cell's "social work"—as opposed to its antireligious propaganda—that had been the major catalyst in these older peasants' decision not to attend church?[82] And, if so, when they decided not to attend church, let alone take on the identity of a nominal *bezbozhnik*, were they trying to assimilate into what they perceived to be a newly forming village political elite? If so, the existence of highly plastic religious identities, as briefly surveyed above, becomes easier to understand.

What, then, *can* we conclude about the impact of antireligious cells in villages such as Malaia Semënovka? To the degree that an antireligious cell constituted a vital presence in antireligious life, villagers took its "culture of godlessness" (*bezbozhie*) into consideration in fashioning their religious identities. Although older male villagers as a rule continued to shun antireligious activities, they were more likely than women to create a public persona in which they exhibited at least some identification with this godless culture—joining an antireligious cell, refusing to attend church, removing Orthodox icons from their huts—to give only three of the many possible examples.[83] Even older male smallholding peasants, who had traditionally been staunch supporters of the priest and the parish church, sometimes forged this kind of public identity, whatever their more private religious attachments may have been. One magnet luring male peasants to public godless culture appears to have been the prestige of science and modern agricultural techniques. When the male members of a village assembly in 1926 engaged in a heated debate about whether to believe in God and about the necessity of priests, the argument turned on whether either could increase the harvest. When the majority concurred that only better agricultural techniques could do so, they decided—perhaps with some outside prompting—to create a godless cell.[84] Some peasants, in fact, implicitly deified science even as they clung to religious beliefs. In 1929, the "entire collective" of teachers and students from a technical school debated religious activists at a "large peasant meeting" in an area of full-scale (*sploshnaia*) collectivization in the Leningrad region. When one "old man" asked a female teacher whether science had proven the nonexistence of God, she answered: "No, science has not proven that."[85]

---

82. It is crucial, of course, to distinguish between what correspondents perceived and what peasants and other villagers experienced.

83. See *Sovetskaia derevnia*, April 15, 1929, for typical complaints that antireligious activities—in this case antireligious lectures—were failing to attract the "adult peasantry." Membership lists of the League of the Godless in Iaroslavl' and Pskov indicate significantly fewer women. Women who held prominent positions in the League's bureaucratic apparatus were rare exceptions. See Daniel Peris's *"Storming the Heavens": The Soviet League of the Militant Godless* (forthcoming), chap. 7.

84. *Bezbozhnik*, April 15, 1926.

85. TsGAOR Leningrada, f. 6307, op. 12, ed. khr. 455, l. 67.

Such cases of *troeverie*—of peasants and other villagers combining elements of Orthodoxy, paganism, and godlessness (*bezbozhie*)—indicate that villagers were often more anxious about the cells than the potency of their activity warranted.[86] Why? Because it was often the Party member who loomed as the most zealous and important antireligious activist in the village, villagers drew a powerful association between the Party cadre and the antireligious process. Peasants, as one Soviet linguist found, defined Communists as "the ones who don't believe in God."[87] This conflation significantly influenced their receptiveness toward the godless cause; their stored anger and hatred of Party members, with whom they associated forced grain requisitioning and other brutalities of the Civil War, shaped their evaluation of the antireligious campaign. In other words, because they feared the Party's power, they may have tried to "pass" as sympathizers or adherents of the godless cause. They may have become anxious when an antireligious cell appeared because they realized that antireligious activity necessarily intersected with the attempt to reshape so many other aspects of rural life—the village political elite, levels of literacy, agricultural practices, sociability, and conceptions of time. The more a cell acted as a vital presence in village life, the more it split the community along religious, social, and, as we will see, political lines.

Institutional Antireligiosity and Popular Cultural Conflict

It would be a serious mistake, however, to view the conflict over religious belief and practice in the village as being synonymous with the League and its rural cells.[88] After all, as we have seen, that conflict long predated not only the existence of a national antireligious organization but the Revolutions of 1917.[89] Moreover, the regime's antireligious efforts extended well beyond the activities of the League, involving, among other things, the use of law as a means of social engineering (e.g., the Decree), and the process of creating a literate and educated populace. How were villagers—sometimes catalyzed by the existence of rural cells and other activities of the League, to be sure—working through such conflict in the years after the Party's proclamation of

---

86. Stites notes the existence of *troeverie*—and even *mnogoverie*—on p. 122 of *Revolutionary Dreams*.
87. Quoted in Sheila Fitzpatrick, *Stalin's Peasants*.
88. In other words, my focus in the analysis that follows is on sociopolitical conflict over religious belief and practice that (1) would have existed even had there been no League and no rural cells and (2) was not directly generated by those cells' formal activities.
89. See also Fitzpatrick, *Stalin's Peasants*, p. 37.

"face to the countryside"? My purpose here is to provide a relatively brief overview of some of the "fields" of conflict in which those hostile or indifferent to religious beliefs and practice carried out their strategic skirmishes and even full-blown attacks: the rural family, education, semiotics, and electoral politics.[90] (These categories were not, in practice, as distinct as this list suggests.) This last category will, of course, be treated in much more depth in the final three chapters of this book.

Members of rural families often came into conflict over issues involving religious belief and practice.[91] Perceiving religious belief and practice as a symbolic legitimization of the power of the family patriarch, younger members of the extended household, for example, expressed their anger at patriarchal dominance by challenging and rejecting various elements of religious belief and practice. Parents and children—especially but by no means exclusively their male offspring—clashed, came to violence, and even killed each other over these issues.[92] A twenty-year-old Komsomolets in Volokolamsk *uezd* ended up killing his father, a long-time church elder, because the latter wanted him to baptize his child. (They had come to blows previously when the son insisted on having a civil marriage.)[93] Another young Komsomolets and *bezbozhnik* wanted to get married without a priest. But he faced so much opposition from aunts, uncles, and his "archreligious [future] mother-in-law" that he ultimately agreed to get married in church. The deciding factor was said to be that his father had promised to buy him a suit if he would get married in church![94]

Villagers also expressed aspects of their religious identity through the clothing they wore. As Sheila Fitzpatrick has recently noted, "sons, and to a lesser extent the daughters, would refuse to wear a cross," a defiant act proudly recounted in peasant verses (*chastushki*) as well.[95] One of these *chastushki* went as follows:

---

90. This analysis is thus informed by Hunter's investigation of what he calls "fields of cultural conflict," as carried out in *Culture Wars*, especially chapters 7 through 12. (He and I differ, to be sure, in our definitions of culture.) To be sure, conflict percolated in these different "fields" prior to 1924–25, as the discussion above suggests. But I introduce these categories here to explore the degree to which the regime's first national antireligious organization, the League of the Godless, was able to harness such conflict for its own purposes.

91. Generational tensions—both a cause and a result of social and political conflict—were in part responsible for the breakup of many extended peasant households during the 1920s. See Hoffmann, *Peasant Metropolis*, pp. 23–24.

92. On the spread of irreligious behavior among young girls (e.g., civil marriages, refusing to pray upon entering the peasant hut), see Murin, *Byt i nravy*, p. 37, and Fitzpatrick, *Stalin's Peasants*, p. 34.

93. For more details, including the trial and lenient sentencing of the Komsomol member, see *Bezbozhnik*, March 24, 1925.

94. For more details, see Murin, *Byt i nravy*, p. 118.

95. Fitzpatrick, *Stalin's Peasants*, p. 37.

To hang out with the Komsomols	S komsomol'tsem shtob guliat'
The same person one can't stay	Nuzhno izmenit'sia:
A neck cross cannot one wear	Krest na shee ne nosit'
and to God cannot one pray	Bogu ne molit'sia.[96]

When adolescent boys donned the military attire also worn by "former soldiers, rural activists, and Komsomols," they were rejecting not just traditional village dress but the benighted world of the village, and especially its traditional religious practices and beliefs—a perception captured as well in peasant verse.[97] One verse particular to the Cherepovets region went as follows:

Ah, let us declare to you	Akh, pozvol'te vam otkryt'sia
Ah, let us tell you	Akh, pozvol'te rasskazat'
One goes to church not to pray	V tserkov' khodiat ne molit'sia
But one's new clothing to display!	A nariady pokazat'![98]

Female adolescents symbolized their hostility to their parents and to village culture, religion included, by wearing makeup and "city" clothes rather than traditional costumes, especially on holidays.[99]

Wives, husbands, and children also had differing ideas about the place of religious imagery in the peasant hut. Its stoves and corners became contested territory.[100] Peasant wives bristled at their husbands' decisions to identify publicly with various elements of godless culture, as the case of Malaia Semënovka suggests. When her husband, a Party member, tried in 1922 to persuade her to remove the icons from their hut and to stop believing in God, the "batrachka" A. A. Poliakova refused. She explained to her husband that although she did not pray, she still didn't know "whether or not God exists"; if he did exist, he would punish her for taking them down. Later, after being elected a delegate to the Party meetings for women (*zhenskie sobraniia*) and learning to read, she sold the two icons and bought herself a short woman's overcoat (*kofta*).[101]

96. See Murin, *Byt i nravy*, p. 140.
97. Quoted in Fitzpatrick, *Stalin's Peasants*, p. 36.
98. See Fenomenov, *Sovremennia derevnia*, 2:97.
99. *Trudy obshchestva istorii arkheologii i etnografii pri Saratovskom universitete* 34:2 (1923): 11; Fitzpatrick, *Stalin's Peasants*, p. 36. Another important aspect of village youth culture—and of young villagers' symbolic representation of their hostility to traditional village culture and to religion more specifically—was the emergence of new forms of sociability and entertainment. As Fitzpatrick has noted: "Urban dances like the tango and the foxtrot were taking the place of the old folk dances in the creations of the young." Ibid. On urban youth culture in the 1920s, see Anne E. Gorsuch, "Enthusiasts, Bohemians, and Delinquents: Soviet Youth Cultures, 1921–1928" (Ph.D. diss., University of Michigan, 1992).
100. See *Sovetskaia derevnia*, December 25, 1927.
101. See ibid.

The rural classroom, like the peasant hut, continued to be a site of intense conflict over issues of religious belief and practice. To be sure, the Bolsheviks regarded secular education as a key weapon in the battle to create a secular society; the Decree on the Separation of Church and State, it will be recalled, stipulated that religious teaching (of the *Zakon Bozhii*) could no longer take place in the schools.[102] It was not just that the Party sought to eliminate religious influences from the schools; it sought to make the classroom—and especially the rural classroom—a place where antireligious education was an important part of the curriculum. To that end, a 1924 circular issued jointly by Narkompros and the Komsomol called for teachers to conduct antireligious propaganda, and there were indeed teachers who organized antireligious cells and gave antireligious lectures.[103] Komsomoltsy and pioneers flocked to rural schools to conduct antireligious activities.[104] Rural teachers were, however, often unlikely enforcers of the Decree and poor antireligious missionaries. As Bukharin himself lamented, priests retained considerable influence on teachers, in part because a significant percentage of the latter came from clerical backgrounds.[105] Often committed believers with active ties to the clergy, many rural teachers ignored the directive to expose their students to antireligious propaganda.[106] In some cases, rural teachers went through the motions of conducting antireligious propaganda in the classroom, only to discredit those efforts by attending religious ceremonies. Even those rural teachers who were true nonbelievers faced significant obstacles in eliminating religion and bringing antireligion to their classrooms. With Sovnarkom's delegation of the financing of rural education to "self-taxation" in 1921, villagers' material support played a role in shaping the curriculum.[107] A teacher's decision to take

102. The text of the Decree is as follows: "Sec. 9. The school is separated from the church. The teaching of religion in state and public schools, as well as in private schools where general subjects are taught, is forbidden. Citizens may study or teach religious subjects privately." Quoted in Curtiss, *Church and State in Russia*, pp. 75–76.

103. See, for example, *Sovetskaia derevnia*, April 15, 1929. On this see Larry E. Holmes, "Schools and Religion in Soviet Russia, 1917–1941," in Sabrina Petra Ramet, ed., *Religious Policy in the Soviet Union* (New York, 1933), pp. 128–29.

104. *Bezbozhnik*, May 1, 1923; TsGAOR, f. 5462, op. 11, ed. khr. 12, l. 32.

105. As of September 1924, 15.4 percent of rural teachers came from clerical backgrounds. See Larry S. Gringlas, "*Shkraby ne kraby*: Rural Teachers and Bolshevik Power in the Russian Countryside, 1921–28" (master's thesis, Columbia University, 1987), p. 57. I thank the author and Mark von Hagen for making this thesis available to me.

106. At the seventh All-Union Congress of Enlightenment Workers in 1930, Lunacharsky claimed that only about 40 percent of all teachers could offer effective antireligious education. TsGAOR, f. 5462, op. 11, ed. khr. 12, ll. 31–32, 41. On teachers' religiosity, see also Sheila Fitzpatrick, *Education and Social Mobility in the Soviet Union, 1922–1934* (New York, 1979), p. 18, and Gringlas, "*Shkraby ne kraby*."

107. Gringlas, "*Shkraby ne kraby*," pp. 34–55, 80. On this see also Fitzpatrick,

the icons off the walls of the school could literally prove quite costly.

When teachers and parents clashed over the place of Orthodox and "secular" icons in the schools, they were involved in a battle to define the symbols and signs—the "semiotics"—of village life.[108] The Party attached even greater urgency to establishing a strong visual presence in the villages—of course secular in nature—when it adopted the policy shift "face to the countryside." It sought to establish a secular visual culture in the countryside through a variety of visual media and artistic forms, such as posters, cinema, and theater.[109] Much of this work was undertaken by the village reading room, which Peter Kenez has aptly described as the "center of [Soviet] 'art' in the village"—when, in fact, a village was "lucky" enough to have one.[110] Intended to serve as a kind of secular village church, the village reading room featured Soviet iconography (e.g., slogans, posters, and pictures, often coordinated with the long list of Soviet anniversaries and holidays).[111] During the period after "face to the countryside," village reading rooms were to put special energy into setting up "Lenin Corners," which were to include pictures of various events in his life.[112]

The other half of the Party's effort to establish a secular visual presence in the village was its battle to subdue and ultimately eliminate the strong visual presence of village Orthodoxy. During the years in question, Party members and other fellow travelers were to pressure priests not to appear in

---

Commissariat of Enlightenment, p. 228, and Holmes, "Schools and Religion," in Ramet, *Religious Policy*, pp. 132–33. The salaries of village teachers were notoriously low, averaging twenty to thirty rubles a year. See Peter Kenez, *The Birth of the Propaganda State: Soviet Methods of Mass Mobilization, 1917–1929* (New York, 1985), p. 139. Contemporaries attributed the renewed teaching of "God's law" to the financial influence of the "kulak." Gringlas, "*Shkraby ne kraby*," p. 70. On the persistence of religious influences in the schools during NEP, see also Holmes, *The Kremlin and the Schoolhouse*, p. 102.

108. Iurii Lotman and Boris Uspenskii, *The Semiotics of Russian Culture*, ed. Ann Shukman (Ann Arbor, Mich., 1984). Somewhat equivalent to "village semiotics" in Hunter's analysis is the "field" of "Media and the Arts." See Hunter, *Culture Wars*, pp. 225–49.

109. On the monumental challenges faced by Party members who traveled to the countryside to show films to peasants, see Kenez, *Birth of the Propaganda State*, pp. 220–22.

110. Ibid., p. 139. Village reading rooms by no means existed in all villages in the RSFSR. In 1925–26, the high point for the NEP period, there were 24,924 reading rooms. In Viazemsk *uezd* of Smolensk province, for example, there were fourteen reading huts in 1924–25. See *Mestnyi biudzhet sovetov Smolenskoi gubernii na 1925–26 god* (Smolensk, 1925), p. 201. In lieu of a village reading hut, the Party tried to set up "red corners," typically in the building that housed the village soviet, in schools, or even in "private" dwellings.

111. On the attempt to create such holidays, see Altrichter, *Die Bauern von Tver*, pp. 110–11, and "Insoluble Conflicts," esp. pp. 199–200, and Stites, *Revolutionary Dreams*, pp. 109–14.

112. The May 1924 issue of the journal *Izba-chital'nia* exhorted reading rooms to set up Lenin corners. See Kenez, *Birth of the Propaganda State*, p. 139. On the Lenin cult, see Nina Tumarkin, *Lenin Lives! The Lenin Cult in Soviet Russia* (Cambridge, Mass., 1983).

public in clerical attire.[113] Although by the "second half" of NEP Party and antireligious leaders recognized the dangers in "administrative" (forced) closings of churches, their ideal scenario was the conversion of the village church into a school or village soviet, a transformation that would of course radically reduce the visual presence of the parish in village life.[114] Although conducted for the most part outside the League, these various efforts were all part of the regime's battle to erode and ultimately eliminate religious belief and practice. The scope of these efforts was limited by some of the same factors that hindered the work of the League: inadequate funds and overworked, insufficiently educated, sometimes far-flung cadres. Nevertheless, during the last three years of NEP, it was the rare peasant (or other villager) who had not been exposed to the regime's efforts to have a Soviet semiotics eclipse the religious "symbols of public culture."[115]

The Party and its rural representatives, however, were of course not alone in wanting—and in scheming—to eliminate religious elements from the semiotics of village life. Village youth, urban out-migrants, and *otkhodniki* had launched this project in the last decades of the tsarist period. What was the relationship, if any, between the Party's efforts "from above" and those that continued to percolate "from below" during the last three years of NEP? How did the popular antagonism toward the religious elements in village semiotics express itself in everyday village life? This is, to be sure, a very broad topic, and my purpose here is simply to outline the general contours of this phenomenon.

Village youth, in particular, behaved in ways that suggested a rejection of the authority of religious symbols in village life. When young males took off their crosses, donned military caps, and danced the fox-trot, they were challenging not only the authority of their elders but also the way in which religious symbolism cemented the patriarchal power structure of the village as a whole. Sometimes these challenges took a destructive turn. In 1925, unidentified individuals in Minusinsk *uezd* seized clerical robes from the local church and distributed them to Komsomoltsy for use in an antireligious performance.[116] On Easter night in 1926, youths from nearby villages gathered at the church in Kovo (Tver' province). They then proceeded to the local cemetery, where they tore out crosses from some graves, pushed over the gravestones, and broke the benches and lampposts.[117] In another case two villagers from the Leningrad region chose to stage their confrontation in the

113. Curtiss, *Russian Church*.
114. This aim was implicit in the Decree on the Separation of Church and State (1918).
115. Hunter uses this phrase in *Culture Wars*, p. 173. On hostile reactions of villagers, see Kenez, *Birth of the Propaganda State*, p. 141.
116. *Bezbozhnik*, May 10, 1925, p. 7.
117. *Bezbozhnik*, July 18, 1926.

church itself. Having entered the building in which the church service was under way, they sang "obscene" songs in order to provoke the worshipers; this was only one of countless episodes in which youth demonstrated that they still believed that cultural transformation could only come through a violent or at least highly intrusive concentration of hostile extremes.[118] Although the Party had formally abandoned Komsomol Easter and Christmas and rejected rough methods, villagers continued to commit such destructively intrusive acts during major religious holidays.[119]

What was the connection of these acts to the antireligious efforts (and the drive to create a secular village semiotics) marshaled by the regime itself? It is quite possible that these village youth spent a good deal of their free time "hanging out" at the village reading room; many would have been inclined to attend antireligious lectures and other events.[120] They may have gained "affirmation" for their hostility to religion—and in particular to the religious element in the visual culture of the village—in these ways. Yet there is every reason to believe that they would have been committing such acts even if the organized antireligious campaign had never existed; after all, they had been expressing hostility to the patriarchal power structure of the village since the last decades of the tsarist period. During the last three years of NEP, their repertoire of violent and intrusive acts continued to create severe anxiety for clergy and lay activists, who could not predict when the next "attack" would occur (despite the fact that they often coincided with major holidays).

In each of the "fields" surveyed thus far—the family, education, and "village semiotics"—popular efforts to reduce and eliminate the role of religious belief and practice well exceeded the relatively small contribution of the League's fragile and unstable network of rural cells. Had there been no League, had the Party not carried on an antireligious "campaign" on a variety of other "fronts" in addition to that of the League, there would still have been a faction of villagers antagonistic to religious belief and practice who would have sought through a variety of means to reduce its influence in village life. This is not to say that this faction remained unaffected by the

118. *Krest'ianskaia pravda*, January 25, 1929. Although the age and political identities of these individuals cannot be discerned, earlier in the article the unidentified author used the term "hooligan" to describe two former Komsomoltsy.

119. Implicitly recognizing the tendency of antireligious sympathizers to commit religiously disrespectful acts, the 1927 plan of the Saratov provincial council of the League for Easter antireligious work instructed that "serious attention should be paid to the prevention of cases of the insult of religious feelings, the trashing of priests [*popoedstvo*], [of] excesses (playing on the harmonica inside the church fence on Easter night, of the theft of eggs, the tearing of Easter decorations from Easter cakes)." *Sovetskaia derevnia*, April 10, 1927, p. 8.

120. Village reading rooms were popular among village youth, but older peasants tended to avoid them. Most directors of reading rooms (*izbachi*) were themselves fairly young. Kenez, *Birth of the Propaganda State*, p. 142.

League and the regime's other attempts to create a secular village—the battle against illiteracy (the ODN and the village reading hut), the regime's efforts to create a Soviet rural educational system, and so on. Nevertheless, as a rule the Party proved unable to channel the popular antagonism toward religious belief and practice into the institutional forms and activities championed by the regime. Villagers instead drew and built on their own "little traditions" of expressing antagonism toward religious belief and practice.[121] The forms in which they expressed that antagonism—the rejection of religious rituals, practices, and symbols, the adoption of secular styles of dress and sociability, and the destruction of church property—were usually quite similar to those chosen in the last decades of the tsarist period.

What, then, of the last "field" to be surveyed, electoral politics? How did the regime and its rural representatives try, in this period, to use rural electoral politics to erode religious belief and practice? The shift in Party policy heralded by "face to the countryside" implied a new and closer relationship between electoral politics and the creation of a secular village. In calling for the "revival of the soviets" and the establishment of "Soviet democracy" in the countryside, Party leaders like Bukharin presumed that participation in rural electoral politics—whether as a voter, elected official, or both—would gradually produce a transformation in *consciousness*. This was the assumption that underlay, following the Party's 1924 decision to "revive the soviets," the institution of preelectoral meetings of poor peasants as a central component of electoral preparations. Designed to raise the poor peasants' political and economic consciousness, the meetings ultimately aimed for an increase in the electoral participation of this targeted stratum, as well as the election of poor and middle peasants to the soviets. Rural Party members, officials from the VIKs, demobilized Red Army veterans, and sometimes rural teachers and students engaged in preparatory electoral activities such as writing and delivering voting notices, reading newspapers and brochures to peasants, setting up exhibits and "performances," and drawing posters.[122]

The regime took a number of other pragmatic steps to "revive" the village soviets, steps that were of potential consequence to parish life. It broadened their access to revenue. As mentioned above, a 1924 decree granted the village assembly, not the soviet, the right to engage in "self-taxation [*samooblozhenie*] for the satisfaction of local social needs."[123] Not until 1928–29 did Moscow entirely remove the barriers that prevented village

---

121. Robert Redfield, *The Little Community: Viewpoints for the Study of a Human Whole* (Chicago, 1955).

122. For details on the 1926–27 voting campaign in Leningrad province, see TsGAOR Leningrada, f. 2552, op. 10, d. 2163, l. 18.

123. Male, *Russian Peasant Organisation*, p. 138.

soviets from acquiring their own budgets.[124] In the meantime, many village soviets created their own "illegal" budgets, which included outlays for religious expenditures.[125] As the existence of illegal budgets indicates, village soviets routinely ignored the law and engaged in self-taxation.[126] Finally, in August 1927, a decree on "self-taxation for local needs" granted village soviets the right to levy "compulsory" taxes.[127] According to this ruling, revenue could be generated for specific public projects such as "building and maintenance of public buildings, roads and bridges, fire precautions, civic amenities and security."[128] Second, it gradually consolidated and enlarged the area that the soviets served, a process referred to as *ukrupnenie*. The number of village soviets declined significantly; the number of village assemblies, on the other hand, remained constant.[129]

Whether or not as a result of these efforts, general electoral participation increased after 1924–25. Moreover, the regime could point to some progress in achieving desired electoral results, such as the election of those classified as "poor" and "middle" peasants.[130] The Party also scored limited success in attracting individuals of the appropriate socioeconomic background, the

---

124. Until 1928–29, by law only exceptionally large soviets could have their own budgets. In 1925–26 only 3 percent of all village soviets in the USSR had them. (The relatively high percentage of soviets with budgets in the Lower Volga region, according to Male, "suggests a greater strength of rural soviet activity there." Ibid., p. 145. In 1927–28, 6 percent (3,479) of rural soviets in the RSFSR had them; by 1928–29, spurred by the enlargement of the soviets, the figure had risen to 14.2 percent (7,791). Prior to the change in legislation, the Party experimented with allowing soviets in some rural areas to have budgets. See ibid. In 1926, for example, it granted "several village soviets in Kostroma *uezd*" their own budgets. See *Izvestiia*, October 30, 1926.

125. A 1926 investigation conducted by the Central Control Commission of the Workers' and Peasants' Inspectorate revealed that in five *volosti* of Kostroma *uezd*, "*de facto* 'illegal' budgets have sprouted up everywhere, not only in village soviets, but in individual settlements." See Male, *Russian Peasant Organisation*, p. 138.

126. Ibid.

127. Its provisions were amplified in an RSFSR decree of January 1928. See ibid., p. 147.

128. Ibid. It could not be used to generate salaries for the staff of the village soviets. The tax was to be "exacted only by a vote at the 'general meeting of citizens,'" thus perpetuating the unrealistic assumption that there could be such a body, consisting only of voters to the rural soviet, separate from the 'land society gathering.'" Depending on the sympathies of the interpreter, religious projects such as the building or repair of new churches could fall into this category.

129. In 1923, there were 80,000 village soviets in the RSFSR, compared to 319,000 communes in the mid-1920s. By January 1929, there were 55,340 village soviets in the RSFSR. Ibid., pp. 87–89. On village assemblies, see John Slatter, "Communes with Communists: The *Sel'sovety* in the 1920s," in Roger Bartlett, ed., *Land Commune and Peasant Community in Russia* (New York, 1990), p. 273.

130. This is Slatter's assessment as made in "Communes with Communists," p. 277. Participation in elections to the village soviets climbed from 22.3 percent of eligible voters in 1922 to 60.7 percent of eligible voters in 1929. For more statistics, see ibid., p. 278. Male takes the position that "revival of the soviets" to some extent did increase the power of the soviets

much-praised poor and middle peasants, into the electoral process.[131] Drawn into the orbit of "Soviet democracy" and its carefully managed forms of political activity, these poor and middle peasants were to find themselves more and more inclined to adopt secular "plans and recipes" as they shared the goals of the regime. An important by-product was that these loyal elements would in fact see to it that the village soviets effected the "separation" of Church and state required by the Decree. And in 1925, with the promulgation of an NKVD circular enhancing the *de jure* role of the soviet in managing public religious ritual (discussed in much more detail in Chapter 8), the responsibilities of the village soviet over the religious life of the village actually increased.

As the mention of this circular suggests, "revival of the soviets" was to eventually extinguish the village assembly's traditionally dominant role in deciding religious matters.[132] Other Party decrees and policies contributed to this goal as well. A 1926 draft circular (*proekt*) of the Central Committee, the "Regulation on Village Assemblies" (*Polozhenie o skhodakh*), banned members of the assembly from discussing religious matters.[133] The circular encouraged members to discuss instead issues such as the "cleaning of roads, bridges, the comfort of the village, sanitary matters, the hiring of firemen and nightwatchmen, the building of fences, the damming of bridges, and so forth."[134] In 1927, the Party sought to prohibit clergy and other *lishentsy*

---

to direct village affairs. For a Soviet treatment that offered roughly the same conclusion, see M. G. Belogurov, "Istochniki ob organizatsii i sostave sel'skikh sovetov RSFSR v period vosstanovleniia narodnogo khoziaistva, 1921–1925" (candidate diss., Moscow University, 1978), p. 46.

131. From 1927 to 1929, the percentage of peasants participating in elections climbed from 48 percent to 61.5 percent, while that of agricultural labors (*batraki*) rose from 46.8 percent to 69.5 percent. For these and other figures on participation by social group, see Slatter, "Communes with Communists," pp. 278–79. Their staffs became more qualified; fewer illiterate peasants manned leadership posts. Since almost all chairs and secretaries were of peasant background, a large percentage were barely literate. See Male, *Russian Peasant Organisation*, p. 127.

132. Despite some superficial legal changes, throughout most of NEP the commune retained virtually the same functions and character as it had before the Revolution. The 1928 decree of the Central Committee, "General Principles of Land Holding and Land Use Measures," marked the end of the relatively unimpaired freedom of the commune that the Land Code of 1922 had perpetuated. See Male, *Russian Peasant Organisation*. On the continued vitality of the village assembly, see also Atkinson, *End of the Russian Land Commune*; Lewin, *Russian Peasants and Soviet Power*; and Taniuchi, *Village Gathering in Russia*. It was rare for the areas served by the commune and the village soviet to coincide. The latter usually served at least several villages. Male, in *Russian Peasant Organisation*, supports the position that in 1927 "there [were] on average three to five land societies [communes] to each rural soviet" (as quoted in *Khoziaistvo i upravlenie* 11–12 [1927]).

133. For a summary of the circular, see *Vlast' sovetov*, September 26, 1926, p. 3.
134. Ibid.

from voting at the village assembly.[135] On a general level, then, Party policies—"face to the countryside," "revival of the soviets," and the decrees of 1926 and 1927—reflected the consequential assumption that controlling the *forms* of rural political activity and eroding religious belief and practice went hand in hand. In sum, the electoral process itself was now more structurally intertwined than ever before with the regime's struggle to eliminate religious belief and practice.

How did Party cadres and fellow travelers on the grassroots level, on the other hand, *perceive* the relationship between electoral politics and the creation of a secular village after 1924-25? We have very little direct evidence that speaks to this issue. To be sure, few rural Party members and Komsomoltsy had read the Bukharinist writings that underlay "face to the countryside" and "revival of the soviets" more specifically. Yet they must have had some appreciation of the strategic importance of the village soviets to the regime's antireligious efforts. Moreover, we have other evidence that demonstrates that Party members and other antireligious activists appreciated the potential contribution of village politics in this realm. Implicitly recognizing the vitality of the village assembly well into the 1920s, Party members and other rural activists appeared at its meetings, exhorting villagers to adopt various antireligious measures, such as closing churches.[136]

It is actually much easier to trace the *villagers'* perceptions of the relationship between electoral politics, antireligious activism, and the popular cultural conflict over religious belief and practice. In excavating these perceptions, it is important to note that in elections to village soviets, most villagers did not—to our great surprise—sift candidates according to whether they were or were not Party members. Having assimilated the notion that candidates to the village soviets (and the VIKs) had to be responsive to their needs, villagers carefully considered the personal qualities (and, when relevant, the previous political service) of candidates, preferring those whom they perceived to be "supportive and amiable."[137] When voting on candidates to the village soviets (and the VIKs), they cared that a candidate up for reelection not have been excessively involved in bribery, and not have

---

135. The Fifteenth Party Congress, held in December 1927, exhorted the Central Committee to devise methods for guaranteeing that persons deprived of voting rights in the soviets be unable to vote at the village gathering. See Male, *Russian Peasant Organisation*, p. 72.

136. Despite its claim that believers decided themselves to close the village church, this is the implication, for example, of an article that appeared in *Bezbozhnik*, September 20, 1925, p. 3.

137. Fenomenov, *Sovremennaia derevnia*, 2:95. Although Fenomenov claimed that villagers believed that the village soviets and VIKs were accountable to them, he stressed that their political horizon stopped short of the *uezd* soviet. Villagers had a very "dim notion" of their right to participate in elections to *uezd* soviets, which they viewed as having an "independent origin." See ibid.

demonstrated "severe rigor" in imposing state decrees, for example, those related to rural religious life.[138] "Don't elect him, he's a god-fighter [*bogoborets*]," for example, was a refrain of clergy during elections to the village soviets.[139] In fact, because the popular conception of a Communist was someone who was opposed to religious belief and practice, villagers made assumptions about a candidate's stance toward religious belief and practice based on Party or Komsomol membership. The more the Party and its rural representatives tried to create "Soviet democracy" in the countryside, the more villagers—and especially clergy and lay activists—saw electoral politics, the antireligious campaign, and the popular conflict over religious belief and practice as being inextricably interwoven.

In the years following "face to the countryside," villagers experienced conflict over the role of religious belief and practice in rural society as part of the fabric of everyday life. A significant and growing faction within the village was antagonistic to religious belief and practice—and especially to its public face within village society—*not*, for the most part, as a result of the regime's various attempts to create a national antireligious organization. As representatives of the Party-state, older peasant smallholders, Red Army veterans, village youth, and women jostled for power, they thus necessarily formulated their competing claims in a discourse about the role of religious belief and practice. Thus the changing faction of antireligious villagers expressed its antagonism in any arena of village life in which relationships of power existed: the family, education, village "semiotics," and electoral politics.

What would be the response of clergy and religious activists to these different and sometimes intertwining attempts to create a secular village? Would they accept passively the attempts of other villagers and Party cadres to subdue and eliminate religious belief and practice? Or would they escalate a culture war whose skirmishes had been a part of everyday life since the last decades of the late tsarist period?

138. Ibid., p. 95.
139. *Bezbozhnik*, March 29, 1925, p. 1.

5

UNEXPECTED RESILIENCE

Western treatments of Russian Orthodoxy in the 1920s implicitly conflate the experience of the central hierarchy and its urban parishioners with that of rural clergy and laity. Focusing on the regime's co-optation and progressive destruction of the upper echelons of the urban Orthodox hierarchy and the provincial episcopate over the course of the 1920s, certain scholars have assumed that the rural Orthodox community likewise capitulated to the same pressures.[1] Although this assumption is highly problematic, it is nonetheless true that parish clergy figured as prime targets in the regime's colonizing designs on the Russian countryside. They were to be not only "outwardly" but "inwardly" assimilated by its laws, discriminatory financial burdens, antireligious activists, persecution, and other predations. Would parish clergy be able to "[make of] the rituals, representations, and laws imposed on them something quite different from what their conquerors had in mind"?[2] How would the prerevolutionary identities and skills of many parish clergy serve them in this new and hostile political conjuncture?

---

1. See, for example, Curtiss, *Russian Church*; Pospielovsky, *Russian Church*, vol. 1, and Regel'son, *Tragediia*.
2. Michel de Certeau, *The Practice of Everyday Life* (Berkeley, Calif., 1994), p. xiii.

National Religious Policy and the Rural Parish Clergy

Throughout NEP, rural parish clergy felt the painful effects of the regime's predations against the Orthodox Church. Deprived by the end of the Civil War of their financial assets, central and diocesan administrations turned to local parishes for financial support. With these administrative structures financially and otherwise emasculated, "the task of registering and defending the parish fell to the faithful themselves."[3] The Church for all intents and purposes stripped of its journals, newspapers, and diocesan gazettes (*eparkhial'nye vedomosti*), parish clergy felt isolated and struggled to stay informed of important developments.[4]

Even when parish clergy were not themselves murdered, tortured, or imprisoned, they were victimized by religious persecution in other ways.[5] To be sure, persecution fell more heavily on the provincial episcopate than on the parish clergy. On the eve of the October Revolution, there were fewer than 130 diocesan and assistant bishops in the Russian Empire.[6] From 1923 to 1926, 50 bishops were murdered.[7] By the winter of 1924–25, 66 bishops were either in exile or prison.[8] According to another source, 117 out of 160 patriarchal bishops were arrested between 1925 and 1927.[9] The episcopate of Saratov province, for example, suffered severe blows during the 1920s. In 1922, the Saratov bishop Dosifei (Protopopov) was placed under house arrest.[10] Bishop Mikhail of Vol'sk was placed on trial in 1923.[11] One Orthodox émigré claimed in 1926 that the emptying of the ranks of the episcopate swelled the "growing influence of the priests and the laity."[12] At the

---

3. Freeze, "Counter-reformation," p. 331. "Assets," as Freeze points out, meant "liquid capital as well as real estate, including land, buildings, typographies, and candle factories."

4. Ibid., pp. 334–36.

5. Village priests went to trial for "counterrevolutionary" activities during the famine of 1921–22 and the ensuing crisis over the confiscation of church valuables. See the Plaskin avtoreferat, p. 13. See also Pospielovsky, *Russian Church*, 1:94–95, for a reprint of a document, attributed by samizdat sources to Lenin, which called for "the maximum possible number of executions" (p. 95) of clergy in connection with the Church's unwillingness to part with church valuables in the industrial town of Shuia, near Moscow, in March and April of 1922.

6. Timothy Ware, *The Orthodox Church* (New York, 1963), pp. 155–56.

7. Ibid., p. 156.

8. Regel'son, *Tragediia*, pp. 534–36.

9. Pospielovsky, *Russian Church*, 1:67. On the persecution of the bishopry, see also E. L., *Episkopy ispovedniki* (San Francisco, 1971), p. 69.

10. According to Regel'son, he was freed only in 1934. *Izvestiia saratovskogo soveta*, June 10, 1922; Regel'son, *Tragediia*, p. 528.

11. *Izvestiia saratovskogo soveta*, August 21, 1923. For other developments in the Saratov episcopate, see Regel'son, *Tragediia*, pp. 523–37.

12. N. [Nikolai Berdiaev], "O russkoi tserkvi," *Put'*, January 1926, p. 8. The number of Old Believer (*popovtsy*) bishops had, by 1925, allegedly increased in comparison to prerevolutionary figures, See *Vestnik sviashchennogo Sinoda* 11 (1926): 17. (Hereafter cited as *VSS*.)

same time, however, the widespread persecution of the provincial episcopate often left parish clergy without spiritual and administrative superiors. Although parish clergy were not as likely as bishops to suffer such a dreaded fate, they still had to live with the uncertainty of not knowing whether they would fall prey to persecution that Nikolai Berdiaev justly characterized in 1926 as haphazard, inconsistent, and illogical.[13] Would the clergy meet a member of the Cheka willing to ignore "anti-Soviet" propaganda or a Party cadre determined to block repeated efforts to close a monastery?[14] Or would they encounter a Chekist or Party member who was intent on trying clergy for crimes committed during the tsarist period or for "merely" mentioning the name of the Patriarch Tikhon?[15] This tortuous uncertainty was a form of persecution in itself.

The church schism of 1922 was another development in national church politics whose corrosive ripples hit the rural parish and its clergy. During the 1922 crisis over the confiscation of church valuables, a group of left-leaning priests staged a coup of the Orthodox Church, temporarily forcing Patriarch Tikhon from its leadership.[16] What exactly were these Renovationists (*obnovlentsy*), as they called themselves? Their roots extending back into radical movements in Orthodoxy during the tsarist period, they were mostly "white" or married clergy who championed a variety of reforms to "renew" or "revitalize" the Orthodox Church.[17] These included certain ecclesiastical reforms in church life, such as the establishment of a nonmonastic episcopate, the "democratization of diocesan administration" (e.g., giving greater power to laity, holding diocesan congresses), and the amelioration of the everyday life

---

13. N., "O russkoi tserkvi," p. 10. But persecution also shrunk the number of parish clergy. Ware claims that by 1926, 2,700 priests had been killed. *Orthodox Church*, p. 156.

14. Throughout the NEP years, one Party member, who at one point even served as the chair of the Kulmyzhinsk district executive committee (Lower Volga Region), repeatedly blocked motions to close a convent. One of his colleagues freed a monk-craftsman (*monakh-kustar'*) from payment of the industrial tax. Thanks to his efforts, the yearly tax on the monastery fell from 15,000 to 1,641 rubles. Protected by local Communists, the monastery survived until 1928. See *Povolzhskaia pravda*, November 2, 1928, p. 3.

15. For related examples, see *Bezbozhnik*, January 18, 1925, p. 8, and February 15, 1925, p. 6.

16. For a detailed discussion of the schismatic development, see Curtiss, *Russian Church*, pp. 129–53. As he notes on p. 142, the Renovationists also spawned several schismatic groups. In August of 1922, Bishop Antonin created the "League of Regeneration of the Church." In October, the "League of Congregations of the Ancient Apostolic Church," led by Dean Vvedenskii, appeared. The "Russian People's Church," located in Vologda, and the "Free Laboring Church," located in Penza, were formed some time later.

17. On March 15, 1905, a group of thirty-two married priests in St. Petersburg sent a memorandum calling for major church reforms to Metropolitan Antonii. This Alliance of Church Renewal, as it came to be called, proposed many of the church reforms later championed by the Renovationists.

of the parish clergy (e.g., allowing priests to wear secular clothes and to remarry if widowed).[18] The Renovationists also advocated religious reforms, including the translation of the liturgy into the Russian vernacular, opening the center doors (*tsarskie vrata*) of the iconostasis so that the laity could see holy rites being performed, and adopting the Gregorian calendar.[19] The Renovationists' embrace of these ecclesiastical and religious reforms went hand in hand with a political accommodation with the Soviet regime. Its leaders vowed their support for the Soviet government and the world socialist revolution; furthermore, they gave their sanction to the regime's confiscation of church valuables, including sacramental vessels. The secret police (OGPU) played a major role in engineering the schism, seeking to use it to weaken and ultimately destroy the Orthodox Church.[20]

Despite the OGPU's indubitable role in the schism, from the start the Renovationists trailed behind the Tikhonite or Patriarchal group in popular support. Although Renovationism began as a movement of parish priests, it subsequently faltered at the local level. Available evidence indicates that the rural laity actually disdained these departures from tradition in everyday religious life, especially the calendar reforms.[21] A 1924 report of the Council of People's Commissars acknowledged the strength of the Tikhon faction in comparison to the Renovationists: "Tikhonism is beating us economically. Their strength in this regard is enormous.... Meanwhile the Renovationists are suffering extreme deprivation, literally a state of poverty (especially in the dioceses of Pskov, Ekaterinoslav, Poltava, and a number of others)."[22] By 1926–27 popular support for the Renovationists had almost completely disappeared. Speaking at the Second Agitprop Conference for the Lower Volga Region in 1929, a Party member claimed that "at the present moment... two religious movements, the Tikhonites and the sectarians, are especially dangerous."[23] A 1929 inquiry into the relative strength of the two factions in Vladimir province revealed that of 184,000 believers, 155,000 considered

18. Freeze, "Counter-reformation," p. 312.
19. Ibid., pp. 312–13. Curtiss, *Russian Church*, pp. 129–74.
20. Volkogonov, *Lenin*, pp. 375–84; Roslof, "Renovationist Movement"; Freeze, "Counter-reformation," p. 311. Some of the documents (drawn from the Presidential Archive) demonstrating the OGPU's role have been published in Nikolai N. Pokrovskii, "Politbiuro i Tserkov', 1922–1923," *Novyi mir*, no. 8 (1994): 186–213.
21. Freeze, "Counter-reformation."
22. TsGAOR, f. 5446-s, op. 55, d. 647, l. 14. See also *VSS* 10 (1926): 8. On the Renovationists' struggle to sustain the movement on the parish level, see also Roslof, "Renovationist Movement," esp. pp. 237–61. Analogously, priests of the Constitutional Church in France enjoyed little support among peasants in certain counterrevolutionary areas, such as Brittany, during the French Revolution. See Donald Sutherland, *The Chouans: The Social Origins of Popular Counter-Revolution in Upper Brittany* (New York, 1982), pp. 237–47, 255–56.
23. *Povolzhskaia pravda*, August 25, 1929, p. 2.

themselves members of the Tikhonite branch, while only 30,000 belonged to Renovationists.[24] In the same year, a provincial correspondent admitted the former territory of Serdobsk *uezd* to be the "center of the Tikhonite movement."[25] Thus even supporters of the Soviet regime, who would be prone to exaggerate the strength of the Renovationists (or to deny their weakness), admitted the depth of popular support for the Tikhonites. Although the Renovationist movement did not meet its ultimate demise until the 1940s, Tikhon's release from prison in 1923 and the subsequent establishment of a separate "Patriarchal" church sealed the movement's failure.

The ultimate triumph of the Tikhon faction notwithstanding, religious villagers wrestled with the question of the affiliation of their parish churches. At times clergy and laity organized forums to work through this issue. In 1924, the priest Plemiannikov organized a debate, "Whom shall we follow?" in Zinov'evko (Petrovsk *uezd*, Saratov province).[26] His defense of Renovationism elicited protest from another village priest, who charged that Renovationist priests had three wives each. Plemiannikov countered as follows: "We marry twice, but they live with women cooks [i.e., have mistresses]." As Plemiannikov's role in organizing and conducting the dispute demonstrates, the schism compelled village priests to take the initiative in attracting other clergy to their chosen affiliation. Renovationists claimed that Tikhonite priests commonly slandered their Synodal counterparts.[27] Calling Renovationists "heretics" and "lacking grace" (*bezblagodatnyi*), Shevalevskii, a former Renovationist priest in Tambov province, was said to typify the slanderous tactics of Tikhonite parish priests.

For the most part, however, rural clergy had very limited and indirect influence in deciding the ultimate affiliation of their parishes. To be sure, they did not invariably want more influence than they in fact had. In some cases they actually looked to the state for direction; in 1922 the clergy in Serdobsk *uezd* (Saratov province) asked the district executive committee to decide their allegiance![28] Most commonly, however, rural clergy had to accept that it was the group of twenty (*tserkovnaia obshchina*), the "meeting of believers,"(*sobranie veruiushchikh*), and the village assembly that decided the parish's ultimate affiliation.[29] Thus the

24. P. Bliakhin, *Kto i zachem stroit tserkvi* (Moscow, 1929), pp. 8–9.
25. *Povolzhskaia pravda*, May 23, 1929, p. 3.
26. *Petrovskaia kommuna*, November 3, 1924, p. 3.
27. VSS 10 (1926): 25.
28. See, for example, the letter written by a priest, printed in *Serp i molot*, September 22, 1922, p. 2.
29. *Vlast' sovetov*, February 1927, pp. 19–20. On the role of the *tserkovnaia obshchina*, see N., "O russkoi tserkvi," p. 8. See also *Bezbozhnik*, February 4, 1926.

schism increased the laity's role in structuring the life of the rural parish.

As the case of the parish church in Lopatko (Petrovsk *uezd*, Saratov province) demonstrates, the laity exercised their power of choice in several ways. In 1924, the village priest decided to affiliate with the Renovationists, but his revenues fell off because his parishioners stopped coming to church.[30] When the priest decided to reaffiliate with the Tikhon branch, the laity questioned his sincerity and demanded he publicly renounce the Renovationists. They even invited a priest from another village to conduct the ceremony.[31] In Lopatko, the village priest had to comply with the wishes of his parishioners in order to retain control of the parish.

Rural clergy in other villages were also obliged to follow their parishioners' lead. Like his counterpart in Lopatko, the priest in Sinodskoe (Petrovsk *uezd*, Saratov province) changed his affiliation to please his parishioners. In the summer of 1922, fearing the loss of his livelihood if he remained attached to the Tikhonites, he joined the Renovationists. But he was assigned to a parish whose laity still considered themselves Tikhonites. They delivered him an ultimatum: leave the Renovationist Church or leave the parish. Submitting to their demand, he went to Saratov to recant formally, accompanied by three witnesses from the village.[32] Neither the parishioners of Sinodskoe nor those of Lopatko trusted their priest's word on his intent to leave the Renovationist Church, a revealing index of their anticlerical attitudes.

Parish clergy also had to depend on their parishioners to resist Renovationist encroachment in the rural parish. From 1922 to 1925, parish councils endeavored with considerable success to bring recalcitrant Renovationist priests back to the Tikhonite camp.[33] Their efforts continued in subsequent years. On March 7, 1926, for example, a church council affiliated with the Patriarchal church arranged a meeting of 140 people in the town of El'nia (El'nia *uezd*, Smolensk province). The gathering forbade the Renovationist bishop Aleksei, who intended to visit the city on March 9–10, to enter the cathedral.[34] According to this report of the district executive committee, "an analogous struggle [against representatives of the Renovationist Church]" was under way "in separate parishes of the countryside." In Smolensk province, religious villagers and town dwellers used the church council to prevent inroads by the Renovationists.

Often motivated by struggles over scarce space and financial resources,

30. For further evidence, see *VSS* 11 (1926): 20.
31. *Petrovskaia kommuna*, June 2, 1924, p. 3.
32. *Petrovskaia kommuna*, June 5, 1924, p. 3.
33. Freeze, "Counter-reformation," p. 332.
34. Smolensk WKP 20, "Otchet El'ninskogo ukoma VKP(b) s oktiabria 1925 po 1-oe apr. 1926 g. na volpartkonferentsii 4 maia 1926 goda."

conflict between Tikhonite and Renovationist supporters sometimes took violent form. A representative incident occurred in Sverdlovsk, when during the winter of 1924–25 the two factions engaged in a physical battle for control of the cathedral. An investigation by the district executive committee, which found that Tikhonites had kept the revenues from the sale of church valuables, catalyzed the conflict. Angered that the executive committee had decided to rent the building to the Renovationists, the Tikhonites attacked their rivals. A Renovationist priest was killed.[35]

Rural Clergy and Parish Democracy

It was by no means only in the context of the schism that rural parish clergy experienced the enhanced power and aggressiveness of their parishioners in parish affairs. Even Patriarchal clergy were the objects of their parishioners' verbal barbs (e.g. "our clergy here are like mould") and sporadic physical blows.[36] Fights between clergy and laity sometimes erupted because of financial disputes. On August 26, 1923, a fight broke out between a priest and layperson in a church in Atkarsk *uezd* (Saratov province). Annoyed that the priest did not read the submitted names (*podannye zapiski*) for the repose of the dead, a parishioner begged him to remember his dead mother. But the priest refused: "For two rubles I won't read [the names]: you should be content that I remember your mother in my mind. If you want me to read [the names] aloud, then pay me twenty rubles."[37] In the winter of 1924–25, local Party representatives in Kursk province decided to close a church when a priest and parishioners engaged in a scuffle.[38]

The clergy's distress over their increased inability to trust parishioners to follow their lead in parish affairs must have rivaled the physical pain produced by such sporadic physical blows. One particularly telling example must suffice here. In July of 1923, a priest called a meeting of parishioners to produce the requisite twenty cosigners for registering the religious community with the district executive committee. Some participants refused their

---

35. *Bezbozhnik*, January 11, 1925, p. 8. The *uezd* executive committee closed the cathedral as a result of the violence. For other examples, see RTsKhIDNI, f. 89, op. 4, d. 118, l. 5, and *Bezbozhnik*, January 2, 1925, p. 2.
36. *Izvestiia Atkarskogo uezdnogo ispolkoma*, March 31, 1923, p. 2. Given the provincial correspondent's investment in portraying villagers' abandonment of religion, such lay denunciations of their priests must, of course, be read with caution.
37. *Izvestiia Atkarskogo uezdnogo ispolkoma*, September 1, 1923.
38. *Bezbozhnik*, January 18, 1925, p. 6.

support: "Why do we need a church? You can pray anywhere. If you want, you can [even] pray in a tavern."[39] To be sure, these villagers were questioning the utility of the church building, not religious belief and practice per se.[40]

Arguably the most dramatic example of parishioners' enhanced influence in parish affairs was the widespread reappearance of *vybornoe nachalo*. Parishioners' rejection of Renovationist priests was but one manifestation of this phenomenon.[41] More and more frequently, villagers only hired priests and other members of the clergy after taking a potential candidate's financial demands into account.[42] In villages such as Sosiakoe, for example, the parishioners cited a priest's financial demands as grounds for refusing to hire him. As of the winter of 1925–26, the parish had been without a priest for a long time. They received the following telegram from a candidate for the post:

> I am at your service and will take from you not much [in financial reimbursement], only enough to feed myself: sixty poods of rice, sixty poods of oats, and, as needed, potatoes from each household, will [need] your hay to feed my two cows, horse and small cattle until fodder feeding.... You will pay the food tax [*prodnalog*], labor tax, and all monetary taxes that I am assessed for. And of course, you'll provide me with an apartment, which you'll supply with wood and light all year round.[43]

At another meeting, parishioners expressed their unwillingness to meet this priest's financial demands. Some villagers asked: "Why does the priest need so much bread, [since] surely there are only three people in his family?" Others wondered: "Why should we pay the agricultural tax [*prodnalog*] for

---

39. A. M. Bol'shakov, *Sovetskaia derevnia, 1917–1925 gg. Ekonomika i byt* (Leningrad, 1928), p. 191.

40. Even workers distinguished between anticlericalism and antireligiosity. See Ia. Shafir, *Gazeta i derevnia* (Moscow, 1923), p. 46.

41. *Izvestiia Saratovskogo soveta*, September 1, 1923, p. 2. Diocesan congresses (*eparkhial'nye s"ezdy*) and superintendants' councils (*blagochinnye sovety*) also underwent democratization. In April 1917 a diocesan congress of clergy and parishioners in Saratov elected a chair, Archpriest Gennady Markovskii. See RGIA, f. 831, op. 1, ed. khr. 146, l. 3 ob. Meeting on May 24, 1917, the clergy and parishioners of a superintendants' council in Saratov *uezd* elected a parish priest, Nikolai Doktorov, a thirty-eight-year-old son of a psalmist, as chair. Ibid., l. 13, l. 13 ob., l. 14 ob. On the reappearance of the analogue of *vybornoe nachalo* in revolutionary France, see Desan, *Reclaiming the Sacred*, p. 149.

42. Fenomenov, *Sovremennaia derevnia*, 2:95. For one of countless examples, see *Sovetskaia derevnia*, May 6, 1924, p. 1.

43. *Bezbozhnik*, February 4, 1926, p. 5.

[his] land, you know on that score there is a decree, [which states that] he who works the land must [be the one to] pay taxes on it." By telegram, the villagers informed the priest that his services would not be needed, a telling example of parishioners' control over the financial side of clerical life. Parishioners also fired priests who made excessive financial demands.[44] When church councils, collectives of believers, and village assemblies decided on expulsion, rural parish priests sometimes complained to higher state bodies (e.g., VIKs), a revealing index of their lingering *étatisme*.[45]

State authorities could not stop the most dramatic example of "parish power," the parish council.[46] Writing from exile in Paris in 1926, an unidentified contributor to the Orthodox journal *Put'* described the emergence of what he called "parish democracy" (*prikhodskaia demokratiia*). Reports from the homeland, he maintained, included "just complaints that the exclusive influence of the laity in the parish sometimes cramps the independence of the priest."[47] In 1928, even P. Krasikov, a former high official at the Commissariat of Justice, admitted that "the clergy itself, of course, does not play any independent role [in the life of the parish]. It is wholly subordinate to those groups [lay organizations such as the church councils], performs their will."[48]

Who comprised these powerful parish councils? Antireligious leaders themselves issued conflicting generalizations on the socioeconomic background of laity who ran the rural church councils during the 1920s. For Iaroslavskii and other leaders of the antireligious campaign, church councils were the organizational tools of the "kulak" and other bourgeois holdovers from the tsarist regime.[49] Speaking on June 11, 1929, at the Second All-Union Conference of the League of the Godless, Iaroslavskii asserted that "these splinters of former classes ... merge with the strata of the kulaks and nepmen and still ... function together, where they can, and in any case, in the

---

44. See, for example, *Sovetskaia derevnia*, January 20, 1924.

45. For an interesting example, see *Izvestiia Saratovskogo soveta*, June 19, 1923, p. 4. In this case Party officials apparently affirmed the priest's right to serve the parish.

46. Freeze, "Counter-reformation," p. 332.

47. N., "O russkoi tserkvi," pp. 8–9. See also Father Trophimus, "Russian Religion," pp. 94–95.

48. *Izvestiia Saratovskogo soveta*, February 17, 1928, p. 2.

49. Contemporaries used various strategic devices to present a distorted image of the socioeconomic makeup of church councils. One ploy was to make assertions on the socioeconomic profile of the councils without providing statistics. For an example, see Bliakhin, *Kto i zachem stroit tserkvi*, pp. 14–15. Another was to use statistics on the membership of church councils in the *towns* to represent the entire province, and especially the countryside. See *Povolzhskaia pravda*, September 15, 1928, p. 3, and Bliakhin, *Kto i zachem stroit tserkvi*, p. 16. Yet another tactic was to distort the socioeconomic composition of the church councils by providing only partial lists of the members. See, for example, *Bezbozhnik*, January 9, 1927.

church councils."⁵⁰ The 1928 edition of the textbook for antireligious workers stated that "kulaks, rich people, and other 'former people' are in control in the church councils and sectarian organizations."⁵¹ But in the same speech at the 1929 conference, Iaroslavskii also admitted that poor and middle peasants could also be found on church councils: "If poor and middle peasants enter these religious organizations [i.e., the church councils], and in some places genuine workers with a long industrial period of service join, this should not deceive us: it means that we still have both among workers and among peasants elements that have not [attained] class consciousness, . . . We have to fight for these elements."⁵² The rural Church and the antireligious campaign, as Iaroslavskii conceded, were competing for the loyalty of members of the same socioeconomic groups. In an unspecified year, the priest Ivenin promoted the "poor peasant" Bur'ianovka to the church council in Stepanovko (Buguruslansk *okrug*).⁵³

Rural church councils, very belatedly fulfilling the mandate of the 1864 *Polozhenie*, sometimes used their considerable power to aid the clergy. Those councils affiliated with the Tikhonites provided financial and material support to a parish clergy struggling to pay taxes, deprived of bread rations, and whose financial requests anticlerical parishioners were spurning in ever increasing numbers.⁵⁴ Reflecting in 1933 on general developments within religious life in the 1920s, a parish priest highlighted the clergy's dependence on their parishioners: "The care that they [the laity] take of their clergy is often very touching."⁵⁵ Dramatizing the dependence of the clergy on the church council, in 1921 the priest of Tokarevo (Kasimov *uezd*, Riazan province) requested the local council to put into practice a schedule for paying him in kind for the performance of various religious rituals.⁵⁶ Rural church councils also mounted resistance to the state's confiscation of church valuables in 1922. Having received a notice concerning the "voluntary" contribution of church objects, the council in Serdobsk *uezd* (Saratov province) called a meeting of believers. During the ensuing discussion, one participant

50. *Stenograficheskii otchet*, p. 54. See also E. Iaroslavskii, "Bor'ba s religiei," in *Voinstvuiushchee bezbozhie za 15 let: Sbornik* (Moscow, 1932), p. 322.
51. A. T. Lukachevskii, ed., *Uchebnik dlia rabochikh antireligioznykh kruzhkov* (Moscow, 1928), p. 273.
52. *Stenograficheskii otchet*, p. 56.
53. I. Eliashevich, *S krestom i evangeliem protiv kolkhozov* (Leningrad, 1930), p. 27.
54. Father Trophimus, "Russian Religion." Throughout the 1920s, *Bezbozhnik* applauded villagers' refusal to receive clergy on religious holidays, when it was customary for parishioners to recompense the clergy for the visit and prayers. See, for example, *Bezbozhnik*, June 3, 1923, p. 2, and August 5, 1923, and *Krest'ianskaia pravda*, December 24, 1929.
55. Father Trophimus, "Russian Religion," p. 96. See also Pospielovsky, *Russian Church*, 1:169.
56. *Petrovskaia kommuna*, March 15, 1921, p. 4.

exclaimed: "We won't give anything! What do they ask of us? The Church is separated from the state and the [government] doesn't give us any financial help for decoration." Apparently swayed by such reasoning, the council decided to give only a large quantity of paper to the committee on famine relief (*Pomgol*).[57] Shouldering considerable responsibility for the financial affairs of the parish, church councils nevertheless focused their energies on caring for the church building.[58] Church sisterhoods (*sestrichestva*) also helped care for churches by cleaning icons placed in them.[59]

Obliged to adopt a deferential stance toward powerful and aggressive parish councils, rural clergy also faced powerful competition from sectarian movements.[60] In a village in Borisoglebsk *uezd* of Tambov province, for example, in 1926 there were more than 300 sectarian households of a variety of affiliations, e.g., Baptists, Molokans, Evangelists, and Subbotniki.[61] Why did various sects grow so tremendously over the course of the 1920s? The mobilizing tactics of sectarians can offer a valuable clue. In 1927, for example, defectors from Orthodoxy to the Baptist sect tried to lure fellow villagers in Sereno (Kamyshin *uezd*, Saratov province) with the promise of religious equality: "Enter our [religious] community, brothers. There is no deceit here. We are equal, and the Lord God himself governs us invisibly. We are [all] the representatives of God on earth."[62] Clearly, the authors of such sectarian propaganda assumed that many villagers were seeking more egalitarian relationships in parish affairs. To be sure, the converts who flocked to the sects over the course of the 1920s may have in fact had different motivations. Nevertheless, there is some evidence that the sects grew so phenomenally *in part* because many villagers preferred a religious community that put all believers on the same footing.[63] In other words, the growth of

57. *Serp i molot*, May 10, 1922. Other examples can be found in Freeze, "Counter-reformation," p. 331.

58. Father Trophimus, "Russian Religion," p. 95; E. L., *Episkopy ispovedniki*, pp. 68–70. The all-Russian *sobor* issued a decree on September 12, 1918 (August 30 Old Style), "On the Protection of the Church's Sacred Objects Against Blasphemous Seizure and Desecration," that explicitly instructed parish communities, when faced with the state's seizure of a church, to support their priest and hold private services. On this see Pospielovsky, *Russian Church*, 1:36–37.

59. Father Trophimus, "Russian Religion," p. 97; M. Shakhnovich, *Zapiski bezbozhnika* (Leningrad, 1933); E.L., *Episkopy ispovedniki*, pp. 168–70; *VRSKhD*, July 1928, 16. Sisterhoods also assisted exiled bishops.

60. The Renovationist press claimed that Tikhonite and Renovationist parish clergy were too busy "fighting" each other to devote much energy to combating the many growing sectarian movements. *VSS* 10 (1926): 21. On sectarians' success in winning converts, see also Stites, *Revolutionary Dreams*, esp. pp. 121–22.

61. *VSS* 11 (1926): 25.

62. *Bezbozhnik*, December 11, 1927.

63. The various sectarian denominations were organized on the national level. In 1926, there were 11,000 members (and 430 communities [*obshchiny*]) of the Adventist sect in the USSR;

the sects should be viewed as part of a larger phenomenon of the continuing renegotiation of the social relationships in religious life.

In sum, rural parish priests and other members of the clergy endured a diminution of their authority within the parish and the village.[64] To be sure, rural clergy experienced this loss in differing—and even in widely differing—degrees. Some rural priests would not have recognized much of their own experience when presented, for example, with an "ideal type" drawn from the most extreme examples given above, such as the starving priest, who, while subjected to constant physical and verbal harassment, also had to deal with competition from the sectarians and the threat of schism. A good many parish priests, especially those of the Patriarchal as opposed to the Renovationist church, even lived somewhat comfortably, enjoying considerable support—financial and otherwise—from their parishioners.[65] Nevertheless, even those priests who fared relatively well had to face challenges to their authority, some of which had been developing since the last decades of the tsarist period. This shift was sometimes represented spatially: priests found themselves unable to reside across from the parish church, as had been customary in tsarist times. Instead, they were obliged to seek more modest quarters (e.g., one or two rooms) on the fringes of the village.[66]

Unable to cope with anticlericalism, financial difficulties, persecution, the schism, sectarians, and the *bezbozhniki*, some parish clergy eventually renounced their calling.[67] How widespread was this phenomenon? Although *Bezbozhnik* and provincial newspapers regularly publicized such cases, a parish priest claimed that "there are some who have renounced the Church, though they are few."[68] Comparison of the number of priests in 1914 with that in 1926 bears him out. In 1914, there were 50,105 deacons and priests in the Russian empire, while in 1926, according to the 1926 census, there were 60,000 priests of various faiths in the USSR.[69]

---

they were in turn organized into six *oblast'* unions and one all-union organization. See *VSS* 11 (1926): 13.

64. Patriarchal priests' perception that they were increasingly subject to the wishes of their parishioners was a phenomenon openly discussed at the plenum of the Holy Synod, held on April 16–21, 1926. *VSS* 10 (1926): 14.

65. On the relatively comfortable financial and material condition of a good many Tikhonite priests (at least in the perception of the financially embattled Renovationists), see, for example, "Ternii obnovlencheskogo pastyria v provintsii," *VSS* 10 (1926): 26.

66. See the description in *VRSKhD*, May 1928, p. 9.

67. There was a distinction between renouncing the church (usually a public event) and simply not functioning as a priest anymore. See Father Trophimus, "Russian Religion," p. 101.

68. Ibid. The number of voluntary abdications of Constitutional clergy during the French Revolution (mostly *l'an* II) was also low. See Vovelle, *Religion et révolution*, p. 83.

69. The 1914 figures are from Curtiss, *Russian Church*, p. 10, and the 1926 figures from Robert Conquest, *The Harvest of Sorrow: Soviet Collectivization and the Terror-Famine* (New York, 1986), p. 202.

The former priests' explanations for their decision to leave the Church attest to the various corrosive pressures on the rural clergy. During their public renunciations of the calling, priests incorporated the vocabulary of the *bezbozhniki* into their criticism of religion and of the Orthodox Church.[70] Village priests in Saratov and Ivanovo-Voznesensk provinces, for example, condemned religious faith as a "narcotic" and a "deception," both favorite terms of the antireligious press.[71] A parish priest heard the following rejection of religion from a former colleague: "It's all nonsense. What sort of God is there? There is no God."[72] For other priests, it was not the propaganda of the *bezbozhniki* but financial difficulties that forced them out of the calling. In 1923, a priest left his parish in Kalachev *uezd* (Briansk province) because one-sixth of his parishioners had stopped attending church.[73]

When necessary, rural parishioners assumed a variety of former clerical functions and responsibilities, including the liturgical functions of the priest. Parishioners improvised collective confessions, prayer meetings, mutual administrations of the eucharist, and mass baptisms.[74] In 1923, peasants in the village Chernevo (Iaroslavl *uezd*, Iaroslavl province) played the role of the priest, deacon, and sexton in a wedding that was held in a peasant hut. The surrogate members of the "lay clergy" held "paltry sieves" (*khudye resheta*) instead of the traditional wreaths (*ventsy*) above the heads of the bride and groom.[75]

Former priests adopted a variety of occupations upon leaving the church. Many took up agriculture or clerical positions in the village.[76] More surprising, some priests, as a member of their ranks put it, "[gave] into the godless teaching."[77] Asked in 1924 whether he had belonged to the Patriarchal or Renovationist Church, a former parish priest from Serdobsk *uezd* replied that "as soon as these church divisions developed, I began to involve myself with antireligious propaganda."[78] A parish priest described a former member

---

70. Given the available evidence, it is difficult to pinpoint the degree to which the *bezbozhniki* compelled them to use such language. See also *VRKhD*, no. 150, 2d ser. (1987): 231.

71. His "ceremony" of renunciation took place in the Serdobsk public house (*nardom*). See *Serp i molot*, October 4, 1924, p. 2; *Izvestiia saratovskogo soveta*, November 27, 1924, p. 2; and *Bezbozhnik*, February 22, 1925, p. 3, and August 7, 1927.

72. Father Trophimus, "Russian Religion," p. 101. For similar (yet rare) cases among Constitutional clergy in France, see Vovelle, *Religion et révolution*, pp. 91–92.

73. It is unclear whether this priest found another parish or had formally renounced the calling. See *Bezbozhnik*, July 29, 1923.

74. Geoffrey Hosking, *The First Socialist Society* (Cambridge, Mass., 1985), pp. 235–36. Unfortunately Hosking does not give his source for this information.

75. *Bezbozhnik*, March 11, 1923, p. 4. As of 1925, 75 percent of all peasant weddings were still held in church. See Stites, *Revolutionary Dreams*, p. 112.

76. See *Bezbozhnik*, April 8, 1923, p. 8.; Father Trophimus, "Russian Religion," p. 101. See also *VRKhD* 2 (1930).

77. Father Trophimus, "Russian Religion," p. 101.

78. *Serp i molot*, October 7, 1924. For analogous developments during the French

of the clergy who now served "in the administrative section in his own former parish, and precisely in the department of religion. He has the look of a convinced Godless."[79] Yet were such former clergy who joined the League of the Godless or otherwise participated in the antireligious campaign *really* true (non)-believers?[80] Why was it that over the course of the 1920s not "friendship and enmity" but priesthood and atheism could be "close neighbors"?[81] Given the clergy's interest in "taming" ostensibly Soviet institutions for their own purposes—and their willingness to shed their clerical identity to do so—there is certainly reason to entertain the possibility that some former clergy were trying to subvert antireligious efforts.[82]

Clergy on the Offensive

Although some priests renounced their calling to escape the financial, ideological, and emotional pressures on the clergy, most, in fact, did not. When they stayed, they did so for a variety of reasons: the uneven weight of the pressures noted above, the lack of other options, and their commitment to their parishioners.[83] How did those priests who did not abandon their calling respond to these various and sometimes overwhelming pressures and, more generally, to the claims made by those antagonistic to religious belief and practice? Did they tolerate passively, for example, the skirmishes waged in the major fields of cultural conflict examined above, namely, the family, education, village "semiotics," and electoral politics? Or did they try and develop strategies to fulfill their personal needs and parish responsibilities in these trying circumstances? In responding to these pressures, how did rural parish clergy draw on aspects of their prerevolutionary sociopolitical identity?

Clergy were limited in their capacity to intervene directly in the conflict that arose within the family around issues of religious belief and practice.

Revolution, see Vovelle, *Religion et révolution*, pp. 102, 104, 106.

79. Father Trophimus, "Russian Religion," p. 101. On former priests taking positions in the Soviet *apparat*, see also *VRKhD*, no. 150, 2d ser. (1987): 231.

80. This is the assumption Peris makes in "Commissars in Red Cassocks." Such "defections" were by no means limited to rural parish priests. The Renovationist archbishop Ignatii, for example, defected to the godless. See *VRSKhD*, October 1928, p. 14.

81. The Russian proverb reads: "Friendship and enmity are close neighbors." Quoted in Kendall Bailes, *Technology and Society under Lenin and Stalin* (Princeton, N.J., 1978), p. 3. See V. I. Dal', *Poslovitsy russkogo naroda* (Moscow, 1957), p. 774.

82. See the discussion below of clergy's temporary renunciation of clerical identity in order to serve on cooperative boards.

83. On this see Figes, *Peasant Russia*, p. 147.

Nevertheless, deeply aware of these tensions, they tried to organize family religious instruction. Their countermobilization efforts in education, village semiotics, and electoral politics were intended to reverberate powerfully in the dynamics of social relationships within the family. For example, they delivered sermons in which they called Komsomol cells "rotten nests" and warned parents not to let their children frequent red corners and reading huts.[84]

As these tactics suggest, clergy did not deny the conflict generated in social relationships within the family over the issue of religious belief and practice. Conceding that antireligious activists (whether popular or "official") had in fact created tremendous tension in family relationships, priests in fact blamed antireligious workers for destroying the foundations of the family: "Only we, believers, have moral families."[85] Clergy also represented *bezbozhniki* as dangerous to the family by calling them "debauchers and libertines" (*bludniki i razvratniki*).[86] In other words, their strategy was to concede and even exaggerate the corrosive impact of *bezbozhniki* on family dynamics, in order to portray antireligious activists as having violated basic moral standards of the peasant community. Clergy were thus using, to different ends, the same strategy employed by correspondents for *Bezbozhnik*. One of the forms in which the conflict over religious belief and practice was played out was a conversation in which each "side" impugned the other for having violated basic conceptions of peasant morality and justice.

Rural clergy's portrayal of *bezbozhniki* as immoral enemies of family life was part of a larger effort to resist and neutralize the tactics of antireligious activists in the "field" of education. This arena of conflict, as noted above, encompassed not only formal education that took place in village classrooms but also the propaganda efforts of the Party, as well as any "counter-propaganda" ventures of groups such as religious activists. In effect, the village itself became a classroom.

In attempting to resist the sometimes feeble and sporadic efforts of Party cadres and their fellow travelers in this "field" of conflict, rural clergy were not completely without resources and opportunities. Until the promulgation of the "Law on Religious Associations" (April 8, 1929), clergy and other religious activists were legally guaranteed the freedom to engage in religious propaganda. Parents had the right to have a priest give their children "private" religious instruction.[87] While the legal infrastructure provided clergy with some opportunities for participating in this field of conflict, their prerevolutionary experience in formal and informal "educational" activities

---

84. *VRSKhD*, October 1928, p. 16.
85. *Izvestiia Saratovskogo soveta*, April 12, 1928, p. 2.
86. Ibid.
87. See Curtiss, *Russian Church*, p. 229.

(e.g., extraliturgical instruction and religious "conversations") provided them with skills potentially useful in this context. Often highly literate, they could "know the enemy" by reading antireligious propaganda such as *Bezbozhnik*. Diocesan gazettes and church programs on the district level routinely instructed clergy to attain "familiarity with antireligious literature." Writing in *Permskie eparkhial'nye vedomosti*, Protopop Byldygin of Perm directed parish priests preparing for antireligious disputes to "read antireligious literature, [and] there, as if having looked in a mirror and seen where you're dirty, you'll know how to wash yourself."[88] To what extent—and how—were rural clergy able to draw on these opportunities and skills in resisting the claims of antireligious activists in the field of education?

Constrained by the low literacy rate of the village population and the virtual absence of an ecclesiastical press, rural clergy had to find ways to reach their audiences other than through the written word.[89] Thus verbal attacks on *bezbozhniki* or other aspects of the antireligious campaign were popular.[90] In 1923, while offering a public prayer for rain, a priest in Ivanovskoe (Kaluga province) attributed all the village's problems to the undermining of religious faith.[91] In 1925, a priest and deacon in Shatskoe (Tambov province) appeared on the porch of the village church and made unspecified charges against the *bezbozhniki*.[92] These examples suggest two more general characteristics of rural clergy's verbal assault on antireligious activists. (Whether clergy distinguished between members of the League and other villagers hostile to religious belief and practice is not clear.) Obliged to seize all possible opportunities to reach the widest possible "audience," rural clergy even integrated their verbal attacks on antireligious activists into traditional events in rural religious life (e.g., public prayers and church services [*bogosluzheniia*]).[93] Second, an important and recurring theme of this discourse was the clergy's contention that antireligious activists were jeopardizing the subsistence of villagers.[94]

---

88. Such an injunction comprised point 1 of the antireligious program of the Tikhonites in Ustiuzhinsk *uezd* (Cherepovetsk province), as reprinted in *VRSKhD*, June 1928, p. 16.

89. Clergy were legally deprived of the right to publish. In the beginning of 1918, the Bolsheviks seized the presses of the Orthodox Church and forbade the publication of religious periodicals, a policy that continued throughout NEP. For details, see Freeze, "Counter-reformation," pp. 334–36. Despite these legal constraints, Tikhonite resolutions on the district level called for the "publication of religious leaflets and brochures." For an example, see *VRSKhD*, June 1928, p. 16.

90. *VRSKhD*, October 1928, p. 15.

91. *Bednota*, July 14, 1923, p. 2; see also *Bezbozhnik*, August 5, 1923, p. 2.

92. *Bezbozhnik*, September 13, 1925, p. 4; August 2, 1925, p. 2.

93. See point 5 of the antireligious program adopted by the Tikhonites in Ustiuzhinsk *uezd*, Cherepovetsk province, reprinted in *VRSKhD*, June 1928, p. 16.

94. On the subsistence ethic, see Scott, *Moral Economy*.

The case of the priest Ivan Ivlev exemplifies how the clergy strategically crafted their verbal attacks on antireligious activists and the regime itself. Ivlev, the son of a trader from Tambov province, served the village Sobinka and the factory "Kommunisticheskii avangard."[95] Refraining from anti-Soviet propaganda, Ivlev publicly used the phrase "each government is from God" to underscore the legitimacy of the regime. But Ivlev adopted a different attitude when speaking with religious villagers. He instructed his parishioners not to frequent the workers' club, the red corner, listen to antireligious speeches and lectures, or send their children to Soviet schools. Dismissing the Bolsheviks as immoral exploiters of workers, Ivlev refused to support the campaign for the seven-hour work day and for discipline in the factories. Preaching "universal Christian love and brotherhood," Ivlev rejected the ideological foundations of the regime: "Communism makes people depraved and incites them against one another."[96] Thus, as circumstances dictated, he shifted from theologically grounded tolerance to uncompromising rejection of the regime.

Although clergy regarded spontaneous verbal snipes at antireligious activists as a useful tactic of self-defense, rural priests in particular recognized that they had to do more than damn the enemy. Resolutions of church councils made note of the clergy's efforts to counteract antireligious activism during "extra-liturgical instruction [*vnebogosluzhebnye besedy*] with parishioners"; clergy in fact accelerated such efforts during anti-Christmas "celebrations," conducting their own propaganda "in churches, in families, in dorms, and on the street."[97] Rural priests offered lectures in which they implicitly attempted to address some of the attacks on religious belief and practice made by antireligious activists. Some speakers, for example, tried to strengthen the religious community by demonstrating the Church's interest in agricultural activities and science, a strategy designed to keep wavering believers. After receiving permission from the district executive committee, on March 15, 1925, a priest in Drozdovo (Podol'sk *uezd*, Moscow province) gave a lecture on natural science.[98] In the Northern Region, a deacon gave a lecture on the topic "Ways of raising [the productivity] of agriculture."[99] Other priests such as Pëtr Petin adapted Christian theology to the new political circumstances.[100]

---

95. Bliakhin, *Kto i zachem stroit tserkvi*, p. 27.
96. Ibid., pp. 46–47.
97. This is a direct quotation from a resolution of the church council of the Nikol'sko-Ozerov church in Tikhvin *uezd*, Cherepovetsk province, an excerpt of which was reprinted in *VRSKhD*, June 1928, p. 16. The continuity of terminology with that of the late tsarist period is striking. On the rural clergy's efforts to conduct discussions to counter anti-Christmas celebrations, see *VRSKhD*, February 1928, p. 17.
98. *Bezbozhnik*, August 9, 1925.
99. N. Matorin, *Religiia i bor'ba s neiu v severnom krae* (Leningrad, 1930), p. 3.
100. Various strands of Christian socialism and Christian radicalism in Russian Orthodoxy

The specifics of Petin's background may explain his blending of elements of the new political culture and Christianity. He had served until 1923 in the Red Army as a cultural enlightenment worker, had taught and become a member of the Union of Cultural Enlightenment Workers (*Rabpros*) after demobilization, and then entered the priesthood, his father's profession; it is not clear whether he was a member of the Renovationist Church. Serving an *artel* in Bol'shaia Syrovatka (Khar'kov province), he preached during the winter of 1924–25 that communism had its roots in the teachings of Christ, the "first communist." Lenin, he maintained, was a religious person.[101] Thus Petin projected both religious attributes onto a political figure and political attributes onto a religious figure.[102] Speaking in June 1929 at the Second All-Union Congress of the League of the Godless, Bukharin warned of the competitive power of a "modernized church" created by priests such as Petin.[103]

Rural clergy competed for the faith of believers not only by offering them opportunities to listen passively to lectures and sermons but also by creating organizations that demanded their active participation. Interested in offering a religious alternative to the Soviet reading huts, by 1925 clergy in Irbitsk, Tobol'sk, Perm, and Nizhne-Tagil'sk districts had organized church groups for public readings and discussion of the Bible.[104] In the winter of 1928–29, a priest organized a "religious-cultural society" (*religioznoe kul'-turnoe obshchestvo*) in Baranyshkovo (Kamyshin *uezd*, Lower Volga), although, as we will shall see, its purpose appears to have been more political than cultural.[105] Clergy also organized choirs; Shakhnovich claimed that from 1924 to 1929 clergy throughout the Russian Republic created choirs to compete with the Soviet club choir.[106]

From 1924 to 1929 rural clergy held special "discussions" (*besedy*) with children, at which they gave the youngsters candy and cookies. Clergy also organized children's choirs and evening parties (*vechera*), offering young-

---

predated the Revolutions of 1917. The Union of Church Renovation, founded in 1905, at one point stressed the Church's obligation to shield workers from capitalist exploitation. See Pospielovsky, *Russian Church*, 1:47–54 and 80–92, for continuities in pre- and post-1917 fusions of political radicalism and Orthodoxy. Pospielovsky, however, focuses solely on urban clergy and national organizations.

101. *Bezbozhnik*, January 4, 1925, p. 6.
102. It is unclear whether he was a member of the Living Church.
103. *Stenograficheskii otchet*, p. 20.
104. *Bezbozhnik*, August 2, 1925, p. 2.
105. *Povolzhskaia pravda*, February 5, 1929, p. 2.
106. Shakhnovich, *Zapiski bezbozhnika*, p. 27; *Bezbozhnik*, December 20, 1925. For the influence of Soviet cultural institutions on the clergy, see Bliakhin, *Kto i zachem stroit tserkvi*, p. 33. Prior to 1917, the parish councils supported choirs. See *Pribavleniia k tserkovnym vedomostiam*, January 29, 1905, p. 212. *Bratstva* also helped form choirs composed of students in the church schools. See Papkov, *Tserkovnye bratstva*, p. 117.

sters the chance to sing and dance and do needlework.[107] In 1927, an instruction on the "Christianization of Children" appeared in the churches of the former territory of Vladimir province. It directed clergy to organize archaeological and zoological walks for the examination of religious questions and to set up children's libraries and corner displays (*ugolki*) with pictures of events from the Bible. It also underscored the usefulness of creating circles of "the baby Jesus" for little boys and of "the baby Mary" for little girls.[108] These activities offered an alternative to those of the Pioneers, the Party organization for children from ages nine to fifteen, as well as to Komsomol activities held at the red corner (*krasnyi ugolok*) and reading huts.[109]

Clergy also developed educational organizations for slightly older youth. By 1925, clergy in villages in Sverdlovsk and Kurgan *okrug*s had organized "circles of youth" for discussion of religious issues and instruction on living the Christian life.[110] During the 1920s, the priest in Ivanovskoe held meetings for youth in the church school.[111] In 1928, clergy in Saratov *uezd* held "evening gatherings [for] youth" (*vecherinki molodezhi*), which featured food, drink, singing, and listening to the gramophone.[112] As a village correspondent for the Lower Volga Region emphasized, rural Orthodox clergy were competing not only with the Komsomol, but with sectarians, as they devised activities for youth.[113]

Rural priests also vied for youthful parishioners by creating their own schools for teaching religious principles. According to Shakhnovich, clergy concentrated on teaching the *Zakon Bozhii*, especially from 1924 to 1929.[114] In 1926, a priest in Komarovko (Syzran *uezd*, Simbirsk province) opened a school in his home and began teaching the *Zakon Bozhii*.[115] A counterpart in the village Tomashevo created the same type of school and taught children how to pray.[116] As the village correspondent noted with disapproval, members of the county soviet invoked the Decree on the Separation of Church and State to explain their acceptance of the school: "Now the Church is separated from the state."

---

107. On this see A. Evdokimov, *V bor'be za molodezh': klassovaia bor'ba v derevne* (Leningrad, 1929), pp. 52–53. On sectarians' success in attracting peasants (roughly of Komsomol age) in Smolensk province, see Tirado, "The Revolution," p. 115.
108. Shakhnovich, *Zapiski bezbozhnika*, p. 27.
109. Evdokimov, *V bor'be*, p. 53. A decree of June 13, 1921, prohibited religious instruction of children below the age of eighteen.
110. *Bezbozhnik*, August 2, 1925, p. 2.
111. M. Kniazev, *Kak kulaki i popy borolis' s kolkhozom* (Moscow-Leningrad, 1930), pp. 6–7.
112. *Bezbozhnik*, January 29, 1928.
113. *Povolzhskaia pravda*, September 16, 1928, p. 5.
114. Shakhnovich, *Zapiski bezbozhnika*, p. 28.
115. *Bezbozhnik*, February 4, 1926.
116. Ibid.

As this remark shows, at times rural priests had difficulty understanding—or accepting—the new legal separation of Church and state. Clergy in several districts of Novgorod province demanded the teaching of the *Zakon Bozhii* in the schools.[117] In 1926 a priest appeared at a village school in Korenevshchina (Lipetsk *uezd*, Tambov province) and stated his intention to teach the *Zakon Bozhii*. Turned away by the school's director, he requested a separate room from the school council.[118]

Rural priests also facilitated the organization of activities for women. Tikhonite resolutions on the district level, for example, called for "the attraction of women to church activities."[119] On March 8, 1925, clergy held a meeting for women in the church in Krasnaia Sloboda (Irbitsk *okrug*).[120] According to Oleshchuk, rural churches sponsored sewing, needlework, and cutting circles, although it is not completely clear that clergy organized them.[121]

To what extent these various activities rekindled the loyalty of wavering parishioners or drained the ranks of various Soviet organizations is hard to say. But in 1928, a village correspondent for the Lower Volga Region attributed the desertion of reading huts and godless circles to the public relations activities of the clergy: "And thus, in the context of such energetic public work of sectarian and Orthodox clergy we see the sickly reading huts, the epidemic absence of cells of *bezbozhniki*, the complete absence of lectures and broad explanatory work. Our cultural enlightenment workers [seem to be] asleep and apparently have no interest in going to the benighted peasant masses."[122] According to this village correspondent, by NEP's end, the clergy of the Lower Volga Region stood out as energetic entrepreneurs, while Soviet propagandists faded into the background as indolent failures. Another testimony to the perceived success of clergy in the educational field was, in fact, the April 8, 1929, law on religious associations. The law replaced the Constitution's guarantee of "freedom of religious and antireligious propaganda" with "freedom of religious worship and antireligious propaganda" and banned religious organizations from engaging in any activities but worship services. Religious associations were forbidden from creating mutual-aid funds and cooperatives, from organizing gatherings for women and youth, from holding Bible study groups and arts and crafts or literary

---

117. Evidence cited in R. P. Makeikina, "Kul'turnoe stroitel'stvo v Novgorodskoi gubernii v 1921–27 gg." (synopsis of dissertation, Leningrad University, 1972).

118. *Bezbozhnik*, February 4, 1926, p. 6.

119. See *VRSKhD*, June 1928, p. 16.

120. *Bezbozhnik*, August 2, 1925, p. 2. For another example, see *VRSKhD*, October 1928, p. 16.

121. Oleshchuk, *Kto stroit tserkvi v SSSR*, p. 36.

122. *Povolzhskaia pravda*, September 16, 1928, p. 5.

meetings, from arranging excursions, and from opening libraries or reading rooms. The legislation annulled the right of parents to have a priest give their children religious instruction.[123] In other words, the law rendered illegal precisely the kinds of activities in which clergy (and, as we shall see, lay activists as well) had, during NEP, invested so much energy, drawing on skills developed in part during the late tsarist period.

Village Semiotics

Village semiotics, like education, was an arena of cultural conflict that had emerged, as we have seen, well before NEP. During the last decades of the tsarist period—and particularly during and after the Revolution of 1905—rural clergy had to face the hostility of some villagers to the physical symbols of religious belief, e.g., the church building and Orthodox icons. Moreover, they had some experience in using a variety of tactics to neutralize that hostility. During NEP, what changed was of course not the *targets* of those hostile to religious belief and practice. Now, however, the assault on the physical symbols of religious belief and practice was underwritten by the Soviet regime and the legal infrastructure of the Decree on the Separation of Church and State. How effectively were rural clergy able to operate within this infrastructure?

Their attempts to avert the state's secularization of the church building offer an interesting insight into this larger phenomenon. The renewal of a church's lease depended on whether the church building itself had been properly maintained. To review the relevant provisions of the Instruction of August 1918, the agreement on use of religious buildings and objects obliged contracting clergy and laity to "undertake repair of the designated property and expenditures connected with the use of property, such as those for heating, insurance, upkeep, the payment of taxes and of local levies, and similar items."[124] According to one parish priest, each member of the rural clergy "almost always [knew] all the latest regulations, instructions, and interpretations of the Soviet Government on this subject."[125] Surveying the worn-down state in which church property lay after seven years of war and ensuing economic hardship, rural clergy must have found this legislation especially overwhelming.[126]

---

123. See Curtiss, *Russian Church*, p. 229.
124. *SU*, 1918, no. 62, art. 758.
125. Father Trophimus, "Russian Religion," p. 96.
126. For descriptions, see L. E. Karunovskaia, "Selo Novoselka-Ziuzino Rostovskogo

They nevertheless attempted to take the necessary financial and administrative steps to avoid secularization. Consciousness of the legal importance of church repair impelled rural clergy to initiate the necessary financial collections among their parishioners.[127] Clergy's experiences in this regard varied significantly from village to village. In some villages, such as Ostashkino (Moscow *uezd* and province) and Edimonovo (Tver' *uezd* and province), priests apparently found parishioners quite willing to donate the necessary funds for church repairs.[128] In fact, to the dismay of antireligious correspondents and other activists, priests competed favorably against secular projects such as the building of wells and conversion to a multi-field agricultural system.[129] In other villages, however, their job was not so easy.

The village priest in Sel'shana (Sumy district [*okrug*], the Ukraine), for example, encountered much more resistance than counterparts in villages such as Ostashkino and Edimonovo. The priest in question decided to repair the parish church in order to fulfill a contract on church use.[130] After soliciting contributions from peasants described as "especially well off and religious," he began the restoration. Finding his financial resources insufficient, the priest approached peasants for an additional contribution of one ruble, but in "most cases" the villagers refused, thereby preventing the priest from finishing the repairs. With the contract for repairs unfulfilled, the district executive committee (*raiispolkom*) informed the priest of its intention to close the church.

This case thus illustrates the more general obstacles faced by many priests who sought to keep their churches in good repair and prevent secularization. Why was the priest in question unable to collect the necessary funds to repair the church? Why, in turn, were most of the villagers unwilling to make the necessary donations? It is very difficult if not impossible to know, for example, whether the primary reason was the villagers' poverty or their hostility (or mere indifference) to religious belief and practice. Most likely both factors were operating. This case thus reminds us that the willingness of villagers to support religious projects such as church repair was by no means

---

uezda," in Tan-Bogoraz, *Revoliutsiia v derevne*, p. 55, and *Vestnik Riazanskikh kraevedov* 1 (1925): 9.

127. In some cases villagers received directives from local Soviet institutions to carry out church repairs. See, for example, *Bezbozhnik*, July 19, 1925, p. 4. On church repair in urban areas, see the John Brophy papers, Box 6 (diaries, 1917–42), Catholic University of America, Washington, D.C.

128. *Bezbozhnik*, March 29, 1925; June 14, 1925, p. 4.

129. In Ostashkino, for example, villagers had declined (most likely at the village assembly) to provide funds to build a well. In Edimonovo, villagers had refused to allot resources for conversion to a multifield system.

130. *Bezbozhnik*, December 13, 1925, p. 6.

constant. It varied in proportion to such interrelated factors as the social composition of the village (i.e., the number of returning army veterans and former *otkhodniki*) and the degree of goodwill that a priest had cultivated with his parishioners over the years. (Parishioners' memories of the priest's political behavior during key political moments such as 1905–7 and 1917, for example, may have very well been triggered when they were presented with such financial requests.) Moreover, as this case reminds us, priests had to interact closely with members of rural political administrative units (e.g., *uezd* executive committees and also village soviets) in their struggles to prevent secularization.

Many rural priests sought not only to maintain important symbols of religious life but to harness various aspects of ritual and material culture in the larger conflict in which they were involved.[131] One case in point is their discovery of the propagandistic potential of inscriptions on gravestones. Instead of typical (prerevolutionary) inscriptions such as "Lord, accept my soul in peace," the following substitutes appeared:

> In the search for holy freedom
> Which path will you take
> Will you go [after] the spirit of negation
> Or for the fiery living faith?
>
> Do not forget, hypocrites
> Judgment and hell await you!
> There is no gentleness, there is no faith
> There is no love and no reward.[132]

While these inscriptions can be read as threats of doom against the *bezbozhniki*, the following offered consolation to believers who were struggling to keep religious activity alive:

> You, whose best strivings
> Perish in vain under the yoke,
> Believe, friends, in deliverance
> We will enter the kingdom of God![133]

---

131. By the terms "ritual" and "material" culture, I am referring to liturgy, liturgical art (e.g., icons), decorations on gravestones, and so on.

132. Bliakhin, *Kto i zachem stroit tserkvi*, pp. 35–36. The Russian version is as follows: "V iskan'iakh istiny sviatoi / Kakoi poidesh' tropoi / Poidesh' li ty za dukhom otritsan'ia / Ili za veroi plamennoi zhivoi?" and "Ne zabud'te, litsemery / Est' dlia vas sud i ad! / Net smiren'ia, net i very / Net liubvi i net nagrad!"

133. Ibid., p. 36. The Russian text: "Vy, ch'i luchshie stremlen'ia / Darom gibnut' pod

The various authors of these inscriptions, whether clergy or laity (or possibly the deceased?), foresaw both the punishment of the unfaithful and the liberation of the devout in some unspecified future.

In sum, rural clergy for the most part participated vigorously in the fields of cultural conflict—family, education, and village semiotics—surveyed thus far. Despite their diminished authority in the parish and in the village at large, they attempted to resist the claims of a socially and politically diverse faction of villagers hostile or indifferent to religious belief and practice. They often succeeded, in fact, in blocking such attacks. Building on the sociopolitical role they had cultivated in the last decades of the tsarist period, they fashioned a new identity, mobilizing human and other resources to an even greater degree than in the past.

Rural clergy came to appreciate the interdependence of what we might call their counterskirmishes in each of the fields surveyed above. For example, to repair the damage that conflict over religious belief and practice had done to social relationships in the rural family, clergy tried to conduct educational propaganda activities among key parts of the village population, such as children and adolescents. They drew on religious elements of village semiotics (e.g., gravestones) in their propagandistic efforts.

Electoral Politics

In particular, rural clergy experienced the interdependence between their struggles in the fields of the family, education, and semiotics and electoral politics (the village assembly, the village soviet, and cooperatives).[134] To generate the funds and other resources needed to offer educational activities and provide "goodies" for children, for example, they sometimes needed to persuade the village assembly to earmark some of its budget for religious purposes. Unlike the rural soviet, which had no independent budget, the village assembly had access to the financial resources necessary to implement its decisions.[135] The commune could generate income through "self-taxation"

---

iarmom, / Ver'te, drugi, v izbavlenie / K svetu bozhiiu pridem!"

134. I include cooperatives here because the members of their boards were elected.

135. According to Male, *Russian Peasant Organisation*, p. 137, the "financial arrangements of the commune were nowhere legally defined, and studies have only been fairly sketchy." The Model Statute of a Land Society, promulgated on January 5, 1926, listed "membership fees, state and co-operative loans and grants, rent from land, forest and communal enterprises" as sources of income (pp. 137–38).

(*samooblozhenie*) for "any kind of local social needs," including support of educational and medical facilities, social security, and civic necessities.[136] In other words, it not only had the right to allot a portion of its general funds for religious purposes but could legally vote a specific tax to meet the needs of the religious community. The village soviet, on the other hand, had to have any request for self-taxation approved by the village assembly. In their efforts in the field of education, rural priests and other members of the clergy appreciated the political importance of not only the village assembly but also the rural soviets. After the promulgation of a 1925 NKVD circular, village soviets had the right to decide whether religious rituals (such as processions of the cross) could be carried out in public places.[137] In Tomashevo, for example, the county soviet allowed the existence of a religious school on the grounds of the legal separation of Church and state. Finally, rural clergy learned the importance of electoral politics in their struggles to preserve and use strategically the religious elements of village semiotics. When they resisted secularization of church property, clergy—and, as we shall see, newly mobilized laity—came into direct contact with officials of village soviets, county, district, and provincial executive committees, and even (admittedly by correspondence) the Central Committee.

As these examples suggest, rural clergy knew that each of these institutions could be useful in multiple ways. As in tsarist times, the village assembly was a potential source of land and income; it was also, as noted above, a potential source of financial and material aid for a variety of religious needs, needs generated in the context of ongoing cultural conflict. Rural cooperatives were likewise important sources of financial aid. And although legally village soviets did not have their own budgets, in practice they created what were called "illegal" budgets. This meant that they were potential sources of funds for various religious needs in addition to being institutions with the *de jure* power to enforce various claims of the Decree and the Instruction. Quite often, as this abbreviated discussion suggests, the clergy discovered that no one rural political institution had sole authority in deciding matters that were important to them and to the parish, a state of affairs reminiscent of the institutional disarray of the Muscovite and imperial periods. In their quest to generate enough material resources (e.g., land) and income to survive, for example, the clergy needed to find ways to harness the powers of all three institutions: the village assemblies, the cooperatives, and the village soviets.

Given the strategic importance of these institutions and the Party cadres

---

136. Ibid., pp. 138–39. Self-taxation was intended to be a specific tax raised for a specific purpose.
137. For more on this circular, see Chapter 8.

who sometimes steered them, it is not surprising that rural clergy tried to cultivate good relationships with them.[138] One of their tactics was to ascribe Christian qualities to rural cadres. In 1928, expressing their gratitude to the local Communist Makevin, chair of the *raion* executive committee, for protecting their monastery in the Lower Volga Region, the monks said: "May the Lord God give Iakov Grigor'evich many years. Although he is a Communist, he has a Christian soul."[139] This type of assessment not only reflected past experience but, we may very tentatively hypothesize, shaped that of the future. As they humanized certain local Communists by ascribing to them Christian attributes, the clergy were also giving themselves permission to create working relationships with members of the *apparat*. And no doubt motivated by a desire to protect themselves, some rural clergy even gave their blessing to the regime. According to participants at the Lower Volga Regional Conference of the League of the Godless, the clergy in many Cossack villages proclaimed the long life (*mnogie leta*) of Soviet power. In one enclosed farm, a priest even cheered the "long life" of the district committee of the Komsomol.[140]

Was the clergy to be content with such implicitly obsequious and indirect attempts to influence rural political actors? Their extensive political activity in the village assembly and with the soviets during the Revolution of 1917–18 and the Civil War leads us to suspect they would not. Could they, in the new political conjuncture of NEP, translate their appreciation of the strategic importance of these rural political institutions into direct and powerful political action (i.e., voting, campaigning for candidates, holding political offices)? How did clergy construct and develop their political identities in these three institutional settings?

Because most clergy had extensive experience in lobbying for various parish and personal needs in prerevolutionary village assemblies, they did not find the idea of doing so even in changed political circumstances a threatening one. Moreover, during NEP, rural clergy actually gained a louder voice in the village assembly. This happened because of how the Land Code of 1922 defined the commune. To be sure, the Code stipulated the commune to be a union of households. But in contrast to the emancipation legislation of 1861, it defined its members as all persons, regardless of age or sex, who belonged to these households.[141] Since a large number of priests derived much of their income from working the land, they qualified as voting members of

---

138. Clergy continued to maintain ties with county executive committees during NEP. See *Bezbozhnik*, March 18, 1923, p. 4, and June 17, 1923, p. 7.
139. *Povolzhskaia pravda*, November 2, 1928, p. 3.
140. *Povolzhskaia pravda*, May 23, 1929, p. 3.
141. Each member over eighteen years of age was accorded full rights, including the

the village gathering.¹⁴² Thus clergy, as we shall see in more detail in Chapters 7 and 8, routinely battled for a wide range of personal and parish needs at meetings of the village assembly. At times they even called—or tried to call—village assemblies to discuss matters pertaining to the parish.¹⁴³ That the Party in 1927 issued a decree prohibiting *lishentsy* (those deprived of voting rights, e.g., clergy) to vote at village gatherings suggests its implicit recognition of the political activity—and the political threat—of clergy in this body.¹⁴⁴

The rural clergy's stance toward the cooperatives, championed by Bukharin as a bridge to socialism, was more ambivalent.¹⁴⁵ Assessing rural cooperatives as a threatening economic adversary, some rural clergy took measures to diminish their economic power. An article that appeared in 1927 in the journal *Bezbozhnik* proclaimed that the clergy had joined the kulaks in opposing the cooperatives.¹⁴⁶ Noting that certain clergy also "agitated" against the electrification of the Soviet countryside, the article portrayed village priests as uncompromising antimodernists, and thus as natural foes of the cooperative, the institutional bridge to both socialism and a modernized village.

Some rural clergy and members of sectarian groups chose to compete with the cooperatives by creating their own economic enterprises. According to a report in *Bezbozhnik* in 1927, a priest in a village in Orel province opened a second-class trading concern (*torgovliia 2 razriada*).¹⁴⁷ Vowing to direct 5

---

possibility of attending the village gathering, as long as he or she worked the land. The Code thus granted women and younger men a say in the commune's affairs for the first time. In practice, however, older men continued to run it. See Male, *Russian Peasant Organisation*, pp. 67–68. On the exceptionalism of women's participation in village assemblies (and the corresponding rarity of their acting as household heads, the necessary prerequisite for such political activity), see Worobec, *Peasant Russia*, p. 175.

142. As discussed earlier, the Fifteenth Party Congress, held in December 1927, exhorted the Central Committee to devise ways to guarantee that persons not eligible to vote in the soviets (*lishentsy*) would also be unable to vote at the village gathering. Since clergy and some laity fell into this category, the change threatened—at least in theory—their capacity to play an active role in the affairs of the gathering.

143. In 1929, a priest in Kustan approached the secretary of the *volkom* with a "request to allow him to call a general meeting of citizens at which he would interpret the essence of communism and would urge [villagers] to strive toward it." The secretary, not surprisingly, refused. See *Bezbozhnik*, March 25, 1923, p. 5.

144. On this decree, see Chapter 4.

145. See Cohen, *Bukharin and the Bolshevik Revolution*, p. 195. There is as yet no English monograph that examines the cooperative movement of the 1920s. For discussions of cooperatives, see, for example, Atkinson, *The End of the Russian Land Commune*; R. W. Davies, *The Socialist Offensive: The Collectivization of Soviet Agriculture, 1929–30*, vols. 1 and 2 (Cambridge, Mass., 1980); Lewin, *Russian Peasants and Soviet Power*; and Yaney, *The Urge to Mobilize*.

146. *Bezbozhnik* 9 (May 1927). The use of "kulak" as an index of rural class stratification here cannot be taken at face value.

percent of all his income to the Church, the priest urged his parishioners to shun the cooperatives. A proclamation of a sectarian group in the Northern Caucasus, the Imiaslavtsy, commanded its adherents "not to join cooperatives and not to get any booklets for members of cooperatives," a precept its members followed.[148]

Building on their prerevolutionary experience in cooperatives, many other village priests, however, sought to harness their financial possibilities for their own ends—and for those of the parish. What prompted clergy to take the lead in creating—or at least attempting to create—rural cooperatives? Priests were constantly scrambling for financial resources for the embattled parish, to be sure. More specifically, it was sometimes their awareness of the limited effectiveness of traditional ways of generating financial resources that led them to take action. A case in point is a priest in the city of Roslavl (Smolensk province), who in 1926 tried to found a cooperative because the church shop (*tserkovnaia lavochka*), which offered candles, crosses, and copies of the Gospel, had failed to attract many customers and was suffering under high taxes.[149] To succeed in their efforts to create cooperatives, rural priests often had to scramble to generate the necessary start-up capital, collecting money from peasants and buying goods on credit.[150]

The clergy faced the equally significant challenge, however, of overcoming the legal and political liability of being disenfranchised. As mentioned in Chapter 2, Soviet legislation prohibited clergy from serving in elected positions to the cooperative. Thus they could not, according to Soviet law, hold positions on the cooperative board (*pravlenie*), its council (*sovet*), or its inspection commission (*revizionnaia komissiia*). How, then, did the rural clergy manage to found cooperatives and serve on their boards? (The two went hand in hand.) To be sure, some clerical entrepreneurs, such as the priest in Roslavl, failed in their attempts.[151] Perhaps learning from these unsuccessful efforts, others left the calling in order to circumvent the legal prohibitions concerning the clergy's holding elected positions in the cooperatives, thereby hoping to further economic interests of the religious community.

The case of a former psalmist in Saratov province illustrates rural clergy's adoption of "musical social identities" in their use of cooperatives to sustain religious life. In 1924, this former psalmist held an unspecified position in a village cooperative.[152] Before lending his services to the cooperative, he sent

148. V. G. Druzhinin, *Po ochagam sektantskogo mrakobesiia* (Moscow, 1928), pp. 20, 22. This may be a paraphrased account.
149. *Bezbozhnik*, February 28, 1926.
150. For an example from Leningrad province, see *Bezbozhnik*, October 25, 1925.
151. The *uezd* soviet rejected the petition signed by church wardens and members of the priest's family.
152. *Petrovskaia kommuna*, December 11, 1924, p. 3.

the local district newspaper, *Petrovskaia kommuna*, a formal renunciation of his clerical position. But after he began serving in the cooperative, he formally rejoined the local religious society.[153] In another instance, a former priest in a village in Saratov province successfully started a cooperative. In 1924, the priest in question gave his word to the county executive committee of the Party that he would not return to clerical service, and that he wanted to "serve the people."[154] At the meeting he organized an agricultural association (*tovarishchestvo*) that attracted two hundred members.[155] The priest, two non-Party peasants, and one Communist comprised the leadership board (*biuro*) of the institution. Given the skeletal nature of this journalistic account, it is impossible to know whether the priest's proclamation of solidarity with Soviet political and economic values was sincere.

Other village priests attained leadership posts in cooperatives without leaving the clergy. During the period of New Economic Policy, Soviet sources reported cases of clerical leadership of cooperatives throughout the RSFSR Clergy occupied leadership roles in the north, where the cooperative movement had developed most strongly; they also held key positions in cooperatives in Briansk, Moscow, Ivanovo-Voznesensk, Viatka, Leningrad, and Saratov provinces.[156] Even OGPU records for the 1920s indicate that clergy served on the boards of cooperatives.[157]

Once in power, clergy sometimes used their position to place their supporters, especially relatives, in other leadership positions in cooperatives. According to an article in *Bezbozhnik* in 1927, a priest in a village of the Northern Caucasus region directed an agricultural *tovarishchestvo*. After attaining this position, the journalistic account implied, he managed to install two of his daughters as accountants in the consumers' cooperative (*potrebobshchestvo*) and one as an accountant in the cooperative artel.[158] Sons of the clergy—including priests and deacons—also held important posts in rural

153. The legal provisions for the formation of a religious society are discussed in Chapter 2.
154. *Sovetskaia derevnia*, May 29, 1924, p. 4.
155. This appears to have been a *tovarishchestvo po obshchestvennoi obrabotki zemli* (*toz*), or, as defined by Moshe Lewin, an "association for the common cultivation of land." For more details, see Lewin, *Russian Peasants and Soviet Power*, pp. 533–34.
156. On clerical leadership of Saratov cooperatives, see *Sovetskaia derevnia*, December 2, 1924, p. 3, and May 15, 1924, p. 4; for cases in Viatka, see *Bednota*, July 21, 1923, and *Bezbozhnik*, February 28, 1926; for Briansk, see ibid., February 14, 1926, p. 5; for an example of a priest as a member of the cooperative's administrative board, see ibid., October 16, 1927; for cases in Moscow province (sons of clergy), see ibid., December 18, 1927.
157. *Fond* numbers are not available for this citation because these archives are still officially closed; however, certain Western researchers have been allowed to see OGPU documents that confirm this information.
158. *Bezbozhnik*, July 3, 1927. There was a greater amount of collectivization in the *artel* than in the *toz*. See Lewin, *Russian Peasants and Soviet Power*, p. 534.

cooperative organizations.¹⁵⁹ At times clergy and their relatives even monopolized all the key positions of power in a given rural cooperative. One particularly colorful example must suffice. In 1923, clergy or their "affiliates" staffed all the leadership positions of a certain rural cooperative in Viatka province.¹⁶⁰ A deacon served as its bookkeeper, while a psalmist was its secretary. The wife and daughter of a village priest worked as its accountants.¹⁶¹ A former psalmist, who now was the regent of the local church choir, also served as a clerical worker. A different priest's wife held the position of copyist.

In other cases, clergy rubbed shoulders with Party members in the councils (soviets) of cooperatives. In 1927 in a village in the Northern Caucasus, three Party members served with a priest in the governing council of the local cooperative. Even a correspondent for *Bezbozhnik*, however, admitted that these Party members had done nothing to counteract the priest's activities in the cooperative.¹⁶² Thus we must avoid assuming that the presence of Party members in such leadership positions effectively curbed the pro-religious activities of their clerical colleagues. To some extent, then, clergy and laity owed their success in using the cooperatives to defend religious interests to the weakness of the rural Party organization.¹⁶³ Party members could not, as a rule, prevent clergy from "taming" cooperatives, from using them for their own purposes rather than those of the state.¹⁶⁴

Rural Party leaders, alarmed by the depth of clerical involvement in cooperatives, drew up plans to purge such undesirable elements from these economic institutions. Regional Party leaders' concern about clerical involvement in cooperatives was exemplified by a plan of the Worker-Peasant Inspectorate (RKI) of the Leningrad Region (*oblast'*) in 1929 for a purge of land organs. Its architects targeted "servitors of the cult" (*sluzhiteli kul'ta*) for expulsion during the examination of roughly five hundred workers in the cooperatives of the region.¹⁶⁵ During the winter of 1929–30, the RKI of Pskov *okrug* expelled an unspecified number

---

159. For an example of sons of priests and deacons staffing the governing board of a new credit cooperative in Moscow province, see *Bezbozhnik*, December 18, 1927, p. 5; see also *Povolzhskaia pravda*, December 21, 1928, p. 2.

160. *Bednota*, July 21, 1923, p. 2. The cooperative was located in Pavlovsk *volost'* of Viatka *uezd*.

161. The Union of Agricultural Cooperatives received inquiries whether priests' wives could be members of cooperatives. See *VSS* 10 (1926): 8.

162. *Bezbozhnik*, July 3, 1927.

163. See especially Thorniley, *Rise and Fall*, pp. 1–71. On rural underinstitutionalization, see Starr, *Decentralization*, and Yaney, *The Urge to Mobilize*.

164. Samuel Popkin has argued that Vietnamese peasants "tamed," or used to their own advantage, the bureaucratic institutions and market structures imposed by capitalist colonialists. *The Rational Peasant* (Berkeley, Calif., 1979), p. 245.

165. *Krest'ianskaia pravda*, March 12, 1929, p. 3. See also ibid., March 12, 1929. Purges

of clergy from cooperative boards in the region.[166]

If clergy often evaded the legal prohibitions on their participation in cooperative boards, how successful were they in circumnavigating legal obstacles to their participation in the village soviets, a key institution of rural electoral politics? Aware of the legal constraints on their direct participation in the village soviets, some clergy opted to work "behind the scenes" to cultivate working relationships with chairs and other officials of the soviets in order to lobby for religious interests.[167] To this end, clergy arranged social gatherings with these political officers. Clergy and members of village soviets were known, on occasion, to drink during their social gatherings, during which they sometimes discussed political matters. In 1925, the "entire presidium" of the Povodimovsko village soviet (Alatyr *uezd*, Simbirsk province) spent three straight days drinking with the priest Arkhangel'skii. During the course of these festivities, members of the soviet promised not to evict him from his apartment.[168]

Not all social get-togethers between clergy and members of village soviets featured alcohol. In 1928, for example, a provincial newspaper published the results of the regional executive committee's (*okrispolkom*) investigation of two religious communes in Pskov province. Members of the investigative committee discovered that the secretary of the village soviet habitually engaged in "soul-saving conversations" with a priest who played an important role in the affairs of one of the communes.[169] During a conversation with the investigators, the latter stressed his "good relations" with the local village soviet.[170] At one of its recent meetings, for example, the chair of one commune had introduced a proposal to hold celebrations of religious holidays (*prestol'nye prazdniki*) in May, June, and October. The plenum approved the request. Thus by building relationships with members of village soviets through drinking bouts and other social encounters, clergy and other religious leaders put themselves in a position to extract favors from this political body.[171]

---

of the cooperative boards (*pravleniia*) began in early spring 1928 in the central organs and then spread to the rural areas. On this see Yanni Kotsonis, "Agricultural Cooperatives in Historical Perspective: The Case of the European North, 1900–1929"(paper presented at the 1991 AAASS Conference in Miami), pp. 25–28.

166. *Krest'ianskaia pravda*, February 15, 1930.

167. *Trud*, for example, described examples of "Red priests" who had cultivated good relationships with soviets. See Siegelbaum, *Soviet State and Society*, p. 163.

168. *Bezbozhnik*, January 11, 1925, p. 7. For another example see *Izvestiia Saratovskogo soveta*, July 22, 1927, p. 2.

169. *Pskovskii nabat'*, November 15, 1928, p. 2.

170. On the friendly, protective relationships between clergy and members of village soviets, see *Krest'ianskii iurist*, November 15, 1928, p. 14, and *Bezbozhnik*, January 30, 1927.

171. Clergy in the non-Russian republics of the Soviet Union also cultivated ties with

Many clergy, however, remained as unsatisfied with such indirect influence as they had been during the Civil War. Still acutely aware of the potential utility of the village soviet in sustaining parish life and in meeting clerical needs, clergy wanted as much direct control over its administrative and political decisions as possible. Thus it was common for clergy to show up at meetings of the soviets. When a certain Comrade Tkachev, chair of the Serdobsk *uezd* executive committee in Saratov province, made a disapproving remark about a priest's presence at the meeting (*aktiv*) of the village soviet, the embarrassed chair conceded: "Well . . . [the priest's here] because we've gotten used to deciding our affairs [of the village soviet] with him. It's impossible to drive him away, because he just keeps coming back to our meetings."[172]

Despite awareness of constraints on their political behavior, clergy considered themselves integral participants in the electoral process. As a village priest from the province of Gomel bluntly stated in 1925: "New elections have been called because, without us, of course, nothing will happen."[173] Village priests contributed to the political defense of religious interests by campaigning for specific candidates.[174] Not surprisingly, a candidate's avowed support of religious interests figured as the most important criterion for winning clerical endorsement. In 1925, Iaroslavskii complained that clergy were appearing at elections and verbally rejecting certain candidates as "godfighters," or members of the League (*bezbozhniki*).[175] Clergy were engaging in one of the key elements of politics, "debate about choice."[176]

Many clergy, however, sought still more direct and powerful influence on the political life of the village soviets: the right—or at least the opportunity—to vote. To be sure, by damning clergy as *lishentsy*, the Constitution had tried to create an insurmountable legal barrier to the direct political participation of clergy in the political life of the village soviet; at the same time, however, it had failed to avoid potential interpretive quandaries concerning clerical

---

members of the lower *apparat*. See A. Mitrofanov, *O chistke i proverke riadov VKP(b)* (Moscow, 1929), pp. 153–54.

172. The village in question was Gulenovskoe. For more details, see *Povolzhskaia pravda*, November 11, 1928, p. 3. The staff of the soviet not only tolerated the priest as an irrepressible participant at its meetings, they courted the current spiritual father with land, which it taxed at what was apparently a low rate (thirty-five rubles, presumably the *per annum* rate) because the village's two previous priests had fled their posts. One of the most influential members of the soviet was the psalmist, who had recently served as chairman.

173. *Bezbozhnik*, March 8, 1925, p. 4.

174. On this see *Bezbozhnik*, March 29, 1925. See also F. Putintsev, *Vybory v sovety i razoblachenie popovshchiny* (Moscow, 1937), pp. 21, 64–65. Enfranchised by the 1936 Constitution, priests were very active in election campaigns to the village soviets in 1937. See Fitzpatrick, *Stalin's Peasants*, pp. 282–83.

175. *Bezbozhnik*, March 29, 1925.

176. Quoted in Eugen Weber, *Peasants into Frenchmen* (Stanford, Calif., 1976), p. 277.

(and lay) voting rights. What kinds of interpretive quandaries did arise, in fact, during NEP? What kinds of political opportunities did these legal ambiguities create for rural clergy? Moreover, how much did the law really matter given that there were so few Party cadres and fellow travelers—not to mention Soviet institutions—in the countryside?

Members of rural voting commissions faced perplexing dilemmas, even before the Party tried to "revive the soviets," as they tried to apply the Constitution's provisions on the voting rights of clergy. As discussed above, the Constitution assumed that clergy would never engage in socially useful labor, a hypothesis belied by reality when rural clergy relied on agricultural work to support themselves to a greater degree in the 1920s than ever before.[177] Because the clergy were supporting themselves through agricultural labor, a necessity imposed partly by the Constitution's legal and financial discrimination against them, they had ceased, ironically, to be "exploiters," the status that had led them to be disenfranchised in the first place.[178] At least this was one possible conclusion that members of voting commissions could and did draw. They had even more reason to be torn about how to classify clergy once the Party's 1924 policy of "revival of the soviets" sought to increase the political participation of "desirable" social groups in rural society. Were clergy really poor or middle peasants, that is, part of the social stratum whose participation the regime deemed vital to the creation of "Soviet democracy"? Or did a priest's *a priori* exploitative nature overshadow his long-standing peasant identity, no matter how enhanced in the difficult 1920s? These are the questions that head-scratching members of voting commissions had to answer.

The 1925 "Instruction on Elections to the Soviets" sought to remove some of these ambiguities. The Instruction reopened the political sphere to certain segments of previously disbarred clergy (and laity, as we shall see).[179] Revising

---

177. *Vlast' sovetov*, January–June 1926, p. 13.

178. Interpretive difficulties were particularly acute with respect to the issue of individuals whose ties to "exploiters" were tenuous. In some cases, for example, village teachers lost their voting rights merely by living with local clergy. See point "g," article 65 of the 1918 Constitution, quoted here as paraphrased in "Perevybory sovetov," *Vlast' sovetov*, August–September 1923, pp. 5–6. In constructing this discussion of voting rights I have benefited from Kathryn Hendley's unpublished paper, "An Analysis of Voting Rights under the Soviet Constitution of 1918" (Georgetown University, December 17, 1986). A Soviet expert on the Constitution, G. S. Gurvich, claimed that (although not supported by the language of the Constitution itself) the denial of voting rights was intended to be conditional for all groups except the Okhrana agents. See his *Istoriia sovetskoi konstitutsii* (Moscow, 1923) and *Osnovy sovetskoi konstitutsii* (Moscow, 1926).

179. See "Instruktsiia o vyborakh v sovety," confirmed by the Presidium of the VTsIK on November 4, 1926, in *SU*, 1925, no. 75, art. 577. All quotations from the text are from the reprint in N. Orleanskii, *Zakon o religioznykh ob"edineniiakh* (Moscow, 1930).

the position on clerical voting rights established by the 1918 Constitution, it offered the franchise to clergy who "for a period of not less than five years have been occupied by productive and socially useful labor and have proved their loyalty to soviet power."[180] Thus, while superseding the 1918 approach to the voting rights of religious activists, the Instruction enfranchised specific groups of clergy (and laity) by citing their secular identity as "workers," the original Constitution's conceptual gateway to enfranchisement.

The 1925 revision also increased the bureaucracy involved in disenfranchisement. Thwarted by the stubborn unpredictability of rural cadres' decisions concerning voting rights or, perhaps more accurately, by their "broad interpretation" of the Constitution's directives, the Presidium of the TsIK sought control through the introduction of fixed criteria and procedures. The Center's revamped instructions required "documented information" from either VIKs, village soviets, or administrative and judicial institutions as grounds for disenfranchisement. It specifically barred individual citizens or groups from preparing motions to revoke voting rights, thereby suppressing a form of independent rural control over local affairs.[181] Thus the periphery's failure to replicate Moscow's normative legal agenda elicited an invisible, yet intensified, bureaucratic presence in the rural world.[182]

Rural cadres found that such increased bureaucracy eliminated neither the interpretive puzzles nor the wily ingenuity of religious villagers. Members of the *apparat* struggled, for example, with the institutional mechanics of disenfranchisement. On April 26, 1926, a new circular of the Presidium of the Central Committee defined the operational role of local voting commissions in the revocation of voting rights. While the commissions were empowered to examine questions "connected with the voting rights of citizens," the circular stipulated that only a court sentence, and not the decisions of executive committees (*ispolkomy*) or voting commissions, could disenfranchise citizens.[183] Another instruction of 1926[184] specified that reinstatement of voting rights could be effected only by voting commissions on the level of the province, with the confirmation of the corresponding executive committee.[185]

---

180. "Lishenie izbiratel'nykh prav," in *SU*, 1925, no. 75, art. 577, in Orleanskii, *Zakon*, p. 117.

181. *Vlast' sovetov*, May 3, 1925.

182. On relations between the Center and periphery see J. Arch Getty, *The Origin of the Great Purges* (New York, 1985); Daniel Brower, "Smolensk Scandal and the End of NEP," *Slavic Review* 4 (Winter 1986): 689–706; and Male, *Russian Peasant Organisation*.

183. *Tsirkuliar* of the Presidium of the VTsIK 26/IV-26 g., No. AP 815/568, as quoted in *Vlast' sovetov*, May 23, 1926, p. 29.

184. "Novaia vsesoiuznaia instruktsiia o vyborakh," as quoted and discussed in *Vlast' sovetov*, October 17, 1926, p. 3.

185. *Vlast' sovetov*, October 17, 1926, p. 3. Where appropriate, i.e., in those parts of the

Thus, according to these clarifications, disenfranchisement, which deployed both the judicial and administrative branches, involved greater institutional complexity than did the process of reenfranchisement, accomplished solely through various administrative organs. The comparative ease of the reinstatement process thus reflected the Center's goal of reviving the rural soviets through increased participation.

The officials of the voting commissions had difficulty with the ambiguous category of "main occupation" in their attempts to conduct a streamlined examination of clerical franchise. A contemporary described the quicksand of ambiguity created by the 1925 Instruction:

> How, then, do we teach the voting commissions to decide correctly the question of whether to strip a cleric ["servitor of the cult," *sluzhitel' kul'ta*] of the right to vote, that is, how [to evaluate] which was or is [the priest's] main occupation—being a priest or being an agricultural laborer? The Instruction provides no answer to this question, nor does it provide any suggestions for resolving the dilemma.[186]

This contemporary went on to suggest that the village soviet should decide whether the village priest had developed a significant relationship to the peasantry through agricultural labor.[187]

Some clerics adopted "fictitious identities" to achieve reinstatement. They took advantage of the ambiguity inherent in point 17 of the 1925 Instruction, which allowed the reinstatement of clergy occupied in socially useful labor. Soviet contemporaries complained that class enemies lingering from the tsarist regime (*byvshie liudi*), such as rural clergy, had "fictitiously" taken up agricultural labor to qualify for reclassification under the new 1925 Instruction. As one contemporary warned, the disappearance of one's opposition to the Soviet regime did not automatically accompany the new occupation.[188] In order to avert the dangers of enfranchising each former priest who "presented a document affirming him to be a peasant as of 1925," he counseled a vigilant examination of each case. Another contemporary disagreed, claiming that because the documents were required to testify that the individual "lived by his own resources and did not exploit someone else's labor," Article 17 provided a clear statement of the conditions for reinstatement.[189] This defense

---

USSR in which the province did not exist, the voting commissions on the *krai* or *oblast'* level had to be involved.
186. *Vlast' sovetov*, January 10, 1926, p. 13.
187. Ibid.
188. *Vlast' sovetov*, January 31, 1926.
189. Ibid., p. 13.

of the article, however, did not address the thorny issue of evaluating loyalty to the regime. Not only did the tactical skill of rural clergy complicate the application of the existing regulations concerning enfranchisement, contemporaries could not even agree on the literal meaning of the regulations themselves.

Pëtr Gnedovskii was a village priest whose struggles to be reinstated dramatize this state of confusion.[190] Unconvinced that he could achieve reinstatement only by relinquishing his clerical identity, in 1925 Gnedovskii bravely approached the local Komsomol cell to obtain a certificate affirming his loyalty to the regime. In effect, the resourceful priest succeeded in convincing the members of the cell of the porous boundaries between the religious calling and loyalty to Soviet power. Striving for persuasive proof of Gnedovskii's political "correctness," the drafters of the certificate marshaled such facts as the priest's membership in several Soviet organizations, e.g., the ODVF, his subscription to a Soviet newspaper, and his nonparticipation in anti-Soviet agitation.[191] Yet despite his efforts he was not reinstated.

Undaunted by such failures, rural clergy became, during the voting campaign of 1926, a tenacious, insistent presence in preelection meetings. The 1926 preelection meetings in Riazan *uezd* (Riazan province) illustrate this phenomenon. Whereas in certain counties the meetings remained open to all, in others only those able to vote could attend. When restricted admission prevailed, those deprived of voting rights (*lishentsy*—unclear whether they were clergy) flocked to the general meeting of citizens (*obshchee sobranie*) and demanded reinstatement: "It is the right of the people [*volia naroda*] to decide ... you took our [voting] rights away, and you can give them back."[192] Such pleas did not necessarily invoke a favorable response. When, for example, clergy arrived at a meeting (perhaps a preelectoral gathering) in the village of Palishcha, the peasants demanded they leave. The priests began to depart with great reluctance, and some even tried to hide in the corners.[193] Clergy regarded themselves as political actors.

The number of clerical *lishentsy* fell as a result of the new bureaucratic procedures, the ambiguous 1925 Instruction, and the rural clergy's own deft maneuvering. During the 1924–25 elections to the village soviets, 110,872 clergy (*sluzhiteli religioznykh kul'tov*) were deprived of the right to vote. This group comprised 20.5 percent of the total (540,830) disenfranchised. In the election campaign of 1925–26, however, the number of disenfranchised clergy dropped to 97,351. This figure actually comprised a relatively larger

---

190. He apparently hailed from Tula province.
191. *Bezbozhnik*, August 23, 1925, p. 5.
192. I. N., "Itogi perevyborov sovetov Riazanskogo uezda," *Vlast' sovetov*, April 4, 1926.
193. Ibid.

percentage (23.4 percent) of the total (416,030) disenfranchised.[194]

Results of election campaigns on the level of the province followed the same pattern. A. Lupolov, an observer from the city of Voronezh, applauded the supposedly profound effect of the new instructions on the 1926 campaign in his province. He commended, for example, the vigilant efforts to eliminate the aberrations caused by an "arbitrary, broad interpretation of [certain] articles of the Constitution (sixty-five, fourteen, the ['old'] twenty-three)," or in less vague terminology, the excessive use of the abstract category of "exploiter" as grounds for disenfranchisement. While guarding against incorrect interpretation of specific articles of the Constitution, organizers of the Voronezh campaign of 1926 also strove for correct application of the revised, 1925 Instruction. Concerning this point, Lupolov claimed that during the 1926 campaign, documentation was required in each case of disenfranchisement. To be sure, given the general recalcitrance of the rural world, the campaign probably never achieved the level of perfection that Lupolov implied. But the statistics for 1926 incontestably demonstrate a significant reduction in the total disenfranchised since 1925. The number of *lishentsy* plummeted from 19,387 in 1924–25 to 11,644 in 1925–26, a drop of 41.4 percent. While the number of disenfranchised clergy fell from 3,357 to 2,773, the number disbarred relative to the total of *lishentsy* actually rose from 17.09 percent to 23.7 percent.[195]

The tide began to turn in 1926–27. Both the province of Voronezh and the USSR as a whole experienced, beginning with the electoral season of those years, a rise in the number of disenfranchised.[196] In Voronezh the number of disenfranchised "servitors of the cult" (*sluzhiteli kul'ta*) grew from 2,773 in 1925–26 to 3,835 in 1926–27.[197] The figure reported for 1926–27 thus exceeded that of 1924–25. Surveying the statistics on disenfranchisement in rural localities for the entire USSR, we see that disenfranchisement fell to its lowest point in 1925–26: 1.1 percent of all rural dwellers could not vote. In 1927, however, the figure climbed to 3.3 percent of all potential rural voters. It again rose to 4.1 percent in 1929.[198]

---

194. These figures appeared in G. S. Gurvich, "Novye sel'sovety i volispolkomy," *Vlast' sovetov*, June 27, 1926. He maintained that the new "instruction on elections to urban and rural soviets," specifically its requirement of documentation to disenfranchise, was primarily responsible for the decrease in the total number of *lishentsy*. He also commented that the execution of the instruction resulted in the reinstatement of several groups of the population (including clergy) previously barred from the electoral process.

195. For these figures and a discussion of the 1925–26 voting campaign in the Voronezh province, see *Vlast' sovetov*, March 21, 1926. The figures quoted do not include the city of Voronezh.

196. On this see also Kimerling, "Civil Rights," pp. 26–27.

197. See *Vlast' sovetov*, April 17, 1927, p. 21.

198. See Slatter, "Communes with Communists," p. 278.

New Strategies

How did clergy, who no doubt lacked access to this statistical information, experience local officials' increasing tendency to rigidify their interpretation of existing legal directives? In answering this question, it is important to keep in mind the general political context in which clergy failed to gain the right to vote. There are two reasons why clergy accorded such failures more significance than their statistical increase might alone suggest. First, they experienced and learned of these failures after they had, with the promulgation and application of the 1925 Instruction, formed heightened expectations for direct political participation in elections to the soviets. These expectations no doubt increased their sense of disappointment. Moreover, they were also disappointed and angry because Party cadres had made increasing efforts to control the political process: they were, for example, holding more and more meetings of poor peasants. The Party made its ambitious efforts to control the electoral process, whether through increased clerical disenfranchisement or other means, in the last two years of NEP. How did clergy respond, if at all, to these strategically and chronologically intertwined efforts?

On the most basic and obvious level, clergy sought direct influence in the voting commissions. To this end they—or their supporters—managed to gain seats in these bodies.[199] The social composition of the commissions thus diverged radically from the administrative norm sought by the regime. The deputy chair of the Leningrad region TsIK admitted in 1928 that disenfranchised individuals were serving on several village voting commissions.[200] The daughter of a village priest sat on a village voting commission in Belebelkov district. The district executive committee removed her, as well as other religious villagers: the wife of a sectarian preacher in the village Chudov, and a prosperous sectarian preacher in Berozov (Novgorod *okrug*). In fact, one village correspondent reported in 1928, the majority of the voting commissions in this district were composed of "well-off" members, who sought to "reinstate kulaks and village priests or sectarian preachers."[201] According to the correspondent, these efforts failed, perhaps as a result of the reputed vigilance of the *uezd* executive committee. While this *uezd ispolkom* apparently thwarted attempts to realign the activity of the voting commissions according to religious needs, we may speculate that the existence of less capable,

---

199. For other examples, see Figes, *Peasant Russia*, p. 201.
200. *Krest'ianskaia pravda*, December 31, 1928, p. 2.
201. See *Krest'ianskaia pravda*, December 28, 1928. The exact wording was "servitors of a religious cult" (*sluzhiteli religioznogo kul'ta*), which I have taken to embrace both Orthodox and sectarian men of the cloth. For other references to "kulaks" serving on voting commissions, see Kimerling, "Civil Rights," p. 39.

more feeble district committees facilitated the success of the religious in other cases.

Religious activists focused their resistance against other elements of the electoral process imposed by the regime, such as the staging of preelection meetings of poor peasants. Proper preparation for the voting process, Party leaders had reasoned, would increase the sought-after participation of the poor peasants. Religious activists countered this institutional threat with an up-to-date tactical repertoire, that is, by intensifying their own preelectoral preparations. Clergy and laity held their own preelection meetings. Resolutions of the Party plenum of July 1926 inveighed against the open and undercover political intrigues of "economic, cultural, and religious organizations" in the context of the election campaign.[202] Contemporary observers, antireligious leaders, and village correspondents decried the open transformation of churches into what one antireligious leader called "clerical [and] sectarian political clubs," which debated candidates and election strategies,[203] the clever camouflaging of such preelection preparations as innocent "Bible readings,"[204] and other religious organizations that held political discussions. Village correspondents offered frequent reports on religious preelection meetings during the 1927–28 electoral campaign.[205] While cadres held a preelection meeting for poor peasants, the priest turned a meeting of the aforementioned "religious-cultural society" in Baranyshkovo into his own preelection gathering. Hoping to steer villagers away from the elections, he instructed them as follows: "When you hear the bell, go immediately to church and listen to the holy epistle. Take with you all sinners."[206] Clergy and laity tapped an autonomous cultural and organizational source to construct their institutional challenge.

Both the Leningrad and Saratov provincial presses, for example, anxiously warned and complained of religious gatherings during the 1928–29 election campaign. In November 1928, a correspondent from the Lower Volga region begrudgingly admitted that "throughout the entire *okrug* one can note the acute activity of clergy [*tserkovniki*] and sectarians . . . the upsurge of the

---

202. *Pravda*, July 21, 1926.
203. On this see Putintsev, *Vybory v sovety*, p. 39.
204. On this tactic see Levin and Suvorov, "Sovety i stroitel'stvo sotsializma," in Pashukanis, *15 let*, p. 453, who date the appearance of these efforts from 1927. A. Angarov, in *Klassovaia bor'ba v sovetskoi derevne* (Moscow, 1929), pp. 29–30, also insisted on the changed nature of the 1926–27 campaign. Peasants he branded "kulaks" used religious organizations to hold secret meetings. On the 1926–27 campaign, see also *Vlast' sovetov*, April 3, 1927.
205. Ignorant of the constraints that may have handicapped the correspondents in covering rural events, we cannot correlate the increasing number of such reports with a corresponding surge in the actual occurrence of this kind of gathering.
206. *Povolzhskaia pravda*, February 5, 1929, p. 2.

religious movement will surely be used in attempts to obstruct the Party line during elections. The church and the sectarian prayer house will, in many cases, really fulfill the role of a kulak voting commission" during the upcoming electoral campaign.[207] Subsequent reports confirmed this prediction, although the church building itself did not always host these meeting. In the Leningrad region, for example, in December 1928, a group labeled the "kulak section" of the village conducted a secret preelection meeting under the cover of a sectarian gathering.[208] At a party given by the village priest in the Liubiansk *uezd* (Leningrad region) in the spring of 1929, unidentified participants discussed matters relating to the election process.[209] Admitting that "we have an intensification of hostile activity, in connection with elections to the soviets, on the part of kulak and organized counterrevolutionary groups, even *tserkovniki* and sectarians," a Central Committee circular summoned the "special vigilance and activity of the party."[210]

In at least one instance, more formal church gatherings served as an institutional point of departure for planning the tactics of election campaigns. Covering an unnamed district in the Petrovsk *okrug* of the Lower Volga region, an embarrassed village correspondent reluctantly conceded that "kulaks and clergy had begun their preparations for elections to the soviets earlier than the party organization."[211] A series of recently held church congresses within the district had included in their agendas a "special point on the relationship to the voting campaign."[212] Since, as we will see in Chapter 6, lay representatives routinely attended these gatherings, especially those sponsored by the Renovationist Church, it can be inferred that clergy did not possess exclusive control over the strategies adopted.

What kinds of strategies emerged from these new institutional formats, and what was the role of the clergy in implementing them? In the Soviet Far East, the clergy conducted propaganda campaigns among the *bednota* in 1927.[213] When they offered poor peasants various kinds of economic assistance, it is quite possible that they were hoping to "buy" their votes and

207. *Povolzhskaia pravda*, November 4, 1928. Clergy and religious activists held similar meetings in the 1930s. On their preelection strategies during the 1937 election campaign for the village soviets, see Fitzpatrick, *Stalin's Peasants*, p. 283.
208. *Krest'ianskaia pravda*, December 31, 1928, p. 2.
209. It is a safe guess that lay members of the church council or lesser "servitors of the religious cult," such as deacons and psalmists, joined the village priest in this discussion. See *Krest'ianskaia pravda*, April 5, 1929, p. 2.
210. *Krest'ianskaia pravda*, January 4, 1929, p. 1.
211. *Povolzhskaia pravda*, January 13, 1929, p. 4.
212. Ibid. Unfortunately, the correspondent did not specify whether these congresses were meetings of the Renovationist or of the Tikhonite "branches."
213. "Obzory mestnoi raboty," *Vlast' sovetov*, March 20, 1927, p. 19. See also *Krest'ianskaia pravda*, December 15, 1930.

nurture other kinds of political and religious loyalties. A few examples can suffice. During the NEP years, a psalmist approached the *volost'* executive committee of Vologda province for permission to work among the poor peasants. Clergy reframed the Church's practice of religious charity in order to compete with Soviet aid to the poor.[214] In the Northern Region, several churches created special "funds for poor peasants" (*bedniatskie fondy*), while priests gave apples to the children of poor peasants in Shenkursk *uezd* (Archangel province). Offering poor peasants cheaper dirges, some priests in the Northern Region applied the principle of the sliding scale to the performance of religious ritual.[215] Increased Party involvement in the voting process, such as the routinization of preelection campaign meetings of poor peasants, did not quickly persuade village clergy that village soviets were institutions of "Soviet" or Communist political power.[216] It merely convinced them of the importance of lobbying poor peasants in a variety of ways.

In addition to "infiltrating" the Party's preelectoral meetings and lobbying poor peasants, the clergy intensified campaign efforts on behalf of "their" candidates. One non-Party peasant testified that the priest had offered personal recommendations for candidates for the position of chair of the village soviet, so as to ensure the election of a reliable person to the post.[217] The Party secretary for Smolensk province complained in 1927 that "religious organizations are trying to obstruct elections to the soviets ... [and] are presenting their own candidates." He also grumbled about the laity and clergy's intensified "agitation against *bednota* and party members during the election campaign" in El'nia and Roslavl *uezd*s.[218] In some instances, rural clergy understandably conflated the categories of "Communist" and *bezbozhnik* in their rejections and endorsements of candidates. During the 1926–27 electoral campaign in the village of Sidorovo (Rostov *uezd*, Iaroslavl province), the village priest insistently urged parishioners not to elect Communists to the village soviets; he

---

214. Oleshchuk, a member of the Central Committee of the League of the Godless, noted that sects also offered economic assistance to the rural poor. See *Kto stroit tserkvi v SSSR*, p. 36.

215. Matorin, *Religiia*, p. 33. In 1919, a priest in Vologda *uezd* organized economic assistance for poor peasants whose sons had died in the World War.

216. In separating the soviets from the regime itself, villagers were, in a sense, replaying a distinction made during the peasant rebellions of the Civil War. As Figes's work has shown, villagers fought anti-Bolshevik "wars" during 1919–21 in the Volga Region in order to "restore the localized village democracy of the revolution." *Peasant Russia*, p. 322. Peasants staged the March 1919 Syzran uprisings to "reestablish the soviets without Party cadres" (p. 329). During both the twilight of NEP and the Civil War, villagers thus continued to believe in the *potential* of the village soviets to be noncommunist institutions, even in the face of increasing Party bureaucratization.

217. *Vlast' sovetov*, April 13, 1927, p. 20.

218. Smolensk WKP 33, "Ob ozhivlenii i razvitii antireligioznoi propagandy v derevne," in *Prilozhenie no. 2 k protokolu No.57 zasedaniia biuro Smolgubkoma ot 17/XI-1927 g.*

commanded them to "elect the reliable non-Party peasant."[219] During the initial phases of collectivization, clergy warned that "if you elect *bezbozhniki*, they will close the churches."[220] Occasionally clergy even offered written recommendations of certain candidates. During the 1928–29 electoral campaign in Petrovsk *uezd* (Saratov province), clergy issued "electoral pamphlets" (*perevybornye listovki*) ordering readers to "vote for their [i.e., the priests'] candidates, rather than those proposed by the [Party] cell."[221]

Some rural priests also campaigned for their own election to the village soviets. During the 1927 voting campaign, in an unspecified village of the Soviet Far East, a priest attending an electoral meeting presented himself for election to the village soviet with this stunning rationale: "The Soviet regime will soon fall. They have already overthrown the Communists in Moscow. Therefore it is imperative to elect the disenfranchised to the soviet."[222] By according the village soviet a lifespan distinct from and longer than that of the regime itself, this priest indicated that he did not regard it as an institution of Soviet power. In other words, he did not believe that the soviets had to be staffed by personnel endorsed by the regime or that these institutions had to fulfill agendas set by the Party. By making such an appraisal, priests armed themselves with an invisible psychological armor that allowed them to disregard the Party's implicit assertions of the "Soviet" essence of the soviets, as well as sidestep the strict legal constraints on clerical participation in the political process. Ostensibly oblivious to the existing legal code, a few audacious members of the rural clergy, such as Pavel Alekseev, even ran as candidates for election to district executive committees. As early as 1923, for example, Alekseev, the warden of the local church, occupied a position in the Kisilevo-Chemizovsnyi VIK (Saratov province) as head of the *volost'* land department.[223] Rumor had it that Alekseev would win a majority of votes and become chair of the county executive committee during the next elections.[224] Electoral successes achieved by religious activists, facilitated in part by these self-liberating judgments, ultimately confirmed the initial appraisal, thereby encouraging additional political ventures.

When all else failed, the clergy got rough. Beginning with the voting campaign of 1926, villagers described as "kulaks" (a label that probably included clergy) were said to have displayed new strategies during the electoral

219. A. Zhukov, "Kulachestvo i dukhovenstvo v perevyborakh sovetov Iaroslavskoi gubernii," *Vlast' sovetov*, April 3, 1927, p. 20.
220. Putintsev, *Vybory v sovety*, p. 78. I include this example from the post-NEP period to demonstrate the continuity in the content of clerical campaigning from NEP through collectivization.
221. *Povolzhskaia pravda*, March 8, 1929, p. 3.
222. Angarov, *Klassovaia bor'ba*, p. 66.
223. *Izvestiia Atkarskogo uezdnogo ispolkoma*, April 12, 1923, p. 2.
224. Ibid.

process.²²⁵ They turned to such methods as the "intimidation of the poor, especially *batraki*, discrediting of poor peasants by inebriating them, bribery of the materially needy, arson, murder of activists—whether the president or other members of the soviet—and village correspondents."²²⁶ The head of the OGPU in the Smolensk region lamented in 1928 that since 1926, "enemy groups," including members of the rural clergy, had intensified their struggle to regain voting rights by bribing and inebriating voting officials.²²⁷

The legal directives of the Decree and the Constitution notwithstanding, the clergy established a strong political presence in the village soviets.²²⁸ Priests, deacons, and psalmists not only gained election to the soviets but in some instances occupied the most influential positions, namely, that of secretary and chair.²²⁹ As we have seen, by 1928 the chair of the village soviet in Gulenovskoe had come to consider the village priest a regular participant in the institution's affairs. As of 1927, "members of the church choir, psalmists, or [other] church assistants" comprised almost the entire staff of the village soviet in Khustianskoe (Smel'iansk *uezd*, Romensk region).²³⁰ Provincial correspondents sometimes commented that members of the clergy served rather lengthy terms of office.²³¹

Available evidence suggests that much to the Party's chagrin, clergy held positions in the village soviet with even greater frequency following the introduction of the "revival of the soviets." After 1924 provincial newspapers, memoirs, and monographs included more reports of clerical participation in the village soviets. To be sure, this increase may have reflected the Party's intensified focus on the weaknesses of this institution, an obsession mirrored in its directives to provincial correspondents, rather than an actual acceleration of what Soviet partisans called the clerical "infiltration" of the soviets. However, the clergy had a number of strong motivations for being interested

---

225. For observations on the animated participation of religious activists in the 1926 electoral campaign in Smolensk province, see Smolensk WKP 13, "Protokol no. 18 zasedaniia volkoma RKP(b) zabolotskoi volosti ot 21 avgusta 1926 g."

226. Levin and Suvorov, "Sovety i stroitel'stvo sotsializma," in Pashukanis, *15 let*.

227. Smolensk WKP 44—Prilozhenie k pr. Biuro GK ot 24/XII 28 g. No. 47—Postanovlenie po dokladu fraktsii VKP(b) Gubizbirkoma t. Liubimovoi i s dokladom: gaz. "Kommuna," i "Golos krest'ianina"—t.t. Murafeva, Kal. TsUK VKP(b)—t. Shubina i nach. OGPU t. Davydova o khode otchetno-perevybornoi kampanii sovetov.

228. There is also evidence that clergy gained election to city (*gorodskie*) soviets and became members of the RKI. See *Bezbozhnik*, July 8, 1928 (8/VII), quoted in *VRSKhD*, October 1928, p. 15.

229. For examples of priests who served as secretaries, see Matorin, *Religiia*, p. 33, and Shakhnovich, *Zapiski bezbozhnika*, p. 130. For examples of deacons who held positions in the soviets, including that of chair, see *Bezbozhnik*, January 17, 1925, and May 3, 1925, p. 6. For cases of psalmists who served as members and officers of village soviets, see *Sovetskaia derevnia*, July 15, 1928, p. 3, and *Povolzhskaia pravda*, November 11, 1928, p. 3.

230. *Bezbozhnik*, January 30, 1927.

231. See, for example, *Sovetskaia derevnia*, July 15, 1928, p. 3.

in establishing a significant political presence in the soviets. The more the regime sought to control the electoral process, the more motivated clergy were to become politically active in the soviets. The financial weakness of the soviets created opportunities for clerical servitors to serve in the institution. Deprived throughout NEP of their own budgets, the soviets relied on the low sums granted by the VIKs to pay their staffs.[232] Consequently, salaries were paltry.[233] Because less well off peasants could not afford to serve in the soviet, villagers with higher outside incomes—such as certain clergy and laity—filled these spots.[234] The political success of rural clergy points to the general truth that it is dangerous and counterproductive for any state to make additional political, social, cultural, and economic claims on its people without having adequate means (i.e., institutions and cadres) to enforce them. Only beginning with the "great turn" was the state more able to impose its will in the countryside. As the process of collectivization accelerated, the Party (more specifically the Workers' and Peasants' Inspectorate [RKI]) grew obsessed with eliminating clergy from the *apparat*. In 1929, the RKI of the Lower Volga region purged forty-three clergy from various rural institutions, apparently including the village soviets.[235]

During NEP, rural parish clergy were, despite their diminished authority in the parish and the village, a social group distinguished by their multidimensional political identity. On the group and even on the individual level, they wore several different political hats, juggling political activity in the

232. Neither the 1924 decree on soviets, "Polozhenie o sel'sovetakh," nor the 1926 regulations on local finance, "Polozhenie o mestnykh finansakh RSFSR," changed this state of affairs, namely, granted the soviets their own budgets. See "Polozhenie o mestnykh finansakh," VTsIK SNK, 19 November 1926, *SU*, 1926, no. 92, art. 668.

233. The average pay for a chair was reported as between twenty-four and thirty rubles a month in 1929. Male, *Russian Peasant Organisation*, p. 127.

234. Ibid., p. 137. According to a major survey of 615,400 households by the Central Board of Statistics, the poor were underrepresented and the more well off were overrepresented, relative to their percentages in the rural population, in the rural soviets. See Male, *Russian Peasant Organisation*, p. 128. This is indirect evidence that at least some rural clergy were in fact relatively well off.

235. During the five or so months preceding April 1929, this branch of the RKI conducted an investigation and purge of "regional institutions, industrial workers, land institutions, and agricultural and consumers' cooperatives." See *Povolzhskaia pravda*, April 6, 1929, p. 3. The instructions of the Central Committee of the RKI for the examination (*proverka*) of the *apparat* dictated that "servitors of religious cults [*sluzhiteli religioznogo kul'ta*] ... should not under any circumstances remain at any position in the lower Soviet *apparat*." See *Krest'ianskaia pravda*, June 11, 1929. Speaking at the Leningrad Region Party Conference in 1929, Iakovlev stated: "You can criticize us or not criticize us, but I'll tell you directly, that we in the presidium of the TsKK decided, that the criterion—being the son or nephew of a priest—is not enough to be purged from the *apparat*; this formal criterion is inadequate, if the person [Party member] shows a conscientious relationship to his work." See ibid., March 15, 1929.

village assembly, the cooperative, and the village soviet. Drawing on the "trained capacity" to be sociopolitical actors developed in the very late tsarist period, they adapted remarkably to the new demands, challenges, and opportunities of the new political conjuncture.[236] Clergy had become, to an unprecedented degree, political entrepreneurs.[237] But how successful and effective were they in using their political skills and presence to contest the claims of villagers indifferent and hostile to religious belief and practice? This depended in part on how much political support and savvy lay religious activists would demonstrate.

---

236. On "trained capacity," see Thorstein Veblen, *Imperial Germany and the Industrial Revolution* (New York, 1939).

237. On clergy as political entrepreneurs, see Popkin, *Rational Peasant*, pp. 259–66.

6

Parish Democracy

When lay activists fulfilled their dreams of exercising more power over their financially, legally, and psychologically embattled clergy, the task of deciding what "laicization" in parish affairs would mean during NEP was by no means behind them. It was one thing to reinstitute *vybornoe nachalo* and to play a much greater role in determining other aspects of the clergy's service in the parish, and another to take on the challenges to parish life generated by the percolating conflict over issues of religious belief and practice. To be sure, those lay activists who had been involved in parish affairs during the late tsarist period had played a public role in this emerging cultural conflict, a role that intertwined with long-standing modes of expressing popular piety (e.g., building and caring for churches and other religious property). This kind of lay activism had continued during the Civil War.

During NEP, however, lay activists faced new considerations that entered into their ongoing decisions about the meaning of laicization in parish affairs. There was now a formally organized antireligious campaign, which although weak, nevertheless had a social base of Party members, returning red Army veterans, *otkhodniki*, and youth; moreover, as we have seen, this diverse contingent's attacks on religious belief and practice went far beyond the narrow confines of antireligious cells. The regime's intensified efforts to create a secular village and to establish its administrative presence in the village went hand in hand, as exemplified by the 1924 policy of the "revival of the soviets." In sum, the "reach of the state," although still erratic and shallow, was significantly greater than during the Civil War. As they faced these more daunting external challenges and obstacles, lay activists also had to decide whether they would allow their anticlericalism to stop them from resisting these intensified challenges to religious belief and practice.

Education, Propaganda, and the Family

To what extent did lay activists become involved, for example, in attempting to subdue the intrafamilial tensions over religious belief and practice? Most likely members of church councils and other lay activists possessed some knowledge of resolutions, such as that adopted by the Tikhonites of Ustiuzhinsk *uezd* (Cherepovetsk province), calling for "religious education to begin from the moment that the child begins to consciously evolve."[1] Whether or not prompted by such resolutions and by discussion of issues relating to the family at meetings of church councils, lay activists joined clergy in portraying antireligious activists and their fellow travelers as immoral enemies of the rural family and its children.[2]

Moreover, whether or not goaded by such resolutions, lay activists resisted antireligious influences in rural education. One of their chief means of resistance was financial. As noted above, with Sovnarkom's delegation of the financing of rural education to "self-taxation" in 1921, villagers' material support played a role in shaping the curriculum.[3] In several *uezdy* in Novgorod province, for example, activists successfully mobilized villagers to stipulate that they would contribute self-taxation funds (*samooblozhenie*) only if "God's law" was taught in the school.[4] In 1921, a district Party appeal in Novgorod province noted that while peasants repaired and heated churches, they failed to commit to the self-taxation necessary to keep the

1. VRSKhD, June 1928, p. 16.
2. See, for example, *Izvestiia Saratovskogo soveta*, April 12, 1928, p. 2.
3. Gringlas, "*Shkraby ne kraby?*" pp. 34–55. On this see also Fitzpatrick, *Commissariat of Enlightenment*, p. 228, and Holmes, "Schools and Religion," in Ramet, *Religious Policy*, pp. 132–33. The salaries of village teachers were notoriously low, averaging twenty to thirty rubles a year. See Kenez, *Birth of the Propaganda State*, p. 139.
4. NPA (Novgorod Party Archive), f. 1, op. 1, ed. khr. 621, l. 17, quoted in Makeikina, "Kul'turnoe stroitel'stvo," p. 6. See also Gringlas, "*Shkraby ne kraby?*" p. 70. On religious influences in the schools during NEP, see also Holmes, *The Kremlin and the Schoolhouse*, p. 102.

schools heated.⁵ Some villagers in Viriatino (Tambov province) kept their children out of schools because of antireligious influences in the classroom.⁶

In addition to using their financial clout to shape the curriculum, lay activists sought to provide alternatives to public schools. In some cases, such as a village in Saratov province, clergy apparently enlisted church councils to join a campaign to close the local school.⁷ But the more typical scenario was for lay activists to demonstrate considerable initiative in providing religious instruction.⁸ In a village in Syzransk *uezd*, for example, a priest's wife opened a private school for teaching "God's law" in 1926.⁹ Mobilized against antireligious influences in rural education, lay activists also resisted antireligious agitation and propaganda in other venues. Because there is reason to believe that they generally had significantly lower literacy rates than clergy, they were somewhat handicapped in this regard. They were thus less able, for example, to familiarize themselves with the antireligious propaganda that trickled into the countryside. These handicaps notwithstanding, lay activists such as those in Tobol'sk and Perm okrugs, for example, created organizations (*obshchestva revnitelei very*) to counter the work of local antireligious cells by conducting "agitation" among villagers.¹⁰ But because the network of antireligious cells was spread so thinly across the Soviet countryside, lay activists made the reading hut their prime institutional target.¹¹

In particular, lay activists fashioned discourses of resistance against villagers who opened and supported the reading huts and red corners. When a reading hut opened in a village in Serdobsk *uezd* of Saratov province, for example, lay activists and clergy warned that "God would punish [villagers for opening the hut] . . . a heavenly fire will consume the blasphemers who use it."¹² In other villages, lay activists adopted a moralistic tone. Shortly after a red corner opened in a peasant's home in a village in Novgorod *okrug*, unidentified villagers wrote the following sarcastic comment on a nearby wall: "If you take the icons from this house [i.e., agree to open a red corner in your hut], you'll get three bundles of firewood."¹³ Invoking the basic principle underlying clerical discourse against the *bezbozhniki* and other villagers hostile to religious belief and practice, lay activists portrayed this villager's

---

5. Gringlas, "*Shkraby ne kraby?*" p. 27.
6. Sula Benet, ed. and trans., *The Village of Viriatino* (Garden City, N.Y., 1970), p. 289.
7. *Bezbozhnik*, February 4, 1926, p. 1.
8. For an example, see ibid., p. 6.
9. Ibid., p. 4. The village in question was Komarovko.
10. *Bezbozhnik*, August 2, 1925, p. 2.
11. *Bezbozhnik*, February 28, 1926; *Krest'ianskaia pravda*, January 28, 1928.
12. *Bezbozhnik*, February 28, 1926. Lay activists also used this discursive strategy against the newly opened cooperative.
13. *Krest'ianskaia pravda*, January 28, 1928.

decision as excessively self-interested and, furthermore, as a violation of community norms of justice. Another important feature of this wall graffiti was what it did *not* say: resistant to "talking Soviet"—that is, mentioning the creation of a red corner—its author(s) instead called the incident the "removal of icons."[14]

Village Semiotics

Lay activists' moralistic warnings about the "removal of icons" were, of course, part of a more general resistance to other villagers' attacks on the religious elements of village semiotics. As we saw in Chapter 1, during the late tsarist period, lay activists—and especially members of church councils—devoted considerable efforts to the upkeep of churches, one of the key expressions of popular piety. Their efforts in this arena continued, despite a radically different political conjuncture, during the Civil War. To what extent did church council members and other lay activists remain committed during NEP to the upkeep of their churches? What means did they use to "keep it alive"?

Church council members and lay activists remained acutely conscious of the legal obligation to repair churches as set forth by the Decree on the Separation of Church and State. In a retrospective account of 1933, a parish priest claimed:

> The believers are constantly occupied in collecting for the maintenance of the church and the priest. There is not a month, not a week, not a day, when the parish commune, if not all together, at least through its executive, does not take thought for the church and its maintenance, and with it for the priest of the parish as such. The church building is always in danger.[15]

The word "danger" is particularly revealing, for it gives us a sense of the anxiety that religious activists felt concerning the existence of the church; moreover, it conveys the urgency that lay activists attached to keeping the

---

14. This is an adaptation of Kotkin's observations on the capacity of Magnitorsk workers to "speak Bolshevik and 'innocent peasant'" as the situation required. See Stephen Kotkin, "Coercion and Identity: Workers' Lives in Stalin's Showcase City," in L. H. Siegelbaum and R. G. Suny, eds., *Making Workers Soviet: Power, Class, and Identity* (Ithaca, N.Y., 1994), p. 303.

15. Father Trophimus, "Russian Religion," pp. 95–96.

church in repair in order to avoid secularization.[16] To be sure, given the pervasive underinstitutionalization of the Soviet countryside, the fears of religious activists may have been generated in part by an unwarranted exaggeration of the state's capacity to enforce the legal claims of the Decree.

Church council members and other lay activists, whether or not responding to an anticipated or actual threat, invested tremendous energy in the various steps involved in completing church repairs.[17] One parish priest claimed that "for collecting the money [for church repairs], and for controlling its expenditure, trustees for the conclusion of the lease are chosen from the members [of the parish]."[18] Church elders went door to door to collect money for repairing the parish church.[19] Typically playing a central role in initiating repair projects, members of church councils also did some of the work themselves.[20] To generate funds and other necessary support, these lay activists also turned to the village assembly and the village soviet, a tactic that, as we will see, brought them into conflict with those villagers indifferent or hostile to religious belief and practice.[21]

Legal deterrents notwithstanding, lay activists also took the initiative in generating the necessary funds and support to build churches. Although in some cases they were trying to rebuild churches (usually made of wood) that had been destroyed by fire, they even, as in tsarist times, constructed churches where none had been before.[22] Lay activists, and in particular members of

---

16. To be sure, we must keep in mind that we are getting the clergy's perhaps erroneous perceptions of lay perceptions here.
17. *Bezbozhnik*, October 23, 1927; TsGAOR, f. 5446-s, op. 55, d. 647, l. 14.
18. Father Trophimus, "Russian Religion," p. 96.
19. *Bezbozhnik*, January 5, 1926, p. 4.
20. As described on pp. 52–53 of Oleshchuk, *Kto stroit tserkvi v SSSR*, sometime in the second half of the 1920s (1928 or before), villagers in Tyntsa (Vladimir province) built a new home for their deacon and repaired the parish church. Initiators of (and financial contributors to) these projects included such prominent lay members of the parish community as the partner of a manufacturer and member of the church council; a former journeyman of a factory and member of the church council; a cement maker (*betonshchik*) at a factory and member of the church council (alleged to be a monarchist); a blacksmith and church elder; and former manufacturer and permanent member of the church council. Interested in discrediting the project by pointing to its supposedly well-off sponsors, Oleshchuk may have exaggerated the role of merchants in its financing. As he noted at the end of his list, "several others" (of unspecified occupation or socioeconomic background) also provided assistance. (Oleshchuk's list included other individuals, all of whom were former manufacturers or traders.) In fact, he maintained that "workers" did the building, allegedly to hide the identities of the project's initiators. Moreover, his list included many *former* manufacturers, who may have assumed more humble, less "incriminating" occupations after the October Revolution, and even some tradesmen (such as the blacksmith).
21. See, for example, *Bezbozhnik*, October 23, 1927, and December 18, 1927, and *Sovetskaia derevnia*, August 26, 1928, p. 4.
22. For discussion of villagers rebuilding churches that had been destroyed, see Oleshchuk,

church councils, also initiated and carried to completion the building of churches in rural factories.²³

The construction of a church in the paper factory "Kommunisticheskii avangard" is an interesting case in point. In an unspecified year, a local priest and members of the church council in the settlement of Sobinko saw the project through to completion.²⁴ According to Oleshchuk, the contingent of lay activists included not only "people of former times" (*byvshie liudi*) such as kulaks and merchants but also former Party members and members of the *apparat*. A former policeman and Communist and a former chair of the Vladimir *uezd* committee occupied leadership positions in the campaign to build the church.²⁵ A priest and former Communists worked side by side to create a place of holy worship!

Along these lines, lay activists integrated ostensibly incompatible religious and political identities into religious art. In a church in Orel, for example, unidentified individuals replaced an icon of Christ that depicted him as the heavenly tsar with another that portrayed him as a carpenter.²⁶ It is unclear how widespread such accommodation of liturgical art to revolutionary circumstances was.

In some cases lay activists even resorted to violence—or threats thereof—in order to resist the encroachment of secular elements in village semiotics. In 1923, for example, members of the church council in the village Temiriazan' (Syzran *uezd*, Simbirsk province) threatened to beat a youth who took a blackboard (said to have been "near" a priest's home) for cultural enlightenment workers' staging of a performance in the public building (*nardom*).²⁷ Peasants described as "kulaks" were accused of tearing out crosses

---

Kto stroit tserkvi v SSSR, p. 8, and *Krest'ianskaia pravda*, July 19, 1929, p. 3. For details on the building of "new" churches, see Oleshchuk, *Kto stroit tserkvi v SSSR*, p. 9. For statistics on the building of new churches during the tsarist period, see the yearly reports of the Holy Synod. In 1911, for example, 250 stone and 343 wood churches were built in the Russian Empire; in 1912, 305 new stone and 321 new wood churches appeared. See *IVO za 1911–12 g.*, p. 77.

23. The Party's investigation of the "Smolensk Affair" in 1928 revealed the construction of a church in a large textile mill, the Iartsev factory. Oleshchuk, *Kto stroit tserkvi v SSSR*, p. 76. Expressing their still strong ties to village culture, in the 1930s "[Moscow] workers of peasant origin contested the closing of churches and contributed money for their restoration." See Hoffmann, *Peasant Metropolis*, p. 170. The strength of workers' religiosity—sometimes said to exceed that of peasants!—became a theme in the antireligious press during the last years of NEP. See, for example *Antireligioznik* 6 (June 1928), cited in *VRSKhD*, October 1928, p. 14.

24. There were six thousand workers at this factory, 60 percent of whom were women. See Bliakhin, *Kto i zachem stroit tserkvi*, pp. 19, 26–27.

25. Oleshchuk, *Kto stroit tserkvi v SSSR*, p. 63.

26. *Povolzhskaia pravda*, November 14, 1928, p. 5. During the very late imperial period, villagers also integrated revolutionary motifs and Orthodox ritual. See Stites, *Revolutionary Dreams*, p. 104.

27. *Bezbozhnik*, August 5, 1923, p. 7.

from graves and then blaming the incident on the local Komsomol, an incident as revealing of the popular association of Komsomol members with violent attacks on religious objects and buildings as of some villagers' intolerance for such tactics.[28]

Thus, like the clergy, lay activists—and church council members in particular—participated vigorously in all three of these "fields" of cultural conflict (the family, education and propaganda, and village semiotics). To be sure, lay activists and clergy sometimes even joined together in resisting the various claims of antireligious activists (e.g., in taking the necessary steps to build churches). When lay activists became involved in these interdependent fields of cultural conflict, they did so in different ways than clergy. Although the clergy took considerable initiative in repairing churches, it was the lay activists who led the campaigns to keep the church buildings—and other religious elements of village semiotics—alive. This was not accidental. For lay activists had, since tsarist times, expressed their piety by building and caring for churches. Moreover, they were anxious because of the legal threat of secularization of church property in early Soviet legislation.

Their efforts focused on maintaining the church building and other religious objects, lay activists were particularly conscious of the importance of electoral politics. To generate funds and support necessary to repair existing churches and build new ones, for example, lay activists needed to harness the financial possibilities of the cooperative, the village assembly, and even the village soviet. To conduct public religious rituals (e.g., processions of the cross) and traditional holiday celebrations, lay activists needed the financial support of these same institutions; moreover, after the promulgation of the 1925 NKVD directive on religious ritual, they needed to be able to secure the necessary permission from the village soviet. Like clergy, lay activists found that their pursuit of parish needs—and their involvement in the cultural conflict over religious belief and practice—created even more cause for political activism than during the Civil War. How successful were they in meeting this challenge? What kinds of political identities did lay activists construct and develop during NEP?

Lay Activists, Church Councils, and Electoral Politics

To meet such financial needs of the rural religious community, members of church councils and other lay activists held important positions in rural

---

28. It is unclear whether kulak was used here as a synonym for clergy, as was often the case in the Soviet press. See E. Iaroslavskii in *Bezbozhnik*, March 29, 1925.

cooperatives throughout the NEP period. This lay contingent consisted of two groups, those with formal titles, such as the church warden and members of church councils, and what might be called the rank and file. During elections to the agricultural association in a village in Smolensk province in 1926, the chair of the church council won the position of steward.[29] In 1928, the church warden (*tserkovnyi starosta*) organized a cooperative machine association in a village in Saratov province.[30] The participation of lay religious leaders in cooperatives complemented that of rural members of the clergy.

Rank-and-file religious activists joined clergy and lay leaders in holding powerful positions in cooperatives. Harder to spot because of their lack of a formal religious title, these individuals nevertheless attended church and observed traditional religious practices. In 1927, the chair of a consumers' cooperative in a village in the Urals, although not a prominent, titled lay leader, allegedly neglected his duties there and instead worked diligently in the church.[31] In 1928, a certain Ivan Ivanovich Olykainen was elected to chair a *sel'khoziaistvennoe tovarishchestvo* in a village in the Leningrad region. Every Sunday he listened to religious broadcasts from Finland on the radio in the association's "cooperative corner," which he had set up after assuming the post.[32] As of 1929, the chair of the managing board of a consumers' cooperative (*potrebobshchestvo*) in the countryside of the Leningrad region reportedly maintained friendly relations with "kulaks" and members of the clergy.[33] The chair of a rural cooperative in the Urals was "always in the first row of any procession of the cross [*krestnyi khod*]."[34] The leaders of six cooperatives in the region closed down their operations on religious holidays in order to attend church. They also shut down the cooperatives on weekdays if they had an opportunity to meet a visiting bishop.[35] In 1929, employees of a rural forestry cooperative in the Leningrad region celebrated the religious holiday of Nicholas Day.[36] One worker marched in the *krestnyi khod*.

For lay activists, the challenge of gaining influence in the village assembly during NEP was of an entirely different nature than that of "taming" the cooperative. While in the case of the cooperative influence hinged on gaining election to the cooperative board, lay activists of course faced no analo-

29. *Pravda*, July 18, 1926.
30. *Sovetskaia derevnia*, July 29, 1928, p. 5.
31. *Bezbozhnik*, February 27, 1927.
32. *Krest'ianskaia pravda*, October 19, 1928, p. 4.
33. *Krest'ianskaia pravda*, June 7, 1929.
34. *Bezbozhnik*, February 27, 1927, p. 8.
35. Ibid.
36. *Krest'ianskaia pravda*, July 5, 1929.

gous hurdle in the case of the village assembly: the Land Code's definition of the commune and of voting rights in the village assembly meant that, in theory, the assembly was more democratic than ever before. The Code even granted women over eighteen who were *not* heads of households the right to participate in the village assembly. (Moreover, women who had been part of a household for more than two years had a right to land if that household broke up; as a result, ten million new peasant households were created between 1917 and 1928.)[37] Thus the key challenge faced by lay activists working for their parishes was to mobilize support in an assembly that had become, at least nominally, much more inclusive. Although all members of the gathering took part in the debates generated by issues of religious belief and practice, church elders and church council members played particularly crucial roles in advocating on behalf of parish needs.[38] It was prominent lay activists of both sexes, for example, who took the initiative in raising such issues at meetings of the assembly.[39]

While lay activists could draw on their pre-1917 experiences in seeking influence in the cooperative and village assembly, they had no such roots in the village soviets. To be sure, lay activists had gained a toehold in the soviets during the Civil War, especially before they became more "bureaucratized" (i.e., before the percentage of Party members and fellow travelers in them began to rise) in 1919–20. As this bureaucratization continued and even gained momentum with the regime's launching of its efforts to "revive" the soviets in 1924, did lay activists stop trying to harness them to their own purposes? And if not, how strong and successful were their efforts to gain influence in them?

Like clergy, religious activists sought to influence the work of the village soviets from behind the scenes. Church elders, for example, even joined priests in socializing with influential members of this political body. To give one of many possible examples, in December of 1926, the church elder of Pokhozhevo appealed to the chair of the village soviet to allow clergy to carry an icon of the Virgin throughout the parish.[40] Symbolizing and cementing their political solidarity, that evening the church elder joined both the priest and the chair of the village soviet for an evening of dancing at the local tavern.

37. On this see, for example, Atkinson, *The End of the Russian Land Commune*, pp. 236, 242–44.
38. See, for example, *Bezbozhnik*, March 8, 1925, p. 4, and Kniazev, *Kak kulaki i popy*, p. 10.
39. *Bezbozhnik*, March 8, 1925, p. 4.
40. The point of this ritual was to collect money from parishioners; the priest was said to have collected one or one-and-one-half rubles from "all" households. See *Bezbozhnik*, June 19, 1927, p. 6.

Lay activists, however, had even less reason than clergy to be satisfied with such indirect influence on the political life of the village soviets. Unlike clergy, their social identity did not automatically subject them to disqualification from political activity either as voters or as candidates. These legal opportunities thus allowed—and even obliged—lay activists to extend the democratization of parish life into the political life of the village soviet as well. The 1918 Constitution's prohibition against electing clergy to Soviet institutions obliged believers, in theory if not in practice, to promote the election of lay leaders.[41] Potentially "safe" candidates, as well as "campaign managers," included members of church councils, the church elders, deacons, psalmists, and close family relatives of clergy.

Lay activists were not, however, completely exempt from legal constraints on their political participation in the village soviets. The Constitution's disenfranchisement of "exploiters" created potential political obstacles for those lay personnel (e.g., members of the church councils and church elders) who also employed hired labor. Interpreting the directive to exclude those employing hired labor, for example, proved very difficult. In some cases, overwhelmed local authorities followed a strict, "letter of the law" interpretation and even disenfranchised *seredniaki* and *bedniaki*. Ignoring these peasants' "material condition," officials revoked voting rights for such trivial infractions as the hiring of nurses and of workers during the harvest of fruit and tobacco.[42] Voting commissions' strict application of the principles of the 1918 Constitution thus excluded from the electoral process rural dwellers possessing even purer class credentials than laboring clergy.

The 1925 "Instruction on Elections to the Soviets" sought to remove some of the ambiguities surrounding lay electoral participation. The "Instruction" guaranteed the voting rights of laity who "through [either] employment or election by religious societies are involved in the administratively economic and technical service of religious buildings and religious societies, such as: watchmen, cleaners, bell ringers, singers, church elders, organists, members of church councils, psalmists, cantors, musicians, and others holding similar positions."[43] However, the amendment also stipulated that these lay functions could not be the "primary occupations" of the individuals in question.[44] Although the absence of adequate sources prohibits any definite conclusions, it was probably, in fact, the goal of obtaining broader participation in the

---

41. Regional newspapers targeted at a rural population sometimes reminded their readership of the legal ban against electing clergy to Soviet institutions. See "Besedy o kooperatsii," published in the Leningrad paper *Derevenskaia pravda*, April 16, 1921.

42. Levin and Suvorov, "Sovety i stroitel'stvo sotsializma," in Pashukanis, *15 let*.

43. Ibid., p. 116. See also [what I presume] is the reprint of the *tsirkuliar* of the Presidium of the TsIK of April 10, 1925, as reprinted in *Vlast' sovetov*, May 3, 1925.

44. *Vlast' sovetov*, May 3, 1925.

process of "reviving the soviets" that motivated the decision to extend the franchise to certain segments of clergy and laity. Such reasoning would implicitly testify to the vitality of lay activity across a broad socioeconomic spectrum of rural dwellers.

In practice, however, members of voting commissions sometimes gave more weight to cultural loyalties than to socioeconomic identity. During the 1927 voting campaign, for example, a lay sectarian leader (i.e., a church elder) lost his voting rights, even though he qualified as a *bedniak* according to prevailing standards of social stratification. The same voting commission disenfranchised other lay leaders of unspecified socioeconomic origin. Seven peasants of the evangelical sect in Tiunelevo *volost'* of the same district lost the right to vote. Local authorities, then, apparently interpreted lay religious activity as a type of "exploitation" prohibited by the Constitution of 1918.[45] Whether they made such strict interpretations out of confusion or radicalism, these cadres thereby deprived the rural political arena of a constituency drawn, in some cases, from the very social strata that had been targeted by the policy of the "revival of the soviets."[46] In order to influence the decisions reached in such ambiguous cases, lay activists joined clergy in serving on the voting commissions.[47]

Lay activists also sought to influence the electoral process by campaigning for specific candidates for election to the village soviets. Conscious of the legal constraints on the clergy's political activity, as well as of the surging anticlericalism of some villagers, lay activists seized a fleeting opportunity to take charge on the campaign trail. The church elder, for example, regularly campaigned for the election of candidates to the village soviets. Relying on his authority within the church community, the elder sometimes took charge of preelection campaigning for a given slate of candidates.[48] Members of the church councils, which as we have seen, included rural residents of varying socioeconomic backgrounds, shared the burden of campaigning for candidates. One anonymous church "official" (*blagovestnik*), underscored the central role of the church council in the electoral process.[49]

Lay activists played a particularly crucial role in electoral preparations once the disenfranchisement of clergy began to rise with the 1926–27 electoral campaign. Chairs and other members of church councils, for example,

---

45. *Vlast' sovetov*, February 6, 1927, p. 2.
46. Local electoral commissions in some cases simply did not have access to the instructions or know the law. See Kimerling, "Civil Rights," pp. 38–40.
47. *Krest'ianskaia pravda*, December 15, 1930. Even by 1930, after the policy to "revive the soviets" had been in effect for six years, some voting commissions failed to meet the Party's expectations. See *Sovetskaia derevnia*, December 22, 1930, p. 3.
48. *Pravda*, February 24, 1926. According to the author, the elder's attempts failed.
49. *Povolzhskaia pravda*, December 5, 1928, p. 3.

apparently took the lead in organizing preelection meetings at which religious activists formulated electoral strategies. In 1929, religious activists in a village in Pskov *okrug* met to discuss electoral strategies at the home of the chair of the church council.[50] While the socioeconomic background and religious status (i.e., whether clergy or laity) of the participants remain unclear, the report does affirm that a layperson, and a woman at that, held the organizational and leadership reins of the meeting. Members of church councils also discussed political issues other than electoral strategies at these meetings. Iaroslavskii, for example, mentioned "cases, when [members of] church councils specifically spent [part of] their meetings discussing how to organize the expulsion of this or that Communist from the Party."[51] A 1925 report of the Workers-Peasants Inspectorate concluded that "*de facto* these organizations (church councils) are the unofficial 'second power' in the countryside."[52] Supported by the institutional authority of the church council, and surrounded by a politically constrained clergy often accorded little respect by parishioners, lay leaders occasionally led religious villagers in their political battles.

Religious activists such as church elders, whether or not prompted by discussions at preelectoral gatherings, sometimes attempted to "buy" votes. In an effort to persuade poor peasants to elect a priest's son to the village soviet, an ingratiating church elder in the Leningrad region offered his targeted clientele bread and conversation. Also seeking to land a priest's son in the soviet, another enterprising church elder from the Leningrad region offered poor peasants the enticement of vodka in addition to bread.[53] Thus religious activists such as church elders used bribery to compete with Party cadres for the political support of the poor peasantry, the very stratum targeted by the policy of the "revival of the soviets."

In fact, especially in the years following the Party's various attempts to control the electoral process, the rural political faction committed to electing religious activists was by no means composed exclusively of church council members and highly visible lay leaders. The political contribution of a socioeconomically broad spectrum of religious activists, for example, characterized an attempt to reelect a religious supporter to the village soviet.[54] During the electoral campaign of 1928–29 in Leningrad region, Andrei Osipov, who had served as a member of the village soviet, again presented

---

50. See *Krest'ianskaia pravda*, February 5, 1929.
51. See E. Iaroslavskii, "Predvaritel'nye itogi," *Bol'shevik* 20 (1929): 15.
52. See A. N. Kolesnikov and I. V. Murugov, *Apparat nizovykh sovetskikh organov* (Moscow, 1926), p. 134.
53. *Krest'ianskaia pravda*, December 31, 1928, p. 2.
54. In 1929, 61 percent of all voters voted during elections to both rural and urban soviets. See Trifonov, *Likvidatsiia*, p. 261.

himself as a candidate for this post. Even villagers whom a provincial correspondent described as middle peasants (*seredniaki*) joined the more well-off peasants in verbally endorsing Osipov's candidacy: "Let Andrei Osipov keep on serving [as a member of the soviet]: he is a devout person and never does [anything] bad."[55] Villagers based their political endorsements not on a candidate's pragmatic effectiveness or on the stand taken on particular issues but on his or her perceived religious identity.

This religious contingent, whatever its changing social complexion, frequently placed its candidates in the village soviets. Members of church councils did hold positions in village soviets during the first few years of NEP, or prior to the "revitalization" of the soviets.[56] An "honorary member" of the collective of believers in 1922 served as chair of the Ulitino-Sleptsovskoe village soviet.[57] In 1923, a member of the church council in Dubrovko (Achinsk *uezd*, Eniseisk province) acted as the chair of the village soviet.[58] During the 1924–25 electoral campaign in Etserishchensk *uezd*, both a member of the church council and a "former" deacon won election to the Khvotnian village soviet.[59]

How did members of church councils and other lay activists fare in their bids to gain election to the soviets following the Party's adoption of "face to the countryside" and "revival of the soviets"? Party leaders, as seen above, assumed that an increase in participation of rural dwellers with the proper class credentials—namely, poor and middle peasants—would result in the election of Party cadres and others loyal to the regime, an assumption that was to some extent borne out after 1924–25. This increased political participation and mobilization notwithstanding, religious activists continued to win seats in the soviets. A. F. Kurinkov, the chair of the village soviet in Osinovko (Saratov region), was said to interpret "all [everyday] events according to the Bible."[60] Other successful candidates included prominent lay leaders. Church elders, who were elected by members of the parish, served as chairs and members of village soviets throughout the RSFSR.[61]

55. *Krest'ianskaia pravda*, January 15, 1929, p. 4.
56. Like clergy, members of church councils and other lay activists also held positions in Soviet cultural institutions such as red corners and reading huts. See *Bezbozhnik*, February 15, 1925, p. 8, and December 18, 1927.
57. *Serp i molot*, December 28, 1922, p. 2.
58. *Bezbozhnik*, June 17, 1923, p. 7.
59. *Bezbozhnik*, January 11, 1925, p. 7.
60. *Sovetskaia derevnia*, October 7, 1928, p. 3. Provincial correspondents reported examples of the attachment of rank-and-file members of village soviets to religious practice rather infrequently. The scarcity of such documentation may or may not have reflected the less concrete and identifiable nature of the phenomenon itself.
61. See, for example *Bezbozhnik*, October 18, 1925, p. 7, and June 28, 1925, p. 5. On church elders as members of soviets, see ibid., February 6, 1927.

Reflecting the importance of family ties in shaping patterns of rural politics in the 1920s, sons of church elders were also frequent and vigorous members and chairs of village soviets.[62] In 1925, for example, a son of a church elder held the chair of the Fedorovskoe village soviet (Skopin *uezd*, Riazan province). An alleged heavy consumer of home brew, he was regularly invited to Orthodox weddings. Attending such an event in the neighboring village of Pakhomovo, he made the following remarks: "Dear people, bless [this couple so that] they travel safely, see God's church, hold the gold wreaths, kiss the cross and the [Holy] Gospel, [and] receive the holy gifts."[63] Although an active participant in the rural political institution that was to be the stronghold of Soviet power in the village, he let religious practice and theology guide his approach to everyday life.

Members of church councils joined church elders and other lay activists in occupying important positions in the village soviets. Lamenting the general overlap between Soviet political institutions and lay activists, one provincial correspondent for the Lower Volga region stated in 1928 that "in church councils there are quite a few members of the village soviets."[64] During the years when the regime was trying so hard to "revive the soviets," members of church councils achieved a broad and deep political presence in them.[65] It was not uncommon for members of a particular church council to occupy several positions—including the most important ones—in a village soviet.[66] In 1925, for example, *all* the members of the church council in the village of Tkharezko (Kamensk *uezd*, Novo-Nikolaevsk province) also served as members of the village soviet. On Sundays and holidays villagers could observe the entire presidium of the soviet perform various functions in the church service. The chair of the soviet usually read the gospel, while his deputy sang. The chair of the peasants' society of mutual aid (KKOV) served at the altar.[67]

Party members and other fellow travelers did, to be sure, know of the vigorous political activity of church council members and other lay activists.

---

62. See *Bezbozhnik*, August 9, 1925, p. 5.

63. *Bezbozhnik*, March 29, 1925, p. 4.

64. *Povolzhskaia pravda*, November 4, 1928, p. 2. See also TsGAOR Leningrada, f. 6307, op. 13, ed. khr. 9, ll. 160–61. Church councils coordinated resistance to collectivization. See Viola, *Peasant Rebels under Stalin*, p. 144.

65. The *caveat* introduced in note 60 concerning sources applies here as well. In other words, although provincial newspapers and other sources published accounts of the involvement of members of church councils in soviets more frequently following 1924, it is impossible to know whether this increase reflected an actual growth in such activity.

66. See, for example, *Krest'ianskii iurist* November 15, 1928, p. 14; *Bezbozhnik*, January 16, 1927, p. 4; and *Povolzhskaia pravda*, December 4, 1928, p. 2. See also *Sovetskaia derevnia*, May 27, 1928, p. 2, and *Pskovskii nabat'*, December 21, 1928, p. 2. For an example from 1928, see *Povolzhskaia pravda*, December 27, 1929, p. 2.

67. *Bezbozhnik*, July 19, 1925, p. 3.

Given the much greater "bureaucratization" (i.e., Party control) of the VIKs and other organs further up the institutional ladder, did such Party cadres try to block such political efforts of religious activists?[68] To be sure, some VIKs expressed alarm on learning that lay activists had gained important positions in the village soviets. Others, however, suffered from varying degrees of paralysis. When, for example, in 1925 a VIK in Bel'sk *uezd* (Smolensk province) learned that a church elder had been serving as chair of the soviet in the village Pochinok, it immediately demanded his removal.[69] Whether because of overwork (*peregruzka*), bribes, or other types of resistance, however, the matter was eventually dropped. Those clergy and lay activists who managed to hold important positions in county and district executive committees may have been able to block such attempts to "purge" the soviets.[70] The political presence of lay activists in the soviets was thus a symptom of the underinstitutionalization of the "Soviet" countryside during the 1920s.

For different reasons, representatives of the church hierarchy were just as alarmed by the political activity of lay activists on the grassroots level. Shortly before his death in 1925, Patriarch Tikhon called on parishes (*prikhodskie obshchiny*) "not to allow any pretensions . . . toward antigovernment activity and to elect to parish councils people . . . [who] are sincere supporters of Soviet power."[71]

Tikhon furthermore made a direct plea for church councils to stay out of politics altogether: "The activity of parish councils should not be directed toward politics [*politikanstvo*], which is completely alien to the Church of God, but to the strength of Orthodox belief, because enemies of Orthodoxy —sectarians, Catholics, Protestants, Renovationists, antireligious activists and the like—are trying to use any pretext to cause harm to the Church."[72] Those further down the institutional chain in the Orthodox ecclesiastical hierarchy echoed Tikhon's fears about the negative ramifications of the

---

68. According to research conducted by the NK RKI (Workers and Peasants' Inspectorate) in early 1925, 84 percent of all VIK chairs were members of the Party, while 13 percent were candidate members of the Party. The percentage of Party members and candidate members in the rank and file of the VIKs was significantly lower (48 percent and 11 percent). Only 63 percent of all VIK members belonged to the Party. For other statistics on other characteristics of VIK chairs and members, see Kolesnikov and Murugov, *Apparat nizovykh sovetskikh organov*, p. 19. As Figes notes, Party presence in the VIKs was actually higher during the Civil War (at the end of 1919). See *Peasant Russia*, pp. 223-24.

69. *Bezbozhnik*, October 18, 1925, p. 7.

70. For an example, see *Pravda*, June 8, 1926.

71. VSS 3 (1925): 5.

72. Ibid. Having in 1918 urged parishes (*prikhodskie obshchiny*) to resist the implementation of the Decree and in 1922 to resist the state's confiscation of church valuables, Tikhon was making an about-face in his stance on lay activism. See VSS 3 (1925): 2.

political activity of church councils. In 1928, for example, an unidentified church official (*blagovestnik*) in the Lower Volga Region expressed alarm concerning the political ambitions of church council members: "Through the church councils they [the members] want to battle with the regime, they want to become [part of] the regime itself, to place themselves in the soviets, in the party. And this is harmful to the Holy Church—the regime can find cause and fall upon [us] with oppression and persecution."[73] The anonymous church official thus implied that clergy could not rein in the poorly considered political activity of the laity, who composed the church councils. In fact, this church official had assumed the duty of "instructing" the clergy to preach the separation of Church and state to their congregation, of demonstrating the "perniciousness of the interference of the Church in worldly affairs."[74] Given the weakness of the ecclesiastical structure, we can speculate that such appeals were made quite infrequently and often failed to reach rural parishes.

Even if clergy and lay activists had heard such injunctions more frequently, however, they would have been disinclined to heed them. Why did warnings to stay out of politics carry so little weight with members of rural parishes? Church officials such as the aforementioned *blagovestnik* were "talking past" rural religious activists in stressing the dangers of political activity.[75] What they felt most threatened by was not the possibility of physical persecution, cases thereof notwithstanding, but the nightmare of a diverse village antireligious faction gaining political hegemony in key rural political institutions. In sum, religious activists on the grassroots level had too much to gain by engaging in extensive rural political activity and too much to lose by choosing not to do so. Those clergy who remained in the church hierarchy, however, were much more susceptible to religious persecution. Therefore, they were much more vigilant about eliminating possible pretexts—such as grassroots political activity—for such persecution. Recalling the ultimately intractable conflicts between the "episcopal party" and the white clergy during the tsarist period, parish clergy and those church officials who staffed what remained of the fragile Orthodox ecclesiastical structure disagreed on the value of political activity because they had differing experiences and interests in the political conjuncture of the early Soviet period.[76]

    73. *Povolzhskaia pravda*, December 5, 1928. This *blagovestnik* may very well have been a Renovationist. During collectivization the OGPU did hold the church council responsible for acts of peasant resistance, such as the *babii bunt*. See Viola, *Peasant Rebels under Stalin*, p. 193.
    74. *Povolzhskaia pravda*, December 5, 1928.
    75. See Mannheim, *Ideology and Utopia*.
    76. Because he does not make this important distinction between the interests of the Orthodox hierarchy and those of lay activists in rural parishes, Roslof mistakenly concludes that "[the Orthodox] displayed a fervent desire to keep Soviet politics out of their parish

In sum, to the chagrin of some rural Party cadres and Orthodox Church officials alike, lay religious activists joined clergy in constructing highly visible political identities during NEP. Like the clergy, lay activists wore several different political hats; on the group and most probably on the individual level, they juggled political activity in the cooperative, village assembly, and village soviet. In fashioning and developing such multidimensional political identities, a good many lay activists drew on political skills honed during the very late tsarist period.

Lay political activists, however, had only so much in common with their clerical counterparts. Their political presence was both potentially and *de facto* larger than that of their nominal spiritual superiors. Moreover, the lay faction, composed as it was of prominent parish leaders (such as church elders) and their relatives, rank-and-file activists, and especially members of church councils, was quite diverse. It comprised, in apparently growing numbers over the course of the 1920s, activists of both sexes. Taking advantage of the relatively greater legal space in which they could maneuver, this diverse and numerically significant lay contingent often overshadowed the political role played by parish clergy. Although lay activists acted as rural political leaders throughout NEP, they became especially mobilized when the Party in 1924–25 began to devote its energies to "reviving" the soviets. Their political activity was an extension of their long-awaited greater voice in and control over parish affairs.

Negotiating conflict over issues of religious belief and practice, Russian villagers discovered the strategic importance of rural electoral politics. Villagers represented differing cultural commitments—religious activists, the indifferent, and those avowedly hostile to religious belief and practice—but all had a sizable political presence in the three main institutions of village politics: the cooperative, the village assembly, and the village soviet. Given the political identities and interests of those villagers who comprised the antireligious faction, how successful would religious activists be in defending and promoting religious interests in village political institutions? What kinds of strategies would they use to do so, and what kinds of political conflicts would emerge?

---

churches." See "Renovationist Movement," p. 265. On the episcopal "party" and its conflicts with the parish clergy, see Freeze, *Parish Clergy*, p. 246.

7

KEEPING THE PARISH ALIVE

Although Russian agriculture recovered much more quickly than industry did from seven years of war and economic devastation, villagers still had relatively limited financial and material resources during NEP.[1] Given the economic constraints that underlay village politics, religious activists would have faced political resistance in their quest for parish resources even if there had been no antireligious faction opposing them. Because they had to contend with a faction of villagers who sought to use these scarce resources for purposes other than the support of the clergy, the securing of general parish resources such as land and money, and the maintenance of church buildings in a difficult legal context, religious activists had to become creative and effective political mobilizers in the village assembly, the village soviet, and (to a lesser degree) the cooperative. They could of course abdicate. But the only way out, to invoke an apt colloquial expression, was through.

---

1. Alec Nove, *An Economic History of the U.S.S.R.* (New York, 1984), chap. 4. To be sure, NEP was indeed the high point of peasant prosperity in twentieth-century Russia, as Martin Malia claims on p. 149 of *The Soviet Tragedy*. But we should resist the temptation to romanticize our portrait of the economic and material situation of the Russian peasantry prior to collectivization. After all, even the so-called kulak only had, as Nove reminds us, "two horses and two cows, and enough land to ensure a square meal the year round, and something to sell." See Nove, *Economic History*, p. 108.

Parish clergy—and parish priests in particular—turned to village political institutions for financial support. When seeking tithes (*ruga*) and other kinds of financial support (e.g., rent), they generally approached the village assembly first, just as they had in tsarist times. In 1921, for example, a priest in the village Klikushie (Luzhsk *uezd*, Petrograd province) appeared at the village gathering and requested a tithe of fifteen pounds (*funty*) of bread for himself and seven pounds for the psalmist and church watchman (*storozh*).[2] The priest warned his parishioners that his services were conditional on payment of the "tribute." Despite the 1926 ban on discussing religious issues at the village assembly, parish clergy continued to negotiate such financial arrangements throughout NEP.

How did village assemblies react to such financial requests? To be sure, in some assemblies and general village gatherings (*obshchie sobraniia*), priests and other clergy encountered little or no opposition to the financial terms they sought.[3] In fact, according to A. Lukachevskii, a member of the Central Committee of the League of the Godless, the village assembly routinely allotted payment in kind to its parish clergy.[4] At the village assembly in Iartsevo (Starodub *volost'* and *uezd*, Gomel province), peasants decided the income of their clergy. In 1925, for example, they agreed to pay their priest and psalmist the following yearly amounts: 150 poods of rice, 300 poods of potatoes, 300 poods of straw, and holiday tithes (*prazdnichnye vznosy*).[5] While village assemblies routinely targeted some of their funds for the clergy, their members, like their counterparts in revolutionary France, in some instances resented and resisted the financial demands of their priests.

Debates in the village assembly in Bezvodnovo illustrate the dimensions of such conflict. In 1924, the assembly debated whether to pay the rent (120 poods) on their priest's apartment. Unidentified church representatives fought on the priest's behalf. Their opponents argued that given the assembly's many other expenditures, the priest should pay his rent out of pocket. One member of the pro-clerical faction asked sarcastically, "[So] this means, citizens, that you don't consider the priest to be necessary?" One of his opponents answered sharply:

> The devil with him and with the priest, let him leave. There's [probably] another piece of this kind of trash staggering around without work. So let's find another priest, a cheaper one. What's the difference, just so he can swing the censer and do what's necessary, and

2. See *Derevenskaia pravda*, September 21, 1921.
3. Klikushie, discussed in the preceding paragraph, is a case in point.
4. *Antireligioznik*, February 1926, p. 6.
5. *Bezbozhnik*, November 15, 1925, p. 5.

then the blessing on them [the members of the parish] is the same. And if worse comes to worse we can get along without him.⁶

Although insulting not only the priest in question but also the entire "soslovie" with the epithet "trash," he did not fundamentally question the assembly's obligation to locate and support a suitable priest: doing without constituted, for him, an extreme, worst case.

This brief speech also reveals other important aspects of the conflict. In Bezvodnovo and assemblies in other villages, the lines were drawn not between the religious and the antireligious but between villagers who were and were not anticlerical. (This is not to say that in other cases antireligious and anticlerical villagers did not form a "united front.") But anticlericalism was, in turn, a smokescreen for another even more fundamental conflict. What the dissenter was really expressing in his invective about finding a cheaper priest was his desire to be able to manage his own affairs; his interjection should be read as an affirmation of rural autonomy. This is by no means to imply, however, that those villagers who wanted to pay the priest's rent had no interest in keeping "the centre of power in the village."⁷ To them, autonomy meant being able to use the resources of the village to support their priest. Villagers were in conflict, then, because they had different understandings of rural autonomy.

When the anticlerical faction prevailed, or when even the friendliest village assemblies could not satisfy their financial needs, clergy made use of other political opportunities. Cooperatives were a popular choice. Staffed by a wide range of members of the rural religious community, cooperatives offered clergy various types of financial support. In some cases, cooperatives gave clergy preferential economic treatment. For example, in 1926, the governing board of a cooperative in a village in Viatka province furnished clergy with all the goods they needed, often at special reduced prices, while allegedly abandoning poor peasants.⁸ An agricultural cooperative also favored clergy: it paid priests one ruble for a pood of bread but offered "peasants" only eighty-five kopecks.⁹

While clergy enjoyed preferential treatment as members of cooperatives, they also benefited from the direct charity of leaders of these economic institutions. Members of the governing board of the aforementioned cooperative in Viatka province in 1926 assigned cooperative members the task of going

---

6. *Sovetskaia derevnia*, May 10, 1924, p. 4.
7. This is an apt phrase used by Figes in *Peasant Russia*, p. 69.
8. *Krest'ianskaia pravda*, February 28, 1926, p. 2.
9. *Krest'ianskaia pravda*, February 27, 1927, p. 8.

door to door to collect the clerical tithe (*popnalog*) when the priest was unable to do so. The priest reportedly blessed the members of the ruling board by saying prayers and performing mass for them "on credit."[10] The governing board of a salt *artel* gave the village priest a free apartment, including heating and light, and also a salary of 50 rubles.[11]

Clergy sought and received many of the same kinds of financial support from village soviets. Their members not only allowed priests, for example, to exact taxes "in kind" from parishioners but also went one step further: they helped do the collecting.[12] Chairs of soviets often proved particularly willing to exert themselves on behalf of parish priests. In 1923, for example, the chair of the soviet in Mar'inka (Atkarsk *uezd*, Saratov province) collected butter, eggs, and other items for the local priest.[13] The chairs of the village soviets in Saratov province were, in 1924, providing priests with carts to collect "tithes" from parishioners. They also notified villagers of upcoming church services.[14]

Although the soviets lacked the financial powers of the village assembly, they nevertheless used what limited resources they had to support the clergy. In 1923, the Gotovitskii village soviet (Saratov province) spent twenty-two rubles and fifty kopecks on entertaining a rural parish priest.[15] In some cases they paid priests in kind (e.g., grain), apparently mimicking the village assembly's practice of providing clergy with *ruga*.[16] Despite allegedly hostile reactions from some villagers, chairs of soviets provided clergy with carts to collect bread from their parishioners.[17] Such support continued even after the Party launched its efforts to "revive the soviets" in 1924–25. The latter's "illegal" budgets included modest financial allotments "for the support of the priest."[18]

When pursuing other needs, clergy did not necessarily have the same range of political options they exercised in their quest for financial support. A case in point was the problem of housing and fuel for heating. Because Soviet legislation made the village soviet (in theory) responsible for overseeing the use

---

10. *Krest'ianskaia pravda*, February 28, 1926, p. 2.
11. *Krest'ianskaia pravda*, February 27, 1927, p. 8.
12. On members of soviets helping clergy to collect taxes from parishioners, see *Bezbozhnik*, September 20, 1925, p. 8, and February 22, 1925. See also *Sovetskaia derevnia*, April 4, 1924, p. 4.
13. *Izvestiia Atkarskogo uezdnogo ispolkoma*, April 18, 1923, p. 2.
14. *Petrovskaia kommuna*, July 3, 1924, p. 3; *Sovetskaia derevnia*, December 6, 1924.
15. *Izvestiia Saratovskogo soveta*, July 8, 1923, p. 3.
16. *Derevenskaia pravda*, January 25, 1922, p. 4.
17. For an example, see *Petrovskaia kommuna*, July 3, 1924, p. 3.
18. The 1926 "illegal" budget in Anisimovo (Kostroma *uezd*, Kostroma province), for example, allotted 3 rubles and 50 kopecks for this purpose. See *Izvestiia*, October 30, 1926.

of property for religious purposes, the clergy were especially dependent on its decisions in this regard.

How successful were the clergy—especially rural parish priests—in obtaining fuel and shelter from village soviets? Judging by the strategies they adopted, this was a matter to which clergy gave considerable thought.[19] A rural priest from the village of Berezovka (Saratov province) exemplified the political initiative often taken by clergy to solve this problem. Elections to the village soviet in Berezovka took place on November 10, 1922. So many voters appeared for the electoral meeting that the gathering had to be moved to the newly constructed people's center. As the crowd trekked to the new location, the village priest approached the chair of the voting commission and requested the right to address the meeting. After discovering that the priest wanted to talk about the heating of his apartment, the chair promised him the floor at the end of the gathering. Standing before the crowd, the priest exclaimed, "Orthodox believers! [*Pravoslavnye*] I don't have [even] a single piece of straw, the cold is coming and I'll freeze to death!"[20] As the crowd was debating whether to fulfill his request, the priest offered to sell them some wine. Cavalierly unconcerned about the priest's plight, and righteously uninterested in the purchase of home brew (*samogon*), the crowd rejected his request for fuel and refused to buy his wine.[21] Both the chair of the voting commission and members of the crowd could have refused him the right to speak; they could have removed him from the building physically or driven him out with humiliating verbal assaults. Instead, they eagerly discussed whether "to give or not to give" the priest straw,[22] viewing the political gathering as a legitimate forum for discussing his humble request. The priest, the chair, and the crowd all believed that the pursuit of religious interests was a legitimate focus of rural politics.

Rather than negotiate political conflicts themselves, in other cases clergy tried to choose advocates they perceived would be effective. Reflecting and accentuating the increased participation of women in rural parish affairs and

---

19. Renovationist parishes also submitted to the VTsIK petitions requesting that clergy be allowed to continue using their homes (*prichtovye domy*) and that quarters previously confiscated be returned to them. See *VSS* 1926 (10): 8.

20. *Serp i molot*, November 30, 1922, p. 2.

21. Village correspondents and other contemporary observers, eager to portray clergy as the evil corrupters of the naive peasantry, claimed that village priests allegedly used alcohol quite frequently to attain political goals. Angarov, on p. 66 of *Klassovaia bor'ba*, for example, maintained that widespread cases of drunkenness, to which clergy contributed, actually prolonged the 1927 electoral campaign. This occurred not only because clergy foisted alcohol on their undisciplined parishioners but also because the campaign coincided with religious holidays and weddings, traditional contexts of intense rural drinking. See also *Vlast' sovetov*, March 20, 1927, p. 19.

22. *Serp i molot*, November 30, 1922.

village politics during the 1920s, they sometimes enlisted peasant women to plead their case before the soviet. In 1924, a priest in Saratov province was alarmed about possible eviction from his apartment; unspecified authorities were apparently planning to turn his apartment into a school. He convinced some of the local peasant women (*bab'i*) to plead his case at the soviet.[23] Despite the efforts of this female contingent, the priest was obliged to vacate his lodgings.

Whether or not they were swayed by such ploys, in a good many cases village soviets did help clergy meet their need for livable housing. A few examples can illustrate this general trend. On March 10, 1924, members of the soviet in the village of Arishevo (Kuznetsk *uezd*, Saratov province) debated whether to grant a public building to the psalmist or to a Soviet club. Aware that a club had once occupied and damaged part of the building, they decided to make repairs so that the psalmist could use it as an apartment.[24] A similar dilemma faced members of the Malyi Meliksk village soviet (Atkarsk *uezd*, Saratov province) in 1927. An unidentified citizen proposed a motion to transfer the red corner to the quarters of the village soviet. At one of its meetings, however, participants protested vehemently against this plan. The village priest, it turned out, lived in quarters adjoining the soviet. Finally the opposing factions within the soviet arrived at the following compromise:

> [that the red corner] occupy [the space] two days per week, on Sunday during the day and on Wednesday evenings until 10 o'clock. After every meeting [those using the red corner] are obliged to clean the floor, take the custodian's astrakhan outside near the building, and avoid loud conversation, so that the priest can hear [the proceedings]. And if these conditions are not met, the red corner will be immediately removed from the [quarters] of the village soviet.[25]

Offering such solicitous support to their parish clergy, village soviets in some cases even dared to defy the decisions of institutions higher in the Soviet state apparatus. A case in point was the battle for space between religious and secular bodies in Khustiansk. For an unspecified period, "two small rooms" of the priest's house had been used for meetings of the village soviet. Maintaining that the village soviet needed all of the building for its activi-

---

23. See *Sovetskaia derevnia*, November 29, 1924, p. 4. On gender as a political strategy in riots against collectivization (e.g., villagers selecting women to lead such rebellious acts), see Lynne Viola, "*Bab'i bunty* and Peasant Women's Protest during Collectivization," *Russian Review* 45:1 (1986): 23–42.

24. *Sovetskaia derevnia*, April 4, 1924, p. 4.

25. *Sovetskaia derevnia*, May 19, 1927, p. 2.

ties, the district executive committee refused to renew the priest's rental contract. But the soviet in fact refused to take over the priest's apartment![26]

In sum, thanks in no small part to the political advocacy of lay supporters (a considerable number of whom held influential political positions), clergy frequently, although not always, benefited from the political decisions made by village assemblies, cooperatives, and village soviets. Given the relatively scarce financial and material resources that these institutions had at their disposal, it was no small achievement that clergy's needs often came before other secular projects championed by some villagers (e.g., funding for a children's cafeteria).[27] But even the most politically ingenious and successful clergy carried considerable anxiety—anxiety that surged to a level unknown even in the very late tsarist period—about whether they would be able to use the opportunities of electoral politics in an effective way. In fact, as clergy mobilized against the sometimes very determined and numerically significant faction of villagers opposed to supporting them, they must have been aware of their changed status in the new political conjuncture of NEP.

Meeting Parish Needs

Even when religious activists did succeed in meeting clerical needs in this new political conjuncture, they faced still more political battles with villagers who had conflicting cultural commitments. This is because, as we have seen, religious activists had other political interests besides providing for their clergy. How did their political agenda of meeting general parish needs, such as financial resources and land, shape village politics? What was the texture of the political battles generated by these differing cultural commitments?

Lay activists led political battles for parish finances. Church elders, for example, sometimes took the lead in drawing the attention of the village assembly to a parish's precarious financial condition.[28] But it was the church councils who assumed the main responsibility for using political means to keep the parish financially viable. To this end, they routinely created "church taxes," packaged in the form of "voluntary self-taxation" in the general village assemblies (*obshchie sobraniia*). In their 1925 investigation into the political and social conditions of a particular village soviet, cadres of the Workers and Peasants' Inspectorate found that even those villagers who did

26. *Bezbozhnik*, January 30, 1927.
27. *Izvestiia Atkarskogo uezdnogo ispolkoma*, April 6, 1923, p. 4.
28. For an example, see *Bezbozhnik*, March 8, 1925, p. 4.

not attend church agreed to such expenditures.²⁹ There were even members of village soviets who enthusiastically collected such taxes on behalf of church councils.³⁰

Lay activists encountered more vocal political opposition in their battle to retain church land, the target of several other competing claimants. One of these was the county land commission (*volzemkomissiia*). When these commissions announced their intent to seize some of a parish church's holdings, clergy and lay activists sometimes mounted considerable and effective resistance. When a priest and deacon in a village in Kineshma *uezd* (Kostroma province), for example, learned that the commission planned to take some of their church's holdings, they began to canvass support from parishioners for overturning the decision.³¹ Finally the village soviet adopted a resolution to cancel the decision of the land commission. While attempting to resist the claims of land commissions, religious activists (in some villages) also faced claims launched by fellow villagers at the village assembly.

Ivanovskoe was one such village. Exemplifying how conflict over religious belief and practice was structured along generational lines, an unidentified number of youthful participants introduced a motion to include church holdings in the general rotation. Prominent lay activists, on the other hand, played a key role in advocating on behalf of the parish. The chair of the church council, for example, declared that "we, . . . the Orthodox people [of the commune] do not want [to be part of] your general rotation."³² Other lay activists followed him in making pleas on behalf of the religious community. These efforts, however, proved fruitless: the assembly voted three times, and each time rejected the demands of the lay contingent.³³ The argument did not end there. Members of the assembly followed certain youths (the proponents of including church land in the general redistribution) into a field. The religious contingent soon joined the new gathering. Another round of argument ensued. When, finally, the leaders of the commune counted the total number of *edokov* (literally, "mouths"), they did not include the priest, his wife, or their children. Shortly thereafter the priest appeared and made a "whining, but spiteful" speech on his own behalf.

Lay leaders in Ivanovskoe, as they tried in vain to keep the motion from passing, invoked a strain of "peasant political discourse" often employed by

---

29. Kolesnikov and Murugov, *Apparat nizovykh sovetskikh organov*, p. 135.
30. For an example from Balashov *uezd* of Saratov province, see *Sovetskaia derevnia*, February 13, 1927, p. 4.
31. The newspaper report's description of this agitation as "anti-Soviet" cannot be taken at face value. (But such language is revealing of the meaning that Soviet cadres attached to resistance mounted by religious activists to the state's claims.) See *Bezbozhnik*, July 1, 1923, p. 4.
32. Kniazev, *Kak kulaki i popy*, p. 10.
33. See *Sovetskaia derevnia*, April 11, 1924, p. 4.

religious activists in political debates in the 1920s.[34] One anonymous speaker warned that "the lord punishes" those who seize church land. The assistant of the church elder (*starosta*) echoed and embellished this threat:

> Go ahead and plunder the temple of God . . . evidently the devils have overcome the holy place . . . go ahead and divide church land as well. Not in vain has it been said in the Scriptures: "And divide my robes into pieces [*i razdelis' rizy moi na kuski*]." Only do not touch our revenue from church land. We offer our revenue toward the splendor of the temple of the Lord. Surely not everyone has sold his [or her] soul to the devil. He who values his soul should not take away [revenue] from the church.[35]

In both the anonymous speaker's brief comment and the assistant elder's lengthy proclamation, we see one of the fundamental characteristics of this strain of peasant discourse: the use of "inherited language" (e.g., the Bible and less specific invocations of Christian theology) to interpret and thereby control political behavior.[36] The threat of losing one's soul was made to prevent members of the village assembly from voting for the motion. Because the religious activists were "talking past" their opponents—appealing to the very cultural precepts that the opposing faction sought to challenge and erode—they failed to sway them to their side.[37] Moreover, we can speculate confidently that when villagers used such provocative discourse, they actually catalyzed greater polarization in the assembly—and in the village—than had previously existed.

Protecting the Church Building

Usually overshadowing clergy in their efforts to mobilize land and financial resources for the parish, lay activists nonetheless had another, arguably more pressing political goal. This was, as we have seen, the cause of maintaining

---

34. I have borrowed the concept "peasant political discourse" from Steven Feierman, *Peasant Intellectuals: Anthropology and History in Tanzania* (Madison, Wis., 1990), p. 3. I thank Clark Sorensen for bringing this book to my attention.

35. Kniazev, *Kak kulaki i popy*, p. 10.

36. Like the Tanzanian peasants that Feierman studied, these Russian villagers were "shaping the inherited language anew to explain current problems." See Feierman, *Peasant Intellectuals*, p. 3.

37. This phrase is taken from Mannheim, *Ideology and Utopia*. Peasants had apocalyptical

the church building as the center of parish and even village life. Whether religious activists (clergy included) were seeking to repair or rebuild an existing church, or build a new one, they needed to secure funds and community support, agendas that propelled them into the political arena. And there—whether in the village assembly or the village soviet, or before the cooperative board—religious activists encountered especially vocal and determined opposition. The origin of this opposition was twofold. Those villagers who comprised the faction hostile to religious belief and practice wanted to eliminate the church building precisely because religious activists attached so much meaning to it; there were some who, like radical antireligious leaders centered in *Bezbozhnik u stanka* and in the Komsomol, equated the destruction of the church with the destruction of religion.[38] Second, they rightly perceived the church building as a drain on the village's limited resources, resources that might be used to build or improve a school, to mention only one of many possible alternative secular projects. While all parish needs claimed scarce village resources, the sums involved in repairing or otherwise maintaining, building, and rebuilding churches were usually relatively large.[39]

Clergy and lay activists encountered significant political opposition, for example, to their attempts to generate funds to make the repairs required by the state. Like their counterparts in revolutionary France, village assemblies debated and sometimes in fact allotted financial expenditures for church repairs.[40] Although the particulars of course varied from case to case, debates on this issue tended to follow a distinct pattern: discussion, opposition by "poor" peasants (or at least this is how provincial correspondents identified this faction), and the proposal of an alternative secular, socially useful project. When, in the winter of 1927–28, participants in the village assembly in Staro-Vasil'evskaia (Egor'evsk *uezd*, Moscow province) opposed spending funds on church repair, they urged the commune to finance the construction of a hospital instead.[41] As indicated by the fact that in this particular case the motion

---

modes of thinking during the 1920s and especially during collectivization. See Viola, "Peasant Nightmare."

38. See the discussion in Chapter 4.

39. Sums collected for church repairs were also significant, ranging, as newspaper reports maintained, from approximately several hundred to several thousand rubles. See, for example, *Bezbozhnik*, May 31, 1925, p. 4; January 4, 1925, p. 2; January 5, 1926, p. 4; and December 18, 1927; and Oleshchuk, *Kto stroit tserkvi v SSSR*, p. 8. Provincial and antireligious correspondents used the relatively large size of these amounts as grounds for portraying religious activists as kulaks, and thus may have exaggerated them somewhat. For an example, see *Sovetskaia derevnia*, March 8, 1928, p. 5.

40. Desan, *Reclaiming the Sacred*, p. 149.

41. *Bezbozhnik*, January 15, 1928.

to allot funds for church repair was defeated, the moment at which the alternative, secular project was introduced was particularly crucial. Although defeated religious activists could and did turn to village soviets for financial support for church repairs, they could not so elude the competition of secular projects and their determined supporters. Their track record there was in fact quite erratic. In some soviets, the cause of church repair lost out to projects such as agricultural needs;[42] in others, soviets under the control of religious activists allotted considerably more funds to church repair than to competing projects such as repairing village bridges and supporting the local school.[43]

When religious activists sought funds for building and rebuilding churches, they often encountered especially vehement opposition. The use of insurance monies to rebuild churches destroyed by fire, for example, required the approval of the village assembly. Moreover, as in tsarist times, they sometimes sought funds to build new churches in places where none had previously existed.[44] As in the case of church repairs, when religious activists introduced a motion to build or rebuild a church, their opponents sought to commit the funds instead to secular projects.[45] In some cases the proposed alternative involved a number of small projects (e.g., repair of school and fire carts, the construction of a reading hut [*izba-chital'nia*], and the purchase of a loudspeaker).[46] Generally, however, villagers proposed alternative projects that rivaled the church in scope and symbolic significance. Bridges and especially schools were popular choices.[47] In debates on these matters that continued even after the 1926 ban on discussion of religious issues at the village assembly, those villagers committed to secular projects sometimes mustered the support to block plans to build and rebuild churches.[48]

Villagers in Morozovo and Novo-Vysel'skoe (Saratov province), for

---

42. See, for example, *Bezbozhnik*, January 5, 1926, p. 3.
43. See *Bezbozhnik*, January 30, 1927.
44. See the 1927 letter of a parish priest in *VRSKhD*, July 1928, p. 13. Echoing this assessment, another contemporary claimed a new building tended to be a small wooden chapel (*chasovnia*) rather than a temple (*khram*). See Bliakhin, *Kto i zachem stroit tserkvi*, p. 11. For descriptions of villagers building new churches, see, for example, *Sovetskaia derevnia*, March 8, 1928, p. 5, and Oleshchuk, *Kto stroit tserkvi v SSSR*, p. 9.
45. Renovationist parishes submitted petitions to the Justice Department of the VTsIK to build churches. *VSS* 1926 (10): 8.
46. See, for example, *Bezbozhnik*, September 4, 1927.
47. For examples of villagers seeking to build a school instead of a church, see *Bezbozhnik* 20 (May 1928); Oleshchuk, *Kto stroit tserkvi v SSSR*, p. 65; (for an example from 1926), Bliakhin, *Kto i zachem stroit tserkvi*, p. 49; *Bezbozhnik*, January 5, 1926, p. 3; and *Sovetskaia derevnia*, May 27, 1928, p. 2. For an example of villagers who sought to build a new bridge instead of a school, see *Bezbozhnik*, April 5, 1925, p. 4.
48. See, for example, *Bezbozhnik*, April 5, 1925, p. 4; Bliakhin, *Kto i zachem stroit tserkvi*, p. 49; and *Bezbozhnik*, January 5, 1926, p. 3, and September 4, 1927.

example, in 1928 debated whether to use funds from an insurance premium to rebuild a church that had burned down the previous year.[49] Curious about the final disposition of the money, on April 14, 1928, the editorial board of a Saratov newspaper sent a fact-finding letter to the Novo-Vysel'skoe village soviet. On May 19, 1928, participants at a general meeting of citizens in Novo-Vysel'skoe debated a motion to build a new church; despite considerable opposition, a majority voted in favor. The next day, "at the initiative of the county Party committee," a meeting was held of the members of the soviet, the KKOV (Peasants' Mutual Aid Society), and politically active peasants (*krest'ianskii aktiv*, or peasants thought to be loyal supporters of Soviet power). In addition to the eighteen members of these various organizations, fifty other peasants attended.

Who supported and who opposed rebuilding the church? Although it is impossible to identify conclusively the social identities of those who comprised the various and shifting factions in villages such as Novo-Vysel'skoe, some important conclusions can be drawn. The most visible supporters of rebuilding the church were titled lay activists and their relatives, such as, for example, a villager whose father held the position of church warden (*ktitor*) of the village church.[50] The conflict in Novo-Vysel'skoe thus illustrated the important role played by family ties in village politics in the 1920s. But it was by no means only clergy, parish officials, and their relatives who tried to mobilize the assembly to build the church; rather, the debates galvanized a broad cross-section of villagers. In fact, the issue of rebuilding the church polarized not only the village but the membership of the village soviet and the KKOV as well.[51] Conceiving of the soviet's institutional role as a mirror rather than molder of public opinion on this religious issue, its members adopted the following resolution: "Because the general meeting had discussed the issue on several occasions, and 'the entire population has insisted on building the church . . . the village soviet suggests that, in light of the persistent desire of villagers [to rebuild the church], further attempts to change their minds will be unsuccessful.'"[52] Dividing the village and the membership of institutions ostensibly identified with "Soviet power," the conflict

49. This case is discussed at length in *Sovetskaia derevnia*, May 17, 1928.

50. In parish churches, clergy and laypersons sometimes used the term *ktitor* interchangeably with church elder (*tserkovnyi starosta*).

51. Given the fact that eight individuals (out of the eighteen whose institutional affiliations are given above) voted at the second meeting for a resolution against building the church, most likely some of the members of both the village soviet and the KKOV must have been in this camp. The resolution read: "We the *aktiv* of Novo-Vysel'skoe, having discussed the question of the disposition of the money received from the insurance premium on the church that burned down, conclude, that all the money [should be] used to build a school and to repair the fire cart." *Sovetskaia derevnia*, May 27, 1928, p. 2.

52. Ibid. Dismayed by the pro-religious stance of this resolution, the editors of the paper

also spread beyond Morozovo and Novo-Vysel'skoe. According to an account published in a local newspaper, "entire villages" (such as Ivanovka, Balashov *uezd*) and "[all those present] at certain gatherings of youth" (in the village Novokreshcheno) protested that the citizens of these villages were planning to fund the rebuilding of the churches.[53] It was in fact these protests that prompted the Saratov newspaper to send its investigatory letter to the Novo-Vysel'skoe village soviet on April 14, 1928.

Some religious activists, perhaps doubting that they could generate support in a conflict whose borders extended beyond the village, initially tried to block discussion of the matter. In the early stages of the conflict, fearing the outcome of a meeting to debate the matter, the priest in Morozovko organized a "choir" to drown out the discussion.[54] The vocalists in fact broke up the meeting.

These early preemptive efforts notwithstanding, religious activists subsequently applied a variety of tactics within the arena of electoral politics itself. They held the first meeting on the grounds of the burned church. Its charred ruins, they believed, would impress upon participants the need to rebuild. Over the course of the conflict, however, they devoted most of their political energy to constructing and applying several different political discourses. At the May 19 meeting, for example, religious activists and their opponents employed discursive strategies very different from those which had emerged in debates in other assemblies over the fate of church lands. A representative of the economic-construction council (*khoziaistvenno-stroitel'nyi sovet*) apparently opened the proceedings by informing those in attendance that a new church would cost 5,600 rubles. His information elicited a flurry of apparently impassioned responses. Bearded peasants shouted: "Build! Let's start to build."[55] Others retorted: "We don't need a church, we need a school." One opponent of the project elaborated: "Yes, we need to allot the insurance money for a school. Our school is crowded and gets in the way of those who want to learn." The chair of the village consumers' cooperative (*potrebilka*) countered: "We won't have a school of the second level [*shkola 2-i stupeni*]. Who will pay the teachers? And we already have one of the first level." Thus, in this and other analogous cases, the arguments for and against building the church were pragmatic, rather than religious.[56] To be sure, it is impossible to state conclusively that it was religious activists' pragmatic

---

recommended that the Balandinsk county executive and Party committees investigate the composition of the village soviet.

53. *Sovetskaia derevnia*, May 17, 1928, p. 5. The role of inter-village social and political conflict in the 1920s has received very little scholarly attention.

54. *Sovetskaia derevnia*, March 4, 1928, p. 3.

55. *Sovetskaia derevnia*, May 27, 1928, p. 2.

56. In another case, more than 400 residents of the Ilansk settlement debated building a new

arguments that proved decisive in convincing the majority of the assembly to vote for the church; in other cases, village assemblies voted not to build churches after engaging in such pragmatic arguments.[57] Clearly, however, this was a strain of peasant political discourse in which religious activists had achieved fluency, as demonstrated by the cooperative chair's spontaneous argument about the infeasibility of this alternative, secular project.[58]

Religious activists introduced still other discursive themes at the next day's meeting. Demonstrating that the "local" aspect of village religiosity could be an important agent of political mobilization of church resources, "believers" spoke first: "Our ancestors believed [in God] and we will believe. The church is our only comfort." They also made arguments that incorporated a knowledge of, and appeal to, national political developments. Along these lines, another participant added: "Kalinin gave us this money only for building a church ... we have a saying: use money [only] for its proper designation."[59] Apparently unmoved by the responses of opponents of rebuilding the church, another participant underscored the parish's firm intent to build the church: "Nothing will dissuade us ... we will build the church."

Some aspects of the Novo-Vysel'skoe case were, to be sure, unique—or at least exceptional. It was rare for a newspaper to send a letter investigating a political conflict over whether or not to rebuild a church.[60] In most cases, villagers decided such conflicts at a single meeting of the village assembly. Even when the conflict proved less protracted, however, the social and political identities of those who supported and opposed rebuilding churches in other villages did not differ fundamentally from those who constituted these respective factions in Novo-Vysel'skoe. In other villages as well, youthful or younger villagers were among those opposed to building or rebuilding churches, while titled lay activists, clergy, and their relatives supported such measures. But the most important lesson demonstrated by Novo-Vysel'skoe

---

church at the general meeting of citizens. Among the peasants and workers who opposed the church was a sixty-year-old peasant Kochnev, who reportedly exclaimed: "We need enlightenment [*prosveshchenie*], we need a school, but a church—what good is it?" See Oleshchuk, *Kto stroit tserkvi v SSSR*, p. 65.

57. In Ilansk, for example, the assembly majority rejected building a church in favor of repairing a school after (though not necessarily because of) hearing pragmatic arguments expressed by the sixty-year-old peasant Kochnev mentioned in the previous note.

58. The village gathering possessed administrative precedence over the village soviet. Even as late as 1928, some village soviets turned over the protocols of the village gathering "for approval." *Bol'shevik*, September 30, 1928, p. 135. This practice meant that the village assembly could veto decisions of the village soviet, such as antireligious measures. In Novo-Vysel'skoe, however, the soviet seems to have abdicated to the assembly's authority on the matter of rebuilding the church.

59. *Sovetskaia derevnia*, May 17, 1928, p. 5.

60. I encountered no other cases of a newspaper sending such a letter.

is the impossibility of deducing a villager's stand on a political issue such as rebuilding a church from his or her political identity, namely, connection to an institution at least nominally associated with support for the regime, such as the village soviet, KKOV, or consumers' cooperative. Moreover, the religious activists in Novo-Vysel'skoe employed discursive themes used by their counterparts in villages throughout the RSFSR, counterparts who both lost and won analogous debates.

In either eventuality, religious activists had other options. They sometimes, for example, used Soviet cooperatives to collect money for the construction of churches.[61] In 1927, a cooperative in a village in the Urals, in the words of a correspondent for *Bezbozhnik*, "played a real financial role" in the construction of a new prayer house.[62]

When religious activists did win their political battles for funds to rebuild churches, they still had to secure the required administrative permission to undertake construction. As the following example demonstrates, it was not uncommon for villagers to devise ingenious methods for obtaining the necessary approval from Soviet institutions for building churches. Seeking permission to build a church, a glass grinder appeared at the village soviet in Urshelo (Vladimir province).[63] According to Oleshchuk (who may have been interested in discrediting the lay activists by publicizing their dishonesty), this individual produced a spurious list of supporters of construction plans. The first list contained fifty signatures, while the remaining 450 identified themselves with a cross, a sign of their illiteracy. The officer of the village soviet objected: he pointed out that a recent census did not reveal any illiterate individuals among the 1,200 workers in the glass factory. The grinder furnished a second list of 1,080 signatures.[64] It would appear that unidentified villagers had compiled the list by calling on the wives of the workers while they were at the factory. One wife not only signed the petition, she even forged the signatures of her four children, one of whom was still an infant! Although they were thwarted in this case, we can safely hypothesize that they succeeded when members of the village soviet or Party exercised less vigilance.

Religious activists used different but no less clever strategies to obtain the required administrative permission for taking control of schools and other buildings being used for secular purposes.[65] One example must suffice. In

61. *Povolzhskaia pravda*, November 4, 1928, p. 2.
62. *Bezbozhnik*, February 27, 1927, p. 8. For more on the different types of support provided by cooperatives to keep churches functioning, see my "Trading Icons: Clergy, Laity, and Rural Cooperatives, 1921–28," *Canadian-American Slavic Studies* 26:1–3 (1992): 329–30.
63. See Oleshchuk, *Kto stroit tserkvi v SSSR*, p. 58.
64. Ibid., p. 59.
65. See, for example, *Petrovskaia kommuna*, March 18, 1924.

1928, a delegation of "believers" from Rep'evko requested permission from the Serdobsk district executive committee (Balashov *okrug*, Lower Volga region) to convert a former gentry home into a prayer house.[66] The committee (*rik*) refused. Soon the lay activists learned of an empty house in the village of Nikol'sko (Bekovo *uezd*). They found that district executive committee quite receptive. Offering the lay contingent a former gentry home, one unidentified member of the committee asserted: "It doesn't matter that a school was slated to open [sometime] during the Five-Year Plan. People also need the church." The persistence of the lay contingent worked in tandem with the religious sympathies of the Party members on the district executive committee to make the new church a reality.

Closing Churches: Methods and Resistance

Although religious activists seized opportunities to convert secular property to religious purposes, more typically they—like their counterparts in revolutionary France—faced the challenge of resisting secularization of church property.[67] As briefly noted earlier, Soviet legislation established clear political and administrative procedures for closing churches. A circular letter of January 3, 1919 ("Circular on the Problem and the Separation of Church and State"), permitted the administrative secularization of church property only if a group of twenty could not be found to take legal responsibility for it.[68] Church buildings could also be secularized if, because of a need for buildings for public purposes, and in response to "demands of the working masses," the local soviet decided to close them. The decision was, ideally, to

---

66. *Sovetskaia derevnia*, December 14, 1928, p. 5.
67. On villagers' resistance to secularization of church property during the French Revolution, see Ozouf, *Festivals and the French Revolution*, pp. 225–27. By "resistance," I assume James C. Scott's definition of acts of a "subordinate class [such as peasants] made on that class by superordinate classes (for example, landlords, large farmers, the state) or to advance its own claims (for example, work, land, charity, respect) vis-à-vis those superordinate classes." See his *Weapons of the Weak*, p. 290.
68. See Tsirkuliar NKIu RSFSR ot 3 ianvaria 1919 g., reprinted in P. V. Gidulianov, *Otdelenie tserkvi ot gosudarstva v SSSR. Polnyi sbornik dekretov, vedomstvennykh rasporiazhenii i opredelenii verkhsuda RSFSR i drugikh sovetskikh sotsialisticheskikh respublikh: UkSSR, BSSR, ZSFSR, Uzbekskoi i turkmenskoi*, 3d ed. (Moscow, 1936), p. 178. The circular letter was issued to correct "excesses" that local authorities had committed while implementing the Decree on the Separation of Church and State and the Instruction of August 1918. See Joshua Rothenberg, "The Legal Status of Religion in the Soviet Union," in Richard H. Marshall, Jr., ed., *Aspects of Religion in the Soviet Union* (Chicago, 1971), p. 67.

be made at a plenary session of the soviet.⁶⁹ To obtain proof of such popular consent, testimony was often sought at the village assembly (*skhod*), where villagers approved and resisted church closings throughout the NEP years.⁷⁰ But this initial legislation empowered either the district or provincial executive committee to make the final decision to close a church.⁷¹

During NEP, however, authorities changed these procedures in response to popular pressure. Disturbed by these bodies' "inexact observance" of 1923 directives on the procedures for closing churches, drafters of an April 4, 1924, circular of the People's Commissariat of Justice transferred decision-making power from provincial Party organs to the Central Committee (VTsIK).⁷² Prior to receiving such approval, neither the district nor provincial executive committees had the right to close a church. While distancing the decision-making process from members of the parish, the new ruling still kept church closings the prerogative of the state. Explaining its decision to revoke the power of the provincial and *uezd* executive committees to close churches, the 1924 circular of the People's Commissariat of Justice cited the Central Committee's receipt of "protests and complaints . . . from groups of believers." These groups, which did have state contracts for the use of their church buildings, complained about local state institutions' improper secularization of church property.⁷³

After 1924, religious activists sometimes made the procedural stipulations of the 1924 circular the basis of their petitions.⁷⁴ On March 3, 1926, for example, the Kaluga provincial executive committee issued a directive in violation

69. Ibid.
70. On the role of the *kombedy* in closing churches during the Civil War, see Chapter 2. For examples of villagers turning parish churches into schools, see *Bezbozhnik*, May 6, 1923, and Bliakhin, *Kto i zachem stroit tserkvi*, p. 49. In at least some instances it was the village soviet that took the lead in putting the issue of closing the church before the village assembly. For an example, see Bliakhin, *Kto i zachem stroit tserkvi*, p. 49.
71. An "Instruction of the NKIu and NKVD" of July 19, 1923, stated the following: "On the basis of a decision of the VTsIK of April 19, 1923, matters concerning the breach of contracts with groups of believers on the use of church buildings and matters concerning the closing of temporary or permanent temples and prayer houses of all cults are resolved by decisions of the presidiums of provincial executive committees without distinction." See Oleshchuk, *Kto stroit tserkvi v SSSR*.
72. Ibid., p. 91. A June 23, 1923, letter of the TsIK to all local Party organizations called for an end to abuses connected with church closings. See Pospielovsky, *History of Marxist-Leninist Atheism*, 1:38.
73. NKIu Circular of April 23, 1924, as reprinted in Oleshchuk, *Kto stroit tserkvi v SSSR*, p. 91.
74. Renovationist parishes also submitted petitions on, for example, the "unlawful seizure from the parish of an area of land with a fruit garden, where the village cemetery had been located." See *VSS* 1926 (10): 8. For analogous examples in revolutionary France, see Desan, *Reclaiming the Sacred*, pp. 17, 95–96, 126, 130–31, 134, 137, 139, 143–45, 154–55, 157, 162, 189, 198. Patriarchal parishes also petitioned the VTsIK for permission to take control of

of these stipulations to close a church in the town of Kozel'sk. In response, "religious citizens" (*veruiushchie grazhdane*) filed a petition with the Central Executive Committee to keep the church open. During the winter of 1926–27, the TsIK overruled the provincial committee and ruled that "the church in question remain in the possession of believers."[75]

What strategies did the authors of these petitions employ? They drafted petitions whose tones and rhetoric varied, to be sure. But the workers Polunin, Vokhmin, and Galanov, who were employed by a factory called "Kommunisticheskii avangard," were not alone in appropriating the language of the Soviet constitution to protest the decision to close their church.[76] In their petition to unspecified "central organizations," the protesters lodged the following claims: "Is not each of us in the Soviet Union really free to go where he [wants], one person to the café or tavern [*kabachok*], another to the brothel [*publichnyi dom*], one to [watch] cockfights and play cards, another to the theater, and another to church?"[77] Referring to the state's decision to close the church, the trio maintained that "this is not freedom . . . but the proletarian dictatorship of pigeons, ignoramuses, and hooligan-workers." By invoking the promise of freedom to lend legitimacy to their claim, the workers were most probably alluding to the Soviet constitution's guarantee of the freedom of religious and antireligious propaganda to all citizens, to its legal guarantee of freedom of conscience (*svoboda sovesti*). It is unclear whether their strategy was successful. Almost equally significant, however, was their incorporation of Soviet political vocabulary into a defense of religious interests. Like their counterparts in revolutionary France, these religious activists may very well have been using legal rhetoric in order to convince central authorities that religious identity and loyalty to the regime were not fundamentally incompatible.[78] Whether or not religious activists in fact were loyal to the regime is, of course, another matter.

Clergy also exercised their right to petition against church closings. One example must suffice here. In 1928, the children of tramway workers petitioned the Maminsk city soviet to convert its church to a school.[79] The provincial correspondent alleged that "all the children's organizations

---

churches (as well as inventory) under the control of the Renovationists. In 1926, the VTsIK received twelve such petitions. See *VSS* 10 (1926): 8.

75. *Vlast' sovetov*, January 9, 1927, p. 29.
76. Oleshchuk, *Kto stroit tserkvi v SSSR*, p. 62.
77. Ibid., p. 63. For examples of petitions made by the village commune to Soviet authorities for the return of priests conscripted by the Red Army or Cheka during the Civil War, see Figes, *Peasant Russia*, pp. 149–50.
78. For parallels see Desan, *Reclaiming the Sacred*, pp. 146–47.
79. *Povolzhskaia pravda*, November 13, 1928, p. 3.

[pioneers] of Saratov" supported the request. In response, the clergy filed counterpetitions (*kontrkhodataistva*) with the city soviet to save the church. They were also preparing petitions to be filed in Moscow. But the clerical petitioners chose to bypass Saratov officials, an indication of their quasi–naive-monarchist belief that the Center would be more sympathetic than intermediary institutions.

Clergy turned to means other than the petition to prevent churches from being closed. Invoking the same discourse of catastrophe that emerged in debates on the fate of church lands, one village priest, for example, responded to the threat of imminent church closings with a prophecy of doom for the village. In 1925 an unspecified state institution or group of individuals decided to close the church in the village of Pavlovka (Saransk *uezd*, Penza province). The priest threatened that the cattle would die if the church indeed shut down.[80] His threat of catastrophe proved powerless to prevent the closing.

Counting Churches

This priest's failure raises the issue of how effective clergy and other religious activists were, on balance, in using political means to "keep the church alive" during NEP. One type of relevant evidence, though not without various interpretive challenges, is statistics on the number of churches that existed throughout NEP.

In antireligious publications and Party newspapers, reports on the efforts of clergy and laity to resist church closings are difficult to find among the frequent proclamations of secularization of church property. It was rare for contemporaries to admit, as did one member of an expedition to the Central Black Earth Region, that *bezbozhniki* had failed to close a church because "the influence of obscurantism is too strong in the dark countryside of the Black Earth Region, and the work of *bezbozhniki* is too weak."[81] By making such admissions only rarely, and by boasting of their successes quite frequently, writers for the antireligious press obscured the painful truth of the large number of functioning churches in the USSR.

Comparison of the number of churches in 1929 with that in 1914 demonstrates the strength of the "physical plant" of Orthodoxy. According to the yearly publication of the Holy Synod, in 1914 there were 54,174 Orthodox

80. *Bezbozhnik*, June 21, 1925, p. 5.
81. Druzhinin, *Po ochagam*, pp. 23–24.

churches in the Russian Empire.⁸² Speaking on June 11, 1929, at the second conference of the League of the Godless, Iaroslavskii admitted that there were 50,000 churches in the Soviet Union.⁸³ The number of churches decreased by only 8 percent from the beginning of World War I to the end of the NEP years. Given the more effective antireligious campaign in urban areas, it is possible that the percentage of decrease would be even lower for the Soviet countryside. In fact, Iaroslavskii estimated that even by 1932 only about one to two percent of all rural churches had been closed.⁸⁴

The rate of decline in the number of churches over the course of NEP varied somewhat from province to province. In 1914 there were 971 churches and 93 chapels and prayer houses in Saratov province, or a total of 1,064 church buildings of various sorts.⁸⁵ It is necessary to estimate/extrapolate the number of churches at the end of NEP. According to a provincial correspondent, in 1928, there were "not less" than 117 churches in the former territory of Serdobsk district. Multiplying that figure by a factor of thirteen (the number of districts in the province before it became part of the Lower Volga Region), we obtain a grand total of 1,521 churches. This estimate is probably too high, because some districts probably had fewer.⁸⁶ Nevertheless, these statistics allow us to make a reasonably safe assumption that the number of churches in the province declined very little during the NEP years.⁸⁷ The number of churches in both Leningrad and Smolensk provinces under-

82. *IVO za 1914 g.* (St. Petersburg, 1916), p. 132. This figure did not include churches for soldiers. In 1916 there were 77,727 church *institutions*. See Veshchikov, "Etapy bol'shogo puti," p. 57.

83. *Stenograficheskii otchet*, p. 52. Oleshchuk, on p. 43 of *Kto stroit tserkvi v SSSR*, also gave the figure of 50,000 urban and rural churches. Although these may have been rhetorical approximations, in 1930, a Soviet journal gave the figure of 51,095 churches. See *Krasnaia niva*, February 15, 1930, p. 15. I thank an acquaintance in Moscow for giving me a copy of this journal.

84. RTsKhIDNI, f. 89, op. 4, d. 41, l. 9 (transcript of Iaroslavskii's meeting with an American delegation led by Sherwood Eddy). To be sure, it is possible that Iaroslavskii sought to hide the truth about religious persecution from the American delegation. Nevertheless, in the same meeting, Iaroslavskii made the revealing distinction between the number of churches that, by 1932, had closed in the entire country (which he estimated at 20 percent), and the far lower number that had been closed in rural areas. With the beginning of collectivization, churches closed more frequently in the cities of the Lower Volga region. On this see, for example, *Povolzhskaia pravda*, May 23, 1929, p. 3.

85. *IVO za 1914 g.*. This figure included 733 parish churches.

86. *Sovetskaia derevnia*, December 30, 1928, p. 6, and *Povolzhskaia pravda*, January 12, 1929, p. 2. Both correspondents actually gave a figure of 117 Orthodox and Old Believer churches, together with 26 prayer houses (11 of which were attached to Orthodox congregations and 15 to sectarian ones) for Balashov *uezd* (excluding Kraikievka and Elan' *volosti*). But they stated that there were "not fewer" churches and prayer houses in the former territory of Serdobsk *uezd*.

87. In 1928, there were 3,892 "prayer buildings" (*molitvennye zdanii*) in the Central Black

went a greater decline than in Saratov. In 1914, there were 816 Orthodox churches and 102 chapels and prayer houses in Smolensk province.[88] In 1925, according to data publicized at the provincial conference of the ODGB, there were 742 "church or religious organizations."[89] Out of this total, 648 were Orthodox, with the remainder distributed among Old Believer, Lutheran, Catholic, Jewish, Evangelist, Baptist, Adventist, and Quaker congregations. In 1914, there were 784 churches in Petrograd province and 1,638 chapels and prayer houses.[90] A very rough and probably low estimate of religious societies in Leningrad province (1924) would be 312. The number of *churches* was probably greater.[91] According to available statistics, the number of churches declined more significantly in Leningrad province than in Saratov or Smolensk, not surprising given the proximity of its countryside to a major urban, industrial center.

Churches closed at different rates on the district level as well.[92] As late as 1927 not one church had been closed in Kasimov *uezd* of Riazan province.[93] During 1928 and 1929, only one church had closed in Krasninsk *uezd* (population 60,480) of Smolensk province.[94] But by 1923, twenty-three churches had closed in Lekhgumsk *uezd* (Tiflis province, Georgia).[95]

To be sure, it would be a mistake to assume that very few village churches

---

Earth Region. See TsGAOR, f. 5263, op. 10, ed. khr. 29, ll. 1a, 24a, 33, 34b, as quoted in V. D. Iudin, "Deiatel'nost' partiinoi organizatsii TsChO po ateisticheskomu vospitaniiu naseleniiav 1928–34 gg." (synopsis of dissertation, Voronezh University, 1970), p. 20. In 1914, there were 1,379 churches and 29 chapels and prayer houses in Tambov province. See *IVO za 1914 g.*, pp. 6–7.

88. *IVO za 1914 g.*, pp. 6–7.

89. *Bezbozhnik*, May 17, 1925. Here is another way to estimate: according to information from Smolensk Party archives, there were eleven churches in Dukhovshchina *volost'* as of August 5, 1926. (This figure may have included other denominations besides Orthodoxy.) Multiplying eleven by the number of counties in the province (267 as of 1921), we get a figure of 2,937. See Smolensk WKP 33, "Zasedaniia agitpropkollegii pri Dukhovshchinskoi volkome VKP 5 avgusta 1926 goda."

90. *IVO za 1914 g.*, pp. 6–7.

91. See Chapter 3 for calculations and explanations. In Volodarsk *uezd*, there were twenty-nine Orthodox religious associations but forty-two Orthodox churches. One "home church" (*domovaia tserkov'*) had recently closed. See TsGAOR Leningrada, f. 1010, op. 1, ed. khr. 103, ll. 86–87.

92. Variation from village to village, though wide, is harder to trace. In 1922, the village of Mitkiro (Serdobsk *uezd*) could claim *three* functioning churches for a population of 350. See *Serp i molot*, December 7, 1922, p. 2.

93. *Bezbozhnik*, October 23, 1927. This case supports Shakhnovich's assessment that the antireligious campaign proceeded with acute difficulty in Riazan province. Interview of October 2, 1987.

94. Smolensk WKP 47, "Svodka po sotsial'no-ekonomicheskomu obzoru Krasninskogo raiona na 25/IX-29 g."

95. *Bezbozhnik*, May 13, 1923, p. 5.

closed during NEP *because* of religious activists' accumulated skills in the arena of electoral politics. Another key factor, of course, was the pervasive underinstitutionalization of the state, which in turn created a political terrain in which religious activists could develop and apply the political skills examined above. Moreover, as we have seen, some of the funds used to repair and rebuild churches were not even generated in institutions of electoral politics; rather, they came from parishioners' direct donations. These other significant factors notwithstanding, religious activists' political savvy in part explains why the church building remained alive and amazingly well during NEP, even though the "material situation" of the parish was in general "not easy."[96]

In sum, in the pursuit of each of the parish needs discussed above, religious activists, especially lay members of church councils, engaged in political battles with villagers who had different cultural commitments. Lay activists even took the lead in using political means to secure clerical needs and interests, a dynamic that became even more pronounced over the course of NEP. In waging their political battles, religious activists employed a variety of political tactics, including symbols (e.g., a charred courtyard) and bribery (e.g., vodka). But it was mainly in the medium of political discourse that religious activists and their opponents negotiated the politics of parish resources. Sometimes following the lead of their opponents, religious activists developed several different discursive strains. These included the centrality of local religion as the basis for political claims; the appeal to national political authority (e.g., Kalinin's supposed designation of money to support churches); the rhetoric of divine catastrophe; the assimilation and refashioning of Soviet legal rhetoric; and the resort to pragmatic considerations. Debates that centered on the pragmatic illustrate especially well that the "real" issues often differed from the particulars being discussed in the village assemblies and village soviets. Villagers were debating more, for example, than the ostensibly self-enclosed issue of whether the church should be repaired or even continue to exist at all. Rather, the real issue behind the debates over the fate of this or that parish church—not to mention those concerning other parish and clerical needs—was much larger. The politics of parish resources was really about rendering a verdict on the future face of the village, on the cultural transformation sought by the regime and its supporters in the village. This is what made the issue of rebuilding a church, as exemplified by the case of Novo-Vysel'skoe, so contentious.

---

96. See *VRSKhD*, July 1928, p. 13.

8

Icons of Power

In his evocative "Peasants," Anton Chekhov described the emotional epiphany experienced by villagers during an annual August religious festival. As the peasants of Zhukovo paraded "the ikon of the Life-Giving Mother of God" through the villages in their *uezd*, claimed Chekhov,

> It was as though they all suddenly understood that there was no void between heaven and earth, that the rich and powerful had not yet taken possession of everything, that there was still a defense against abuse, bondage, that oppressive, unendurable poverty, and the horrors of vodka.[1]

Although Chekhov was describing a single religious procession, he nevertheless managed to portray public ritual as part of the very fabric of village life, in all places, at all times. This deep and pervasive attachment notwithstanding, Chekhov implied that peasants could nevertheless infuse public ritual and religious celebrations with new, even spontaneously improvised meanings. During this annual religious festival, the peasants of Zhukovo had

---

1. Anton Chekhov, "Peasants," in *Selected Stories*, trans. Ann Dunnigan (New York, 1982), p. 270.

the "sudden understanding" that they could choose whether to defer to the institutional, human, and material sources of their domination and exploitation. Peasants may have engaged in these collective rituals in order to display genuine religious feeling, or they may have done so out of habit, but in the process they discovered that their anger was the key to finding a door to a new political and social world. Their collective rituals both harvested and sowed seeds of political resistance, resistance couched in a highly symbolic and necessarily camouflaged form.[2] Russian villagers found ritual and collective religious celebrations so attractive and meaningful, implied Chekhov, because it gave them faith in their power to control and remake the secular.[3]

Religious Ritual and the Village Assembly

By the 1920s, roughly twenty years after Chekhov wrote "Peasants," the place of ritual and holiday celebrations in village life was more ambiguous than his Zhukhovo villagers would have thought possible. By that juncture, those villagers who continued to regard the public display of religiosity as an integral part of village life faced opposition not only from the growing ranks of other, often more youthful villagers but also from the Soviet state and the *bezbozhniki* in particular—hardly, as we have seen, mutually exclusive categories. The Soviet government even tried to convince villagers to switch their allegiance from the many traditional religious holy days and holidays that punctuated the agricultural calendar to a series of new secular holidays, such as International Labor Day, Journalism Day, and Harvest Preparation Day.[4] To what extent was cultural conflict over the fate of religious ritual and ceremony—both private and collective—played out in village politics, that is, in the village assembly and the village soviet?[5] In the turbulent social, cultural, and political conjuncture of the 1920s, what political meanings did religious activists and their opponents assign to religious

   2. Eric Hobsbawm and George Rudé have noted the connection between the annual village feasts and the form of labor protests in early nineteenth-century England. See their *Captain Swing* (New York, 1968), pp. 66–67. On the relationship between local, ostensibly apolitical traditions and organizations and subsequent resistance and overt political challenges to the domination of elites, see Scott, *Moral Economy*, p. 207n. Scott, in fact, uses *Captain Swing* in his analysis. On the distinction between the dominant and the hidden transcript, see Scott, *Domination and the Arts of Resistance*, p. xii and passim.
   3. This is a reference to Geertz's concept of religion. See his *Interpretation of Cultures*.
   4. Altrichter, "Insoluble Conflicts," pp. 199–200.
   5. By "public ritual and ceremony—both private and collective," I understand religious holidays (traditional Orthodox holidays, feasts of the saints, and local holidays), religious

ritual and public religious celebrations? Did they, like the villagers of Zhukovo, explore the political uses of religious ritual, and, if so, what were their discoveries?

The village assembly necessarily debated a wide range of issues connected with the fate of collective religious ritual in village life. Decisions to hold a procession of the cross, to hold a public prayer service, to bring an icon in from a nearby village, all involved a commitment of funds and village resources, since, for example, priests would have had to be paid for their services. Because the village assembly was the organ responsible for deciding how to allot the funds of the commune, it had to be involved in the types of cases listed above.

But some villagers, comprising an antiritual faction whose size varied from village to village, sought to harness the assembly for new political purposes. Now open for discussion, for example, was the issue of celebrating traditional religious holidays, whether "pagan" ones such as the holiday of Frol and Lavr, protectors of cattle (August 18), or Orthodox ones such as the Day of St. George (April 23 and November 26).[6] Even when villagers agreed that a specific holiday should continue to be celebrated, they often debated their differing visions of the place of ritual in those holiday celebrations. The village assembly in Timino (Iur'evetsk *uezd*, Ivanovo-Voznesensk province), for example, in 1925 argued about whether to conduct a procession of the cross on the Day of Dmitrii (October 26). In some cases, villagers framed the debate in more global terms, namely, whether to prohibit members of the village society (*sel'skoe obshchestvo*) from working on holidays.[7] Nor was the place of ritual in village life on nonholiday occasions less contentious.[8]

Lay activists played a paramount role in mobilizing support during these debates. Given the overwhelmingly lay composition of the village assembly, that fact in itself is not surprising. It is indeed noteworthy, however, that lay

---

festivals, processions of the cross, as well as the ostensibly more private rituals of what might be called pagan Orthodoxy. For a good discussion of how villagers celebrated what Altrichter calls the "sequence of holy days and feast days that interrupted the rural routine and broke the year up into smaller, more comprehensible parts," see his "Insoluble Conflicts," pp. 195–200. As we shall see, the boundaries between private and public religious observance in this rural *dvoeverie* were very fluid; villagers often regarded an individual's decision to engage in religious rituals as a matter of community concern.

6. For an example of debates on whether to discuss "pagan" holidays, see Kursanovskaia, "Selo Novoselka-Ziuzino," in Tan-Bogoraz, *Revoliutsiia v derevne*, p. 72; for an example of debates on the fate of Orthodox holidays, see *Bezbozhnik*, January 25, 1925. For details of the spring celebration of St. George's day, see M. Zabylin, *Russkii narod: Ego obychai, obriady, predaniia, sueveriia i poeziia* (Moscow, 1990), p. 98.

7. See *Bezbozhnik*, January 13, 1924, p. 6.

8. *Bezbozhnik*, January 8, 1925, p. 4.

activists, rather than clergy, even introduced motions involving issues of religious ritual. A case in point, for example, is the aforementioned village assembly in Timino. There individuals whom a correspondent described as "older peasants" introduced the motion to conduct a procession of the cross on the Day of Dmitrii.[9]

While these peasant advocates in Timino were almost certainly men, women activists also took—or threatened to take—the initiative in involving the village assembly in the fate of ritual in village life. As the following case from Atkarsk *uezd* in Saratov province demonstrates, women activists even regarded the village assembly as a legitimate arbiter of the place of ritual in an individual's private life. One particularly rich example can illustrate this more general trend. During Easter week in 1927, the delegate Maria Tsibisova refused to allow the priest to come into her home: "You, little father [*batiushka*], go away, we don't need you."[10] This behavior elicited the wrath of her religious husband, who in fact was a member of the village soviet. The scorned priest informed the rest of the village that Maria Tsibisova did not believe in God.[11] At this point a group of eight women descended on Tsibisova's home and threatened her: "If you don't believe in God, we will [use] the village assembly to throw you out of the village."[12] The enraged group of women thus saw the political institution of the village assembly as the legitimate enforcer of religious belief, which they apparently equated with participation in traditional religious practices. In viewing themselves as potentially effective political actors, these women villagers displayed a political self-conception radically different from that of prerevolutionary peasant women (*bab'i*), who very rarely participated in the affairs of the village assembly.[13] Paradoxically, they were assuming this public political persona in order to determine the place of ritual in the ostensibly "private" life of a Russian villager, rather than to secure public and collective ritual in village life. It is impossible to state conclusively, however, that during NEP women and men tended to occupy "separate spheres" in political battles involving the place of ritual in village life. If so, such a gendering of the politics of ritual would then have paralleled the gendering of economic responsibilities in the peasant household, where women's contributions generally took place in the private spaces, such as the peasant hut and its gardens, while men's

9. *Bezbozhnik*, November 8, 1925, p. 4.
10. *Sovetskaia derevnia*, May 22, 1927, p. 4.
11. This is an unusual reversal of the typical patterns reported by the Soviet press, in that the wife was actually *less* religious than her husband.
12. *Sovetskaia derevnia*, May 22, 1927, p. 4.
13. See Chapter 2 on the exceptionalism of women's participation in the affairs of the village assembly in the prerevolutionary period. Taniuchi maintains that women peasants rarely attended the village assembly even in the Soviet period. See *Village Gathering in Russia*, p. 41.

economic activities occurred in public spaces, such as the family's allotment fields.[14]

What were the social identities of those villagers who sought to reduce, if not eliminate, the place of ritual in village life? Outsiders, whether anthropologists or rural correspondents, frequently noted the comparative youth of those villagers who opposed celebrating religious holidays or holding public rituals during debates in the village assembly. In Timino, reported an antireligious correspondent, village "youth" balked at the suggestion to conduct the procession of the cross on the Day of Dmitrii.[15] In another case, villagers whom an anthropologist described as the "more youthful and smarter" members of the assembly opposed celebrating Il'in Day.[16] Although these and other references are cryptic, it would appear that village youth, Red Army veterans, and urban out-migrants transformed their free-floating hostility to religious belief and practice into political activism.[17] Although they were not necessarily using the political issue of religious ritual in a

14. For a discussion of the roles of women and men in the Russian peasant household of the post-emancipation period, see Christine Worobec, "Peasant Women and Patriarchy," in Kingston-Mann and Mixter, *Peasant Economy, Culture, and Politics*, p. 184, and *Peasant Russia*; and Engel, *Between the Fields and the City*.

15. *Bezbozhnik*, November 8, 1925, p. 4.

16. Kursanovskaia, "Selo Novoselka-Ziuzino," in Tan-Bogoraz, *Revoliutsiia v derevne*, p. 72. While it is appropriate to raise a skeptical eyebrow at the assertion of the higher intelligence of these villagers, we should not automatically discount the claim about their age. To what extent, and why, should we trust the latter observation? To be sure, correspondents had ideological and pragmatic reasons for hoping to find youth leading the political battle against ritual in the village assembly, since such would have been evidence—or so they thought—of a new, utopian future for the village. On the utopian mentality in NEP political culture, see Eric Naiman, "The Case of Chubarov Alley: Collective Rape, Utopian Desire, and the Mentality of NEP," *Russian History* 17:1 (Spring 1990): 1–30. Was it then the case that the correspondents willfully distorted the ages of the participants in debates on ritual in the village assembly? (For reasons elaborated in the Introduction, it is highly unlikely that village correspondents intentionally lied in this case.) Given the degree to which village correspondents saw themselves as having a stake in the political future of the village, what is possible is that the correspondents selectively reported the ages of the participants. In this way they could reassure themselves and their superiors (not to mention their readers) that the future would bring the cultural transformation they were seeking. (Archival reports most likely exhibit such selective reporting as well.) Faced with the "cognitive dissonance" of finding younger villagers behaving as religious activists in the village assembly, they may have conveniently (either consciously or unconsciously) neglected to report such information. The reports of rural correspondents do qualify as evidence that younger villagers opposed the celebration of holidays and public rituals, though they do not establish that no youth or younger villagers sought to preserve the place of ritual in village life. (Nor do they establish that older villagers invariably sought to maintain the place of ritual in village life.)

17. I do not mean to imply that social identity and political activism necessarily went hand in hand. Because a villager's latent political goal—eliminating displays of religiosity from village life—could be enjoyed even by those who had not contributed to the political struggle, the

consciously instrumental way (since they may not have understood the origins of their antireligiosity themselves), the younger and almost invariably male faction that opposed public rituals and celebrations was after not only the power to dictate the cultural future of the village but the very reins of village power. This potentially diverse contingent was necessarily challenging the authority of the *bol'shaki* to control the affairs of the village. Thus their political opposition to religious holidays and collective rituals, as voiced in the village assembly, was as much an expression of their generational and economic conflict with the village elders as one of their antireligiosity per se.

As the size and strength of this faction varied from village to village, so did the centrality of religious ritual as a political issue. Because these urban exiles did not spread themselves out evenly over the vast expanse of the Russian countryside, and because the dynamics of *otkhod* also varied over time, the social base of the antiritual faction—and the frequency and intensity of the political conflicts they instigated—varied considerably from village to village.[18] The emergence of religious ritual as an issue in some village assemblies may have followed the shock waves produced when the deurbanized and demobilized returned at sporadic intervals; the aforementioned "drying up" of *otkhod* opportunities in Saratov province in the mid-1920s is a case in point. In some villages, then, members of the village assembly may have found themselves debating the place of ritual in village life sporadically rather than constantly.

Seeking to dissolve the power of the *bol'shaki*, these younger and often less rooted villagers tried to demonstrate what their elders' mistaken choices were (both metaphorically and literally) costing the village. While the exact content of such debates varied enormously from case to case, some general patterns can be observed. As in the political debates that emerged in conflict over parish resources, younger members appealed to secular criteria such as increased agricultural productivity to try to convince the assembly to abandon holiday celebrations and public rituals. Better harvests of grain existed, explained village "youth" in Timino, in countries where the population was atheistic and did not carry out such religious processions. Rather than present such fairly involved arguments concerning the economic cost of religious celebrations, in other cases villagers simply urged their peers to spend holidays working in the fields.[19]

Russian villagers in question experienced what political scientists have called a "free-rider" dilemma. For a discussion of how rational choice or rational actor theorists have approached "free-rider" dilemmas in rural collective action, see Daniel Little, *Understanding Peasant China: Case Studies in the Philosophy of Social Science* (New Haven, Conn., 1989), esp. p. 39.

18. See the discussion in Chapters 2 and 3.
19. Kursanovskaia, "Selo Novoselka-Ziuzino," in Tan-Bogoraz, *Revoliutsiia v derevne*, p. 72.

Their opponents countered with arguments appealing to the very kind of cultural "mechanisms" that younger villagers were seeking to erode, if not destroy. Examples gleaned during an expedition to the Black Earth Region, for example, illustrate the type of arguments brought to bear on those who would discard religious celebrations in favor of increased agricultural productivity. At times villagers threatened opponents of religious holidays and ritual with punishment from a transcendental source. Seeking to win approval for celebrating Il'in Day, for example, villagers warned the assembly that "Il'ia [the patron of the holiday] is a serious master, and doesn't like joking."[20] Although shorn of such an obvious reference to religious forces, other arguments likewise refracted superstitious beliefs in ways to magnify peasants' power to control a hostile world.[21] Seeking to persuade the assembly to celebrate the holiday of Frol and Lavr, villagers warned that previous failures to observe these holidays had caused deluges. During the same debate, these religious activists also reminded the gathering that in the past the commune had imposed a fine on anyone who failed to go to church on this day. Whether religious activists argued from tradition or by threatening punishment from a transcendental source, they were, as in some debates on parish resources, "talking past" their opponents.[22] This lack of cultural consensus suggests that the debates were most likely quite acrimonious.

Their outcomes varied. In Timino, for example, the opponents of the holiday celebration were victorious. Members of the assembly decided not to celebrate the holiday or receive the icons and bought a threshing machine with the savings. Calling for the elimination of one or more religious holidays, resolutions adopted by other villagers instructed households to donate money for secular projects (e.g., the construction of a school). The village assembly in Bukholovo, for example, adopted a resolution to eliminate two holidays, the Day of Gregory (November 26) and the Day of St. Elijah (May 20). It instructed each household to donate one ruble for the construction of a school.[23] As an alternative, the assembly sometimes decided on a compromise reflecting the cultural allegiances of the differing factions. In the case of the debate about whether to celebrate Il'in Day, for example, the assembly resolved to celebrate for half a day and work in the hay meadow after dinner.

These victories of the "antiritual faction" notwithstanding, there is compelling evidence that those villagers who sought to preserve or even extend

20. Ibid.
21. Samuel C. Ramer, "Traditional Healers," in Kingston-Mann and Mixter, *Peasant Economy, Culture, and Politics*, p. 216.
22. Mannheim, *Ideology and Utopia*.
23. *Bezbozhnik*, January 25, 1925.

the place of ritual in rural life very often enjoyed success. Writing in 1926, Lukachevskii made the general assessment that "the village assembly decides, for example, to bring in an icon from a neighboring village, to hold a public prayer service."[24] The difficult-to-enforce 1926 ban on the discussion of religious issues, including ritual and religious celebrations, at village assemblies testifies to Party leaders' perception that the outcomes of such discussions were too often at variance with their goals on the "cultural front."[25] They must have been equally if not more horrified when assemblies not only adopted resolutions that maintained the customary place of ritual in village life but enlisted the village soviet to enforce their provisions. During the winter of 1923–24, for example, participants at a general meeting of citizens (Eniseisk province) resolved to prohibit members of the village society (*sel'skoe obshchestvo*) from working on holidays. The measure, which was certified by the village soviet, obliged disobedient villagers to pay a fine of two poods of grain. The resolution also targeted members of the soviets and the village militia to enforce the new law.[26] In agreeing to these procedures, the villagers ironically empowered an institution of Soviet power to enforce compliance with traditional norms of behavior.

Religious Ritual and the Village Soviet

The role played by some village soviets in the conduct of collective ritual reminds us that while villagers accorded the fate of ritual an important place in debates in the village assembly, that organ by no means had a monopoly on the politics of this significant issue. During the first few years of NEP the village soviet offered the village assembly very little real competition for reasons elaborated above in our discussion of the politics of parish resources. The years 1925–26 marked a change in this regard. Assuming that a dramatic increase in relevant newspaper reports corresponds to an actual change in social reality, it was at this juncture that the village soviet began to play a significantly greater role in deciding the scope of ritual in village life. This increase, then, coincided chronologically with the Party's "face to the countryside" campaign, which as we have seen, was an attempt to achieve greater control and presence (the two were perceived to go hand in hand) in the

---

24. *Antireligioznik*, February 1926, p. 6. He charged that these practices violated Article 13 of the Soviet constitution, which guaranteed freedom of conscience (*svoboda sovesti*), because the authority of the assembly's "general will" rendered these financial levies compulsory.

25. For more on this circular, see Chapter 4.

26. *Bezbozhnik*, January 13, 1924, p. 6.

recalcitrant "rural nexus." One expression of that policy shift was an NKVD circular of February 1925 on religious ritual.

Like the 1926 ban on the discussion of religious issues at village assemblies, this measure was designed to transfer legal responsibility for deciding the fate of public rituals and holidays from the assembly to the village soviet. Basing its provisions on the 1918 Decree on the Separation of Church and State, this NKVD circular defined the relationship of the village soviet (as well as other units of provincial political power) to the sphere of religious ritual. The circular stipulated the following:

> The right of giving suitable permission for the completion of religious rituals on streets, squares, and similar [places], such as processions, processions of the cross, prayers, and similar [rituals] belongs to local political organs, that is, to the village soviet, if the ritual is executed within the boundaries of one village, to the *volost'* executive committee, if the ritual covers two or more villages, and to the *uezd* police and the department of provincial administration, if the ritual is carried out in a district or provincial city.[27]

The directive implicitly saddled clergy and other religious activists with the duty to request permission for such activity from the village soviet.

What was the hidden agenda of this circular? Its architects clearly sought to bring yet another aspect of rural religious life under the control of an institution ostensibly aligned with Soviet goals on the "cultural front"; moreover, they were no doubt attempting to strengthen the village soviet by according it more administrative prerogatives. Did they also hope that the presumably loyal cadres' refusal to grant the requested permission would reduce and eventually eliminate public ritual from village life, thereby contributing to the secularization of the village? That the promulgation of the circular coincided chronologically with the creation of the League of the Godless is powerful evidence that this more radical agenda was operating as well. The fulfillment of either agenda required that two conditions be met.

First, villagers and the officers of the village soviets alike had to be familiar with the circular. Not unlike tsarist reformers, who had also exaggerated the reach of the state into the Russian countryside, Party leaders were no doubt engaging in wishful thinking when they assumed that this would be so. To be sure, it is impossible to know whether, in general, villagers and the

---

27. Tsirkuliar NKVD 12/II-1925 g. (first printed in *Biulleten' NKVD*, February 24, 1925), as reprinted in *Vlast' sovetov*, March 8, 1925. In addition to the Decree, one precedent for this ruling appeared in Article 31 of an instruction of the People's Commissariat of Justice of August 25, 1918.

officers of the soviets knew of this particular circular. But there is good reason to doubt it. One delegate to the Fourteenth All-Russian Congress of Soviets, for example, stated that "a mass of laws come down to the chair [of the village soviet], but he usually finds it difficult to read them, let alone do anything about them."[28]

Second, those who drafted the circular assumed that rural political actors, once aware of the circular, would accord it legitimacy. Yet whatever their knowledge of the decree, many chairs and other officers of the soviets did not act in consonance with the antireligious goals of the regime, as the circular implicitly assumed they would. Rather than either defiantly withhold or grudgingly concede the permission for public religious activity sought by religious activists, chairs and other officers of the soviets sought to use their power to preserve its place in village life. Some village soviets went to extra lengths to obtain the necessary permission for clergy to hold prayer services, while others dug into their illegal budgets to pay clergy for services rendered in connection with public religious activities.[29]

The actions of a chair of the village soviet in Mashaga (Novgorod province) demonstrate the extent to which many such officers made facilitating public ritual one of their political goals. In the summer of 1925, the chair issued the following order: "Furnish for the procession of the cross the necessary quantity of carts, beginning with this [certain] household and do not skip anyone."[30] As reflected in the wording of this order, the chair in question was not simply using his power to allow the procession of the cross to take place, the legal role set out for him by the NKVD circular. Going well beyond its letter and spirit, he was using his office to assure enough material and financial resources for the procession to take place. The phrase "do not skip anyone" is especially telling, because it betrays not only an anxiety about generating the necessary finances but quite possibly his intent to compel each household to make a donation for such public religious activity. This chair, like many of his counterparts in village soviets throughout the RSFSR, regarded himself as an advocate of public religious practice.

Even more surprising is the degree to which chairs considered the role of ritual in the individual lives of villagers to be a political matter. At times they interceded on behalf of villagers for whom the village priests refused to perform the Orthodox sacraments of marriage, burial, or baptism.[31]

The chair of the soviet in the village of Korzhovo was one such ally. In

28. Fillipov, *XIV All-Russian Congress of Soviets. Stenographic report*, as quoted in Male, *Russian Peasant Organisation*, p. 127.
29. *Bezbozhnik*, August 9, 1925, p. 4; *Izvestiia*, October 30, 1926; *Vlast' sovetov*, April 25, 1926, p. 21.
30. *Bezbozhnik*, July 26, 1925.
31. *Bezbozhnik*, January 11, 1925.

1925, some peasants refused to register when the priest was drawing up the list of believers (*spisok veruiushchikh*). He then threatened not to marry, bury, or baptize anyone who had not registered. At this point the chair of the soviet jumped into the game. He reprimanded the priest for making such threats. But he also assured the recalcitrant villagers that the priest did not have the right to refuse to perform these rituals. Through the agency of [Soviet] personnel sympathetic to the needs of the laity, even the new discourse of "civil rights" laid out in the Soviet constitution could come to the aid of villagers whose access to clerical services was jeopardized.[32]

While suggestive of the political attitudes of chairs of village soviets, the incident also demonstrates that villagers felt that they had to anticipate the political consequences of practicing their religion. Most likely the villagers in question refused to register because they feared the consequences of being identified in state records as believers. Did their refusal at the time betray an antireligiosity, or even an anticlericalism? Though the evidence is ambiguous, the answers to these questions would seem to be negative; apparently the villagers themselves enlisted the chair's aid in assuring their access to the priest's services. Their decision, then, has two important implications. First, the number of villagers who valued the services of their priest exceeded the number willing to assume legal responsibility for the upkeep of the church or to be identified as "believers" in state records. Second, it meant that the villagers in question perceived that they could count on the chair to provide for their religious needs.

By no means exclusively made up of lay partisans, village soviets assured priests access to lay revenue in return for performing rituals. The actions of a member of the soviet in the settlement of Favetovko (Semipalatinsk province) demonstrate the length to which officers of that organ went to mobilize economic resources for village priests. In 1925, he called a meeting of the village assembly, at which he exhorted villagers to have their children baptized. Interested parties, he maintained, would have to bring a certificate of registration to the village soviet. Three days later he arranged for another meeting, at which he urged villagers to register their children. The goal of registration, for which a fee was apparently required, was to generate 120 poods of bread for the priest.[33] It can be inferred that the priest, like the villagers of Korzhovo, perceived that he could count on the village soviet to be his political advocate, an assumption that turned out to be well founded.

32. Clergy also used legal phrases from the Constitution to defend their right to engage in certain religious activities. Appearing before the Central Committee, a priest connected with the building of a church in the factory "Kommunisticheskii avangard" stated: "We ... the workers of the factory 'Kommunisticheskii avangard' ... have the right to build a church." He then produced a petition with 2,540 signatures. See Oleshchuk, *Kto stroit tserkvi v SSSR*, p. 55.

33. *Bezbozhnik*, May 10, 1925, p. 4.

True Believers or Opportunists?

By the mid-1920s, then, chairs and other officers of the village soviets had acquired a reputation as allies of those who wished to preserve the place of ritual in the village and in the private lives of individual villagers, if indeed the two spheres can be separated. That they used their political power in this way, however, does not necessarily mean that they had the same needs and interests as the religious activists who sought and received their political advocacy. The political history of Russia, not to mention that of other European nations and the United States, offers countless examples of religious interests being championed by politicians with secular, and even philistine, motivations. Key Bolsheviks, for example, regarded themselves as political advocates of sectarians persecuted by the tsarist state.[34]

Unlike the Bolsheviks, the officers of the village soviets did not leave a rich verbal record of their motivations. They did, however, leave other valuable evidence that speaks to the issue of why they often used their political power to keep the display of ritual, whether public or private, a part of village life.

To find it, we need look no farther than the walls of the buildings in which the business of the soviet took place. Those walls were indeed contested territory. In the vision of Party leaders, those walls were to be adorned with appropriate Soviet political art. Pictures of Lenin, Kalinin, and others would not only attest to the presence of Soviet power, they believed, but in subtle ways influence members of the soviet to act in accord with Party policy. In village soviets throughout the provinces of the RSFSR, however, members had chosen to decorate their walls with Orthodox icons rather than with the secular iconography of the Communist regime. In one case, members of the soviet elected Kalinin as their honorary chair while an icon of the Virgin Mary hung on the walls of the building![35] Did these choices reflect the religious attachments of the members of the soviets? Or when the soviet appropriated space that had been used for other purposes, did its members leave the icons undisturbed because they had too much on their minds, or because they could not find any Soviet political art to put up instead?

In some cases, members may have left the icons hanging because they were indifferent or lacked resources. But they generally had other motivations for covering the walls of the soviets with religious art. Many times officers of the soviet themselves decided to adorn its walls with icons. Fearing the com-

---

34. On the Bolsheviks' interest in sectarians, see, for example, Robert C. Williams, *The Other Bolsheviks: Lenin and His Critics, 1904–1914* (Bloomington, Ind., 1986), pp. 24–27.

35. *Bezbozhnik*, May 20, 1923; *Sovetskaia derevnia*, May 17, 1924, p. 4. See also *Izvestiia Saratovskogo soveta*, May 7, 1924, p. 4.

ing of the Antichrist, for example, the chair of the Kuzhutki village soviet (Nizhegorod province) put up an icon.[36] The behavior of staff and participants of the village soviets attests even more conclusively to their religious attachments. Villagers (church elders and those described by village correspondents simply as "peasants") and officers of the soviet alike crossed themselves and prayed in front of icons that hung in the corners of the building.[37] When challenged by villagers of a more secular inclination, chairs even defended the presence of icons in their chanceries. "They are not disturbing anyone," replied the chair of the village soviet in Svatsovko (Saratov *uezd* and province) in 1924 to villagers who wanted to remove the icons from the walls of the chancery.[38]

A case from Orel province demonstrates that many officers of the soviets really did want icons in the chanceries. As of late 1925, the chancery of the Chern' village soviet (Orel province) was set up in the home of a certain Kisilev, who was apparently the chair of the soviet and "chair of the district and a member of the Zlynka *volost'* executive committee."[39] He had decorated its corner with "icons of various shapes and sizes." On Orthodox holidays, Kiselev lighted lampadas in front of the icons. Commenting on the case, the correspondent lamented that there were "many such chanceries throughout Zlynka *volost'*; they are visited by members of the county committees, the Komsomol, the *volost'* and *uezd* executive committees, and no one pays attention to it."

As the example of Kisilev suggests, the icons were only one manifestation of a general devotion to Orthodox ritual. Although usually neither prominent lay activists or relatives thereof, the chairs of the village soviets continued to engage in a variety of religious rituals throughout NEP. Officers of the soviets (chairs and secretaries) had traditional Orthodox wedding ceremonies and had their children baptized. In 1924, for example, the secretary of a village soviet in Saratov province was planning an Orthodox wedding, even though he had joined the Party in 1920.[40] Officers of the soviets engaged not only in the Orthodox rituals that punctuated the life cycle of the human being but also in those rituals that accompanied the ebbs and flows of rural

---

36. *Bezbozhnik*, June 3, 1923, p. 4.
37. *Izvestiia Saratovskogo soveta*, January 4, 1924, p. 4; *Petrovskaia kommuna*, May 29, 1924, p. 3; *Bezbozhnik*, September 20, 1925.
38. *Izvestiia Saratovskogo soveta*, January 4, 1924, p. 4.
39. *Bezbozhnik*, December 1, 1925, p. 5.
40. *Sovetskaia derevnia*, February 4, 1924, p. 4. This secretary, who was not of poor peasant stock, had allegedly opposed the October Revolution. In 1919 he deserted from the Red Army, was caught, and was transferred to a workers' brigade. Although the operator of a private, unregistered school, he had not completed the village school. See also *Sovetskaia derevnia*, April 11, 1924, p. 4.

agriculture. In 1925, for example, the "entire presidium" of the village soviet in Malye Iagurye led a religious procession that a village priest had formed in order to pray for rain.[41]

When officers practiced religious rituals and attended services, they interfered with the functioning of the soviet. According to a 1924 newspaper report, for instance, the chair of the soviet in Kordil (Balashov *uezd*, Saratov province) spent an entire week worshiping in church. During this period he is said to have completely neglected his official duties.[42] Although the business of the soviet seems to have proceeded without him, in many cases officers' participation at religious ceremonies, such as weddings and funerals, and also at holiday celebrations actually shut down the soviets.[43] The impact of officers' commitment to religious practice on the political life of the soviets is brought to life by the case of an individual who served as both chair of the soviet and psalmist in Aleksandrovko (Kursk province). He regularly attended baptisms, funerals, weddings, and wakes (*pominki*). On an unspecified holiday in 1925 he arrived at the soviet in a drunken state. Fed up with the demands of the crowd, he dismissed them: "Why did you come today, today is a holiday, a nonworking day—come tomorrow."[44]

There is still more dramatic evidence of the religious commitments of officers of the soviets. The latter sometimes even allowed public religious celebrations to displace official business. On November 21, 1924, an Orthodox wedding took place in the Surov village soviet (Pugachev *uezd*). According to the account of a provincial correspondent, its chair lay in a drunken stupor underneath a bench.[45] While the correspondent may have exaggerated the chair's degree of intoxication, it is nevertheless important to note that this official not only allowed the ceremony to take place in the chancery of the soviet but was an active participant in its festivities. Given his behavior, it is easy to imagine him using his political power to maintain public religiosity in village life.

Or is it? Eager to hang icons in the corners of chanceries, inclined not only to engage in Orthodox ceremonies and rituals but to put off their political responsibilities to do so, replacing the business of the soviet with religious festivities—were many officers of the soviets, whether or not they were clergy or self-identified religious activists, really committed on a personal level to a wide variety of religious practices? Did these personal attachments account for their willingness—even their determination—to use their political power to maintain the place of ritual in the public life of the village and in the quasi-

41. *Bezbozhnik*, July 19, 1925, p. 3.
42. *Sovetskaia derevnia*, April 23, 1924, p. 4.
43. *Pskovskii nabat'*, December 21, 1928, p. 2.
44. *Bezbozhnik*, July 19, 1925, p. 3.
45. *Sovetskaia derevnia*, December 24, 1928, p. 2.

private lives of villagers? We must consider the possibility that officers of the village soviets succumbed to the bribes of village priests and lay activists, extracting *samogon* (home brew) and cash in return for political favors.

Bribery had, of course, been a part of village life during tsarist times;[46] oblique references to clergy and officers of the village soviet occasionally drinking together, whether at holiday celebrations, weddings, or social gatherings can be read as implicit evidence of bribery. (It is important to recognize, however, that villagers typically drank together on such occasions.)[47] If the officers of the soviets took bribes, were they motivated exclusively by them as they used their power to promote and defend religious interests? That officers of the soviets *spontaneously* defended the presence of icons in the chancery, or sent callers away on holidays, is strong evidence that their own attachments to religious belief and practice also played a significant role in shaping their political and administrative decisions.[48] Thus the taking of bribes, if it existed, was the political equivalent of icing on the cake, since officers of the village soviet also stood to lose access to religious practice unless they used their political power in the ways described above. Given this identity of interests, religious activists would have bribed the politicians of the soviets in order to reassure themselves, much like an anxious traveler who orders a wake-up call even though he has a functioning alarm clock. The politics of ritual and religious practice was a politics of identity, not extraction.

In sum, the officers of village soviets used their political power to support ritual and religious practice more generally because of their own attachments to these threatened elements of village life. Propelled by their own religious loyalties, these village politicians, in the NEP years after the scissors crisis and the ensuing shift in Party policy heralded by the "revival of the soviets" and "face to the countryside" campaigns, helped created a political culture in which the village soviet helped sustain the place of public ritual and religious practice. Villagers' commitment to collective and individual displays of religious ritual helped them create an autonomous political culture—both in spite of and because of the Party's attempt to bring the rural nexus under its political control.

---

46. On the commune's use of bribery in the first decades of the nineteenth century see, for example, Steven L. Hoch, *Serfdom and Social Control in Russia: Petrovskoe, a Village in Tambov* (Chicago, 1986), pp. 32, 134, 142–46.

47. On rural drinking, see David Christian, "Traditional and Modern Drinking Cultures in Russia on the Eve of Emancipation," *Australian Slavonic and East European Studies* 1:1 (1987): 61–84; Herlihy, "Joy of the Rus'."

48. For a somewhat analogous argument in which the spontaneity of religious activists' assertions is used to deduce internal beliefs and motivations, see Desan, *Reclaiming the Sacred*, pp. 146–47.

Ritual as Weapon

In the aftermath of the scissors crisis, however, religious activists used ritual as more than just a catalyst for political mobilization. They also used it as a political tool. To give but one example, rural clergy promoted successful fulfillment of religious ritual as a criterion for election to the village soviet. Lukachevskii noted that during the mid-1920s, Ukrainian clergy made the renewal of icons a political criterion: "The icons renewed themselves for the most part in the homes of kulaks, and on this basis clergy agitated: 'Elect to the soviets those for whom the icons renewed themselves.'"[49] This priest's electoral command reflected an appreciation of the triangular bond that linked internalized authority, religious symbolism, and political action. He counted on the power of religious symbolism to channel internalized religious authority into the achievement of political goals. Not unlike Calvinists who believed that wealth was evidence of a state of grace, clergy regarded renewal of icons as a sign of being part of the political "elect" of the village, a perception that once again revealed a reluctance to draw clear boundaries between the secular and the sacred.

Religious activists continued to wield ritual as a political weapon, as the Party, beginning in 1926, began to hack away at rural political autonomy. With the resurgence in clerical disenfranchisement that began with the 1926–27 electoral campaign, as we have seen, activists experimented with new strategies in response to the Party's efforts to control elections to the village soviets. They chose ritual and religious practice to resist these new and suddenly imposed restrictions on their political activity.

It was the refusal of religious activists to reconcile themselves with the changes in the electoral process that underlay sectarian activities during the 1926–27 voting campaign in Nikolaevka. Reputedly angered by the disenfranchisement of clergy, members of the Molokan community orchestrated a public ritual during a crucial moment of the campaign.[50] Their procession, punctuated by group prayer and song, startled the "audience" as it sprang "from behind the corner" just as the oral voting on candidates was about to take place. While claiming that the clergy had organized this unexpected

---

49. Lukachevskii, *Uchebnik*. The exact date of this event is unclear. But since the book appeared in 1928 and the author claimed the event took place "several years ago," we can guess that it occurred somewhere around 1924–26. When an icon "renewed" itself, its blackened surface miraculously regained color until the image had retained its original appearance.

50. The Molokans, a Protestant sect with affinities to the Baptists, first appeared at the end of the eighteenth century in Tambov province. At the beginning of the twentieth century there were 1.2 million members of the sect in Russia. For more on them, see, for example, V. D. Bonch-Bruevich, "Sektantstvo i staroobriadchestvo v pervoi polovine XIX v.," in *Izbrannye sochineniia*, vol. 1 (Moscow, 1959).

interruption, the Soviet journalistic account did not directly address the respective contributions of clergy and laity to the staging of this public procession (*krestnyi khod*). Certainly the report did try to create an image of an aggressive, conspiratorial clergy successfully manipulating a passive, politically indifferent laity. Examining the account more closely, however, we learn that the initial participants, whether clergy or laity, could not control the course of subsequent developments: the women's section (*zhenskaia chast'*) of the *skhod* suddenly joined the procession, stayed with it for a brief time, and then returned inexplicably to the voting arena. The elections resumed after momentary confusion.[51] While ostensibly intended to underscore the greater vulnerability of women to unharnessed "outbursts" of religious enthusiasm, this detail actually affirmed the undeniable contribution of the laity to the procession.

The "deep structure" of this public ritual should not escape careful elaboration. Potentially seen as a brief, simplistic, and inconsequential disturbance of the main event (i.e., the voting process), the sectarians' interjection in fact fleshed out their basic convictions about the relationship between religion and politics. For the Molokans of Nikolaevka, religious ritual had become a form of political protest. The sectarians *selected* religious ritual to express acute dissatisfaction with certain aspects of the political sphere.[52] By choosing to juxtapose public ritual against a crucial segment of the electoral process, the Molokan sectarians of Nikolaevka expressed their anger at the unjust exclusion of their leaders from the political arena. Surely it was not accidental that they staged the interjection to coincide with the very moment of voting. The procession enacted an instantaneous reversal in which the nearly equal participation of all replaced the exclusion of disenfranchised clergy from the political process. It is necessary to qualify this description of the ritual with the words "nearly equal participation," because it can be inferred that clergy led the procession, just as Father Gapon led workers to the Winter Palace in January 1905. By recognizing this distinction, we can appreciate the brilliant symmetry of the procession's inversion of the electoral order: politically marginalized clergy, shorn of their voting rights, now occupied a commanding position in the public procession. Ritual encapsulated the sectarians' normative vision of the political process.

As the Party, beginning in 1928–29, took even more severe measures against rural political autonomy, religious activists continued to fashion religious ritual as a political weapon that expressed their perceived exploitation. Omens threatening the existence of rural politics included the narrowing of the interpretation of voting rights, closures of churches provoked by electoral

51. *Vlast' sovetov*, March 20, 1927, p. 19.
52. On peasants as rational decision makers, see Popkin, *Rational Peasant*, p. 31.

successes, and the importation of ideologically charged urban workers to the villages, best exemplified by the 25,000ers, assigned the task of imposing a cultural, economic, and political revolution on the countryside.[53] In this context activists sometimes marshaled the physical symbols of religious belief, as well as ritual, to distract voters from preelection meetings of poor peasants. In the beginning of 1929,[54] an Orthodox priest in the village of Baranyshkovo (Kamyshin *okrug*, formerly Saratov province) scheduled a sermon to coincide with the preelection meeting of poor peasants: "When you hear the [church] bell, go quickly to church and listen to the message of God.... Bring along with you all sinners."[55] Despite the priest's efforts to compete directly with the established preelection agenda, the village correspondent noted, 280 persons or 42 percent of the village population attended the meeting.[56] Regrettably, the correspondent did not furnish statistics on attendance at the sermon.

In selecting this technique, the priest demonstrated his perception of the authority of religious symbolism among villagers, whatever their level of anticlericalism. The priest designed his event under the assumption that the church bell's authority, internalized by the villagers, could enable them to challenge the political legitimacy of the meeting. Religious symbolism released the stored power of a religio-political legacy, a tradition predating the 1917 watershed by many years, empowering believers to resist and reshape the emerging components of the revolutionary rural political order. Ritual and religious symbolism remained the inalienable political property of believers, a tool in the struggle for political power.

Sectarians used the same tools to resist the encroachment of preelection meetings on rural political autonomy. In the village of Poga (Detskosel'sk *uezd*, Leningrad region), sectarians sought to disrupt a preelection meeting in 1929 by scheduling a religious gathering to coincide with it.[57] This tactic had important symbolic implications. It implied an unequivocal and intransigent denial of the legitimacy of the Soviet electoral process. It was not incidental that this stubborn and impatient rejection of a component of the mainstream political order appeared in 1929, after several years of the Party's intensified attempts at controlling the rural political arena. The sensation of

---

53. On the 25,000ers, see Lynne Viola, *The Best Sons of the Fatherland: Workers in the Vanguard of Soviet Collectivization* (New York, 1987).

54. The exact date of this incident cannot be determined. Although the newspaper report appeared in February 1929, the incident could have occurred in the latter part of 1928.

55. *Povolzhskaia pravda*, February 5, 1929, p. 2.

56. Ibid. This meeting was labeled an *otchetnoe sobranie*. During the election, 335 persons, or 50.3 percent of eligible voters in the village, eventually voted; 63 percent of them were men and 37 percent were women.

57. *Povolzhskaia pravda*, April 5, 1929, p. 2.

facing and battling a relentless political opponent thus elicited the most intransigent, yet also the most creative, retaliatory strategies.

Religious activists, in what was the most radical fashioning of ritual and religious practice as political resistance, targeted the complete package of political activities on election day. During the 1928–29 voting campaign, clergy and their unidentified allies intentionally scheduled religious services for election day in villages in the Lower Volga Region.[58] Confronted with this threat to their authority, members of the Party cell decided to bargain with organizers of the service in order to reach a satisfactory compromise. After lengthy discussion, the party entourage and the clerical contingent came to the following agreement: the prayer service would last from noon to eight P.M., with elections scheduled to follow. In another case, local clergy slated a grand funeral for election day. Once again, Party representatives, such as the director of the voting campaign and the representative from the regional (*okrug*) executive committee ultimately decided to postpone elections until after the funeral ceremony.[59] While such agreements prohibited the service from directly obstructing the voting process, the worship service had changed the initial political agenda.

Party workers in the Volkhov district of Leningrad region, however, failed to react quickly enough to public rituals held during the 1930–31 electoral campaign. Icon-bearing village priests leading parishioners in a *krestnyi khod* distracted a large group of voters on election day in the area encompassed by the Ekovo, Nikhinsk, Karpino, and Izsad village soviets.[60] When the Party officials acted too slowly, religious activists accomplished two key goals: they rejected the legitimacy of the voting campaign and Soviet political institutions, and they undermined the Party's control of the most crucial moment of the electoral process.

Through the channel of collective religious activity, religious activists—often led by clergy—honored the "collective memory" of rural politics.[61] Clergy and laity refused to forget their brief but intense experience of politics as a struggle for power between legitimate contenders; they recoiled at submissively redefining it as an incontestable demonstration of will. By mounting such resistance, they both reflected and deepened the inexorable split between those who sought to maintain rural political autonomy and those who either wished to effect, or were willing to accept, its demise.

58. See *Povolzhskaia pravda*, January 24, 1929, p. 3.
59. Ibid.
60. *Krest'ianskaia pravda*, December 15, 1930.
61. On "collective memory," see Maurice Halbwachs, *The Collective Memory* (New York, 1968).

Committed to ritual and religious practice, religious activists transformed rural politics in two key ways during NEP. As the Party, in the wake of the scissors crisis, tried to establish a political presence in the village soviets, so too did religious activists expend greater political efforts in that organ in their attempts to maintain various types of public and private religious practice. To be sure, they continued to debate these issues in the village assembly after the momentous shift in Party policy of 1924–25 and its epiphenomenon, the ban on discussion of religious issues at the village assembly. Yet the politics of ritual occupied an increasingly important place in the affairs of the soviet. Religious activists succeeded to a large degree in using the soviets to maintain religious practice, whether public rituals, holiday celebrations, or even "private" ceremonies such as baptisms, weddings, and funerals. They did so in spite of—in fact *because* of—the regime's seeking to use the village soviets for the interrelated goals of eliminating public religious practice and rural political autonomy.

A different "politics of religious ritual" emerged in this new institutional setting. What activists' use of collective ritual tells us, in fact, is that by the end of NEP it was the fate of rural politics itself that had become the burning political issue of the day. While before 1926 such specific and local issues as the disposition of the church building, support for rural clergy, and the future of religious holidays had been at the center of rural politics, thereafter villagers were more often concerned with the abstract and national issue of rural political autonomy. This would indicate that rural political life had become less defined, as is typical of everyday village politics, by village factions pursuing opposing interests, and increasingly characterized by a good many villagers' use of religious ritual to present a defiant stance against the exploitative intrusion of outsiders.[62] In this, religious activists of the late 1920s could see themselves as the descendants of Chekhov's Zhukovo villagers. But what meaning did the Soviet regime's cadres, whether Party leaders or village correspondents, attach to religious activists' determined practice and defense of rural political autonomy?

---

62. On the prevalence of factions in peasant politics, see Hamza Alavi, "Village Factions," in Theodor Shanin, ed., *Peasants and Peasant Societies: Selected Readings* (New York, 1987), pp. 346–56.

9

FASHIONING THE ENEMY

Western historians of the early Soviet period have generally refrained from investigating the discursive strategies employed in the revolutionary transformation of Russian society. Their reluctance to view revolutionary rhetoric as a text amenable to literary analysis in part reflects their disdain for Bolshevik ideology.[1] The marginality of Soviet revolutionary discourse—the implicit assumption that the Soviets spun propagandistic lies, whereas French revolutionaries, for example, crafted language that can and should be a proper subject of historical analysis—is a legacy of what Stephen Cohen has called the "Cold War consensus."[2] A case in point is the discourse of the antireligious campaign. For the most part its historians have implicitly regarded the rhetoric of the *bezbozhniki* as the linguistic crystallization of evil, a rhetorical epiphenomenon of the terrible religious persecution of the 1920s and 1930s, and beyond. They would agree with Nikolai Berdiaev that "In its anti-religious propaganda Soviet literature stands at a very low intellectual level.... It is quite the most inferior sort of literature in Soviet Russia."[3]

1. See Lynn Hunt, "The Rhetoric of Revolution," in *Politics, Culture, and Class*, especially her methodological manifesto on pp. 21–25.
2. See Cohen, *Rethinking the Soviet Experience*, esp. pp. 8–19.
3. Berdiaev, *The Origin of Russian Communism* (New York, 1937), p. 198.

In the discussion that follows, however, I rehabilitate Soviet revolutionary language, treating it as historical evidence amenable to the same type of analysis conducted by historians of other revolutionary processes. In particular, I explore the rhetoric of antireligious activists (correspondents for Party, provincial, and antireligious newspapers; rural cadres; and antireligious workers), tracing their changing image of rural religious activity, with particular focus on the political activity of religious activists. (These images in turn shaped the very process of the antireligious campaign itself.)

Antireligious Discourse and "Militarized Socialism"

Provincial and antireligious correspondents used military rhetoric to describe antireligious activity throughout NEP, a reflection of what Mark von Hagen has called the "militarization of political culture" characteristic of the 1920s as a whole.[4] During the early years of NEP, even before the League of the Godless had become the major institutional player in the antireligious campaign, Party publications heralded antireligious activists as the "army of *bezbozhniki*."[5] Throughout NEP, activists routinely conceived of the arena of antireligious activity as a "front": they wrote of the successes and failures on the "ideological front," the "godless front" (*na bezbozhnom fronte*), and the "antireligious front."[6] In general, correspondents used military rhetoric to advertise the successes and lament the failures of *bezbozhniki*, clergy, and laity. The newspaper *Povolzhskaia pravda*, in a 1928 article called "Before a General Offensive," warned of the involvement of "sectarians and *tserkovniki*" in the village soviets of the region. A reflection of the fact that Soviet political and military leaders as well as Party rank and file viewed war and struggle "as the norm for international and domestic relations," such rhetoric also *transformed* the character of antireligious activity, lending it the reality of a "war" on religion.[7]

---

4. See von Hagen, *Soldiers in the Proletarian Dictatorship*, pp. 331–32, for a discussion of the fact that this militarized political culture predated the first five-year plan. Civil War veterans used rhetoric that "resembled those of military campaigns" in speeches and printed statements on challenges facing the regime. See ibid., p. 335.

5. *Bezbozhnik*, May 27, 1923, p. 4.

6. On the "ideological front," see *Povolzhskaia pravda*, September 4, 1928, p. 2. For references to the "godless front," see "Na bezbozhnom fronte," *Bezbozhnik*, May 3, 1925, p. 8. On the "antireligious front," see "Na antireligioznom fronte," *Izvestiia Saratovskogo soveta*, February 6, 1924; "Ne oslabliaiite bor'bu na antireligioznom fronte," *Krest'ianskaia pravda*, December 14, 1928, p. 6; and Iaroslavskii, "Vyrovniat' antireligioznyi front," *Pravda*, June 24, 1930.

7. On this see von Hagen, *Soldiers in the Proletarian Dictatorship*, p. 335.

Antireligious activists' use of military discourse and metaphors changed significantly in response to the increased political activity of religious villagers after 1924.[8] When activists used the word "front," they were implicitly conceptualizing the religious as the enemy and churches, temples and prayer houses as enemy territory to be conquered. But not until the end of NEP, however, did these activists actually use the term "enemy" when describing religious activists, especially their political forays.[9] The author of a 1927 article in *Vlast' sovetov* branded the clergy (designated here by the pejorative term *pop*) an "enemy element" in connection with their activity during elections to the soviets.[10] A statement of the Party's Central Committee, which was reprinted as the lead article of the January 4, 1929, issue of the Leningrad Party daily *Krest'ianskaia pravda*, warned: "We have a strengthening of enemy activity in connection with elections to the soviets on the part of kulaks and organized counterrevolutionary activity, right up to *tserkovniki* and sectarians."[11] Several months later, the author of an article in the same newspaper denounced as "class enemies" visible lay members of the rural religious community, such as a church elder and a member of a religious society, who had won election to the governing boards of cooperatives.[12]

As this excerpt from *Krest'ianskaia pravda* suggests, by the end of the 1920s antireligious correspondents had changed the substantive meaning of *tserkovnik*. In the late tsarist period, for example, the term referred mainly to either a junior deacon (*prichetnik*) or a "person of ecclesiastical calling, but [who was] not ordained"; it could also mean an Orthodox parishioner.[13] Activists used the category's flexibility to capture the clergy's increasing dependence on the laity during the 1920s, as well as the fluid ambiguity of each contingent's respective contribution to sustaining parish life. During the first few years of NEP, they tended to use *tserkovnik* as a synonym for "clergy."[14] Thereafter, however, journalists and other antireligious activists

8. See Hunt, *Politics, Culture, and Class*, p. 26.
9. Provincial correspondents and Party leaders also accused the religious of being "enemies" without mentioning their political activities. See *Povolzhskaia pravda*, September 4, 1928, p. 2, which warned of the "revival [*ozhivlenie*] of anti-Soviet hostile forces: the growth of the religious movement."
10. A. Zhukov, "Kulachestvo i dukhovenstvo," *Vlast' sovetov*, April 13, 1928, p. 20. See also "Vragi nagleiut," *Povolzhskaia pravda*, September 15, 1928, p. 8, and *Krest'ianskaia pravda*, December 14, 1928.
11. *Krest'ianskaia pravda*, January 4, 1929.
12. *Krest'ianskaia pravda*, April 16, 1929, p. 5. Speaking in January 1930, one Party leader in the Leningrad Region condemned the "resistance [*soprotivlenie*] of the class enemy in the person of the kulak and priest [*pop*], clergy and sectarian" to collectivization. See TsGAOR Leningrada, f. 6307, op. 13, ed. khr. 9, l. 49.
13. "Tserkovnik," *Entsiklopedicheskii slovar'* (St. Petersburg, 1912–24), p. 1258.
14. See, for example, "Bor'ba tserkovnikov," *Izvestiia Saratovskogo soveta*, June 21, 1922, p. 2.

seemed confused about what a *tserkovnik* indeed was; they often used the term in different ways within the same article or document, using it both to refer to clergy alone and as a shorthand for both clergy and laity. Iaroslavskii's lead article in the March 29, 1925, issue of *Bezbozhnik* deemed *tserkovniki* not only a "people, capable of doing anything" but illustrated this "praise" with the example of "village kulaks" who tore out some crosses from graveyards and then blamed this on Komsomoltsy.[15] His subsequent admonition to keep *tserkovniki* out of politics (namely, the village soviets), however, refers to the clergy (*pop*).[16] We find the same ambiguous construction of the category of *tserkovnik* in a 1927 protocol of the Smolensk provincial party organization.[17] Having resolved this ambivalence, other Soviet authors seemed to have clarified to themselves that *tserkovnik* should refer to Orthodox clergy and laity; during the period of 1927–29, they used it to mean the opposite of "sectarian."[18] Antireligious journalists and Party cadres alike adjusted the meaning of *tserkovnik* in response to both the laity's increasing involvement in village politics and assumption of responsibility for parish life.

In the process, *tserkovnik* ceased to be solely a religious category. Instead the *tserkovnik* became a political as well as a religious actor. Activists gradually identified the *tserkovnik* with an Orthodox priest or layperson active in the village soviets and cooperatives, the institutions the regime had hoped and expected to be run by individuals who, by virtue of their socioeconomic background (e.g., poor and middle peasants), subscribed to "Soviet" values (such as atheism). By comparison, Soviet authorities used other terms for clergy and laity, such as *dvadsatki* and *dukhovenstvo*, when discussing Orthodox villagers' administrative (as opposed to political) activity.[19] *Tserkovnik*, then, implied a social and political identity associated with the frustration of Soviet goals and expectations.

Antireligious activists revealed their perception of independent social groups in their rhetoric of the politically active layperson or priest (*tserkovnik*) as enemy. Not only, as we have seen, did *tserkovnik* denote a

15. E. Iaroslavskii, "Tserkovniki na vyborakh," *Bezbozhnik*, March 29, 1925, p. 1.
16. Ibid.
17. "Ob ozhivlenii i razvitii antireligioznoi propagandy v derevne. Prilozhenie no-2 k protokoly no. 57 zasedaniia Biuro Smolgukoma ot 17/XI-1927 g." Used at different points as an antonym to both "believers" and sectarians, *tserkovnik*, by implication, stands for both clergy and the Orthodox population.
18. See *Izvestiia Saratovskogo soveta*, December 18, 1927, p. 3; *Povolzhskaia pravda*, September 13, 1928, and November 4, 1928, p. 2; and *Krest'ianskaia pravda*, January 4, 1929, and April 5, 1929, p. 2.
19. See the discussion of the administrative registration of religious societies in "Doklad o rabote Volodarskogo raiispolkoma c 1/XII do 1/IX 24 g. na plenume Gubispolkoma (September 3, 1923)," in TsGAOR Leningrada, f. 1010, op. 1, ed. khr. 103, ll. 86–87.

Fashioning the Enemy 257

Fig. 12. "We Will Unmask the Anti-Soviet Plans of Capitalists and *Tserkovniki*. Long Live the World Proletarian Revolution!" Date not available. Antireligious activists were increasingly frustrated by the efforts of priests and politcally active religious laypersons (*tserkovniki*), whom they publicly targeted as enemies. Courtesy, Poster Collection, Hoover Institution Archive, Stanford University. Artist: Dmitrii S. Moor.

sectarian or Orthodox villager active in institutions that the Party had intended as reliable administrative strongholds and agents in the construction of a socialist countryside. As the excerpt from *Krest'ianskaia pravda* indicates, *tserkovnik* had, by the end of NEP and beginning of collectivization, acquired military as well as hostile connotations, as Figure 12 shows. As NEP wore on, antireligious leaders and journalists increasingly saw independent social initiative, such as the religious villagers' involvement in local soviets and cooperatives, as the activity of an internal foe. Participating in the practice of trying to maintain consensus by verbal exclusion that had characterized Russian political culture since Muscovite times, they were also crafting a rhetorical strategy of mobilization by damnation.[20] Antireligious

20. Marc Raeff has noted the tendency in Muscovite political culture to brand those who rejected social norms as foreigners and/or enemies. We can substitute "Bolshevik" or "Communist" for "tsar" and "holy Moscow" in the following analysis: "Any deviation from the social norms automatically implies rejection of the system and hence renunciation of the tsar as supreme protector. Indeed, deviation was seen as tantamount to social treason. This gave rise to a Manichean world view: one was either a subject of holy Moscow or a foreigner and, by definition, an enemy." See *Understanding Imperial Russia: State and Society in the Old Regime*, trans. Arthur Goldhammer (New York, 1984), p. 14.

activists worried continually about both attaining and maintaining unanimous commitment to Bolshevik values, just as French revolutionaries carried what Hunt has described as "an enormous collective anxiety about the solidity of the new consensus."[21]

When antireligious correspondents used sarcastic rhetoric, they were also expressing their frustration with the religious villagers who had thwarted their dream of a homogenous Bolshevik political world. Correspondents employed this rhetorical device after the Party proclaimed its policy of "revival of the soviets" in 1924, a policy that had the unintended consequence of bringing more religious villagers into the political process. Dismayed that a member of a church council and a former deacon had won seats in a village soviet during the 1924–25 electoral campaign, an exasperated village correspondent exclaimed: "Now, I suppose, all that's left is to close the church, hoist up a cross over the [building housing the] village soviet, and hold mass!"[22] This correspondent's irony betrayed a deep sense of powerlessness, a sign of the regime's inability to control the processes of rural politics.

Antireligious correspondents tended to engage in ironic overstatement, a habit that both reflected and intensified this mood of powerlessness. Correspondents for *Bezbozhnik*, for example, condemned the involvement of religious villagers in the soviets in such articles as "Not a Village Soviet, But a Chapel" (1925) or "Not a Village Soviet, But a Cathedral of Believers" (1927).[23] Such correspondents were committing a cognitive error of substituting the part for the whole, of taking the election of clergy or committed laypersons to the village soviets to mean a complete loss of control over these institutions. (Hence we see the tendency to recast them conceptually and rhetorically as religious institutions.) Titles such as "God in the Village Soviets" (1925) and "The Artel Saved by God" also reflected such an interpretation.[24] Although these correspondents may have intended to use this rhetoric to mobilize activists to intensify their battle against religion, this strategy may have backfired: by conceding the village soviets were completely controlled by religious activists, such titles heightened their readers' (not to mention their authors') exasperation with the existence of any factional politics in the village.

---

21. Cf. Hunt's comment on p. 32 of *Politics, Culture, and Class*: "The reverse side of the mythic present of national regeneration was an enormous, collective anxiety about the solidity of the new consensus."

22. *Bezbozhnik*, January 11, 1925, p. 7.

23. "Ne sel'sovet, a chasovnia," *Bezbozhnik*, December 1, 1925, p. 4; P. Bol'shak, "Ne sel'sovet, a sobor veruiushchikh," *Bezbozhnik*, January 30, 1927.

24. "Bog v sel'sovetakh," *Bezbozhnik*, July 19, 1925; "Bogospasaemaia artel'," *Povolzhskaia pravda*, February 10, 1929.

Conflating Kulak and Clergy

Like their use of sarcasm, the antireligious activists' identification of kulak and clergy both expressed and intensified their fear of rural religious activity. In 1929, Iaroslavskii declared war on the "kulak-clergy front" (*kulatsko-popovskii front*) at the second all-union congress of the League of the Godless.²⁵ This new rhetoric paralleled the antireligious correspondents' tendency to associate and even equate clergy with kulak, a very frequent habit in the years following the Party's decision to "revive" the soviets. To be sure, village correspondents linked the priest and kulak, both of whom were deprived of voting rights by the Soviet Constitution, even before 1924.²⁶ Yet the more the Party increased its efforts to place "reliable elements" (e.g., poor and middle peasants) in the village soviets, the more correspondents and Party leaders complained that "kulaks and clergy," or some variant thereof, were working in tandem to stall the process.

Antireligious activists developed several variants of the rhetorical association of clergy and kulaks. Reviewing Party and antireligious publications of 1927–29, for example, we find clergy represented as the manipulated "dupes" of the kulaks: a 1927 article in *Vlast' sovetov* accused kulaks of having "seduced" (*poodsobliali*) clergy to campaign against Communist candidates during elections to the soviets.²⁷ In a related vein, the same publications condemned kulaks' use of religious organizations and personnel, such as the Bible readings mentioned above, as a "cover" for their anti-Soviet activities during election campaigns to the soviets.²⁸ In 1928, a provincial correspondent asserted that during preelection preparations in Khopër *okrug* of the Lower Volga Region, "the church and sectarian prayer house will, in many cases, really serve the function of a kulak voting commission."²⁹ To be sure, articles in *Pravda* as well as provincial newspapers applauded the failure of the priest and kulak to place their candidates in the soviets.³⁰ Yet it is

---

25. On the 1929 congress, see Peris, "The 1929 Congress of the Godless."
26. See, for example, "Komu doroga tserkov'?—popam i kulakam," *Izvestiia Atkarskogo uezdnogo ispolkoma*, March 31, 1923, p. 2; *Izvestiia Saratovskogo soveta*, April 6, 1923, p. 3.
27. A. Zhukov, "Kulachestvo i dukhovenstvo," *Vlast' sovetov*, April 3, 1927, p. 20. See also "Obzory mestnoi raboty," ibid., March 20, 1927, p. 19; *Izvestiia Saratovskogo soveta*, February 17, 1928, p. 2; *Krest'ianskaia pravda*, December 14, 1928; and A. T. Lukachevskii, "Antipaskhal'naia kampaniia 1929 goda," in Lukachevskii, ed., *Antipaskhal'nyi sbornik* (Moscow, 1929), p. 6.
28. See, for example, Levin and Suvorov, "Sovety i stroitel'stvo sotsializma," in Pashukanis, *15 let*, p. 453; Angarov, *Klassovaia bor'ba*, pp. 29, 83; and "Kulatskaia aktivnost' budet bita!" *Krest'ianskaia pravda*, December 31, 1928, p. 2.
29. *Povolzhskaia pravda*, November 4, 1928, p. 2.
30. See, for example, *Pravda*, February 24, 1927, and *Krest'ianskaia pravda*, December 28, 1928, p. 3.

significant that authors of articles in the same publications reluctantly heralded the achievements of the joint efforts of clergy and kulaks in the political arena. What a provincial correspondent from Leningrad in 1929 branded the "kulak-clergy front" drew admiration for its organizational skills, for its early campaign preparations, for its deft exploitation of "each temporary difficulty" facing the Soviet regime.[31] Correspondents as well as antireligious and Party leaders represented the clergy-kulak team as effective political actors or, we might infer, as a capable political "party." Like French revolutionaries after 1789, antireligious propagandists demonstrated a hyper-vigilant unmasking of conspiracy, in this case, of a kulak-clergy subterfuge that had bred factional politics.[32] The 1929 statement of the Central Committee, quoted above, called for "special vigilance" (*osobaia bditel'nost'*) on the part of the Party in unmasking the counterrevolutionary threat of groups such as "*tserkovniki* and sectarians" during elections to the soviets."[33]

By 1928–29, antireligious correspondents had collapsed the conceptual boundary between priest and kulak even further. Dismissing the need to investigate the actual socioeconomic backgrounds of particular priests, they appeared to assume that clerical standing alone was enough to identify a kulak. A case in point is a 1928 article in *Krest'ianskaia pravda*. Illustrating his claim that "kulaks aren't dozing and are very actively preparing for elections to the soviets," the author cited the daughter of a priest, the wife of a sectarian preacher, and a Baptist preacher, all of whom had gained positions in village voting commissions.[34] An article that appeared in *Krest'ianskaia pravda* in 1929 followed a similar pattern. Asserting that "kulaks are trying with all their might to creep into cooperative organs," a provincial correspondent illustrated his claim with the examples of a church elder, a member of a religious society (*chlen tserkovnoi 'dvadtsatki'*), and a former priest.[35] While the author accused the church elder of being a "wealthy peasant," he did not mention the actual socioeconomic backgrounds of the others.

As correspondents conflated the clergy and the kulak, they influenced the

---

31. For comparison of the "kulak-clergy" (*kulatsko-popovskii*) front to the front defended by poor and middle peasants, see *Krest'ianskaia pravda*, February 5, 1929, p. 5. For acknowledgments that the kulak-clerical contingent had begun their election preparations earlier than the Party and its cadres, see *Povolzhskaia pravda*, January 13, 1929, p. 4, as well as *Krest'ianskaia pravda*, April 5, 1929, p. 2. On the clerical-kulak contingent's skillful exploitation of situational difficulties faced by the regime, see especially Putintsev, *Vybory v sovety*, p. 58.

32. On "unmasking," see Hunt, *Politics, Culture, and Class*, p. 39.

33. See *Krest'ianskaia pravda*, January 4, 1929.

34. *Krest'ianskaia pravda*, December 31, 1928, p. 2. The author of the article was Comrade N. I. Ivanov, deputy chairman of the executive committee of the Leningrad *oblast'* Party organization.

35. "Kulaki vsemi silami staraiutsia prolezt' v organy kooperatsii," *Krest'ianskaia pravda*, April 16, 1929, p. 5.

perception of priests and religious activity in general. For the Bolsheviks, the "kulak," the greedy peasant who (in theory) made a living by exploiting labor for profit, loomed as a symbol not only of capitalism but also of the failure of socialism to take root in the countryside. As the personification of economic and cultural backwardness, the "kulak" served, for the "military socialists" who increasingly steered the regime and served as rank-and-file cadres, as the figure onto whom they projected their impatience with NEP and their anxiety about achieving a homogenous community based on shared proletarian identity.[36] Moreover, these military socialists disdained the kulak, as von Hagen has noted, precisely because his secular activities in the capitalist economic sphere negated and threatened their ethos of self-sacrifice and rejection of worldly pleasures.[37] For these reasons they created a stigmatized and even demonized being: the kulak, "evil" personified. "Kulak" had become a moral category denoting an absence of revolutionary virtue. Suggesting a pursuit of particularistic interest at odds with revolutionary goals, it was to the political culture of the early Soviet period what *soslovnost'* was to that of the late imperial period. The Russian nobility had to protect themselves from being accused of the pursuit of private as opposed to general interest (or neutralize the charge); the peasant's relationship to the damning label of "kulak" was the same.[38]

Ironically, by merging the priest and the kulak, creators of the antireligious word were, by implication, ironically "demonizing" the priest, the committed layperson, and religious activity in general, both Orthodox and sectarian. We can infer that they also stigmatized the clergy in this fashion to affirm their ethos of self-sacrifice and its concomitant disdain of secular pleasures, temptations to which they perceived the clergy as having succumbed in their financial "extortion" of impoverished parishioners who paid them for various services. As both recent scholars and contemporaries have pointed out, however, Russian Marxists as well as Bolshevik leaders and rank-and-file cadres drew inspiration from Christian values and models even as they militantly rejected and fought against institutionalized religion.[39] The

36. On "militarized socialism," see von Hagen, *Soldiers in the Proletarian Dictatorship*, pp. 332, 334.
37. On this see ibid., pp. 332–33.
38. On this see Leopold H. Haimson, "Conclusion: Politics of the Countryside," in Haimson, ed., *The Politics of Rural Russia, 1905–1914* (Bloomington, Ind., 1979), p. 275.
39. Jay Bergman, "The Image of Jesus in the Russian Revolutionary Movement: The Case of Russian Marxism, "*International Review of Social History* 35 (1990): 220–48; Williams, *The Other Bolsheviks*, esp. pp. 49–65. In *A Radical Worker*, even after Kanatchikov had formally rejected the institutional and ritual component of village Orthodoxy championed by his father, the symbolic aspects of this religious experience continued to be part of his cultural frame of reference. For Kanatchikov, secular experiences (machines and the factory) elicit what Clifford Geertz would call religious moods and motivations, while the peasant-worker's invocation of

Bolshevik ideal of collective self-sacrifice, embodied in Lenin's vision of the quasi-ascetic, disciplined Party member, had cultural origins in the kenotic strain of Russian Orthodoxy and Christ's model of personal sacrifice. Ironically, then, "militarized socialists" implicitly drew on Christian (Orthodox) values and models—most notably Christ's martyrdom and rejection of this world—as they developed the anticlerical, conspiratorial strain of their antireligious propaganda.[40] For the Bolsheviks, the Word of God helped invisibly to forge the godless Word.[41]

By implication, many antireligious activists were giving "kulak" a very different meaning than it had had in, say, the late tsarist period. They were not using it to designate a wealthy peasant who profited from hiring labor. Rather, as our examination of the antireligious periodical press and Party documents shows, the meaning of "kulak" now spanned political and cultural categories. Correspondents, for example, assigned peasants this damning, conspiratorial identity on the basis of a combination of cultural identity (namely, religion) and political activity (namely, involvement in the village soviets and/or cooperatives and related electoral activities). While radical French revolutionaries developed what Hunt has called their "systematic obsession" with conspiracy only when they "confronted the novelties of mass politics," Bolshevik revolutionaries succumbed to similar thought patterns in response to religious villagers' creation of interest-group politics in the Soviet countryside.[42]

---

religious symbols (e.g., taking St. Petersburg to be the "Promised Land") seems to elicit secular moods and motivations (i.e., revolutionary political activity). See Geertz's definition of religion as elaborated in *Interpretation of Cultures*, p. 90. For a related assessment, see Nicholas Berdiaev, *The Origin of Russian Communism* (New York, 1937). For somewhat analogous developments in China, see David S. Nivison, "Communist Ethics and Chinese Tradition," reprinted in John A. Harrison, ed., *China: Enduring Scholarship Selected from the Far Eastern Quarterly—The Journal of Asian Studies, 1941–1971* (Tuscon, Ariz., 1972), pp. 207–30. I thank Philip J. Ivanhoe for bringing this article to my attention. In *Politics, Culture, and Class*, Hunt acknowledges François Furet's insistence on the importance of religious values in molding the plot theories devised by French revolutionaries. See ibid., p. 42, as well as François Furet's *Penser la Revolution française* (Paris, 1978), p. 78.

40. Bergman, for example, shows that certain Russian Marxists were influenced by Jesus' resurrection and divinity. Certain Soviet journalists deified Lenin as a Christlike figure. Here Bergman cites, for example, Lev Sosnovskii, the editor of *Bednota*, which, incidentally, carried reports on antireligious activities among the peasantry. See Bergman, "The Image of Jesus," pp. 239, 243. On the representation of Lenin as "Christlike," see also Tumarkin, *Lenin Lives!* esp. pp. 83–84.

41. Cf. the following assessment by Berdiaev: "The best type of communist . . . is a possibility only as the result of the Christian training of the human spirit, of the re-making of the natural man by the Christian spirit. The result of this Christian influence upon the human spirit, frequently hidden and unperceived, remains even when the people consciously refuse Christianity, and even become its foe." See *Origin of Russian Communism*, pp. 206–7.

42. Hunt, *Politics, Culture, and Class*, pp. 42, 44.

Even M. M. Khataevich, a leader of the *apparat* in Ukraine, realized that cadres in the countryside often treated "kulak" as a political rather than economic category:

> It was quite often the case in the countryside, and still is, that assignment of this or that peasant to [the ranks of] the "kulaks" proceeds not so much from the agricultural condition and his property, as from the content of his behavior. It is clear, that in the majority of cases the kulak comes out against the Party and against Soviet power in the countryside but not every act against the [Party] cell, or against a Party member from the county executive committee or village soviet is an anti-Soviet act. Not every opponent [*vystupaiushchii*] should and can be designated as a kulak, of whom there are in general significantly fewer in the countryside than many of our rural Party members suggest.[43]

Unable to find any kulaks in the traditional sense and in response to the Russian peasantry's lack of socioeconomic differentiation and to its political cohesiveness, Bolshevik bureaucrats, journalists, and Party leaders improvised.[44] They created their enemy by changing and broadening the category's defining characteristics, by making "kulak" a much more elastic concept.

The more the propagandists so redefined the kulak, the more they portrayed religious involvement in rural politics as both an economic and political roadblock to the building of socialism. (See Figure 13.) A 1927 protocol of the Smolensk provincial Party organization (*gubkom*) warned that

> in connection with . . . international relations and the growing threat of war, the activity of clerical and sectarian organizations has especially quickened in recent times. Religious organizations are attempting to disrupt elections to the soviets, cooperatives, to present their own candidates . . . and in general are a serious brake in the path of socialist economic development . . . All these facts bear witness to the aspiration of religious organizations to use the difficulties and contradictions of economic growth in the USSR for their own interests.[45]

---

43. Khataevich section, "O iacheikakh i partiitsakh derevni," in Rylkin and Truntaev, *Iacheika i sovety*, p. 10.

44. See Theodor Shanin, *The Awkward Class: Political Sociology of Peasantry in a Developing Society. Russia, 1910–1925* (New York, 1972).

45. Smolensk WKP 33, "Ob ozhivlenii i razvitii antireligioznoi propagandy v derevne" (Prilozhenie no. 2 k protokoly no. 57 zasedaniia Biuro Smolgubkoma ot 17/XI-1927 g.); E. Iaroslavskii, "Kul'turnaia revoliutsiia i antireligioznaia propaganda," in *Prosveshchenets na antireligioznom fronte* (Moscow, 1929), p. 33.

Fig. 13. "The Battle Against Religion Is the Battle for Socialism." 1929–33. Party propagandists sought to keep religious villagers out of rural politics, blaming them for the perceived failure of socialist economic goals. This poster calls for "mass appearance in the cells of the League of the Godless." Courtesy, Poster Collection, Hoover Institution Archive, Stanford University.

They held politically active religious villagers responsible for the perceived failure of socialist economic relations to materialize in the countryside, a perception echoed by Iaroslavskii in 1929.[46]

Most antireligious activists perceived such frustration of socialist economic goals—not to mention other forms of rural religious activity—as "counterrevolutionary." In 1925, a correspondent for *Bezbozhnik* published an article documenting cases of clerical and lay initiative; the author noted with dismay that priests were summoning *bezbozhniki* (rather than vice versa) to a dispute and that "*tserkovniki* [were] showing great interest in usurping [*k zakhvatu*] posts in lower Soviet and social [*obshchestvennye*] organs."[47] He titled the article "The Attacking *Popovshchina*" ("Nastupaiushchaia popovshchina"), rhetoric that may have called to mind movements of opposition to regimes throughout Russian history, whether the "Pugachevshchina" of 1773–74 or, more recently, the "Antonovshchina" in

---

46. Iaroslavskii, "Kul'turnaia revoliutsiia." He called religious organizations a "serious block in the path of the fundamental socialist transformation of society."
47. "Nastupaiushchaia popovshchina," *Bezbozhnik*, August 2, 1925.

Tambov province.[48] (See also Figure 14.) A 1929 statement of the Central Committee also interpreted religious villagers' involvement in rural politics as a movement of political opposition to the regime: "We have an intensification of hostile [*vrazhdebnaia*] activity in connection with elections to the soviets on the part of kulaks and organized counterrevolutionary groups, even *tserkovniki* and sectarians."[49] The same document warned that "illegal groups of Trotskiists," which had formed a "counterrevolutionary Menshevik organization," were aiding these religious contingents in their political forays.[50] In the same year, Fedor Oleshchuk, a member of the Central Committee of the League of the Godless, warned that closing churches against the wishes of believers could motivate "enemies of Soviet power" to stage "counterrevolutionary agitation."[51] While Oleshchuk may have had actual anti-Soviet protests or destruction of state-owned property in mind, the other authors quoted above are remarkable for deeming "counterrevolutionary" political activity that, for the most part, fell within the boundaries allowed by Soviet law. Antireligious propagandists, as well as Party leaders, took a religious villager's self-defensive political autonomy to be a counterrevolutionary act. Calling to mind developments Hunt has traced in the rhetoric of French revolutionaries after 1792, these antireligious propagandists recast specific events of the antireligious campaign along the lines of a literary "romance" in which heroic *bezbozhniki* staved off the menacing attacks of demonic, villainous, counterrevolutionary religious villagers.[52]

Gendering the Antireligious Campaign

What was the place of religious belief in this conspiratorial image of religious villagers, and especially of their political activity? By 1929, the standard line in antireligious circles was that religious "ideas" were used in "every possible way [*vsemerno*] by class enemies . . . in their battle against the building of socialism and against soviet power."[53] (In Figure 15, we see

---

48. In 1937, Putintsev titled a monograph on clerical and lay involvement in institutions of Soviet power, such as village soviets, *Vybory v sovety i razoblachenie popovshchiny* (Elections to the soviets and the unmasking of a "conspiracy of priests"). On the Pugachev rebellion, see Paul Avrich, *Russian Rebels, 1600–1800* (New York, 1972), pp. 180–273. On Antonov, see Radkey, *Unknown Civil War*.
49. See *Krest'ianskaia pravda*, January 4, 1929.
50. Ibid.
51. Oleshchuk, *Kto stroit tserkvi v SSSR*, p. 18.
52. I draw here on Hunt's use of Northrop Frye's categories as developed in *Anatomy of Criticism: Four Essays* (Princeton, N.J., 1957). See Hunt, *Politics, Culture and Class*, pp. 34–39.
53. *Stenograficheskii otchet vtorogo s"ezda*, p. 3.

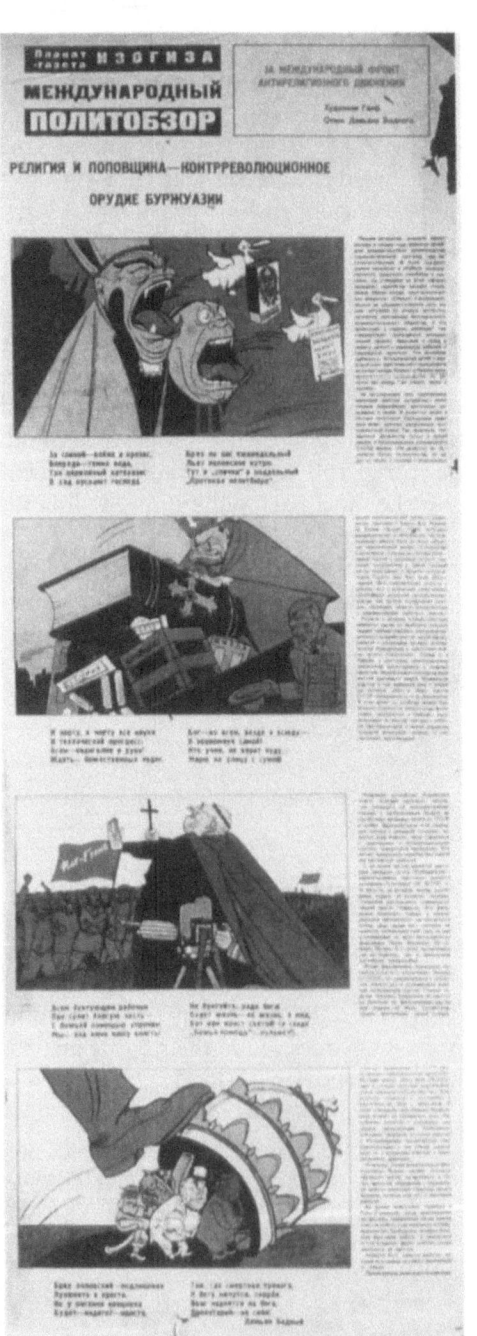

Fig. 14. "Religion and the *Popovshchina* Are the Counterrevolutionary Weapons of the Bourgeoisie." 1933. The cartoon at the top shows the pope and a priest with their "fangs" exposed. The second cartoon from the top shows a priest crushing school buildings with a giant Bible. In the third cartoon from the top, a priest urges workers not to rebel "for the sake of God." The last two stanzas of the verse that accompanies the cartoon at the bottom read: "The enemy places its hope in God. The proletariat—in itself." Courtesy, Poster Collection, Hoover Institution Archive, Stanford University. Poem by Demian Bednyi. Artist: Iurii Ganf.

this theme depicted on the cover of a 1929 issue of *Bezbozhnik u stanka*.) This held even for "superstition" (*sueverie*, most likely a reference to "pagan" elements of rural religiosity), which antireligious leaders and correspondents, like Plekhanov and Lenin, even routinely if not invariably conflated with religiosity itself.[54] Although religious ideas were said to be used by *all* religious activists in a factional politics that necessarily threatened the building of socialism, antireligious discourse typically portrayed the woman peasant (*krest'ianka*) as the preserver of religious belief in general, and especially of superstition.[55] Women played this role, as the story went, because they had urgent emotional needs—for comfort, for the allaying of anxiety—that only religiosity could satisfy. An important theme of antireligious discourse was in fact the playing off of a binary opposition between "female" religious superstition and "male" rationality or science (which antireligious propaganda itself was claimed to exemplify).[56] Because the role of women was to safeguard religious superstition, to be a male religious activist/"kulak"/ *tserkovnik* thus implicitly meant to be in the woman's domain, to be open to being controlled by women, a shameful fate worse almost than death for a male peasant. Religious activists thus threatened the very existence of patriarchal social relations. The implication was clear: to avoid the stigma of being emasculated, and to keep the patriarchy intact, the only option was to break with religion and join the antireligious campaign. By gendering the antireligious campaign, antireligious activists could threaten powerful negative incentives for not taking these steps and, in turn, for not extending the reach of the Soviet state into the Russian countryside.

Did the antireligious discourse of 1927–29 offer any positive incentives for converting to atheism and enlisting in the antireligious campaign? Given that antireligious leaders and correspondents tended to emphasize the power and aggressiveness of religious activity, especially in the realm of electoral politics, the answer seems to be no. In devising titles for their articles, provincial correspondents chose metaphors to convey their perception of the danger posed by religious activity, especially in the political realm. "Novo-Vysel'skie *Tserkovniki* Are Pressing the Buttons," the title of a 1928 article in a Saratov paper, portrayed religious villagers as strong and

54. At its May 23, 1929, meeting, the Commission on the Closing of Churches faulted local Party organizations for "underestimating the percentage of the believing population, [and] the extent of its enduring (*neizzhitie*) religious superstitions." See RTSKhIDNI, f. 89, op. 4, d. 125, l. 4. (The commission was composed of Krasikov, Tolmachov, and Tuchkov.)
55. For one of many examples, see *Bezbozhnik*, February 15, 1925, p. 4. ("At this point the woman peasant of the Soviet countryside is still full of belief in god, she is still very superstitious and dark [*sueveria i temna*].") See also Viola, "*Bab'i bunty*."
56. For some of the countless examples of antireligious propaganda being portrayed as "scientific," see *Stenograficheskii otchet vtorogo s"ezda*, pp. 10, 69, 82.

Fig. 15. 1929 cover of *Bezbozhnik u stanka* (The Godless at the workbench), showing a factory worker sweeping away God and religion, the tool of the "class enemies." Courtesy, Poster Collection, Hoover Institution Archive, Stanford University.

powerful.⁵⁷ Such titles emanated from the more general premise that religious activists were actually on the "attack," or were preparing for a "general attack."⁵⁸ While portraying religious activists as aggressive military conspirators, at the same time leaders and correspondents expressed a clear conviction that *bezbozhniki* could remedy particular problems besetting the antireligious campaign. In 1928, for example, a correspondent from the Lower Volga region wrote an article on the antireligious campaign titled "Enough Sleep and Indifference."⁵⁹ *Bezbozhniki*, he implied, indeed had the power to wake up and transform themselves into committed fighters on the "godless front." More boldly, and with article titles such as "Kulak Activity Will Be Smashed," they prophesied future victory in particular "battles" on the antireligious front, as well as the eventual triumph of the antireligious campaign over atheism and the kulak.⁶⁰ Correspondents developed a discourse of optimism and faith: despite temporary setbacks, the antireligious campaign was moving on schedule toward the creation of an atheist society.⁶¹ This optimism was also conveyed visually: a 1931 cover of *Bezbozhnik u stanka*, for example, showed a Red Army soldier spearing god as he marches swiftly along. Were antireligious correspondents and leaders simply succumbing to "black or white" thinking, oscillating erratically between the extremes of portraying *bezbozhniki* as either completely powerless over religious activity or capable of erasing problems simply by naming them and willing them to go away? Or was there an underlying unity to these ostensibly contradictory strains?

These contradictory strains in fact existed for good reasons. To be sure, with religious activists portrayed as dangerous aggressors, antireligious actions were in effect justified (at least on paper).⁶² But this discursive strategy had an even more vital function: to sound an alarm that would mobilize and sustain fighters on the antireligious front in a class war against the kulak-religious activist. And this was, in fact, a war that antireligious cadres were said to be sure to win. To understand this, we need to review the Marxist

57. "Novo-Vysel'skie tserkovniki nazhimaiut knopki," *Sovetskaia derevnia*, May 27, 1928, p. 2.
58. See, for example, Nikolai Ignat'ev, "Pered general'nym nastupleniem," *Povolzhskaia pravda*, November 4, 1928, p. 2.
59. "Dovol'no spiachki i blagodushestva," *Povolzhskaia pravda*, December 14, 1928.
60. B. Zernov, "Kulatskaia aktivnost' budet bita!" *Krest'ianskaia pravda*, December 31, 1928, p. 2.
61. "Ponemnogu osvobozhdaiutsia," *Bezbozhnik*, March 11, 1923, p. 4. See also A. M., "K bezbozhnikam potianula," ibid., May 24, 1925; "Na boga ne nadeiutsia," ibid., April 25, 1927; "Bezbozhniki organizuiutsia," *Sovetskaia derevnia*, January 22, 1928; "Organizatory novoi, sovetskoi derevni," *Krest'ianskaia pravda*, February 22, 1928; and "Bezbozhie rastet," *Izvestiia Saratovskogo soveta*, April 14, 1928.
62. Peris, "Storming the Heavens," p. 268.

script, as amended by Lenin. Marx had made capitalism not only the chronological precursor but also the womb, so to speak, of socialism; Lenin transferred this prediction to the Russian countryside, maintaining that a socialist countryside would be born from the victory of the poor and middle peasants over the kulak. In Lenin's revised script, the rise and fall of the kulak was a necessary precondition to the emergence of socialism in the countryside and in Russia at large. Thus Lenin accorded the kulak what we might call a "Janus-faced" identity and role: threatening because it meant capitalism still existed, the kulak's presence nevertheless consoled and soothed because only his obliteration would mean the triumph of socialism. The kulak was the welcome adversary. Antireligious propagandists, not to mention Party leaders, preserved the "deep structure" of this drama by recasting the kulak's religious identity and political activity as the threat to be overcome. They substituted alternative cultural loyalties and political autonomy for capitalist economic behavior. Moreover, antireligious discourse translated this "deep structure" into the idiom of gender by representing the kulak-religious activist as a dangerous woman (dangerous because autonomous) but also as a (peasant) woman who could and would be controlled by male rationality.

I have argued that many antireligious activists perceived, by the end of NEP, the involvement of religious villagers in Soviet institutions such as the village soviets and cooperatives as a quasi-demonic military conspiracy, powerful yet doomed because of its alleged femininity. It is important to review the steps of this conceptualization. First, antireligious correspondents, *bezbozhniki* in rural godless cells, and Party leaders alike all acquired extensive familiarity with the political activity of rural clergy and laity. These architects of a new Soviet society interpreted such factional politics as the shattering of a sacred Bolshevik consensus based (in theory) on the unanimous attainment of "proletarian consciousness."[63] As Sheila Fitzpatrick has noted, the Bolsheviks interpreted the latter to mean "active involvement in the building of a new socialist society, whether at the factory bench or elsewhere."[64]

The transformation of antireligious rhetoric reflected the "militarized socialist" perception that, as religious activists participated in rural politics, they had blocked the attainment of a consensus based on shared proletarian identity. *Tserkovnik* became a synonym for a factional politician of the rural world. As we have seen, however, *tserkovnik* was also a military category.

---

63. Sheila Fitzpatrick, "The Bolsheviks' Dilemma: The Class Issue in Party Politics and Culture," in *The Cultural Front: Power and Culture in Revolutionary Russia* (Ithaca, N.Y., 1992), p. 35.
64. Ibid.

Pursuit of "private" as opposed to "proletarian" interests made the *tserkovnik* a military enemy of the regime.⁶⁵ (By comparison, the rhetoric of French revolutionaries and of *déchristianisation* in particular seems to have lacked a military element.)⁶⁶ Dissolving the conceptual boundary between kulak and clergy or layperson, antireligious activists added a conspiratorial, demonic element to their image of the political activity of religious villagers. It did not matter that religious villagers perceived themselves as Orthodox (or, in the case of sectarians, at least as Christian) rather than demonic, as civil political actors rather than soldiers and generals, or, if military, then as embattled defenders rather than cunning aggressors. The "militarized socialists" clung to their image as if it were the Holy Grail. And during collectivization, as they warred on the rural religious community, they unleashed that image's brutal power.

---

65. Radical French revolutionaries perceived private interests as the "betrayal of a nation united." See Hunt, *Politics, Culture and Class*, pp. 44–46.

66. See Vovelle, *Religion et révolution*, and Hunt, "The Rhetoric of Revolution," in *Politics, Culture, and Class*.

Conclusion

During the NEP years, clergy and laity revived factional politics in the Soviet countryside. With religious life jeopardized by antireligious activity, by legal constraints on religious activity, and by the persecution of clergy and sometimes laity, religious villagers entered the realms of both traditional and Soviet politics. The struggle to generate the money to repair churches and support their priests, to secure the necessary permission to hold public rituals and build new churches, and even to take direct measures against the *bezbozhniki* (to name only a few crucial tasks) turned the attention of the rural religious toward the world of village politics. Clergy and laity continued to raise religious issues and even to pass measures on behalf of the religious community, at the village assembly, just as they had before the Revolution.[1] With increasing frequency over the course of the 1920s, they

---

1. Religious activists' use of the assembly to defend religious belief and practice thus calls for a recasting of our historiographical portrait of this key institution of rural life. While both Western and Soviet historians have described the village assembly's *administrative* eclipse of the village soviet during the NEP period, in the battle to decide the place of religion in rural life, villagers turned the assembly into a *political* institution. For a discussion of such scholarship, see the Introduction. Although the commune's village assembly may have been expected to fulfill state Interests in the prerevolutionary period, its religiously committed members used the institution to oppose the antireligious policy of the Soviet regime.

perceived the village soviet to be an institution useful for defending religious interests, hardly a consequence Party leaders had intended. For this reason they developed social relationships with its chairs and other officers, campaigned for their own candidates during elections, and often even held important positions within the institution. In short, like their counterparts in revolutionary France, they engaged in politics to maintain the possibility of being religious.[2] They even continued to do so during the assault on rural religious life that was so much a part of the *velikii perelom*.[3]

A constellation of factors made possible their political forays and successes. The most critical element was the weakness of the Communist antireligious campaign itself. Hampered by structural inadequacy, the indifference or incompetence of its cadres, and ineffective and even counterproductive tactics, the *bezbozhniki* failed to generate enough public support to destroy the foundations of religious life in the countryside. Even by the end of the decade, when Stalin abandoned NEP, the network of the League of the Godless had penetrated only weakly into the countryside, where 80 percent of the population still resided. The religious ties of some members of the Party and the Komsomol, teachers, and demobilized Red Army veterans dampened their commitment to antireligious activity and rendered them tolerant of clergy and laity's participation in politics. As certain *bezbozhniki* applied the military techniques of the Civil War to the antireligious campaign, they did not fulfill their dreams of annihilating religion instantaneously so much as catalyze clergy and laity to defend religious interests. Even those activities that did not display the influence of military training so obviously, such as antireligious debates and disputes, stimulated the villagers' interest in religious questions.

Although the new political, legal, and social contexts unquestionably inflicted severe blows on the rural religious community, at the same time they allowed its members to create some of their tools of survival. With the rural clergy riven and oppressed by financial hardship, persecution, factional struggles, and legal constraints, the laity had to take more responsibility for the life of the rural parish. This struggle for survival impelled laity to revitalize the church councils, which both clergy and laity had often disregarded during the period between their creation with the church reforms of 1864 and the Revolutions of 1917. With political upheaval chiseling away at the foundations of traditional rural society, clergy and especially laity experimented with new forms and content in theology, ritual, and religious organization.

2. See Desan, *Reclaiming the Sacred*.
3. See Viola, *Peasant Rebels under Stalin*; Young, "Rural Religion and Soviet Power," pp. 440–56; Richard L. Hernandez, "Rural Religion and Anti-Religious Activism, 1928–32" (Ph.D. diss., Stanford University, forthcoming).

As the example of the church council indicates, these innovations not only changed the complexion of religious life and the parish community but in certain cases proved to be essential tools for the political struggle of religious villagers. Personifying the influence of the tsarist social structure on the creation of Soviet society and rural politics, religious activists demonstrated how the adaptation of traditional theology, ritual, organizations—and their experience in the cultural skirmishes of the late tsarist period—could in turn contribute to the remaking of society and politics in the new revolutionary context.[4]

The varying impact of Soviet legislation on rural religious activity illustrates the inconsistent relationship between state and civil society during NEP. At times villagers structured religious activity along the guidelines of Soviet legislation but at other times they operated either in violation or ignorance of the imperatives of Soviet law.

When rural clergy and laity allowed legislation to structure religious life, they demonstrated the influence of the Soviet state on traditional rural society. Their struggle to keep the Church alive—to repair old churches, rebuild those razed by fire, and build new ones from scratch—dramatized the powerful impact of legislation on everyday religious life. Their actions reflected that impact in two ways. Legislation on the use of church buildings shaped the everyday lives of religious villagers by motivating them to repair churches, an enterprise that involved collecting money and generating public support. Perhaps even more important, the concrete provisions of the legislation, which obliged clergy and laity to deal with local Soviet officials and institutions to keep the church building in existence, threw them into contact with the day-to-day business of the Party *apparat*. Specific provisions of relevant legislation heightened religious villagers' appreciation of the importance of politics.

And yet, as we know, clergy and laity often ignored legal directives for the conduct of religious life. Well after the 1926 ban on discussing religious topics at the village assembly, they continued not only to bring religious matters up for debate but also to effect measures on behalf of the religious

---

4. I have encountered some historians of the Soviet period who assert that in 1928–29 the NKVD "collected fragmentary accounts and carefully selected petty details to paint a scene that would allow the use of extralegal means for eradicating religion." See Roslof, "Renovationist Movement," p. 265, whose argument is based to a significant extent on M. I. Odintsov, "Gosudarstvo i tserkov': Istoriia vzaimootnoshenii, 1937–1938 gg.," *Kul'tura i religiia* 11 (1991): 36–37. To perhaps belabor the obvious, there are several reasons why this argument is implausible. It is an example of *ex post facto* reasoning. As seen above, archival and press reports of such involvement long predated arrival of the *velikii perelom*; in fact, they dated from the very first days of Soviet power. Even in 1928–29, the Party leadership lacked the control over rural correspondents—and the cadres who wrote the archival reports cited above—that this explanation assumes.

community. As we saw in Chapter 8, sympathetic members of the village soviet often ignored the article of the 1918 "Instruction on the Implementation of the Decree on the Separation of Church and State" that forbade the performance of religious rituals and ceremonies, as well as the display of religious objects such as icons, in state and other public buildings. To generalize, religious villagers frequently ignored legislation that sought to repress their political activity, a pattern that showed how much the political defense of religious interests meant to them. When legislation defined segments of everyday religious life, such as requirements for the repair and building of new churches, they complied much more readily. Although this inconsistency may appear paradoxical to us at first glance, clergy and laity's anxiety about the very existence of religious life motivated their differing responses to both types of legislation. Religious villagers retained control over the law by choosing whether to obey, a dynamic that showed the central Party leadership (not to mention local officials) the limited and erratic influence of legislation.

Soviet leaders also realized that legislation had limited power to control religious activity because local officials inconsistently interpreted circulars, directives, and laws. As we saw in Chapter 8, the Instruction of 1918 and an NKVD circular of February 1925 required clergy and laity to obtain permission to hold public religious rituals from local organs of power. In practice, however, officers of the village soviet sometimes harnessed the power of their positions to facilitate public rituals. And as rural cadres, especially members of voting commissions, decided which clergy and laity to disenfranchise, they made choices that disturbed the central Party leadership and bureaucrats. Moscow tended to deal with its lack of control by producing more legislation, such as the 1925 revision of voting rights that required "documented information" from local political and administrative organs for disenfranchisement. As the application of this particular directive demonstrated, such increased legislative encroachment into rural political life only heightened the confusion of officials, once again confronting Moscow with its lack of control over the rural sphere.

The legal arena, however, comprised only one element of rural clergy and laity's broader confrontation of the Party with the limits of its power over the Soviet village of the NEP years. As villagers made religious concerns a part of Soviet political life, as they adopted Soviet political techniques (such as the use of the petition) and language (the constitutional guarantee of religious freedom), they demonstrated the adaptability of the bearers of traditional Russian culture to the new Soviet political context. Clergy and laity made rural religious life so tenacious not by cutting themselves off from the new political order but by exploring and harnessing its opportunities. They were the assimilators, not the assimilated. And as they brought the world of

Soviet politics within the orbit of everyday religious life, clergy and laity reminded central Party leaders and local cadres of their failure to build socialism in the countryside. They confronted the Party with the autonomy of the peasantry, the last independent social group in Soviet society.

In this sense clergy and laity's reintegration of religion and politics underscores why the Bukharin alternative, allowing Soviet villagers to "grow into" socialism, did not seem feasible to Stalin and other Party leaders. Despite the inroads made by the antireligious campaign in certain villages and among particular parts of the population, studying rural religious activity convinces us of how tightly villagers, even members of the Party and the Komsomol, clung to certain strands of traditional rural culture. These cultural commitments, which villagers' steadfast attachment to religious life exemplified so well, had political consequences. That religious activity changed the face of village politics makes Stalin's decision to proceed with collectivization more understandable.[5]

To be sure, by transforming rural politics, religious activists did not "cause" Stalin to embark on the path of collectivization. But we need to remember that the Party leadership's image of this development as a quasi-demonic military conspiracy, as transmitted by the rhetoric of Iaroslavskii and other antireligious activists, intensified its impatience with and disdain for NEP society. More specifically, religious villagers' factional politics reminded Stalin and his loyal coterie of all that the Party had *not* accomplished in the countryside: its failure to bring Soviet cultural norms to the village, its incapacity to imprint a Soviet ideological stamp on political institutions in the countryside, and, in general, its weak or nonexistent control over what Moshe Lewin has called the "rural nexus."[6] Religious activists,

---

5. Neither those historians who support the notion of "revolution from above" nor those who favor "revolution from below" regard culture as a motor of transformation in the *velikii perelom*. Those insisting on "revolution from above" regard Stalin and other leaders as responding to political concerns, sometimes thinly disguised as economic motivations, rather than cultural preoccupations. For the partisans of "revolution from below," the independent variable or catalyst was the upward social mobility of peasants and workers, with cultural transformation simply a consequence of that process. See, for example, Cohen, *Bukharin and the Bolshevik Revolution*, esp. pp. 270, 295, 312, 314, 322, 336–37, 359, 363, 385, and *Rethinking the Soviet Experience*, esp. p. 68; Robert C. Tucker, *Stalin in Power: The Revolution from Above, 1928–1941* (New York, 1990); Sheila Fitzpatrick, "Editor's Introduction," in Fitzpatrick, ed., *Cultural Revolution in Russia, 1928-1931* (Bloomington, Ind., 1984), p. 7; and Lewin, *Making of the Soviet System*.

6. Lewin, "Introduction: Social Crises and Political Structures in the USSR" in Lewin, *Making of the Soviet System*, p. 12. See, for example, Stalin's famous speech to business executives in February 1931: "No, we refuse to be beaten! One feature of the history of old Russia was the continual beating she suffered for falling behind, for her backwardness. She was beaten by the Mongol Khans. She was beaten by the Turkish beys. She was beaten by Swedish feudal

so often reflexively equated with the kulak, personified the backwardness that Stalin and his cadres had come to view as a secular Antichrist to be destroyed at any cost.[7] As clergy and laity outmaneuvered the *bezbozhniki* and shaped rural politics, they may have helped to convince Stalin and his supporters of the need for a profound and violent restructuring of the cultural, economic, and political life of the Soviet countryside.

This study, then, offers a rather ambiguous answer to one of the central questions posed in the Introduction: Did the involvement of religious activists contribute to the development of a vital "political society" in the countryside, or did it remain confined to the arena of administration? It would be too simple to conclude that religious activists revived rural politics during NEP and leave it at that. This is not to deny the resilience and the vitality of the political world they helped to revive and remake. Nor is it to deny that their political activism was the expression of a rural civil society that, for a time, eluded the reach of the state (such was not the case in urban Russia).[8] Their weapons of the weak were very powerful indeed. But their power was, after all, contingent in nature. The NEP era in the Russian countryside was the calm before the proverbial storm: the regime and its cadres grudgingly tolerated rural political autonomy, but they by no means gave it legal and ideological sanction. Rural politics existed because the regime, for the time being, lacked the institutional means—and the ideological fire—with which to cripple and eliminate it. In this lay the fragility of rural political autonomy. Moreover, religious activists and other villagers lacked the wherewithal to eliminate this insecurity.[9] To do so, they would have needed weapons—organization on a national scale, military might and the inclination to use it, to name only two possibilities—that they did not have and could not acquire.

Finally, what does the story told in this book contribute to the broader historiographical conversation on state-society relations during NEP? The politics of rural religious activists conforms to neither of the paradigms used to conceptualize the period of New Economic Policy, namely, "creeping totalitarianism" and "pluralism."[10] As shown by the regime's increasingly intense

---

lords. She was beaten by Polish and Lithuanian gentry. She was beaten by the British and French capitalists. She was beaten by Japanese barons. All beat her—for her backwardness: for military backwardness, for political backwardness, for industrial backwardness, for agricultural backwardness." *Problems of Leninism* (Moscow, 1940), p. 365.

7. Ibid.

8. This is the conclusion reached by Siegelbaum in *Soviet State and Society*. See p. 84.

9. I adapt here a point made by Siegelbaum in *Soviet State and Society*, p. 51: characterizing civil society in tsarist Russia as "stunted and insecure," he concludes that no "means for overcoming this insecurity" existed.

10. The basic "pluralist" manifesto is Stephen Cohen, *Rethinking the Soviet Experience*.

efforts to control rural politics and especially the politics of religious activists after 1924, politics was not a sphere that the regime decided to grant autonomy, but one that increasingly became the object of its hegemonic designs. It was not to be part of the allegedly pluralist social, economic, and cultural sectors of NEP society.

Nor does this study, when viewed in the context of ten years of NEP historiography, support the "creeping totalitarian" model, if we conceive of that model as pointing to both the regime's intended and actual control of society. For the more the state tried to intervene in rural politics and other spheres of society by championing new and already existing institutional "forms" (e.g., the village soviet), the more religious activists and other members of NEP society, such as the NEPmen, resisted those claims through those very institutional forms.[11] In response to the Party's increased efforts to control the rural political process in 1926–28, religious activists innovated in the political forms they themselves used. The more the Party and its cadres tried to control the political life of the village soviets, the more religious activists drew on elements of religious life—for example, religious ritual—to resist the claims of the state. Thus, the very institutional "forms" championed by the regime to promote socialist consciousness (or, stated in negative terms, to eliminate bourgeois hegemony) in this case proved to be the institutional forum in which religious activists resisted the claims of the state.

In fact, the story of religious activists' political resistance in the village soviets has deep structural parallels in other areas of NEP "society." To give just one example, as the Party took various repressive measures against the NEPmen in 1926–27, so too did the latter "capture" the *arteli*, which the regime regarded as part of the socialist sector, for their own purposes.[12] The NEPmen's creation of false *arteli*, which disguised the capitalist activity that went on inside them, was analogous to religious activists' "capture" of the village soviets. This is not to claim that religious activists were as successful in colonizing the soviets as the NEPmen were in colonizing the artels. Religious activists were not invariably in the majority in the leadership of village soviets. Even when they were, they were not necessarily—or even usually—exercising power in the name of the entire village. Even when that "best-case" scenario did prevail, their power was open to challenge by villagers with other political allegiances. These qualifiers notwithstanding, the important continuity remains: when the regime intensified, after 1924–25, its championing of "socialist" institutional forms, it ironically catalyzed the expression of prerevolutionary identities as a means of resistance to the

---

11. Alan M. Ball, *Russia's Last Capitalists: The Nepmen, 1921–29* (Berkeley, Calif., 1987).
12. The *artel* was a producers' collective. See Ball, *Russia's Last Capitalists*, pp. 141–44.

state's claims. (An important parallel can be drawn to the tsarist regime's cameralist efforts, especially in reshaping popular piety, and its unintended eliciting of political resistance in which "local" religion was a key mobilizing lever.) By 1928–29, religious activists had presented the regime and its cadres with a stark choice: *either* give up its agenda for political, economic, and cultural transformation *or* use militaristic and violent means to achieve that goal. Taking the latter course meant expending greater resources of various kinds. Had this great expenditure of resources produced political and economic equilibrium, one can viably argue that all would have been well. But such was not the case. For when the Soviet state violently assaulted an insecure rural civil society—when it implemented forced collectivization—it inadvertently saddled itself with long-term economic and political vulnerability. It brought on, of course, the dire economic and political consequences of the chronic underproductivity of collectivized agriculture.

This is the ultimate sense in which the regime's championing of the village soviets was one chapter in a fascinating yet repetitive story: the "perverse counterproductivity" of the power of the Soviet state.[13] In fact, this dynamic bears deep structural affinities to the way in which the regime's promotion of ethnic *forms* of identity ultimately resulted in the very sources of political resistance (and in the construction of identities) that proved fatal to the Soviet regime.[14] When placed in this context, state-society relations during NEP appear representative of, rather than discontinuous with, the historical trajectory of the Soviet experience and the dynamics that brought about the end of the Soviet experiment.[15]

---

13. On the "perverse counterproductivity" of state mobilization, see also Orlando Figes, "Stalin's Oblomovs," *Times Literary Supplement*, January 13, 1995, p. 26. I thank Frank Conlon for bringing this review to my attention.

14. Ronald G. Suny, *Revenge of the Past: Nationalism, Revolution, and the Collapse of the Soviet Union* (Stanford, Calif., 1993); Yuri Slezkine, "The USSR as a Communal Apartment or How a Socialist State Promoted Ethnic Particularism," *Slavic Review* 53 (Summer 1994): 414–53.

15. For an exposition of the opposite view (i.e., NEP as an "aberration" in Soviet history), see, inter alia, Malia, *Soviet Tragedy*, p. 48. Although he notes the oscillation between the NEP and War Communist models throughout the Soviet period, he does not give a precise elaboration of the processes that caused it. His explanation amounts to indicting Communism's "genetic code" (the ideological imperatives of the "socialist choice") for its "too relent[less] demands" on the Soviet population. See pp. 495–96.

Select Bibliography

ARCHIVAL SOURCES

Archives in Russia

Central State Archive of the October Revolution, Moscow (TsGAOR SSSR).
 fond 5462. TsK soiuza rabprosa.
Central State Archive of the October Revolution, Leningrad (TsGAOR Leningrada).
 fond 566. Ispolnitel'nyi komitet Novinskogo volostnogo soveta rabochikh, krest'ianskikh i krasnoarmeiskikh deputatov Tikhvinskogo uezda Cherepovetskoi gubernii (Otdel narodnogo obrazovaniia).
 fond 596. Moloskovshchkii volostnoi ispolnitel'nyi komitet, Kingiseppskogo uezda Leningradskoi gubernii.
 fond 748. Kapshinskii volostnoi ispolnitel'nyi komitet soveta, Tikhvinskogo uezda Pskovskoi gubernii.
 fond 1010. Otdel upravleniia Novoladozhskogo uezdnogo ispolkoma.
 fond 2552. Leningradskii gubernskii otdel narodnogo obrazovaniia.
 fond 3106. Protokoly sobranii grazhdan i studencheskikh konferentsii, 1925–25.
 fond 6307. Leningradskii oblastnoi komitet profsoiuza rabotnikov prosveshcheniia.
 fond 7576. Kingiseppskii uezdnyi politprosvet.
Rossiiskii tsentr khraneniia i izucheniia dokumentov noveishei istorii (RTsKhIDNI) [Russian Center for the Preservation and Study of Documents (Records) of Modern History, formerly the Central Party Archive of the Institute of the Theory and History of Socialism of the CPSU Central Committee].
 fond 89. Emel'ian Iaroslavskii.
Russian State Historical Archive (RGIA).
 fond 831. Kantseliariia Patriarkha Tikhona.

Archives Outside Russia

Bakhmeteff Archive of Russian History and Culture, Columbia University.
 Lodyzhenskii Papers. Petrus (pseudonym). "Religious Communes in the USSR." Unpublished manuscript by émigré.
Catholic University of America. John Brophy Papers.
Hoover Institution Archive, Stanford University. Soviet Poster Collection. Wrangel Collection.

282   Select Bibliography

Keston College Archives. Oxford, England. "Iz zhizni odnogo sviashchennika." Part 1, "Ostraia luka."
Library of Congress, Washington, D.C., Manuscript Division. Alexis Babine Papers.
Smolensk Party Archive 1917–41. The National Archives, Washington, D.C.

INTERVIEWS

Mikhail Shakhnovich, October 2, 1987. Leningrad.

NEWSPAPERS AND PERIODICALS

Antireligioznik. Moscow.
Bednota. Moscow.
Bezbozhnik (journal). Moscow.
Bezbozhnik (newspaper). Moscow.
Bogoslovskii vestnik.
Bol'shevik. Moscow.
Derevenskaia kommuna.
Derevenskaia pravda. Petrograd.
Derevenskii iurist. Moscow.
Etnografiia. Moscow.
Golos zhivoi very (dvukhnedel'nyi Tambovskii eparkhial'nyi zhurnal). Tambov.
Iaroslavskie eparkhial'nye vedomosti.
Izvestiia. Moscow.
Izvestiia Atkarskogo uezdnogo ispolkoma. Atkarsk.
Izvestiia Kurskogo gubernskogo obshchestva kraevedeniia. Kursk.
Izvestiia Saratovskogo soveta rabochikh i krest'ianskikh deputatov. Saratov.
Izvlecheniia iz vsepoddaneishego otcheta ober-prokurora sviateishego sinoda po vedomstvu pravoslavnogo ispovedaniia (1880–84). Renamed in 1885 *Vsepoddaneishii otchet ober-prokurora sviateishego sinoda po vedomstvu pravoslavnogo ispovedaniia* (1885–1917). St. Petersburg.
Khristianin. Kostromskie eparkhial'nye vedomosti. Kostroma.
Krasnyi arkhiv.
Krasnaia niva. Moscow.
Krasnaia nov'. Moscow.
Krasnye rezervy. Krest'ianka. Moscow.
Krest'ianskaia pravda. Leningrad.
Krest'ianskii iurist. Moscow.
Kurskii krai.
Missionerskoe obozrenie.
Nauka i religiia. Moscow.
Novaia zhizn'.
Petrovskaia kommuna. Petrovsk.

Povolzhskaia pravda. Saratov.
Poznai svoi krai. Izdanie Pskovskogo obshchestva kraevedeniia. Pskov.
Pravda. Moscow.
Pskovskii nabat'. Pskov.
Put'. Paris.
Saratovskie eparkhial'nye vedomosti. Saratov.
Serp i molot. Serdobsk.
Sovetskaia derevnia. Saratov.
Sovetskoe gosudarstvo. Moscow.
Tambovskaia pravda. Tambov.
Tambovskie eparkhial'nye vedomosti. Tambov.
Trudy obshchestva istorii arkheologii i etnografii pri Saratovskom universitete. Saratov.
Tserkovnyi vestnik.
Vestnik Riazanskikh kraevedov. Riazan.
Vestnik russkogo khristi anskogo dvizheniia. Paris.
Vestnik sviashchennogo Sinoda.
Vlast' sovetov. Moscow.
Zhizn' iskusstva. Moscow.

CONTEMPORARY RUSSIAN-LANGUAGE SOURCES

Amosov, N. *Kolkhoznyi stroi i religiia*. Moscow, 1930.
Angarov, A. *Klassovaia bor'ba v sovetskoi derevne*. Moscow, 1929.
Antireligioznyi sbornik. Moscow, 1940.
Astaf'ev, G. *Pochemu liudi veriat v boga*. Bezbozhnik, 1930.
Aver'ev, V. N., ed. *Komitety bednoty: sbornik materialov*. 3 vols. Moscow-Leningrad, 1933.
Batalin, A. B. *Doklady o tserkovnoi zhizni*. Kaluga, 1927.
Bezbozhniki sotsialisticheskoi derevni navstrechu 4-mu godu piatiletki; antirozhdestvenskiis bornik. Edited by M. Flerov. Moscow, 1931.
Bliakhin, P. *Kto i zachem stroit tserkvi*. Moscow, 1929.
Bogoraz, V. G. *Khristianstvo v svete etnografii*. Moscow-Leningrad, 1928.
Bogovoi, Ivan. *Chto nuzhno znat' k perevyboram sovetov (k kampanii 1927 goda)*. Moscow, 1927.
Boldryev, M. F. *Novaia oblast'*. Stalingrad, 1928.
Bol'shakov, A. M. *Sovetskaia derevnia 1917–25 gg. Ekonomika i byt*. Leningrad, 1928.
———. *Vvedenie v kraevedenie*. Leningrad, 1929.
Bonch-Bruevich, V. D. *Zhivaia tserkov' i proletariat*. 4th ed. Moscow, 1929.
Brandt, A. *Gatchina: antireligioznaia vystavka dvortsa muzeia*. Moscow-Leningrad, 1931.
Bukharin, N. *O rabkore i sel'kore*. Moscow, 1925.
Burkin, N. *Monastyri v Rossii, ikh eksploatatorskaia i kontrrevoliutsionnaia rol'*. Moscow, 1931.
Burov, Ia. I. *Rabochie obshchestva dlia shefstva nad derevnei*. Edited by V. Karpinskii. Moscow, 1925.

Chetyre goda raboty: otchet II-mu vsesoiuznomu s"ezdu bezbozhnikov. Moscow, 1929.
Chugunov, S. I. *Chto pokazali poslednie perevybory sovetov*. Moscow-Leningrad, 1926.
Druzhinin, V. G. *Po ochagam sektantskogo mrakobesiia*. Moscow, 1928.
———. *Molokane*. Leningrad, 1930.
Eliashevich, I. *S krestom i evangeliem protiv kolkhozov*. Leningrad, 1930.
Enisherlov, M., ed. *Voinstvuiushchee bezbozhie v SSSR za 15 let*. Moscow, 1932.
Evdokimov, A. *V bor'be za molodezh': klassovaia bor'ba v derevne*. Leningrad, 1929.
Fenomenov, M. I. *Sovremennaia derevnia: opyt kraevedcheskogo obsledovaniia odnoi derevni. (Derevnia Gadyshi, Valdaiskogo uezda, Novgorodskoi gubernii)*. 2 vols. Leningrad, 1925.
Flerov, I. *Voinstvuiushchee bezbozhie v shkole*. Moscow, 1933.
Garkavenko, F., ed. *O religii i tserkvi: sbornik dokumentov*. Moscow, 1965.
Gurvich, G. S. *Istoriia sovetskoi konstitutsii*. Moscow, 1923.
———. *Osnovy sovetskoi konstitutsii*. Moscow, 1926.
Gurskaia, I. "Tserkov' i reforma 1861 g." *Krasnyi arkhiv* 52 (1983).
Iakovlev, Ia. A. *Derevnia kak ona est'*. Moscow-Leningrad, 1925.
Iaroslavskii, E. *Protiv religii i tserkvi*. 3 vols. Moscow, 1932–35.
———. *Razvernutym frontom. O zadachakh i metodakh antireligioznoi propagandy. (Doklad na vtorom vsesoiuznom s"ezde soiuza bezbozhnikov)*. Moscow, 1929.
———. *Religiia i R.K.P.* Moscow, 1925.
Izbiratel'naia kampaniia po R.S.F.S.R. v 1923 godu. K XI vserossiiskomu s"ezdu sovetov R.S.F.S.R. Moscow, 1924.
Izvlecheniia iz vsepoddaneishego ober-prokurora Sv. Sinoda po vedomstvu pravoslavnogo ispovedaniia. St. Petersburg, 1866–84. New series title: *Vsepoddanneishii otchet oberprokurora Sv. Sinoda po vedomstvu pravoslavnogo ispovedaniia*. St. Petersburg, 1886–1915.
Kak stroit' soiuz bezbozhnikov. Moscow, 1927.
Kaminskii, Grigorii N. *Kolkhoznoe stroitel'stvo v Moskovskoi oblasti*. Moscow, 1931.
Kavraiskii, B., and I. Khamarmer. *Sel'sovet i sotsialisticheskoe pereustroistvo derevni*. Novosibirsk, 1930.
Kniazev, M. *Kak kulaki i popy borolis' s kolkhozom*. Moscow-Leningrad, 1930.
Kolesnikov, A. N., and I. V. Murugov. *Apparat nizovykh sovetskhikh organov*. Moscow, 1926.
Kochin, N. I. *Pochin pochinok; ocherk o kolkhoze-gigante imeni Stalina*. Moscow, 1931.
Komsomol'skoe rozhdestvo; sbornik pod obshchei red. TsK RKSM. Moscow, 1923.
Kooperatsiia v 1923–24 godu i v 1924–25 godu. Moscow, 1928.
KPSS v rezoliutsiiakh i resheniiakh s"ezdov, konferentsii i plenumov TsK. Moscow, 1970.
Krainiuk, Z. *Piatiletka i religiia*. Moscow, 1931.
Krivtsov, S. S., ed. *Leningradskaia oblast' i Karel'skaia SSSR*. Moscow-Leningrad, 1928.
Lenin, V. I. *Polnoe sobranie sochinenii*. 55 vols. Moscow, 1971–75.
Lukachevskii, A. T. *Uchebnik dlia rabochikh antireligioznykh kruzhkov*. Moscow, 1931.

———, ed. *Antipaskhal'nyi sbornik*. Moscow, 1929.
———. *Izuchenie sotsial'nykh kornei religii SSSR*. Moscow, 1930.
Lunacharsky, A. *Religion and Socialism*. St. Petersburg, 1908–11.
Luzhin, A., and M. Rezunov, eds. *Nizovoi sovetskii apparat (sel'sovet i volispolkom)*. Moscow, 1929.
———. *Ot volosti—k raionu (reorganizatsiia volosti v RSFSR)*. Moscow, 1929.
Mariinskii, A. P. *Protiv popov i sektantov*. Moscow-Leningrad, 1929.
Martsinkovskii, V. F. *Zapiski veruiushchego. Iz istorii religioznogo dvizheniia v Sovetskoi Rossii (1917–1923)*. Prague, 1929.
Matorin, N. *Religiia i bor'ba s neiu v severnom krae*. Leningrad, 1930.
Mestnyi biudzhet sovetov Smolenskoi gubernii na 1925–26 god. Smolensk, 1925.
Miliutin, N. A. *Razvitie krest'ianskoi vzaimopomoshchi*. Moscow, 1924.
Miliutin, V. P., ed. *Kooperatsiia v SSSR za desiat' let*. Moscow, 1928.
Mitrofanov, A. Kh. *O chistke i proverke riadov VKP(b)*. Moscow, 1929.
Murin, V. A. *Byt i nravy derevenskoi molodezhi*. [Moscow], 1926.
Murugov, I., and A. Kolesnikov. *Apparat nizovykh sovetskikh organov. Po materialam obsledovaniia NK RKI RSFSR 1925 g.* Moscow-Leningrad, 1925.
Obichkin, G. D. *Kto skryvaetsia za religiei; kontrrevoliutsiia pod flagom religii*. Moscow, 1930.
Obzor khoziaistva i kul'tury Saratovskogo okruga. Edited by A. Ia. Grinshteina and G. A. Timrota. Saratov, 1929.
Okninsky, A. *Dva goda sredi krest'ian: vidennoe, slyshannoe, perezhitoe v Tambovskoi gubernii s noiabria 1918 goda do noiabria 1920 goda*. Riga, 1936. Reprint. Newtonville, Mass., 1986.
Oleshchuk, F. *Kto stroit tserkvi v SSSR*. Moscow-Leningrad, 1929.
———. *XVII s"ezd VKP(b) i zadachi antireligioznoi raboty*. Moscow, 1934.
———. *Shkola i vospitanie aktivnykh ateistov*. Moscow, 1928.
Orleanskii, N. *Zakon o religioznykh ob"edineniakh*. Moscow, 1930.
Papkov, A. A. *Tserkovnye bratstva. Kratkii statisticheskii ocherk o polozhenii tserkovnykh bratstv k nachalu 1893 godu*. St. Petersburg, 1893.
Pashukanis, E., ed. *15 let sovetskogo stroitel'stva*. Moscow, 1932.
Perepiska sekretariata TsK RKP(b) s mestnymi partiinymi organizatsiiami. Moscow, 1957–72.
Pervyi Tambovskii s"ezd krest'ianok-obshchestvennits. Tambov, 1925.
Polozhenie o raionnykh i gorodskikh sovetakh SVB. Moscow, 1933.
Prot. M. L—v. *Tserkovno-prikhodskaia zhizn' v 1896 godu*. Tobol'sk, 1897.
Programma po obsledovaniiu religiozno-bytovoi zhizni mestnogo naseleniia. Pereslavl'-Zalesskii, 1930.
Prosveshchenets na antireligioznom fronte. Moscow, 1929.
Protokoly eparkhial'nogo sobraniia dukhovenstva i mirian Tambovskoi eparkhii maiskoi sessii. Tambov, 1918.
Putintsev, F. *Vybory v sovety i razoblachenie popovshchiny*. Moscow, 1937.
Rozanov, Aleksandr. *Zapiski sel'skogo sviashchennika. Byt i nuzhdy pravoslavnogo dukhovenstva*. St. Petersburg, 1882.
Rylkin, G., and V. Truntaev. *Iacheika i sovety v derevne*. Edited by Ia. Iakovlev and M. Khataevich. Moscow-Leningrad, 1925.
Sbornik materialov i statei po kooperatsii i posobie dlia agitatsionno-politicheskikh kooperativnykh kursov. Moscow, 1921.
Sel'sovety i volispolkomy. Sbornik statei i materialov. Edited by Ia. Iakovlev and M. Khataevich. Moscow-Leningrad, 1925.

Shafir, Ia. *Gazeta i derevnia.* Moscow, 1923.
Shakhnovich, M. *Zapiski bezbozhnika.* Leningrad, 1933.
Sobranie uzakonenii i rasporiazhenii rabochego i krest'ianskogo pravitel'stva. Moscow, 1918.
Sostoianie sel'skogo khoziaistva i rabota v derevne na Urale. Sverdlovsk, 1929.
Soveshchanie po voprosam sovetskogo stroitel'stva 1925 g. Moscow, 1925.
Stalin, V. I. *Problems of Leninism.* Moscow, 1940.
Stenograficheskii otchet vtorogo vsesoiuznogo s"ezda soiuza voinstvuiushchikh bezbozhnikov. Moscow, 1930.
Tan-Bogoraz, V. G., ed. *Revoliutsiia v derevne (ocherki).* Vol. 1. Moscow, 1924.
Toshchakov, N. A. *Kolkhoz "Volia" Prisheksninskogo raiona, Leningradskoi oblast': zapiski bor'byi pobed.* Moscow-Leningrad, 1931.
Trophimus, Father. "Russian Religion on the Defensive." *Slavonic and East European Review* 12 (July 1933).
Tseli i zadachi soiuza bezbozhnikov. Ul'ianovsk, 1928.
Ulasevich, Viktoriia, ed. *Zhenshchina v kolkhoze.* Moscow, 1930.
Ustav soiuza bezbozhnikov SSSR. Moscow, 1925.
Virganskii, V. *Sel'iacheika, sel'sovet i krest'ianstvo.* Leningrad, 1925.
Voinstvuiushchee bezbozhie za 15 let: sbornik. Moscow, 1932.
Vsesoiuznoe soveshchanie po voprosam perevybornoi kampanii sovetov 1929 goda. Stenograficheskii otchet. Moscow, 1928.
Zybkovets, V. *Bezbozhniki i sotsialisticheskaia perestroika derevni.* Moscow, 1930.

RUSSIAN LANGUAGE SOURCES SINCE 1945

Abramov, V. A., and T. K. Kocharli. "Ob oshibkakh v odnoi knige (pis'mo k redaktsiiu)." *Voprosy istorii KPSS* 5 (1975).
Alekseev, V. A. *Illiuzii i dogmy.* Moscow, 1991.
———. *Shturm nebes otmeniaetsia?* Moscow, 1992.
Andreeva, M. S. "Agitatsionno-propagandistskaia i politiko-prosvetitel'nia rabota Kommunisticheskoi partii v vosstanovitel'nyi period (1921–1925)." Doctoral dissertation, Moscow University, 1968.
Arutunian, Iu. V. "Iz opyta sotsiologicheskikh obsledovanii sela v dvadsatye gody." *Voprosy istorii KPSS* 3 (March 1966).
Baranov, Iu. D., Vladimir B. Ostrovskii, Iurii B. Suslov, Georgii A. Malinin, and Z. E. Gusakova. *Kul'turnoe stroitel'stvo v Saratovskom povolzh'e.* Vol. 1, *1917–1928 gg.* Saratov, 1985.
Belogurov, M. G. "Istochniki ob organizatsii i sostave sel'skikh sovetov RSFSR v period vosstanovleniia narodnogo khoziaistva, 1921–1925." Candidate dissertation, Moscow University, 1978.
Birger, L. I. *Kul'turnoe stroitel'stvo na srednei Volge v gody pervoi piatiletki.* Synopsis of dissertation by Birger. Kuibyshev University, 1966.
Bonch-Bruevich, V. D. *Izbrannye sochineniia.* Vols. 1 and 2. Moscow, 1959.
Dal', V. I. *Poslovitsy russkogo naroda.* Moscow, 1957.
Danilov, V. P. "Nekotorye itogi nauchnoi sessii po istorii sovetskoi derevni." *Voprosy istorii* 2 (1962).

———. "Sel'skoe naselenie soiuza SSR nakanune kollektivizatsii (po dannym obshchenarodnoi perepisi 17 dekabria 1926 g.)." *Istoricheskie zapiski* 74 (1973).
———. *Sovetskaia dokolkhoznaia derevnia: sotsial'naia struktura, sotsial'nye otnoshenie.* Moscow, 1979.
Danilov, V. P., and S. A. Krasilnikov, eds. *N. I. Bukharin.* Novosibirsk, 1990.
Dunaev, Vladimir Nikolaevich. "Sotsial'no-politicheskaia orientatsiia i deistviia pravoslavnykh tserkovnikov v period podgotovki i provedeniia velikoi oktiabr'skoi sotsialisticheskoi revoliutsii v pervye gody sovetskoi vlasti (1917–1922). Na materialakh Voronezhskoi Kurskoi, i Tambovskoi gubernii." Candidate dissertation, Voronezh University, 1972.
Eingorn, I. D. "Reaktsionnaia rol' dukhovenstva i tserkovnykh organizatsii. Zapadnaia Sibir' nakanune perioda massovoi kollektivizatsii." Synopsis of doctoral dissertation by Eingorn. Tomsk University, 1966.
E. L. *Episkopy ispovedniki.* San Francisco, 1971.
Emeliakh, L. I. *Istoricheskie predposylki preodoleniia religii v sovetskoi derevne (Sekuliarizatsiia derevni nakanune Velikogo Oktiabria).* Leningrad, 1975.
Ermakov, V. T. "Sovetskaia kul'tura kak predmet istoricheskogo obsledovaniia." *Voprosy istorii* 11 (1973).
Fain, L. E. *Istoriia razrabotka V. I. Leninym kooperativnogo plana.* Moscow, 1970.
Iablokov, I. N. *Sotsiologiia religii.* Moscow, 1979.
Iudin, V. D. "Deiatel'nost' partiinoi organizatsii TsChO po ateisticheskomu vospitaniiu naseleniia v 1928–34 gg." Synopsis of doctoral dissertation, Voronezh University, 1970.
Iz istorii partiinogo stroitel'stva (Na materialakh partiinykh organizatsii nizhnego povolzh'ia). Saratov, 1975.
Karevskii, F. A. "Likvidatsiia kulachestva kak klassa v srednem povolzh'e." *Istoricheskie zapiski* 80 (1967).
Kartashev, A. V. *Ocherki po istorii russkoi tserkvi.* Vol. 2. Moscow, 1991.
Kirichenko, M. G. *Svoboda sovesti v SSSR.* Moscow, 1985.
Klibanov, A. I. *Religioznoe sektantstvo i sovremennost'.* Moscow, 1969.
———. *Religioznoe sektantstvo v proshlom i nastoiashchem.* Moscow, 1973.
Kollektivizatsiia sel'skogo khoziaistva v srednem povolzh'e, 1927–37 gg. Dokumenty i materialy. Kuibyshev, 1970.
Konovalov, V. N. "Problemy teorii i praktiki ateizma v SSSR v 1920–1930 gg." Candidate dissertation, Moscow University, 1968.
Kozlov, V. A. *Kul'turnaia revoliutsiia i krest'ianstvo, 1921–27 (po materialam Evropeiskoi chasti RSFSR).* Moscow, 1983.
Krasikov, N. P., ed. *Po etapam razvitiia ateizma.* Leningrad, 1967.
Krasnov-Levitin, A. E. *Likhie gody, 1925–1941. Vospominaniia.* Paris, 1977.
Kukushkin, Iu. S. *Sel'skie sovety i klassovaia bor'ba v derevne.* Moscow, 1968.
———. "Sovety v vosstanovitel'nyi period." *Voprosy istorii* 3 (March 1966): 43–52.
Leninskii komsomol: ocherki po istorii VLKSM (1918–1941 gg.). Moscow, 1969.
Levitin, Anatolii, and Vadim Shavrov. *Ocherki po istorii russkoi tserkovnoi smuty.* 3 vols. Zürich, 1978.
Makeikina, P. "Kul'turnoe stroitel'stvo v Novgorodskoi gubernii v 1921–27 gg." Synopsis of doctoral dissertation by Makeikina. Leningrad University, 1972.
Malazkova, A. I. *Dukhovnye khristiane.* Moscow, 1970.

Morozov, L. F. *Ot kooperatsii burzhuaznoi k kooperatsii sotsialisticheskoi.* Moscow, 1969.
Ocherki istorii Leningradskoi organizatsii VLKSM. Leningrad, 1969.
Odintsov, M. I. "Gosudarstvo i tserkov': istoriia vzaimootnoshenii, 1927-1938 gg." *Kul'tura i religiia* 11 (1991).
Opalikhin, F. I. *Bor'ba kommunisticheskoi partii za provedenie v zhizn' politiki ozhivleniia sovetov v derevne.* Synopsis of doctoral dissertation by Opalikhin. Leningrad University, 1953.
Parkhomenko, M. M. "Klassovaia bor'ba v Checheno-Ingushetii v pervye gody novoi ekonomicheskoi politiki (1921-25 gg.)." Synopsis of doctoral dissertation by Parkhomenko. Leningrad University, 1975.
Persits, M. N. *Otdelenie tserkvi ot gosudarstva i shkoly ot tserkvi v SSSR.* Moscow, 1958.
Plaskin, R. Iu. *Krakh tserkovnoi kontrrevoliutsii, 1917-1923 gg.* Moscow, 1968.
Plekhanov, G. V. *O religii i tserkvi: izbrannye proizvedeniia.* Moscow, 1957.
Regel'son, Lev. *Tragediia russkoi tserkvi, 1917-1945.* Paris, 1977.
Saratovskaia partiinaia organizatsiia v gody vosstanovleniia narodnogo khoziaistva. Dokumenty i materialy, 1921-1925 gg. Saratov, 1960.
Savel'ev, S. N. *Emel'ian Iaroslavskii-propagandist marksistskogo ateizma.* Leningrad, 1976.
Selivanov, A. M. *Organizatsionnoe upkreplenie sovetskogo gosudarstvennogo apparata v 1921-1925 gg. (na materialakh verkhnei Volgi).* Synopsis of doctoral dissertation by Selivanov. Tomsk University, 1975.
Seregina, Inna Gennad'evna. "Sotsial'no-ekonomicheskoe razvitie derevni tsentral'nogo promyshlennogo raiona v 1921-25 gg. i ego regulirovanie sovetskim gosudarstvom." Synopsis of candidate dissertation by Seregina. Kalinin University, 1982.
Shakhnovich, M. *Lenin i problemy ateizma.* Moscow, 1961.
Skvortsov-Stepanov, I. I. *Izbrannye ateisticheskie proizvedeniia.* Moscow, 1959.
Sheinman, M. *Khristianskii sotsializm.* Moscow, 1969.
Tepliakov, M. K. "Problemy ateisticheskogo vospitaniia i preodoleniia religii v prakticheskoi deiatel'nosti Voronezhskoi organizatsii KPSS (1917-1970 gg.)." Doctoral dissertation, Voronezh University, 1972.
Trifonov, Ivan Iakovlevich. *Klassy i klassovaia bor'ba v SSSR v nachale NEPa, 1921-23 gg.* Leningrad, 1964.
——. *Likvidatsiia ekspluatatorskikh klassov v SSSR.* Moscow, 1975.
——. *Ocherki istorii klassovoi bor'by v SSSR v gody NEPa, 1921-1937.* Moscow, 1960.
Veshchikov, A. "Etapy bol'shogo puti." *Nauka i religiia* 11 (November 1962).
Vorontsov, G. V. *Leninskaia programma ateisticheskogo vospitaniia v deistvii (1917-1937 gg.).* Leningrad, 1973.
Zabylin, M. *Russkii narod: Ego obychai, obriady, predaniia, sueveriia i poeziia.* 1880. Reprint. Moscow, 1990.
Zaitsev, Kirill (Sviashchennik). *Pravoslavnaia tserkov' v sovetskoi Rossii.* Part 1. Shanghai, 1947.

SECONDARY SOURCES IN LANGUAGES OTHER THAN RUSSIAN

Alavi, Hamza. "Village Factions." In *Peasants and Peasant Societies: Selected Readings*, ed. Teodor Shanin. New York, 1987.
Altrichter, Helmut. *Die Bauern von Tver: Vom Leben auf dem russischen Dorfe zwischen Revolution und Kollektivierung*. Munich, 1984.
——. "Insoluble Conflicts: Village Life Between Revolution and Collectivization." In *Russia in the Era of NEP: Explorations in Soviet Society and Culture*, ed. Sheila Fitzpatrick, Alexander Rabinowitch, and Richard Stites. Bloomington, Ind., 1991.
Anderson, Paul B. *People, Church, and State in Modern Russia*. New York, 1944.
Ascher, Abraham. *The Revolution of 1905: Authority Restored*. Stanford, Calif., 1992.
Atkinson, Dorothy. *The End of the Russian Land Commune, 1905–30*. Stanford, Calif., 1983.
Avrich, Paul. *Russian Rebels, 1600–1800*. New York, 1982.
Bailes, Kendall. *Technology and Society under Lenin and Stalin: Origins of the Soviet Technical Intelligentsia*. Princeton, N.J., 1978.
Ball, Alan. *Russia's Last Capitalists: The Nepmen, 1921–29*. Berkeley, Calif., 1987.
Bartlett, Roger, ed. *Land Commune and Peasant Community in Russia*. New York, 1990.
Belliustin, I. S. *Description of the Clergy in Rural Russia: The Memoir of a Nineteenth-Century Parish Priest*. Edited and translated by Gregory L. Freeze. Ithaca, N.Y., 1985.
Benet, Sula, ed. and trans. *The Village of Viriatino*. New York, 1970.
Berdiaev, Nicholas. *The Origin of Russian Communism*. New York, 1937.
Berenson, Edward. *Populist Religion and Left-Wing Politics in France, 1830–1852*. Princeton, N.J., 1984.
Berger, Peter L., and Thomas Luckmann. *The Social Construction of Reality: A Treatise in the Sociology of Knowledge*. Garden City, N.Y., 1967.
Bergman, Jay. "The Image of Jesus in the Russian Revolutionary Movement: The Case of Russian Marxism." *International Review of Social History* 35 (1990): 220–48.
Brooks, Jeffrey. *When Russia Learned to Read: Literacy and Popular Literature, 1861–1917*. Princeton, N.J., 1985.
Brower, Daniel. "Smolensk Scandal and the End of NEP." *Slavic Review* 4 (Winter 1986).
Bourdeaux, Michael. *Opium of the People: The Christian Religion in the USSR*. London, 1965.
Bushnell, John, Ben Eklof, and Larissa Zakharova. *Russia's Great Reforms, 1855–1881*. Bloomington, Ind., 1994.
Carr, E. H. *Socialism in One Country, 1924–26*. Vol. 1. London, 1958.
Chaianov, A. V. *The Theory of Peasant Economy*. Translated and edited by Daniel Thorner, Basile Kerblay, and R.E.F. Smith. Madison, Wis., 1987.
Christian, David. "Traditional and Modern Drinking Cultures in Russia on the Eve of Emancipation." *Australian Slavonic and East European Studies* 1 (1987): 61–84.

Christian, William A., Jr. *Local Religion in Sixteenth-Century Spain.* Princeton, N.J., 1981.
Chulos, Chris. J. "Peasant Religion in Post-Emancipation Russia: Voronezh Province, 1880–1917." 2 vols. Ph.D. diss., University of Chicago, 1994.
Cohen, Stephen F. *Bukharin and the Bolshevik Revolution: A Political Biography, 1888–1938.* New York, 1973.
———. *Rethinking the Soviet Experience: Politics and History Since 1917.* Oxford, 1985.
Conquest, Robert. *The Harvest of Sorrow: Soviet Collectivization and the Terror-Famine.* New York, 1986.
———. *Religion in the USSR.* New York, 1968.
Curtiss, John S. *Church and State in Russia: The Last Years of the Empire, 1900–1917.* New York, 1965.
———. *The Russian Church and the Soviet State, 1917–1950.* Boston, 1953.
Davies, R. W. *The Socialist Offensive: The Collectivization of Soviet Agriculture, 1929–30.* Vols. 1 and 2. Cambridge, Mass., 1980.
Davis, Natalie. *Society and Culture in Early Modern France.* Stanford, Calif., 1975.
de Certeau, Michel. *The Practice of Everyday Life.* Berkeley, Calif., 1994.
Delaney, Joan. "The Origins of Soviet Antireligious Organizations." In *Aspects of Religion in the Soviet Union, 1917–1967*, ed. Richard H. Marshall, Jr. Chicago, 1971.
Desan, Suzanne. *Reclaiming the Sacred: Lay Religion and Popular Politics in Revolutionary France.* Ithaca, N.Y., 1990.
de Tocqueville, Alexis. *Democracy in America.* New York, 1966.
Deutscher, Isaac. *Stalin: A Political Biography.* New York, 1967.
Duara, Prasenjit. *Culture, Power, and the State: Rural North China, 1900–1942.* Stanford, Calif., 1988.
Eklof, Ben. *Russian Peasant Schools: Officialdom, Village Culture, and Popular Pedagogy, 1861–1914.* Berkeley, Calif., 1986.
Ellis, Jane. *The Russian Orthodox Church: A Contemporary History.* London, 1986.
Emmons, Terence, and Wayne Vucinich. *The Zemstvo in Russia: An Experiment in Local Self-Government.* New York, 1982.
Engel, Barbara. *Between the Fields and the City: Women, Work, and Family in Russia, 1861–1914.* New York, 1994.
———. "Peasant Morality and Pre-Marital Relations in Late Nineteenth-Century Russia." *Journal of Social History* 23:4 (1990): 695–714.
Engelstein, Laura. *The Keys to Happiness: Sex and the Search for Modernity in Fin-de-Siècle Russia.* Ithaca, N.Y., 1992.
Fainsod, Merle. *Smolensk Under Soviet Rule.* Cambridge, Mass., 1958.
Farnsworth, Beatrice. "Village Women Experience the Revolutions," in *Bolshevik Culture: Experiment and Order in the Russian Revolution*, ed. Abbott Gleason, Peter Kenez, and Richard Stites. Bloomington, Ind., 1985.
Feierman, Steven. *Peasant Intellectuals: Anthropology and History in Tanzania.* Madison, Wis., 1990.
Figes, Orlando. "Peasant Farmers and the Minority Groups of Rural Society: Peasant Egalitarianism and Village Social Relations During the Russian Revolution (1917–1921)." In *Peasant Economy, Culture, and Politics of European Russia, 1800–1921*, ed. Esther Kingston-Mann and Timothy Mixter. Princeton, N.J., 1991.

———. *Peasant Russia, Civil War: The Volga Countryside in Revolution (1917-1921)*. New York, 1989.
———."The Russian Peasant Community in the Agrarian Revolution, 1917-18." In *Land Commune and Peasant Community in Russia: Communal Forms in Imperial and Early Soviet Society*, ed. Roger Bartlett. New York, 1990.
———."Stalin's Oblomovs." *Times Literary Supplement*, January 13, 1995, p. 26.
Fisher, Ralph Talcott, Jr. *Pattern for Soviet Youth: A Study of the Congresses of the Komsomol, 1918-1954*. New York, 1955.
Fitzpatrick, Sheila. "The Bolsheviks' Dilemma: The Class Issue in Party Politics and Culture." In *The Cultural Front: Power and Culture in Revolutionary Russia*. Ithaca, N.Y., 1992.
———. "The Civil War as a Formative Experience." In *Bolshevik Culture: Experiment and Order in the Russian Revolution*, ed. Abbott Gleason, Peter Kenez, and Richard Stites. Bloomington, Ind., 1985.
———. *The Commissariat of Enlightenment: Soviet Organization of Education and the Arts under Lunacharsky, October 1917-1921*. New York, 1970.
———, ed. *Cultural Revolution in Russia, 1928-1931*. Bloomington, Ind., 1984.
———. *Education and Social Mobility in the Soviet Union, 1922-1934*. New York, 1979.
———. "The Problem of Class Identity in NEP Society." In *Russia in the Era of NEP: Explorations in Soviet Society and Culture*, ed. Sheila Fitzpatrick, Alexander Rabinowitch, and Richard Stites. Bloomington, Ind., 1991.
———. *The Russian Revolution, 1917-1932*. Oxford, 1982.
———. *Stalin's Peasants: Resistance and Survival in the Russian Village after Collectivization*. New York, 1994.
Fletcher, William C. *A Study in Survival: The Church in Russia, 1927-42*. New York, 1965.
Frank, Stephen. "Popular Justice, Community, and Culture: 1870-1900." In *The World of the Russian Peasant: Post-Emancipation Culture and Society*, ed. Ben Eklof and Stephen P. Frank. London, 1991.
———. "Simple Folk, Savage Customs: Youth Sociability and the Dynamics of Culture in Rural Russia, 1856-1914." *Journal of Social History* 25 (Summer 1992): 711-36.
Frankel, Edith Rogovin, Jonathan Frankel, and Baruch Knei-Paz, eds. *Revolution in Russia: Reassessments of 1917*. New York, 1992.
Freeze, Gregory. "A Case of Stunted Anticlericalism: Clergy and Society in Imperial Russia." *European Studies Review* 13 (April 1983): 177-200.
———. "Counter-reformation in Russian Orthodoxy: Popular Response to Religious Innovation, 1922-1925." *Slavic Review* 54 (Summer 1995): 305-39.
———. "Handmaiden of the State? The Church in Imperial Russia Reconsidered." *Journal of Ecclesiastical History* 36 (January 1985): 82-102.
———. "The Orthodox Church and Serfdom in Prereform Russia." *Slavic Review* (Fall 1989): 361-87.
———. *The Parish Clergy in Nineteenth-Century Russia: Crisis, Reform, Counter-Reform*. Princeton, N.J., 1983.
———. *The Russian Levites: Parish Clergy in the Eighteenth Century*. Cambridge, Mass., 1977.
———. "The *Soslovie* (Estate) Paradigm and Russian Social History," *American Historical Review* 91 (February 1986): 11-36.

———. "Subversive Piety: Religion and the Political Crisis in Late Imperial Russia." *Journal of Modern History* 68 (June 1996): 308–50.
———, ed. *From Supplication to Revolution: A Documentary Social History of Imperial Russia*. New York, 1988.
Frye, Northrup. *Anatomy of Criticism: Four Essays*. Princeton, N.J., 1957.
Furet, François. *Penser la Révolution française*. Paris, 1978.
Galili, Ziva. *The Menshevik Leaders in the Russian Revolution*. Princeton, N.J., 1989.
Geertz, Clifford. *The Interpretation of Cultures*. New York, 1973.
Gerth, H. H., and C. Wright Mills, eds. *From Max Weber: Essays in Sociology*. New York, 1958.
Getty, J. Arch. *The Origin of the Great Purges*. New York, 1985.
Gorsuch, Anne E. "Enthusiasts, Bohemians, and Delinquents: Soviet Youth Cultures, 1921–1928." Ph.D. diss., University of Michigan, 1992.
Gringlas, Larry S. "*Shkraby ne kraby:* Rural Teachers and Bolshevik Power in the Russian Countryside, 1921–1928." Master's thesis, Columbia University, 1987.
Haimson, Leopold. "Civil War and the Problem of Social Identities in Early Twentieth-Century Russia." In *Party, State and Society in the Russian Civil War*, ed. Diane P. Koenker, William G. Rosenberg, and Ronald Grigor Suny. Bloomington, Ind., 1989.
———, ed. *The Politics of Rural Russia, 1905–1914*. Bloomington, Ind., 1979.
Halbwachs, Maurice. *The Collective Memory*. New York, 1980.
Hanson, Stephen. *Time and Revolution: Marxist Ideology and the Design of Soviet Institutions*. Chapel Hill, N.C., 1997.
Hendley, Kathryn. "An Analysis of Voting Rights Under the Soviet Constitution of 1918." Georgetown University, December 17, 1986.
Herlihy, Patricia. "'Joy of the Rus': Rites and Rituals of Russian Drinking." *Russian Review* 50 (April 1991): 131–47.
Hernandez, Richard L. "Rural Religion and Anti–Religious Activism, 1928-32." Ph.D. diss., Stanford University, forthcoming.
Hobsbawm, Eric. "Peasants and Politics." *Journal of Peasant Studies* 1 (1973).
Hobsbawm, Eric, and George Rudé. *Captain Swing*. New York, 1968.
Hoch, Steven L. *Serfdom and Social Control in Russia: Petrovskoe, a Village in Tambov*. Chicago, 1986.
Hoffmann, David L. *Peasant Metropolis: Social Identities in Moscow, 1929–1941*. Ithaca, N.Y., 1994.
Holmes, Larry E. *The Kremlin and the Schoolhouse: Reforming Education in Soviet Russia, 1917–1931*. Bloomington, Ind., 1991.
Hosking, Geoffrey. *The First Socialist Society*. Cambridge, Mass., 1985.
Hunt, Lynn. *The Family Romance of the French Revolution*. Berkeley, Calif., 1992.
———. *Politics, Culture, and Class in the French Revolution*. Berkeley, Calif., 1984.
Hunter, James Davison. *Culture Wars: The Struggle to Define America*. New York, 1991.
Johnson, Robert E. *Peasant and Proletarian: The Working Class of Moscow in the Late Nineteenth Century*. New Brunswick, N.J., 1979.
Keane, John. *Civil Society and the State: New European Perspectives*. London, 1988.

Kenez, Peter. *The Birth of the Propaganda State: Soviet Methods of Mass Mobilization, 1917–1929.* New York, 1985.
Kimerling, Elise. "Civil Rights and Social Policy in Soviet Russia, 1918–1936." *Russian Review* 41 (January 1982): 24–46.
Kingston-Mann, Esther, and Timothy Mixter, eds. *Peasant Economy, Culture and Politics of European Russia, 1800–1921.* Princeton, N.J., 1991.
Koenker, Diane. "Urbanization and Deurbanization in the Russian Revolution and Civil War." In *Party, State, and Society in the Russian Civil War*, ed. D. P. Koenker, W. G. Rosenberg, and R. G. Suny. Bloomington., Ind., 1989.
Kopelev, Lev. *Education of a True Believer.* Translated by Gary Kern. New York, 1980.
Kotkin, Stephen. "Coercion and Identity: Workers' Lives in Stalin's Showcase City." In *Making Workers Soviet: Power, Class, and Identity*, ed. Lewis H. Siegelbaum and Ronald Grigor Suny. Ithaca, N.Y., 1994.
Kotsonis, Yanni. "Agricultural Cooperatives in Historical Perspective: The Case of the European North, 1900–1929." Paper presented at the 1991 AAASS Conference in Miami, Florida.
Kravchinsky, Sergei M. *The Russian Peasantry: Their Agrarian Condition, Social Life, and Religion.* 1888. Reprint. Westport, Conn., 1977.
Kuromiya, Hiroaki. *Stalin's Industrial Revolution: Politics and Workers, 1928–1932.* New York, 1988.
Lewin, Moshe. *Lenin's Last Struggle.* Translated by A. M. Sheridan Smith. New York, 1968.
———. *The Making of the Soviet System: Essays in the Social History of Interwar Russia.* New York, 1985.
———. *Political Undercurrents in Soviet Economic Debates: From Bukharin to Modern Reformers.* Princeton, N.J., 1974.
———. *Russian Peasants and Soviet Power: A Study of Collectivization.* New York, 1975.
———. "Russia/USSR in Historical Motion: An Essay in Interpretation." *Russian Review* 50 (July 1991).
Little, Daniel. *Understanding Peasant China: Case Studies in the Philosophy of Social Science.* New Haven, Conn., 1989.
Liu Shao-ch' i. *How To Be a Good Communist.* Peking, 1951.
Lotman, Iurii, and Boris Uspenskii. *The Semiotics of Russian Culture.* Edited by Ann Shukman. Ann Arbor, Mich., 1984.
Luukanen, Arto. *The Party of Unbelief: The Religious Policy of the Bolshevik Party, 1917–1929.* Helsinki, 1994.
Male, Donald. *Russian Peasant Organisation Before Collectivization: A Study of Commune and Gathering.* New York, 1971.
Malia, Martin. *Comprendre la Révolution russe.* Paris, 1980.
———. "A Fatal Logic." *The National Interest* 31 (Spring 1993): 80–90.
———. *The Soviet Tragedy: A History of Socialism in Russia, 1917–1991.* New York, 1994.
Mally, Lynn. *Culture of the Future: The Proletcult Movement in Revolutionary Russia.* Berkeley, Calif., 1990.
Mannheim, Karl. *Ideology and Utopia: An Introduction to the Sociology of Knowledge.* New York, 1936.
Manning, Roberta Thompson. *The Crisis of the Old Order in Russia: Gentry and Government.* Princeton, N.J., 1982.

Marx, Karl. *The Eighteenth Brumaire of Louis Bonaparte*. New York, 1981.
McCullagh, Captain Francis. *The Bolshevik Persecution of Christianity*. London, 1924.
Meyer, Jean A. *The Cristero Rebellion: The Mexican People Between Church and State, 1926–1929*. New York, 1976.
Michelet, Jules. *Histoire de la Révolution française*. 2 vols. 2d ed. Paris, 1868.
Migdal, Joel S. *Peasants, Politics, and Revolution: Pressures toward Political and Social Change in the Third World*. Princeton, N.J., 1974.
Mironov, Boris. "The Russian Peasant Commune After the Reforms of the 1860s." *Slavic Review* 44 (Fall 1985).
Naiman, Eric. "The Case of Chubarov Alley: Collective Rape, Utopian Desire, and the Mentality of NEP." *Russian History* 17 (Spring 1990): 1–30.
Neuberger, Joan. *Hooliganism: Crime, Culture, and Power in St. Petersburg, 1900–1914*. Berkeley, Calif., 1993.
Nichols, Robert L., ed. *Russian Orthodoxy under the Old Regime*. Minneapolis, 1978.
Nivison, David S. "Communist Ethics and the Chinese Tradition." In *China: Enduring Scholarship Selected from the Far Eastern Quarterly—The Journal of Asian Studies, 1941–1971*, ed. John A. Harrison. Tucson, Ariz., 1972.
Nove, Alex. *An Economic History of the USSR*. New York, 1984.
Odom, William. *The Soviet Volunteers: Modernization and Bureaucracy in a Public Mass Organization*. Princeton, N.J., 1973.
Ozouf, Mona. *Festivals and the French Revolution*. Cambridge, Mass., 1988.
Pascal, Pierre. *The Religion of the Russian People*. Translated by Rowan Williams. Crestwood, N.Y., 1976. First published as *La religion du peuple russe* (Lausanne, 1973).
Peris, Daniel. "Commissars in Red Cassocks: Former Priests in the League of the Militant Godless." *Slavic Review* 54 (Summer 1995): 340–64.
———. "The 1929 Congress of the Godless." *Soviet Studies* 43:4 (1991): 711–32.
———. "'Storming the Heavens': The League of the Militant Godless and Bolshevik Political Culture in the 1920s and 1930s." Ph.D. diss., University of Illinois at Urbana-Champaign, 1994.
Perrie, Maureen. "Folklore as Evidence of Peasant Mentalité." *Russian Review* 48 (1987): 119–43.
Plaggenborg, Stefan. "Volksreligiosität und antireligiöse Propaganda in der frühen Sowjetunion." *Archiv für Sozialgeschichte* 26 (1992): 95–130.
Popkin, Samuel. *The Rational Peasant*. Berkeley, Calif., 1979.
Pospielovsky, Dmitry. *A History of Marxist-Leninist Atheism and Soviet Antireligious Policies*. New York, 1987.
———. *A History of Soviet Atheism in Theory and Practice, and the Believer*. New York, 1987.
———. *The Russian Church Under the Soviet Regime, 1917–1982*. Vol. 1. Crestwood, N.Y., 1984.
———. *Soviet Antireligious Campaigns and Persecutions*. New York, 1988.
Powell, David E. *Antireligious Propaganda in the Soviet Union: A Study of Mass Persuasion*. Cambridge, Mass., 1975.
Pretty, Dave. "The Saints of the Revolution: Political Activists in the 1890s in Ivanovo-Voznesensk and the Path of Most Resistance." *Slavic Review* 54 (Summer 1995): 276–304.
Rabinowitch, Alexander. *The Bolsheviks Come to Power: The Revolution of 1917 in Petrograd*. New York, 1976.

Radkey, Oliver H. *The Unknown Civil War in Soviet Russia: A Study of the Green Movement in the Tambov Region*. Stanford, Calif., 1976.
Raeff, Marc, ed. *Russian Intellectual History: An Anthology*. New York, 1986.
———. *Understanding Imperial Russia: State and Society in the Old Regime*. Translated by Arthur Goldhammer. New York, 1984.
———. "The Well-Ordered Police State and the Development of Modernity in Seventeenth- and Eighteenth-Century Europe." *American Historical Review* 80 (1975): 1221–43.
———. *The Well-Ordered Police State: Social and Institutional Change Through Law in the Germanies and Russia, 1600–1800*. New Haven, Conn., 1983.
Raleigh, Donald J. *Revolution on the Volga: 1917 in Saratov*. Ithaca, N.Y., 1986.
Ramer, Samuel C. "Traditional Healers and Peasant Culture in Russia, 1861–1917." In *Peasant Economy, Culture, and Politics of European Russia, 1800–1921*, ed. E. Kingston-Mann and T. Mixter. Princeton, N.J., 1991.
Ramet, Sabrina, ed. *Religious Policy in the Soviet Union*. New York, 1993.
Redfield, Robert. *The Little Community: Viewpoints for the Study of a Human Whole*. Chicago, 1955.
———. *Peasant Society and Culture: An Anthropological Approach to Civilization*. Chicago, 1956.
Robinson, Geroid. *Rural Russia Under the Old Regime: A History of the Landlord-Peasant Revolution of 1917*. Berkeley, Calif., 1932.
Rosenberg, William G., ed. *Bolshevik Visions: First Phase of the Cultural Revolution in Soviet Russia*. Ann Arbor, Mich., 1984.
Roslof, Edward. "The Renovationist Movement in the Russian Orthodox Church, 1922–1946." Ph.D. diss., University of North Carolina at Chapel Hill, 1994.
Rothenberg, Joshua. "The Legal Status of Religion in the Soviet Union." In *Aspects of Religion in the Soviet Union, 1917–1967*, ed. Richard H. Marshall, Jr. Chicago, 1971.
Rothstein, Frances. "The New Proletarians: Third World Realities and First World Categories." *Comparative Studies in Society and History* 2 (1986): 218–24.
Sablinsky, Walter L. *The Road to Bloody Sunday: Father Gapon and the St. Petersburg Massacre of 1905*. Princeton, N.J., 1976.
Schapiro, Leonard. *The Communist Party of the Soviet Union*. New York, 1960.
Scott, James C. *Domination and the Arts of Resistance: Hidden Transcripts*. New Haven, Conn., 1990.
———. *The Moral Economy of the Peasant: Subsistence and Rebellion in Southeast Asia*. New Haven, Conn., 1976.
———. *Weapons of the Weak: Everyday Forms of Peasant Resistance*. New Haven, Conn., 1985.
Shanin, Theodor. *The Awkward Class; Political Sociology of Peasantry in a Developing Society: Russia, 1910–1925*. New York, 1972.
Shatz, Marshall S., and Judith E. Zimmerman, trans. and eds. *Signposts: A Collection of Articles on the Russian Intelligentsia*. Irvine, Calif., 1986.
Siegelbaum, Lewis H. *Soviet State and Society between Revolutions, 1918–1929*. New York, 1992.
———. *Stakhanovism and the Politics of Productivity in the USSR, 1935–1941*. New York, 1988.
Skocpol, Theda. *States and Social Revolutions: A Comparative Analysis of France, Russia, and China*. New York, 1979.
Slatter, John. "Communes with Communists: The *Sel'sovety* in the 1920s." In

Land Commune and Peasant Community: Communal Forms in Imperial and Early Soviet Society, ed. Roger Bartlett. New York, 1990.
Slezkine, Yuri. "The USRR as a Communal Apartment or How a Socialist State Promoted Ethnic Particularism." *Slavic Review* 53 (Summer 1994): 414–53.
Smolitsch, Igor. *Geschichte der russischen Kirche, 1700–1917*. Vol. 2. Berlin, 1990.
Starr, S. Frederick. *Decentralization and Self-Government in Russia, 1830–1870*. Princeton, N.J., 1972.
Stites, Richard. *Revolutionary Dreams: Utopian Vision and Experimental Life in the Russian Revolution*. New York, 1989.
Suny, Ronald G. *Revenge of the Past: Nationalism, Revolution, and the Collapse of the Soviet Union*. Stanford, Calif., 1993.
Sutherland, Donald M. G. *The Chouans: The Social Origins of Popular Counter-Revolution in Upper Brittany*. New York, 1982.
Taniuchi, Yuzuru. *The Village Gathering in Russia in the Mid-1920s*. Birmingham, Eng., 1968.
Thorniley, Daniel. *The Rise and Fall of the Soviet Rural Communist Party, 1927–39*. New York, 1988.
Tian-Shanskaia, Olga Semyonova. *Village Life in Late Tsarist Russia*. Edited by D. L. Ransel. Bloomington, Ind., 1993.
Tirado, Isabel A. "The Revolution, Young Peasants, and the Komsomol's Anti-Religious Campaigns (1920–1928)." *Canadian-American Slavic Studies* 26:1–3 (1992): 97–117.
Treadgold, Donald W. "The Peasant and Religion." In *The Peasant in Nineteenth-Century Russia*, ed. Wayne Vucinich. Stanford, Calif., 1968.
Tucker, Robert C. *Stalin in Power: The Revolution from Above, 1928–1941*. New York, 1990.
Tumarkin, Nina. *Lenin Lives!: The Lenin Cult in Soviet Russia*. Cambridge, Mass., 1983.
Ulam, Adam. *The Bolsheviks: The Intellectual and Political History of the Triumph of Communism in Russia*. New York, 1965.
Veblen, Thorstein. *Imperial Germany and the Industrial Revolution*. New York, 1939.
Viola, Lynne. "*Bab'i bunty* and Peasant Women's Protest during Collectivization." *Russian Review* 45:1 (1986).
———. *The Best Sons of the Fatherland: Workers in the Vanguard of Soviet Collectivization*. New York, 1987.
———. "The Peasant Nightmare: Visions of Apocalypse in the Soviet Countryside." *Journal of Modern History* 62 (December 1990).
———. *Peasant Rebels under Stalin: Collectivization and the Culture of Peasant Resistance*. New York, 1996.
Volkogonov, Dmitri. *Lenin: A New Biography*. New York, 1994.
von Geldern, James. *Bolshevik Festivals, 1917–1920*. Berkeley, Calif., 1993.
von Hagen, Mark. "Civil-Military Relations and the Evolution of the Soviet Socialist State." *Slavic Review* 50:2 (Summer 1991).
———. *Soldiers in the Proletarian Dictatorship: The Red Army and the Soviet Socialist State, 1917–1930*. Ithaca, N.Y., 1990.
Vovelle, Michel. *Les métamorphoses de la fête en Provence de 1750 à 1820*. Paris, 1976.
———. *Religion et révolution: La déchristianisation de l'an II*. Paris, 1976.

Ware, Timothy. *The Orthodox Church*. New York, 1963.
Weber, Eugen. *Peasants into Frenchmen*. Stanford, Calif., 1976.
Wildman, Allan K. *The End of the Russian Imperial Army*. 2 vols. Princeton, N.J., 1980, 1988.
Williams, Robert C. *The Other Bolsheviks: Lenin and His Critics, 1904–1914*. Bloomington, Ind., 1986.
Worobec, Christine. *Peasant Russia: Family and Community in the Post-Emancipation Period*. De Kalb, Ill., 1994.
———. "Victims or Actors? Peasant Women and Patriarchy." In *Peasant Economy, Culture, and Politics of European Russia, 1800–1921*, ed. Esther Kingston-Mann and Timothy Mixter. Princeton, N.J., 1991.
Yaney, George L. *The Urge to Mobilize: Agrarian Reform in Russia, 1861–1930*. Urbana, Ill., 1981.
Young, Glennys. "'Into Church Matters': Lay Identity, Rural Parish Life, and Popular Politics in Late Imperial and Early Soviet Russia, 1864–1928." *Russian History / Histoire Russe*, 1996 (1–4).
———. "Rural Religion and Soviet Power, 1921–1932." Ph.D. diss., University of California, Berkeley, 1989.
———. "Trading Icons: Clergy, Laity, and Rural Cooperatives, 1921–28," *Canadian-American Slavic Studies* 26:1–3 (1992): 315–33.
Zelnik, Reginald. "Introduction: Kanatchikov's *Story of My Life* as Document and Literature." In *A Radical Worker in Tsarist Russia: The Autobiography of Semën Ivanovich Kanatchikov*. Stanford, Calif., 1976.
———. "On the Eve: Life Histories and Identities of Some Revolutionary Workers, 1870–1905." In *Making Workers Soviet: Power, Class, and Identity*, ed. Lewis H. Siegelbaum and Ronald Grigor Suny. Ithaca, N.Y., 1995.
———. "Russian Bebels: An Introduction to the Memoirs of Semën Kanatchikov and Matvei Fischer." *Russian Review* 35 (July 1976) and (October 1976).
———. "Russian Workers and the Revolutionary Movement," *Journal of Social History* 6:2 (Winter 1972–73).
———. "'To the Unaccustomed Eye': Religion and Irreligion in the Experience of St. Petersburg Workers in the 1870s." *Russian History* 16:2–4 (1989): 297–326.
———, trans. and ed. *A Radical Worker in Tsarist Russia: The Autobiography of Semën Ivanovich Kanatchikov*. Stanford, Calif., 1986.
Ziegler, Adolf. *Die russische Gottlosenbewegung*. Munich, 1932.

Index

(Illustrations are denoted by page references in italics.)

adolescents. *See* youth
Alexander II, 15 n. 19
Alliance of Church Renewal, 149 n. 17
All-Union Congress of Enlightenment
  Workers (1930), 138 n. 106
All-Union League of Active Atheists, 82 n. 12
anti-alcohol propaganda, 25–26, 42
anticlericalism
  of Bolsheviks, 92
  of parishioners, 13, 27–28, 28 n. 87,
    44–45, 47, 213
  postrevolutionary increases in, 52–53
antireligious activists. *See bezbozhniki*
antireligious campaign, 2, 96–99. *See also*
    posters
  obstacles to, 87–94, 130–32
  role of science in, 130
  tactics of, 96 n. 81, 96–97
  weakness of, 274
antireligious cells (League of the Godless),
    116–35
  and *Bezbozhnik*, 116–35, 119–20
  impact of, 134–35
  and members' identity, 127
antireligious circles, 82–87. *See also*
    antireligious cells
Anti-Religious Conference, 116
antireligious discourse. *See* vocabulary:
    antireligious discourse
antireligious groups. *See* antireligious cells;
    antireligious circles
apportionment, 60 n. 52. *See also*
    disenfranchisement
archpriest (*protoierei*), 12 n. 3
art, 198–99. *See also* posters
Ascher, Abraham, 40 n. 149
"assembly of laity" (*obshchestvo*
  grazhdan), 24
atheism, practice of, 52, 100–105

baptism, 88
"The Battle Against Religion Is the Battle
  for Socialism" (poster), *264*
Belinsky, Vissarion, 13
Belliustin, I. S., 15
Berdiaev, Nikolai, 149, 253–54, 262 n. 41
Bergman, Jay, 262 n. 40
besedy. *See* discussions
bezbozhniki (antireligious activists)
  activities of, 2–3
  antiritual stance of, 237–39
  and "campaign," 96–99. *See also*
    antireligious campaign
  impact of, 239–40
  parish clergy on, 161–63
  vocabulary for, 254–58
"The *Bezbozhnik* Is a (Scientific)
  Experimenter" (poster), *131*
Bezbozhnik (newspaper), 98–99, 120,
  120
  and antireligious cells, 116–35
  on clergy, 156 n. 54
  cover of, *268*
  portrayal of clergy in, 122–23, 126,
    173
  See also newspapers
bishops, numbers of, 148, 148 n. 12
Black Hundreds, 40
Bogdanov, Aleksandr, 80
Bogoraz, Vladimir, 126
Bogoslovskii vestnik, 40
Bolsheviks
  anticlericalism of, 92
  as catalysts of peasant uprisings, 66
  and Civil War, 68
  and infrastructure building, 55, 68–78
  and "kulak-clergy" vocabulary, 261
  membership of, 68 n. 94
  peasant support for, 49–50

Bolsheviks *(continued)*
  and village social and political structure, 55–56
  See also Communist Party
bribery, 247
Bukharin, Nikolai Ivanovich, 112, 113, 138, 142, 164
Bunakov, N. F., 29
burning, of religious effigies, 101

Central Black Earth Region, 229
Central Committee, 88 n. 45, 144 n. 132, 265
Central Committee (League of the Godless), 115 n. 14, 116, 265
Central Committee (VTsIK), 227
chanters. *See* churches: readers
Cheka, 65. *See also* NKVD; OGPU
Chekhov, Anton, 233–34
children, and parish clergy, 164–65
Christian, William, 13 n. 5
Christianity, concept of rural, 13 n. 5
"Christianization of Children," 165
Christian radicalism, 163–64 n. 100
Christmas celebrations, of Komsomol, 101–2, 103, 107–8
church brotherhoods (*bratstva*), 18–19 n. 40, 23 n. 61
church buildings
  and "Instruction on the Implementation of the Decree on the Separation of Church and State," 167–68
  and "Instruction on the Implementation of the Decree on the Separation of Church and State" (1918), 58
  obstacles to repair of, 220–22, 224–25
  preservation of, 16, 25, 25 nn. 70 and 72, 45, 168–69, 168 n. 129, 196–99, 197 n. 20, 219–26, 220 n. 39
church councils. *See* parish councils
church sisterhoods (*sestrichestva*), 157
churches
  buildings of. *See* church buildings
  closings of, 226–29, 231
  numbers of, 229–32, 230 n. 83, 231 nn. 89 and 92
  cinema, as substitute for religion, 98 n. 90, 103
  civil marriage. *See* marriage: civil
Civil War, 67–78, 92–93

"The Clergy's Folk Dance" (poster), *121*
clerical estate, structure of, 12 n. 3
clergy. *See* parish clergy
clothing, and religious identity, 136–37
Cohen, Stephen, 6, 253
collectivization, 122 n. 46, 277
Commissariat of Justice, 69 n. 98
Committees of the Village Poor. *See kombedy*
communes
  function of, 17 n. 29, 144 n. 132
  and land issues, 53, 56–57
  and "separators," 54–55 n. 26
  and taxes, 170–71
Communist Party
  and antireligious circles in infrastructure building, 82–87
  Central Committee of, 88 n. 45, 144 n. 132, 265
  duties of members of, 94–95, 94 n. 74
  and election procedures, 62–63
  and "face to the countryside" campaign, 112–13
  and implementation of Decree of the Separation of Church and State, 64–65
  influence of in NEP, 79–81
  membership of, 94 n. 71
  and parish clergy, 176–77, 177 n. 167, 177–78 n. 171
  peasantry on, 135, 146
  role of members of, 85–86
  and VIKs, 207, 207 n. 68
  weakness of antireligious campaign of, 274
  See also Bolsheviks
Constitution of the Russian Republic (1918), 2, 56, 60–63
  Article 57, 60
  Article 65, 61
  and franchise, 178–79. *See also* disenfranchisement
  on role of parish clergy, 61–62, 61 n. 58
  on village soviets, 60–62
cooperatives
  nepotism in, 175–76
  and parish clergy, 173–77, 213–14
  and religious activists, 200
  rural, 171
Council of People's Commissars, 150

Counterreform era, 17 n. 31, 22–34
"creeping totalitarianism," 6, 278–79
culture, definition of, 2 n. 5, 277 n. 5
Curtiss, John S., 38 n. 139, 40 n. 149

deacons, 12 n. 3
Decree of 1890, 22
Decree on "General Principles of Land Holding and Land Use Measures" (1928), 144 n. 132
Decree on Land (1917), 52, 56
Decree on the Separation of Church and State (1918), 56, 57–58, 196, 241
 abuses of, 65, 76–78
 and education, 138 n. 102, 138–40
 Orthodox Church's condemnation of, 70
 resistance to, 68–78
 See also "Instruction on the Implementation of the Decree on the Separation of Church and State" (1918)
"Defiance of Youth" (poster), 106
dioceses, role of, 42
discussions (besedy), 17–18 n. 34, 17–20, 18 nn. 36 and 39, 18–19 n. 40, 19 n. 42
 and antireligious campaign, 96–98
 failures of, 99–100
 parish clergy use of, 164–65
 and politics, 19, 35–36
 topics for, 19
disenfranchisement
 and "Instruction on Elections to Soviets," 179–80
 numbers of, 183, 183 n. 194
 and parish clergy, 56, 61, 144–45, 173 n. 142
 and teachers, 179 n. 178
Dobrokhim (Society of the Friends of Chemistry), 114 n. 10
Duara, Prasenjit, 45 n. 171
Dukhobors (Spirit-Wrestlers), 90, 90 n. 54

Easter celebrations, of Komsomol, 101–2, 103, 107–8
Edict of Toleration (1905), 41
education, 17–18, 75–76, 138–40, 165–66, 194–96, 225–26
1864 Regulation, 26, 26 n. 81

Eighth Party Congress, 77
elders, church, 38 n. 138, 205, 217, 222 n. 50
electoral politics, 142–46, 143–44 n. 130, 145 n. 137
 and parish clergy, 170–91
 procedures for, 62–63, 182
 and religious activists, 199–209, 223–25
 and ritual, 248–49, 251–52
 and voting commissions, 184, 203 n. 47, 276
 See also disenfranchisement
Emancipation Proclamation (1861), 11–12, 16–17
Emeliakh, L. I., 37 n. 133
"enemy," vocabulary for, 255, 255 nn. 9 and 12, 263
"Enough Deception" (poster), 125
"episcopal party," 208
ethnographers, 132–33 n. 75
Evdokim, Arkhimandrit, 39, 40
extended families, and generational conflicts, 136

"face to the countryside" campaign, 112–45, 116–17 n. 25, 240
Fedorovich, Apollon, 20 n. 49
Fenomenov, M. I., 145 n. 137
Fifteenth Party Congress, 145 n. 135, 173 n. 142
Figes, Orlando, 50, 54, 63, 66–67, 187 n. 216
Fitzpatrick, Sheila, 126, 136, 137 n. 99, 270
Fourteenth Party Congress, 112
free riders, 66–67, 238 n. 17
Freeze, Gregory, 12 n. 3, 28, 40 n. 149
Frye, Northrop, 265 n. 51
"Fulfill Lenin's Precepts" (poster), 112
Furet, François, 262 n. 39

Gapon, Georgii, 20 n. 49
Geertz, Clifford, 2 n. 5, 261–62 n. 39
Geldern, James von, 101
generational conflicts, 30–34, 136, 136 n. 91. See also parents, role of
gentry, loss of rights by, 11 n. 11
Glavpolitprosvet (Political Education Department), 68–69
Gnedovskii, Pëtr, 182

gravestones, propagandistic potential of, 169–70
"Great Reforms," 6, 11–12, 20

Haimson, Leopold, 7 n. 23
Hanson, Stephen, 95 n. 78
Harvest Day, 130, 130 n. 65
Hobsbawm, Eric, 234 n. 2
Holy Synod, 17, 17 n. 29
  and establishment of parish councils, 38
  on parish clergy's political role, 41
  on politics, 35–36, 46–47
  yearly reports of, 26
Hunt, Lynn, 7 n. 24, 258, 262 n. 39, 265, 265 n. 52
Hunter, James Davison, 136 n. 90

Iaroslavskii, Emel'ian, 2 n. 5, 99, 108 n. 134, 230 n. 84
  on antireligious activity, 114–15 n. 13
  on "kulak-clergy," 259
  and League of the Godless, 8 n. 26
  on number of churches in Soviet Union, 230
  on parish councils, 155–56
  on religious organizations, 264
icons, 104, 125, 248 n. 49
identity, sociopolitical, 21–22, 127, 136–37, 155 n. 49, 222–23, 237–38 n. 17
illiteracy. *See* literacy rate
"industrialization debates," 111 n. 1
in-migrants, 51–52, 54, 54 n. 22. *See also* outmigrants
"Instruction on Election to Soviets" (1925), 179–80, 202–3
"Instruction on Election to Soviets" (1926), 180
"Instruction on the Implementation of the Decree on the Separation of Church and State" (1918), 56, 58–59, 59 n. 45, 167–68, 276
insurance monies, for church repair, 221
International Organization to Aid Imprisoned Fighters for the Revolution. *See* MOPR
Ivanhoe, Philip J., 262 n. 39
Ivlev, Ivan, 163

Kalinin, M. I., 77, 111

Kanatchikov, Semën Ivanovich, 30–34, 31 n. 107
Kenez, Peter, 139
Khataevich, Mendel M., 113 n. 5, 263
KKOV (Peasants' Mutual Aid Society), 222
kombedy (Committees of the Village Poor), 71–72, 71 n. 112, 72 n. 114, 227 n. 70
Komsomol
  Christmas and Easter celebrations of, 101–2, 103, 107–8
  rural membership of, 93 n. 66, 93–94, 94 n. 69
korenizatsiia, 113 n. 9
Kostelovskaia, Mariia Mikhailovna, 115 n. 13
Kotkin, Stephen, 196 n. 14
Krasikov, P., 155
Kravchinsky, Sergei, 4 n. 10, 27
Krest'ianskaia pravda, 255
kulaks (well-off peasants), 122 n. 46
  parish clergy viewed as, 7, 104, 173, 199 n. 28, 278
  and parish councils, 155–56
  religious actvists viewed as, 220 n. 39
  vocabulary for, 256, 259–65, 270
Kurinkov, A. F., 205

land
  and communes, 53, 56–57
  decree on "General Principles of Land Holding and Land Use Measures," 144 n. 132
  parish, 39 n. 143, 69–70, 218–19
  and parish clergy, 36–37, 56–57
  peasant seizures of, 50–51, 52, 70
  and Russian Orthodox Church, 37 n. 131
Land Captain (*zemskii nachal'nik*), 11 n. 11, 23
Land Code (1922), 172, 172 n. 141, 201
landless peasants, 63. *See also* land: peasant seizures of
"Law on Religious Associations" (1929), 161, 166–67
laws and legislation, 275–76
  on civil marriage, 57
  Constitution. *See* Constitution of the Russian Republic
  Decree of 1890, 22

Decree on Land, 52, 56
decree on local finance, 190 n. 232
decree on soviets, 190 n. 232
Decree on the Separation of Church and State. *See* Decree on the Separation of Church and State
"Instruction on Election to Soviets," 179–80
"Instruction on the Implementation of the Decree on the Separation of Church and State," 56, 58–59, 59 n. 45
Land Code, 172, 172 n. 141, 201
"Law on Religious Associations," 161, 166–67
NKVD circular on religious ritual, 241–42
Regulation on Parish Councils, 23
"Regulation on Village Assemblies," 144
lay activists. *See* religious activists
League of the Godless, 83, 111–45
  antireligious activities prior to, 109–10
  and antireligious cells, 116–18, 117 n. 31, 118 nn. 32 and 36, 264
  and collectivization, 122 n. 46
  Cooperative Central Council of, 122 n. 46
  criticism of, 119
  goals of, 114, 122 n. 46
  membership of, 134 n. 83
  second conference of, 230
  structure of, 115–16, 115 n. 14
legislation. *See* laws and legislation
Lenin, V. I., 80, 82 n. 13, 104, 112, 262 n. 40
Lewin, Moshe, 5 n. 13, 8 n. 25, 13 n. 5, 277
literacy rate, 120 n. 44, 144 n. 131, 162
Lukachevskii, A., 83, 212, 240, 240 n. 24
Lunacharsky, Anatole, 97 n. 85, 138 n. 106
Lupolov, A., 183

Malaia Semënovka (Saratov province), 127, 133–34
Male, Donald, 143 n. 130
Malia, Martin, 211 n. 1
manorial justice, 11 n. 11
marriage
  civil, 57, 74–75
  religious, 88, 159, 159 n. 75, 245

Marx, Karl, 28 n. 87
Mikhail of Vol'sk, Bishop, 148
Model Statute of a Land Society, 170 n. 135
Molokans, 248, 248 n. 50, 249. *See also* sects
MOPR (International Organization to Aid Imprisoned Fighters for the Revolution), 95, 95 n. 75, 114 n. 10
Moscow Society of the Godless, 82 n. 12

Narkompros, 69 n. 95
NEP (New Economic Policy), 4, 211 n. 1, 278
nepotism, 175–76, 206
New Economic Policy (NEP), 4, 211 n. 1, 278
newspapers, role of, 120, *120*, 202 n. 41, 218 n. 31, 249. *See also names of individual newspapers*
NKVD (Soviet People's Commissariat for Internal Affairs), circular, on religious ritual, 241–42. *See also* Cheka; OGPU
nonordained clergy, 14
Novyi byt (New Everyday Life), 114 n. 10

Obshchestvo Doloi negramotnost', 95
Obshchestvo druzei detei (ODD) (Society of the Friends of Children), 114 n. 10
Obshchestvo druzei radio (ODR) (Society of the Friends of Radio), 114 n. 10
Obshchestvo pomoshchi studenchestvu (Society to Aid Students), 114 n. 10
Obshchestvo smychka goroda s derevnei (Society for the Alliance of the City and the Countryside), 114 n. 10
October Manifesto, 41
ODD (Obshchestvo druzei detei) (Society of the Friends of Children), 114 n. 10
ODP (Obshchestvo doloi prestupnost') (Society to End Crime), 114 n. 10
ODR (Obshchestvo druzei radio) (Society of the Friends of Radio), 114 n. 10
OGPU (secret police), 150
Old Belief, 46 n. 175
Oleshchuk, Fedor, 197 n. 20, 225, 265
"On the Protection of the Church's Sacred Objects Against Blasphemous Seizure and Desecration" (Orthodox Church), 157 n. 58

ordained clergy, 12 n. 3
Orthodox Church. *See* Russian Orthodox Church
Osoviakhim, 95
outmigrants (*otkhodniki*), impact of, 23, 28–34, 42–43, 81, 81 n. 11

Panin, V. N., 14
parents, role of, 89–91, 91 n. 57. *See also* generational conflicts
parish clergy, 12–14, 163
  abdications of, 158–60, 158 nn. 67–68
  after Emancipation Proclamation, 17
  and antireligious campaign, 99–100. *See also* antireligious campaign
  and autocracy, 35
  benefits to of extraliturgical discussion, 19–20
  on *bezbozhniki*, 161–63
  and church closings, 228–29
  and Communist Party, 176–77, 177 nn. 167 and 171
  and Constitution of 1918, 61–62, 61 n. 58,
  and cooperatives, 173–77, 213–14
  dependency of on parishioners, 21, 158, 168 n. 129, 212–13
  disenfranchisement of, 56, 61, 144–45, 173 n. 142
  and early Soviet legislation, 59
  elective positions of, 188, 189 n. 228
  and electoral politics, 170–91
  and extraliturgical discussions. *See* discussions
  financial sources for, 170–71
  franchise of, 178–83
  image of, 7, 13, 69 n. 97, 120 n. 45, 153, 199 n. 28, 278
  and involvement in education, 165–66
  and land reform, 56–57
  legal rights of, 61–62, 162 n. 89
  and Lenin, 82 n. 13
  and national religious policy, 148–53
  nonordained, 12 n. 3
  and parish democracy, 153–60
  and popular verses about, 123, 126
  portrayal of in newspapers, 122–23, 126, 173. *See also* newspapers
  reaction to Bolsheviks' infrastructure building, 69–78
  and religious activists. *See* religious activists
  and renovationists, 151–53
  roles of, 20–21, 41–42
  sociopolitical identity of, 21–22
  and state, 13–15, 17, 21, 39–40, 160–67, 169, 183–91
  support for, 215–16
  as targets of political resistance, 36–37
  trials of, 148, 148 n. 5
  use of alcohol by, 215 n. 21
  and VIKs, 60–61 n. 54, 61 n. 58
  and village assemblies, 171–72
  and village soviets, 63–64, 72–73, 189, 214–17, 243–44
  violence against. *See* violence: against parish clergy
parish councils (*prikhodskie sovety*), 24 n. 63, 38
  activities of, 24–25
  and kulaks, 155–56
  membership of, 38–39, 39 n. 141, 69 n. 98
  and parish clergy on antireligious activism, 163
  parishioners' use of, 25–26, 155
  and religious activists, 23–24, 199–209
  resistance of to state, 26–27, 65–66
  sociopolitical identity of, 155 n. 49
  strength of, 45 n. 173
  and support for clergy, 156–57
parish democracy, 153–60, 193–209
parishioners
  anticlericalism of, 13, 27–28, 28 n. 87, 44–45, 47, 213
  donations for church buildings, 25, 25 nn. 70 and 72, 45
  and parish democracy, 153–60
  and Renovationists, 152
  resistance to state by, 16 n. 26
"parish question," 37–39
parish record books, 73–74
partnagruzka (party load), 94 n. 74
Party Congresses
  Eighth, 77
  Fifteenth, 145 n. 135, 173 n. 142
  Fourteenth, 112
  Tenth, 2
  Twelfth, 108
Pascal, Pierre, 4 n. 10

peasant justice. See *samosud*
peasantry
  on Communist Party, 135, 146
  landless, 63
  literacy rate of, 120 n. 44, 144 n. 131, 162
  seizures of land by, 50–52, 70
  small-holding, 55–56, 67–68, 123
  uprisings of, 66, 187 n. 216
Peasants' Mutual Aid Society (KKOV), 222
People's Commissariat of Justice, 227
peregruzka (overload), 94 n. 74
Peris, Daniel, 122 n. 46
Petin, Pëtr, 163–64
Plemiannikov, 151
"pluralism," 6, 278 n. 10, 278–79
political development, theories of rural, 4–5
Political Education Department (*Glavpolitprosvet*), 68–69
pomoch', 56. See also land
Popkin, Samuel, 176 n. 164, 249 n. 52
popular verses, about parish clergy, 123, 126
Pospielovsky, Dmitry, 164 n. 100
posters
  "The Battle Against Religion Is the Battle for Socialism," 264
  "The *Bezbozhnik* Is a (Scientific) Experimenter," 131
  "The Clergy's Folk Dance," 121
  "Defiance of Youth," 106
  "Enough Deception," 125
  "Fulfill Lenin's Precepts," 112
  "Religion and the *Popovshchina* . . . ," 266
  "Religion and the Woman," 128
  "Religion is the Narcotic of the People," 104
  "The Spider and the Flies," 124
  "We Will Unmask the Anti-Soviet Plans of Capitalists and *Tserkovniki*," 257
  "The Working Woman: Into the Battle for Socialism. Into the Battle Against Religion," 129
preelection meetings, 182, 185, 250
priests. See parish clergy
provincial councils, 115 n. 14, 116
Provisional Government, 50
Pryzhov, Ivan, 97 n. 85

public ritual and ceremony, definition of, 234–35 n. 5

Raeff, Marc, 257 n. 20
raion councils, 115 n. 14
readers. See churches: readers
reading huts, village, 139, 141, 141 n. 120, 164, 195–96, 205 n. 56
Red Army veterans, 91, 102 n. 114. See also outmigrants
"Red priests," 177 n. 167
reforms, church, 15, 15 n. 19, 16. See also Decree on the Separation of Church and State (1918)
refugees, 51–52, 68
Regulation on Parish Councils, 23
"Regulation on Village Assemblies" (1926), 144
religion, concept of local, 13 n. 5
religion and politics, studies of, 3–5
"Religion and the *Popovshchina* . . ." (poster), 266
"Religion and the Woman" (poster), 128
"Religion Is the Narcotic of the People" (poster), 104
religiosity, definition of, 132–34, 234–35 n. 5
religious activists, 199–209
  and church building repair, 196–99, 219–26, 220 n. 39
  and church closings, 227–28
  and cooperatives, 200
  and education, 194–96, 225–26
  and electoral politics, 199–209, 223–25
  and parish councils, 23, 199–209
  and parish lands, 218–19
  political agenda of, 217, 219–20
  resistance of to state, 279–80
  sociopolitical identity of, 222–23
  and taxes, 194
  use of ritual by, 248–52
  viewed as "kulaks," 220 n. 39
  and village assemblies, 200–201, 235–36, 273 n. 1
religious art, 198–99
religious instruction, role of, 17–18
religious organizations, 57–58
religious societies, 83 n. 16
Renovationists, 149–53, 157 n. 60, 208 n. 73, 227 n. 74

Rethinking the Soviet Experience (Cohen), 6
Revolution of 1905–7, 35–40
Roslof, Edward, 208–9 n. 76
Rozanov, Aleksandr
    on church councils, 27
    on duties of priests, 22
    on impact of "Great Reforms," 20
Rudé, George, 234 n. 2
rural Christianity, concept of, 13 n. 5
rural clergy. *See* parish clergy
rural cooperatives. *See* cooperatives
rural political development, theories of, 4–5
Russian Orthodox Church, 37 n. 131
    All-Russian Council of, 70
    and Communist Party members, 87–92
    decree on "On the Protection of the Church's Sacred Objects Against Blasphemous Seizure and Desecration," 157 n. 58
    schism of 1922, 149–50

salaries. *See* teachers: salaries of
samosud (peasant adjudication or mob law), 66
science, role of in antireligious campaign, 130
"scissors crisis," 111, 111 n. 1, 247, 248
Scott, James C., 12 n. 4, 66 n. 87, 122 n. 47, 226 n. 67, 234 n. 2
secret police (OGPU), 150. *See also* Cheka; NKVD
sects, 157–58, 157–58 n. 63, 248, 248 n. 50, 249
secularism, 33, 75–76
sel'kor (village correspondent), 8 n. 26
"separators" (*otrubniki*), 54–55 n. 26
Shakhnovich, Mikhail, 92, 92 n. 61, 102, 116–17 n. 25
Shevalevskii (former Renovationist priest), 151
Siegelbaum, Lewis, 132–33, 278 n. 9
Skvortsov-Stepanov, Ivan, 102, 108–9
Slatter, John, 143 n. 130
"Smolensk Affair" (1928), 198 n. 23
social identity. *See* identity: sociopolitical
Society for the Alliance of the City and the Countryside (Obshchestvo smychka goroda s derevnei), 114 n. 10

Society of the Friends of Chemistry (Dobrokhim), 114 n. 10
Society of the Friends of Children (Obshchestvo druzei detei), 114 n. 10
Society of the Friends of the Newspaper *Bezbozhnik* (ODGB), 2, 83–85, 84 n. 21, 100
Society of the Friends of Radio (Obshchestvo druzei radio), 114 n. 10
Society to Aid Students (Obshchestvo pomoshchi studenchestvu), 114 n. 10
Sosnovskii, Lev, 262 n. 40
Special Commission on Church Reforms, 15, 15 n. 18
"The Spider and the Flies" (poster), *124*
Stalin, Josef, 277–78, 277–78 n. 6
Stites, Richard, 97 n. 85, 130 n. 65
Stolypin, Pëtr, 41
superstitions, 267 n. 54
Syzran uprisings, 187 n. 216

taxes, 17 n. 29
    and communes, 170–71
    industrial, 149 n. 14
    for parish finances, 217–18
    and religious activists, 194
    and village soviets, 143, 143 n. 128, 171
teachers
    as antireligious missionaries, 138 n. 105, 138–40
    salaries of, 139 n. 107, 194 n. 3
    See also education
Tenth Party Congress (1921), 2
Tikhon, Vasily Ivanovich, 82 n. 13, 149, 207–8
Tocqueville, Alexis de, 4 n. 12
trials, of clergy, 148, 148 n. 5
Trotsky, Leon, 98 n. 90, 103
Trud, 177 n. 167
tserkovnik, 255–57, 256 n. 17, 270–71
Twelfth Party Congress, 108

uezd councils, 115 n. 14
Union of Agricultural Cooperatives, 176 n. 161
Union of Church Renovation, 163–64 n. 100

VIKs. *See volost'* soviet executive committees

village assemblies, 24
  as financial source for parish clergy, 171–72
  functions of, 16–17
  historians on, 5
  and land issues, 53
  and parish finances, 212–13
  postrevolutionary, 51
  and "Regulation on Village Assemblies," 144
  and religious activists, 200–201, 235–36, 273 n. 1
  and religious ritual, 234–40
  role in parish affairs, 24, 37–38
  vs. village soviets, 63 nn. 66 and 67, 111–12, 224 n. 58
village electoral commission (*izbirkom*), 62
villager, definition of, 2 n. 5
village soviets
  budgets of, 143, 143 n. 124
  Constitution on, 60–62
  effectiveness of, 64–67
  historians on, 5
  numbers of, 143 n. 129
  officers of and ritual, 244–47
  and parish clergy, 63–64, 72–73, 189, 214–17, 243–44
  preelection meetings for elections for, 182
  and religious activists, 201–2, 205–6, 274
  and religious ritual, 240–44
  revival of, 142–45, 179
  role of, 60
  and state, 71–72
  and taxes, 143, 143 n. 128, 171
  vs. village assemblies, 63 nn. 66–67, 111–12, 224 n. 58
violence
  electoral, 188–89
  against parish clergy, 53–54, 65, 153
  as ritual, 105–10, 141, 141 n. 119
vocabulary
  in antireligious discourse, 254–58, 255

nn. 9 and 12, 263, 265, 267, 269–70
  for "kulak-clergy," 256, 259–65, 270
  Soviet political, 228, 243 n. 32
volost' soviet executive committees (VIKs), 5 n. 17, 17 n. 29
  and Bolsheviks infrastructure programs, 68, 68 n. 94
  and Communist Party, 207, 207 n. 68
  election of, 60
  and parish clergy, 60–61 n. 54, 61 n. 58
  and parish record books, 73 n. 122
volost' soviets, 5 n. 17
voluntary associations, 113–14, 114 n. 10
voting commissions, 183, 203 n. 47, 276
Vovelle, Michel, 105 n. 125

wall newspapers, 120, *120*. See also newspapers
War Communism, 112
"We Will Unmask the Anti-Soviet Plans of Capitalists and *Tserkovniki*" (poster), *257*
"white" clergy (nonmonastic), 12 n. 3, 208
women
  and antireligious discourse, 265, 267
  antireligious publications for, 126–27, *128*, *129*, 249
  and Land Code, 201
  in League of the Godless, 134 n. 83
  and parish councils, 38–39, 39 n. 141
  as rebels, 66 n. 86
  religious activities for, 166
  and support for parish clergy, 215–16
  and village assemblies, 236
Workers' and Peasants' Inspectorate (*RKI*), 176–77, 190, 204
"The Working Woman: Into the Battle for Socialism. Into the Battle Against Religion" (poster), *129*
World War I era, 46–48

youth, role of, 106, 136–37, 140–41. *See also* generational conflicts; parents, role of

www.ingramcontent.com/pod-product-compliance
Lightning Source LLC
Chambersburg PA
CBHW031545300426
44111CB00006BA/178